"NEILL! NEILL! ORANGE PEEL!"

"NEILL! NEILL! ORANGE PEEL!"

An Autobiography by

A. S. NEILL

HART PUBLISHING COMPANY, INC.
NEW YORK CITY

Pictures on pages 349 and 364 are reprinted from INSIDE SUMMERHILL *by Joshua Popenoe, copyright 1970 Hart Publishing Company, Inc.*

The photograph on the jacket of this book is a reproduction of a painting of A. S. Neill rendered by Ishbel McWhirter of London. Grateful acknowledgement is made to the artist for permission to reproduce this painting, as well as the pen sketch on page 358.

Contents

II THOUGHTS ON SUMMERHILL

III THOUGHTS AT THE END OF A LIFE

Photographs and Illustrations

"NEILL! NEILL!
ORANGE PEEL!"

I

MY LIFE

A Note about the Title

Years ago, Hetney, a little boy at Summerhill, went round muttering to himself: "Neill! Neill! Orange Peel!" The phrase caught on and has lived for more than twenty-five years. To this day, small children follow me around chanting the words, and my usual reaction is: "Wrong again. Not orange peel—banana peel."

I have selected this rhyme as the title of my autobiography, because it sums up my life with children; indeed, it might be the motto for Summerhill, if we believed in mottoes. These words tell the whole story of my school and my life. They show how the gulf between generations can be bridged—or rather abolished—for they do not connote *cheek* or *hate*: they mean love; they mean equality. If every kid in the world could call his teacher Orange Peel, or an equivalent, my mail would not be filled with letters beginning: "I hate my school; can I come to Summerhill?"

The little boy's chant shows that there is no necessity for a gulf separating pupils from teachers, a gulf made by adults, not children. Teachers want to be little gods protected by dignity. They fear that if they act human, their authority will vanish and their classrooms will become bedlams. They fear to abolish fear. Innumerable children are afraid of their teachers. It is discipline that creates the fear. Ask any soldier if he fears his sergeant major; I never met one who didn't.

The Summerhill rhyme tells the world that a school can abolish fear of teachers and, deeper down, fear of life. And it is not only Neill that the kids treat with equality and fun and love; the whole staff are treated as pals and playmates. They do not stand on their dignity, nor do they expect any deference because they are adults. Socially, the only privilege the teachers have is their freedom from bedtime laws. Their food is that of the school community. They are addressed by their first names and seldom are given nicknames; and if they are, these are tokens of friendliness and equality. For thirty years, George Corkhill, our science master, was George or Corks or Corkie. Every pupil loved him.

Years ago, in one of my books, I wrote that when interviewing a prospective teacher, my test was: "What would you do if a child called you a bloody fool?" It is my test today, except that *bloody*—never a real swearword outside British realms—has been changed to a more popular expletive.

More and more, I have come to believe that the greatest reform required in our schools is the abolition of that chasm between young and old which perpetuates paternalism. Such dictatorial authority gives a child an inferiority that persists throughout life; as an adult, he merely exchanges the authority of the teacher for that of the boss.

An army may be a necessity, but no one, barring a dull conservative, would argue that military life is a model for living. Yet our schools are army regiments or worse. Soldiers at least move around a lot, but a child sits on his bottom most of the time at an age when the whole human instinct is to move.

In this book, I explain why the powers that be try to devitalize children as they do, but the mass of teachers do not understand what lies behind their discipline and "character molding," and most do not want to know. The disciplinary way is the easy one. ATTENTION! STAND AT EASE! These are the orders of the barrack square and the classroom.

Obey! Obey! they say, but people do not *obey* equals; they obey superiors. Obedience implies fear, and that should be the last emotion encouraged in a school.

In the U.S.A., it is the student's fear of bad grades—idiotic grades that mean nothing of importance—or fear of not passing exams; in some countries—Britain among them, I hate to admit—it is still fear of the cane or the belt, or the fear of being scorned or mocked by stupid teachers.

The tragedy is that fear also exists on the teacher's side—fear of being thought human, fear of being found out by the uncanny intuition of children. I *know* this. Ten years of teaching in state schools left me with no illusions about teachers. In my time, I, too, was dignified, aloof, and a disciplinarian. I taught in a system that depended on the *tawse,* as we called the belt in Scotland. My father used it and I followed suit, without ever thinking about the rights and wrongs of it—until the day when I myself, as a headmaster, belted a boy for insolence. A new, sudden thought came to me. What am I doing? This boy is small, and I am big. Why am I hitting someone not my own size? I put my tawse in the fire and never hit a child again.

The boy's insolence had brought me down to his level; it offended my dignity, my status as the ultimate authority. He had addressed me as if I were his equal, an unpardonable affront. But today, sixty years later, thousands of teachers are still where I was then. That sounds arrogant, but it is simply the raw truth that teachers largely refuse to be people of flesh and blood.

Only yesterday, a young teacher told me that his headmaster had threatened him with dismissal because a boy had addressed him as Bob. "What will happen to discipline if you allow such familiarity?" he asked. "What would happen to a private who addressed his colonel as Jim?"

I believe that in the Russian Army after the Revolution there were no barriers between officers and men. They were all pals. But the system failed, I am told, and the army returned to its old ways of class division and stern discipline.

Neill! Neill! Orange Peel! is a title that may shock the "dead" teachers. But it will be understood by students in all lands—barring those in Iron Curtain countries who are never allowed to hear of Summerhill.

Why do I get hundreds of letters from children? Not because of my beautiful eyes—nay, but because the idea of Summerhill touches their depths, their longing for freedom, their hatred of authority in home and school, their wish to be in contact with their elders. Summerhill has no generation gap. If it had, half of my proposals in our general meetings would not be outvoted. If it had, a girl of twelve could not tell a teacher that his lessons are dull. I hasten to add that a teacher can tell a kid that he is being a damned nuisance. Freedom must look both ways.

I do not want to be remembered as a great educator, for I am not. If I am to be remembered at all, I hope it will be because I tried to break down the gulf between young and old, tried to abolish fear in schools, tried to persuade teachers to be honest with themselves and drop the protective armor they have worn for generations as a separation from their pupils. I want to be remembered as an ordinary guy who believed that hate never cured anything, that being on the side of the child—Homer Lane's phrase—is the only way to produce happy schooling and a happy life later on. As I am "Neill! Neill! Orange Peel!" to my little pupils, so I would like to be to all the children in the world—one who trusts children, who believes in original goodness and warmth, who sees in authority only power and, too often, hate.

Soon I must shuffle off this mortal coil, but I hope that coming generations will look back at the education of our time

and marvel at its barbarity, its destruction of human potentialities, its insane concern about formal learning. I hope,
against everything that makes me pessimistic: the wars, the
religious suppression, the crimes. Cannot those who yell for
the hanging of criminals see that they are treating a rup-
tured appendix with aspirin? Will not society recognize that
it is our repressive system, plus the poverty of our mean
streets, plus our soulless, acquisitive society, that is making
criminals and neurotics?

I confess to dithering. One day, when I think of the
challenge of the young, I am optimistic; next day, when I
scan the newspapers and read of rape and murder and wars and
racialism, I become engulfed by pessimism. But I guess that
ambivalence is common to us all.

Alexander Sutherland "Orange Peel" Neill

Summerhill
1972

My Beginnings

I was born on the 17th of October, 1883, in Forfar, Scotland. Forfar, which today is the Angus County seat, is not far from Dundee and the Firth of Tay. The MacNeill clan originally came from the island of Barra and later joined Bonnie Prince Charlie. Those said to have deserted him before or after the battle of Prestonpans—before, I should guess—settled down in and around the village of Tranent near Edinburgh.

The MacNeills became coal miners, and my grandfather, William MacNeill, worked in the pits for many years. But as I first remember him, he had already left the pits and set up a fish shop in Edinburgh. He came to visit us sometimes, a tall, distinguished-looking man with a fine profile and long-fingered, sensitive hands. His hobby was fiddle-making. As a boy, I was afraid of him, for he had a sarcastic tongue and I still recall one occasion when I fell under its lash after trying to sharpen a pencil with his new hollow-ground razor. I think my father was afraid of him, too, for he was always a little strained when the old man came to stay with us.

Though all my uncles had gone to work in the pits, my father was of less tough clay, and having a flair for learning, was sent to be a student-teacher. I never knew why he dropped the Mac from his name. Indeed, I never knew much about my father's early life, for he was not a communicative man. But I recollect his being very angry when his sister Maggie told us about his boyhood days.

My mother was Mary Sutherland. Her mother had been a Sinclair, and her maternal grandmother a Gunn. Granny Clunes Sinclair was one of a family of about twenty sons and daughters, born to a farmer with small holdings in Caithness. They all died of tuberculosis except herself. My Granny went to Leith (now part of Edinburgh) as a servant girl, married Neil Sutherland who had something to do with the docks, and began to rear a family on fourteen shillings a week. Then one night my grandfather was found drowned, and Granny had to take in washing to support the family.

How it came about that my mother—her only daughter— became a teacher, I do not know. It must have meant tremendous self-sacrifice on the part of Granny. My father and mother taught in the same school in Leith, and so their courtship began.

I have one or two of my father's love letters, beautifully written in copperplate. They are not real love letters and resemble the letters I used to write home: *Today it was raining . . . Jim Brown sprained his ankle last week.* My mother had kept them all tied up in pink ribbons, but she had taken care to burn all her letters to him. Only as a postscript did my father usually send his love, yet I have a hazy memory of once uncovering something more. This happened at the age of twelve when I was prowling about the lumber room and found a box of Father's letters. I recall being a little shocked at one of them. He had just been reading *Venus and Adonis,* and his letter showed the eroticism aroused by this poem. Reading it then, I was sure my mother must have been morally outraged; now I am not so sure.

Granny Sinclair lived with us until her death when I was fourteen. As her favorite grandchild, I think I must have loved her as much as a boy can love an old woman. She used to suck peppermints, and her way of showing her love was to kiss me while shoving a peppermint from her mouth into mine. She was very religious, read much in the family Bible, and liked to tell us that as a girl she had walked nine miles to church every Sunday and nine miles back. Her faith was a simple one of sheep and goats, with no doubts, no skepticism whatsoever. I remember discovering the word *bugger* when I was about seven, and Granny making me kneel down beside her to ask God for forgiveness. My early fear of hell must have come from her.

She made us read aloud to her from various books of sermons, including Boston's *Fourfold State*. Boston, apparently, had no doubts either. For me, the most terrifying passage of that book was one in which the Man of God, as Granny called him, gave a minute description of the pains of hell. It began in this fashion: "If you want to know what the torments of hell are like, just light a candle and hold your finger in the flame." And because Granny and Boston had no doubts about what was going to happen to sinners, I also had no doubts, but knew, as if by instinct, that hell was my destination. Yet there was no hate in Granny. She was a very human, loving old woman, and one of her joys was to listen to the often obscene gossip of the woman from the cottage over the road.

My sister Clunes (named after Granny) had less timidity and faith than I had. She wouldn't have hell at any price; and when she took the next step and wouldn't have God and his heaven, I actually feared that she might be struck down dead on the spot. My fright was caused by a grim story in Granny's annotated *Shorter Catechism* about a servant girl accused of stealing a silver spoon. "May God strike me down dead if I stole the spoon!" she cried; and, of course, she fell down dead there and then, the silver spoon tinkling on the floor. I reminded the atheistic Clunie of this tale more than once, but she laughed me to scorn, and threatened to commit the unforgivable sin—blasphemy against the Holy Ghost. She never did, but when my oldest brother Willie, at the age of thirteen, stood out in a thunderstorm and invited the Almighty to strike *him* down dead for asking God to perform an unnatural act on the Holy Ghost, I was terrorstruck. As the thunder crashed, I shut my eyes tight, opening them to whatever degree of skepticism I was capable of having in those days, for Granny's silver-spoon story had lost some of its glory. It is of interest to note here that Willie became a minister.

When the psychologists say that our early experiences rule our lives, one is apt to question. But I have had no doubts about this since 1918, when my dearly beloved sister Clunie died of pneumonia at the age of thirty-four. In all her years, she had never compromised her atheism. To her the Christian religion was both superstition and a cruel humbug. Yet on her deathbed she kept muttering the prayers she had learned as a baby, imploring God to save her soul. In the weakness of dying, she returned to emotions that had slumbered for thirty years. To me, that was convincing proof that the feelings of early childhood live on for a lifetime.

My granny was psychic. She had none of that second sight so often mentioned in Scottish tales I heard all my youth—tales like the one about Old Tamson touching Mrs. Broon on the shoulder in the kirk, and whispering: "Better go home, for your laddie has just broken his neck"; after which Mrs. Broon drives the seven miles home to discover that exact calamity. Many such stories were told in my boyhood, but it was always a case of "I know a man who heard about it from the beadle." No, Granny contented herself with more simple phenomena: her special department was knocks. "I'm no' long for this life," she would say, coming down from her room of a morning, very very depressed. "I heard three warning knocks, loud and clear. My Maker has called me." And she would go upstairs again to get her death linen in order. Naturally, we grew accustomed to her premonitions, but suffered some remorse in the end when she died after hearing her knocks.

It is difficult to look back and come to any conclusion about the over-all influence the old woman had on me. She used to say to my mother: "Allie will be the best of the family to you in your old age." And it is true that I never neglected my parents in their old age, although other members of the family may have given them more practical help than I did. I do think that what older folks say to a child may have a great effect on later behavior and thought. One of our neighbors once looked sadly at me when I was about ten. "Eh, Mrs. Neill," she said, "that laddie has death written in his face. He winna live lang." That remark haunted my life for years.

Death was no stranger to me. I had been at the burial of little members of the family more than once, and knew the trappings of death and the tears—yes, and the airy relief after the body was left in the grave. I must have attended three funerals before I was ten. Counting a still-born infant, my mother had thirteen children in all. Years later, when we used to criticize her for having so many, she indignantly told us that it was God's will, and she got furious with Clunie for saying: "That's all very well, but you had no right to have me eleven months after Allie; and if you call that God's will, He is to blame for my poor health."

Father walked back and forth to his school at Kingsmuir, two miles out. Later, when I was about eight, we moved there after a new schoolhouse had been built. My earlier memories of Forfar are vague and hazy. We lived in a third- or fourth-story flat, and one of my pleasant recollections is playing trains in the long hall. Saturday morning was market time for the farmers' wives who brought in their butter and eggs; a hopeful time for a small boy who might get tuppence for holding a horse, though my fear of horses then makes me wonder how I had the pluck to go near one. To this day I pass a horse's heels uneasily. Sometimes on those Saturdays, we did manage to pick up a penny or two, largesse from kindly farmwives whose bairns were at Kingsmuir School. This had to be accepted surreptitiously, for one of my mother's stern rules forbade us to accept money or food from other people under any circumstances. For her, to have the children accept little presents from others would have been classing her family with the lowest orders. But we children found it hard to give a reasonable excuse for refusing Mrs. Findlay's offer of a delicious piece of bread with thick fresh butter and damson plum jam.

One day when I proudly told Mother that I had refused such a tempting dainty, she smiled and told me I was a good boy.

"Of course you said you weren't hungry, didn't you?"

"No," I said with confidence, "just 'Thank you, but my ma says I mustn't take it.'" And she slapped me hard.

She was a proud wee woman, my mother. To us her rule seemed cruel: naturally, we did not understand the fear of patronage that lay behind it, a fear that came from her lowly upbringing in a humble Leith home. Mother had high ambitions for herself and her family. She was a snob, and she made us snobs.

The brothers and sisters of both my parents were poor folk of the working class, speaking in dialects you could cut with a knife. Gradually, we came to believe they were beneath us, and we acquired the well-known "poor-relation" complex. My mother dexterously managed to keep her own relatives from visiting us—they were a hundred miles away—with one exception.

Eccentric Uncle Neil was a barber in Brechin—a most unsuccessful one. He would suddenly lock up his shop and go for a long walk. Legend said that on one occasion he went off for a stroll in the midst of shaving a customer, leaving the man with one cheek unshaved. He talked to himself a lot, which may explain his lack of success: a barber who talks to himself while handling a razor will not build up a large business. But he was a harmless man, and we were all very fond of him. When his business failed shortly after Granny's death—she had been helping him with her saved-up coins—he came to live with us. After a while, Mother began to suggest it was time he did something for a living. One morning he got annoyed with her, bundled up his few belongings, and left. We never saw nor heard of him again. The children missed him, for he was always generous with sweets. I often wondered what happened to him.

Father's people, apparently, were less immune to hints and sometimes would come to stay with us. Old William MacNeill, my grandfather, was a man of strong convictions. He had all the dourness of the Scot, and any subtle suggestion made him stiffen. My mother could not forgive him his neckwear; he refused to wear a collar but wore a black handkerchief instead. As I have said earlier, he was a distinguished-looking man; in my mother's eyes, however, a man whose neckwear betrayed his low-class origin. He could make a fine fiddle with a penknife; he could make wonderful furniture with hidden dovetails; he could tackle any mechanical job with skill and some art, but he would not wear a collar. Worse yet, he always had a cackle in his throat and would spit anywhere. Even as a child, I felt a tense atmosphere between my mother and him. He had definite ideas about women: they were something lower than men in the scale of humanity; they had to be kept in their place. Possibly Mother could have forgiven him his neckwear and his spitting if only he had given her the right to be at least as important as he was.

There also was some confused story of my father's family having spoiled Mother's wedding in some way: something about the MacNeills' keeping father to themselves when he ought to have started on his honeymoon. To her, the old man remained a bossy old interferer.

Saturday mornings stand out as happy times. I can still

smell the fresh, unsalted butter in the market, still see the farmers' gigs with their smart ponies. By midday, the ponies had all taken their masters home—literally—for in those days many of them got so drunk that the pony had to find its own way without guidance. When motors came in and an agent tried to sell Farmer Mosside one, Mossy looked at him beerily. "Here," he said, "if you can sell me a car that'll bloody well take me home when I'm fu', I'll buy it."

Glory departed with the gigs; Saturday afternoon was dreary and dull. We wandered around the gray streets, often searching the gutter for treasure. Sammie Clark averred he had once found a penny, but search as we might, we never found money. The richest treasure I recollect was a cap gun with a broken trigger. Sometimes the town band would play, and we would march along the street to the music. Clunie and I followed the band one day to the Market Muir, a long way from home for toddlers' feet. I had a sanitary accident; and when I got home, my irate mother marched me down to the outside washing house, took off the offending pants, and sent me running home with a hearty slap on the bum. I must have been about six, yet I still can recall my fear that someone would meet me in that pantless sprint. Mother seemed to get some amusement out of the incident, for years later she referred to my speed that day as a criterion for swiftness.

Sundays always seemed a depressing time, when we were rigged up in Sabbath clothes with starched collars and cuffs. We were accustomed to the collars, because Mother prided herself on the fact that her boys wore genuine stiff collars even on weekdays. She spoke bitterly of the lazy limmers who dressed their sons in ordinary waterproof ones.

Getting ready for the kirk was hateful to us. We struggled with clumsy cufflinks: we resentfully stood to have olive oil rubbed into our hair. We were all dressed up with nowhere to go—nowhere, at any rate, that we wanted to go. We knew there lay before us an hour and a half of extreme boredom, of sitting on a hard pew with upright back—only the rich had cushions—of listening to dull psalms and hymns and a seemingly interminable sermon by Dr. Caie. The one bright spot in the somber picture was the tight-laced woman who had the pew in front of ours. Her waspish waist had been gained at the expense of internal gurgles, and we beguiled the time during the sermon by counting the intervals between gurgles. As the sermon dragged on, we found that we had enough to do just keeping our sense of gravity. Occasionally, I imagine, the sounds from the wasp-waisted one were drowned by our own unsuppressed splutters of merriment. I don't think the lady was conscious of our ribald attentions, for she often turned around and gave us peppermints.

I was just getting on to Sunday School age when, luckily, the schoolhouse (our new home) was finished, and we moved to Kingsmuir. Evidently my parents did not think it necessary to send us to a Sunday School two miles away. Moving to the country stands out as a happy milestone in my life. At five, I had gone to school in Forfar, daily toddling the long two miles while holding my father's hand. He was always a fast walker— even at seventy-five he could outpace me—and my childish steps must have irritated him.

My father did not care for me when I was a boy. Often he was cruel to me, and I acquired a definite fear of him, a fear that I never quite overcame in manhood. I see now that Father did not like *any* children; he had no contact with them. He did not know how to play, and he never understood the child's mind. The boy he admired was the boy who could beat the others in lessons; and since I never had any interest in lessons and could not learn, I had no hope of gaining Father's interest or affection. But in the time I am writing of—the time I attended school as a toddler—the lesson element had not yet appeared on the horizon. To him, I was merely a drag who made him late for school. He had a lady assistant at that time, a long-legged girl who kept up with him athletically, and I still see myself falling behind and whimpering in dread of being left.

I also remember another fear of those days: cattle. The Forfar cattle market was held on Mondays, and the roads were full of cattle droves. I soon found that the droves frightened Father, who sometimes even jumped a dyke with me when we met what looked like a dangerous beast. In the manner of all boys, I believed that my father could fight a score of lions, and to see him scuttle ignominiously over a wall to escape a herd of bulls must have pricked the bubble of my faith. Like his father before him, he was a timid man.

Old William MacNeill was so afraid of the dark that when he was courting my grandmother, she had to come from her village to meet him in his. My father always feared the dark, and in later years when he returned from Edinburgh by the midnight mail, my brothers and I had to meet him at the station about two in the morning.

My mother was fearless, partly because she had less imagination than Father. I recall the day she set off to town, presumably to shop. She returned, having had all her top teeth extracted. Local anesthetics were then unknown, and only the rich could afford gas.

We certainly were not rich. My father's salary was never more than 130 pounds a year, and how they brought up eight children, sending three of us to the university, is a mystery. Only great self-sacrifice could explain it. My mother augmented our meager income by dyeing and curling feathers, and my father spent nothing on himself. He neither smoked nor drank. Other teachers could have their golf and their bowls; he had no games and no hobbies. Once he tried to join in a village game of quoits, but my mother put her foot down: "George Neill, think of your position! You can't lower yourself to play games with plowmen and railwaymen."

I fear that mother's emphasis on social position cramped our style. In summer, when the whole school went barefoot, we children alone had to wear hot stockings and boots—also those stiff starched collars.

Mother had a mania for laundry, and she washed well and ironed perfectly. If her family did not become ladies and gentlemen, it would not be her fault. We had to speak English in the house, but of course we spoke broad Forfarshire outside. How we managed to change slickly from one to the other is astounding: we never seemed to make a mistake. The inside *boots* automatically became *bates* when we talked to Jock Broon.

One of our grievances was not being allowed to work as the common children did. In the potato-harvest holidays, they all went gathering on the farms. In the berry season, they all went picking strawberries. The "aristocratic" Neills could not be allowed to behave as menials. But a day came when economic circumstances overruled snobbery. Then thirteen, I was sent to the strawberries and potatoes, and hated the toil. Snobbery gave way because my oldest brother Willie was acting the spendthrift at St. Andrews University.

Moving to the new schoolhouse in Kingsmuir broadened our view of life. In Forfar, our horizon had been the churchyard; here it extended farther. The smell of new wood always takes me back to that house; to us it was heaven, and for many years, the center of my world. Clunie died in the wee bedroom where I had slept for years—Clunie, the playmate I loved so much; for my two elder brothers left me out of things and I was forced to make her my chum. The strange thing is that I can look at that schoolhouse now without any emotion. I cannot sentimentalize what has gone, and perhaps that is a good thing, for hankering after the past often denotes a disappointing present. If we go backward to find our emotions, something is far wrong; equally wrong is the forward look, toward bliss in the next world.

Father's school was on one side of the road; our dwelling, the schoolhouse, on the opposite side. The house had a parlor, dining room, kitchen, and five bedrooms. Our loo was an earth closet far up the garden. I cannot remember if we appreciated the fact that instead of a two-mile uphill walk to school each morning, we simply had to cross the road. I may have, but my brothers soon had to go to Forfar Academy and walk two miles again, morning and evening.

The penny-farthing bicycle was then in use, though we never knew it by that name and simply called it a "high" bicycle. The "safety," growing in popularity, had solid rubber tires, rather like those of a baby carriage, and was displaced by the "cushion," a bicycle with thicker solid tires. I cannot remember when the "pneumatic" came in, but have a vague recollection of seeing the great racer Killacky riding a cycle with inflated tires about as big as the modern low pressure automobile tire. But bicycles were unknown to the poor in those days, and my brothers had to walk.

Forfar Academy was the stepping stone to a university education. To my father, advancement in life meant advancement in learning. We were to be scholars, and Willie led the way. In the Academy, he topped his class in most subjects, and won the gold medal—or, rather, tied for it with a boy called Craik, son of an important jute manufacturer in town. My mother strongly believed that Craik was in the tie only because of his bigwig father, a natural opinion for her to have. But Willie was the hope of the house. His brilliance as a scholar seemed remarkable. Without visibly doing any work, he managed to go to university at sixteen and win further medals there. His method was to sit up for three nights before the exam with a wet towel around his head, and his memory was prodigious.

Willie's brilliance had unhappy effects on all the members of the family. Neil, who came between Willie and me, also went to the Academy. He was no great scholar and he did not worry much when the teachers made nasty comparisons between his work and Willie's.

When it came my turn to go to the Academy, I was not sent. I was the only one of the family who never went to the Academy. The sad truth is that it would have been useless and hopeless to send me there, for I could not learn. My father still did not care much for me, and little wonder: I was obviously the inferior article, the misfit in a tradition of academic success, and automatically I accepted an inferior status. If there was a particularly hard and unappetizing heel to a loaf, my father would cut it off with a flourish; with another flourish, he would toss it over the table in my direction, saying: "It'll do for Allie."

Clunie used to wax indignant at the way I was treated, but she never had the courage to attack my father on the subject. I recall her vigorous protest against my having to wear Willie's cast-off clothes; but adoring Willie so much at that time, I may have given her a clump on the ear for interfering. In all fairness, I still do not know why all the others were sent to the Academy. Clunie was clever but no prizewinner, and the other sisters did nothing important academically.

I was the only one who began and completed his schooling in the village. This was unfortunate, for it kept me tied to the old folks too long and prevented my measuring myself against the more sophisticated boys in the town. Not that Forfar Academy would have helped me at all educationally; there I surely would have been near the bottom of every class.

Early Schooldays

Kingsmuir School was a two-roomed building divided into the "big" and "little" rooms. In the big room, my father had Standards IV to ex-VI, ex-VI being composed of the few boys who remained in school after age fourteen. The "'Missy" kept the younger children in the little room.

If Father was to give Class V a lesson in geography, he told a boy to hang the map on the blackboard. While this was being done, test cards in arithmetic were given out to Standard III. Standard IV might be ordered to learn its spelling, while Standard VI read. Heaven only knows what the ex-VI's were doing. My father would stand at the map, and I can still hear the geography class shouting in unison: "Leeds, Bradford, Halifax, Wakefield." After a few minutes, he would leave this class to its own devices and take the reading of the VI's. Naturally, it was a noisy room. We spent much of our time talking, also drawing on our dirty slates, which we cleaned by spitting on them and then rubbing them with the palm of the hand. We never seemed to tire of tilting our slates so that the spittle would make slimy designs.

It was in the main a happy school. Sometimes my father used the strap a lot, especially when exasperated by the dunces, for his salary depended on the number of Standard V students he passed. For some obscure reason, Standard V came to be the parking place of dunces; as Inspection Day approached, and my father got more and more irritable, the blows of the strap grew many and hard. Lest he be accused of favoritism, he punished his family as severely as the others, and I came in for more than my fair share when the strappings were given for noise or mischief: as a Neill, I ought to have kept away from the bad boys.

I feared my father much at that time. He had a nasty habit of taking me by the cheek and pinching me hard between thumb and forefinger. Often he pinched my arm painfully. There must have been something very unlikable about me then, for the other members of the family received fairer treatment. I was clumsy, preoccupied with scraps of iron in my pockets, and my unprepossessing appearance did not help. My stuck-out ears earned me the nickname Saucers, and my feet grew suddenly to the size they are now. I was much ashamed of the enormous boots I wore. Because my toes turned in, I clattered along the road with those great boots hitting each other, sometimes tripping me up. I was certainly not the kind of son desired by a father who sought high academic distinction for his family. This aim was apparent in our evening homework. The rural scholars, destined to be hewers of wood and drawers of water, had none. But we were different. Every night at a certain hour, our games with the village lads were sadly and roughly interrupted by a dog whistle my father blew at the back door.

"Time for the dogs to ging hame," cried our chums, and the dogs went home with their tails between their legs— Neilie and Clunie and me. Willie, a law unto himself, required neither driving nor coaching. The rest of us trooped into the nursery and attempted to turn our thoughts from "smuggle the gig" to Allen's *Latin Grammar.*

How I hated that book! Tags from it still linger in memory: *A dative put with show and give, tell, envy, spare, permit,*

believe: to these add succour, pardon, please. .Neilie and
Clunie had no great difficulty in learning such things, but I
never could; and often I had to sit poring over the stuff when
they had been allowed to go back to the village lads and their
play.

On Sundays my mother took command, and we had to
stay in until we had learned set verses of a psalm or paraphrase. Again I was left behind, tearfully muttering to myself
the meaningless lines. Sometimes dear old Granny Sinclair
would surreptitiously slip me one of her peppermints to show
that she was on my side. My failure to learn Latin angered
my father, but my inability to learn even two lines of a psalm
gave my mother more sorrow than anger. What did anger her
was my forgetting "messages" when sent to town. As the only
child who didn't go to the Academy, my job of a morning was
to walk to Forfar with the Academy lot and fetch household
supplies.

"Now are you sure you can remember the list?" my mother
would ask. "Pound of flank and a marrow bone, two pounds
of sugar, mustard, bottle of vinegar, and"—here my mother
whispered—"a bottle of aqua." In those days, aqua—our word
for whiskey—was 2/10d. a bottle, Melvin's best; but when
Grandfather was coming, or when Donald Macintosh, the School
Board Clerk, was expected, we had to have it in the house. It
was always a luxury.

So off I'd trudge to town in my big boots. When I got
to the East Port, however, I had completely forgotten the
items. Sometimes I made wild guesses, but the result of bringing home sugar when I had been told to get salt was too painful, and I took to telling feeble lies about Lindsay and Lows'
being out of sugar at the moment. Then I was given a written list, though sometimes I lost even that.

Coming back from town with my awkward parcels was
an unpleasant experience. No one ever thought of inventing a

rucksack, and although I could have taken a basket, it seemed an effeminate thing to do. So I trudged up the braes with my heavy parcels, pausing every few steps to see if Will Clunie's milkcart was coming, for Will was always kind to the children and never passed without giving me a lift.

Often empty gigs would pass, but my plea for a hitch: "Hi, mannie, see a lift fae ye," was met by indifference. They were a dour, unfriendly crowd, the Angus farmers. Most of them wouldn't allow even a "hing ahent," when you gripped the backboard and ran behind.

Those farmers, most of them long since dead, affect me to this day. When motoring, I seldom pass a child or an old person on the road without offering a lift. On long journeys, like going to Scotland, I often give lifts to tramps, partly for company but mainly because I suffered so much as a child from selfish drivers.

I got into the way of lingering on the road until Will Clunie came along to pick me up. He left town rather late, however, and Father got exasperated because I was too long in bringing him his *Scotsman*. Then I was forbidden to wait for milkcart lifts.

This "going messages" to Forfar was not only tiring but alarming. Every boy who did not live in one's own village was regarded as an enemy; and if a Letham boy walked through Kingsmuir, we did our duty; that is, we chased him with stones. In Forfar, of course, we Kingsmuir "skites" were the strangers, and therefore regarded as enemies.

The way into town was through a street called the Ha'en, a queer name in an inland town. The Ha'en had its squad— gang, nowadays—and every morning there were dangers to face. I cannot recall being severely beaten up, possibly because I ran like hell when I saw them. But there are also vague memories of sometimes being friendly with the Ha'en squad, and I can only guess that immunity was won by flattery and humility.

This hatred of strangers was very strong when I was a boy. A few sons of well-to-do farmers had ponies on which they rode to the Academy. We continually attacked them with sticks and stones. I don't know why, for they were harmless fellows who gave no offense.

Kingsmuir and Lunanhead were both called Landward schools, the only two in the Forfar area. They had a common school board, and this board stupidly arranged a joint picnic for the two schools during the celebration of the Queen's Jubilee in 1897. Students of each school marched to the picnic grounds, and there we stood staring sullenly at each other. The Lunanhead lads were bigger and beefier than ours, so when one of them, seeing me, asked what I was laughing at and did I want "my face ca'd up amongst my hair," I looked away hurriedly. Unfortunately, our bruiser Jake Hanton had left school a few weeks before. When competitions began, and the rival schools began to express their enmity by charging and kicking, we looked at Lunanhead's shock brigade as we whispered to each other: "Oh, if only Jake Hanton was here!"

Suddenly, a small boy came running to us, and told us that not only had Jake Hanton come down after his day's work but also that Dave Wyllie, another pugilist, was with him. Then, I fear, we smaller, weaker ones behaved in a low-down fashion. We began to make insulting remarks to the Lunanhead louts; whereupon they took off their coats, turned up their sleeves, and told us they would "knock us into jelly." We smiled and signaled to our champions. The Lunanhead lads lost the battle, and as they sidled away, pretended not to hear Jake's sporting offer to "fecht any five o' them with one hand."

Jake Hanton was a dunce, with one talent—fighting, and he fought like a bulldog. His name alone could quell any boy in the neighborhood. He liked me and became my protector, and for some months my life was made soft and easy by the magic phrase: "If you touch me, I'll tell Jake Hanton."

We seem to have fought a tremendous lot, though seldom in anger. For example: I would have a quarrel with Jock Broon about anything at all, maybe a marble or a piece of skiley—a slatepencil. I'd threaten to sock him in the nose; and Jock, who of course was younger than I, would reply: "Ye wudna say that to Dave Wyllie."

Now Wyllie was a hefty lad, a good fighter who could beat me to a standstill in a few seconds; but when Jock insinuated the truth, that I was afraid of Wyllie, honor compelled me to say that I had no fear of Wyllie. So Jock would tell Wyllie, who would look over the schoolroom at me, put his fist to his nose, and say: "Wait till fower o'clock." And so at four o'clock I would be facing the champion Wyllie up the Back Dykes, scared stiff and hopeless, beaten before the fight began. The shattering effect of that "wait till fower o'clock" is with me still.

Like my father and grandfather, I was a coward, but a coward with a difference. Like my father, I feared the dark, but unlike him, I did not avoid the dark. A dread of the dark haunted me in those early days, especially when I had to walk home from Forfar after dark, a distance of two long miles with only one house. This house was kept by two old women, but to me it seemed a sort of halfway sanctuary from the dangers of the road. I never doubted that the two old women could protect me when "the man wearing the cheesecutter bonnet" came after me with a knife. He had sprung out on Jeem Craik, a grown man. He had held up plowmen with the demand: "Your money or your life!" His favorite spot was the stile at the bottom of Welton Brae. Needless to say I never saw him, for he existed only in the imagination of Eck Smith.

My fear was proportionate to the lateness of the hour. Winter nights seemed safe until six o'clock, for the factory

girls were on the road then. Seven wasn't so bad because one
of the girls might have stayed behind to do some shopping,
and sometimes lovers wandered slowly out the Kingsmuir Road.
One night a couple, annoyed because I walked close behind
them, accused me of trying to listen to their conversation. I
hadn't the courage to tell them the truth, that I was afraid to
be alone.

Leaving the town was the worst of it. I trailed slowly up
Easter Bank Brae, fearful to leave the light of the gas lamps. At
the last lamp I would stop and stare into the black night ahead
of me, glancing back in the hope that a gig would be coming
along behind. There was small hope of getting a lift, but if I
hurried into the dark road, I'd get as far as the High Dykes
before the gig passed me. Then, when the pony had to walk up
Welton Brae, I could overtake the gig by running. Once up the
brae, I was within sight of the first twinkling lamps of Kingsmuir. In any event, the man with the cheesecutter bonnet had
not been known to operate above the brae.

Although the major terror was the road from Forfar, there
were minor fears attached to shorter journeys. I had to go to
Granny Hutchison's every night for the milk. Her place was
just round the corner, and I never had any fear going there;
but when I turned to come back, it seemed that all the
murderers in the world were after me. I had a similar emotion
about going to the water closet, or rather the *closet,* for it was
a dry one at the top of the garden. Going up there in the
dark made me uneasy, for who knew who might be sitting
on the seat? But coming back was something like the speed
of the wind. Taking a lantern was doubtful help. It certainly
gave a kind of protective companionship; on the other hand, it
told the man with the cheesecutter bonnet where you were.

Somewhere back in this period, I discovered that on a
lonely dark road it was advantageous to stop and urinate; for
I had only to begin when someone's footsteps would be

heard. Of course, I had to move on hastily. Nevertheless, it proved an infallible way to attract company.

I must have relied mainly on my legs to escape the terror, but I can recall arming myself. Willie brought home a real skullcracker that could slip easily into an overcoat pocket. I also had a Gamage water pistol filled with cayenne-peppered water, and must have been somewhat disappointed that I never got the opportunity to test its efficiency on some bad man's eyes. Later, our Skye Terrier completed my armament, although he was a poor bodyguard. Boulot kept at my heels all the way to town, when I didn't need him, but went off on his own when we entered the town, and straggled home hours later, wet, bedraggled, and very, very guilty.

Still, Boulot gave me ideas. When passing the worst danger—the stile at the foot of Welton Brae—I kept whistling for an imaginary dog, calling "Wolf" or some such name that would let the man with the cheesecutter bonnet know that my dog was a huge maneater. Another technique was to shout back to an imaginary companion: "Come on, Jock," when I thought that danger was near.

I never knew if the other children had similar fears. We did not mention such things, because we knew that to be a coward was the greatest of all social sins. Like the sin against the Holy Ghost, it was unforgivable. I do not know how we acquired this standard. It may have had something to do with our literature, which was of the penny-dreadful variety. (We called the booklets *penny horribles,* or *bloods.*)

Our school readers always contained a few stories of heroes, inclined to moral courage. One was the tale of a British officer in a far-out Empire post, sick with fever, speared in the leg by the natives—gangrene had set in—and facing a tribal uprising with no other weapon that his belief in God and Queen Victoria. I cannot recall how he triumphed, but he did; and with his dying breath he thanked God that he had done his duty. I'm afraid we preferred the godless heroism of the penny horribles.

It cannot be easy for younger generations to imagine village life at the end of the last century. Every village boy of today is within reach of a cinema; he has, or he can hear, a radio; he watches television, and he sees the world go by in automobiles, trucks, and buses.

In my childhood, life went by slowly, in gigs and on bicycles. The only entertainment was a very occasional concert in the schoolroom, or a visit from an itinerant juggler. There was, other times, old Professor Thomson, unwashed and smelling of drink. He usually arrived in the morning. My father told us to bring our price of admission (a ha'penny) in the afternoon. We were thrilled, of course, to see the professor draw ribbons from his mouth by the yard, and find eggs in Jock Broon's pocket. When the magician breathed forth fire after swallowing balls of colored paper, I was at once excited and alarmed. To this day, I have the same attitude toward conjuring: I simply stare like a rustic, vainly wondering how it is all done.

Once a year, we had a school picnic. That was a swell affair. We went in farmers' carts, and the plowmen spent nights polishing their harnesses and grooming their horses. Of all the days in the year, that one was nearest heaven; the day following was the deepest hell. On the day after the school picnic, I invariably plumbed the depths of bitter despair, weeping in sheer misery. The glory had departed and would never come again. I tried to perpetuate the emotion of the picnic by attaching some of it to the people who had been there. Because a man called Jake Kenny had driven the cart I rode in, Jake became my hero for weeks. I had a vague feeling that Jake and I were bound together for eternity as two souls having shared a great spiritual experience.

On the other 364 days of the year nothing happened in

Kingsmuir. This monotony of life was broken only by an occasional wedding or funeral. We welcomed both but preferred marriages. They were often forced ceremonies, the couple having "cut the wedding cake before the marriage," as the saying went. Sometimes a boy was present at his parents' wedding. Kingsmuir had no false modesty about such marriages.

The part of the ceremony that interested us was the departure of the bridal pair. Not that we had any special interest in them, but their departure was the proper time for the best man to "scatter." He had a bag of sweets, and sometimes he included a few coppers. These he scattered on the road as the carriage drove away, and we all scrambled for the goodies in the mud or dust. We had no fine feelings about eating the sweets: any of us would lift one from a pile of horse dung and shove it into our mouth. I compromised by spitting out the first suck, but one lad considered it a sentimental waste to spit out anything.

It was the chance of picking up coppers that drew us to the marriages. Money was almost unknown to us, for we had no pocket money as most children do nowadays. The possession of a ha'penny marked a red-letter day. Then we went to Nanzy Tam's wee shop window and glued our little noses to the panes. The window was not a good window as shop windows go: all it contained was a row of sweetie bottles, a few laces or sticks of sugarella and jaw-sticker, and one or two lucky bags. These last were my favorite purchase. I never got anything lucky in them, but never lost hope of finding a new golden ha'penny wrapped up in tissue paper. Later, lucky something-or-others appeared with red bits of toffee in thin paper. They had ha'pennies inside. I once got a lucky one—and then lost the golden ha'penny.

Games had their special periods: marbles when the March dust was blowing, tops later in the spring. We all had marbles and tops, and iron hoops which we called girds, but I never knew how we got them. Marbles in the shops were expensive—ten a penny at one time—yet when the season began, poor ragged boys would appear suddenly with their "pooches full of bools." Some at least were stolen from Nanzy Tam's shoppie, and more than once I helped raid the coalshed where she kept empty lemonade bottles. We took the bottles to a dark corner and broke their necks to get out any glass marbles inside. We made poor catapults from the rubber rings. It never occurred to us that poor Nanzy would have to pay for the empties. Possibly the marbles originated from small sons of the more well-to-do farmers.

I cannot recall many other attempts on our part to steal from shops. We'd ask Nanzy for something we knew she kept in the kitchen, and while she was away we'd pinch chewing gum or chocolate, but that was petty crime. A milk-delivery boy, who freely supplied me with penny horribles and *Chips* and *Comic Cuts,* had some elaborate system of robbing a newsagent's shop. Exactly how he managed this I was not curious enough to inquire, no doubt because knowledge would have made me a guilty accomplice. We were an honest crowd, mainly because there wasn't anything to steal. We did the usual raiding of orchards; our moral standard made stealing money a heinous offense, whereas orchards were pure sport.

Money was a very necessary adult concern on two Saturdays of the year—the May and November "Terms." Those were the days on which the plowmen were engaged or fee'd. (I was brought up among words or phrases that no Englishman or American ever knows: *fee, public roup, ashet, ground to feu, avizandum,* for example.) Twice a year, on Market Day, masters and men met in town to bargain. Plowmen were engaged from term to term, but why they changed masters so often I cannot understand, for the wages were standard (very low) and the perquisites of meal and milk seem to have obtained on all farms. For us children, *any* Market Day meant entertainment. Each Friday we peeped excitedly at booths and tents going up in the High Street—at hobby horses and swing boats. The anticipation made us sleep badly every Friday night.

The sons of the farmers had a lot of money to spend at the Market, the Adams family as much as half a crown each. We poor Neills never had more than sixpence apiece; it was all our parents could afford. Sometimes I augmented mine by looking soulfully up into Mrs. Adams's eyes and asking if her rheumatism were better. She was always kind to us bairns. On Market Day, I displayed quite a lot of anxiety about the health of farmers and their wives, and could turn my sixpence into eightpence, or sometimes even ninepence. The spending was a ticklish business. Hobby horses cost a penny, so did the swinging boats. The boxing saloon, from the front of which Jimmy Lavin bellowed an offer of five pounds to any man who would knock out his boxer, was too dear; and I had to take the easier road of sneaking under the tent canvas when Jimmy Lavin was concentrating his attention on the boxing. No one ever won the five pounds. The plowmen went in with their arms swinging like flails, and the scientific boxer knocked them down easily with straight lefts.

I was conservative in my spending on Market Days. My procedure was always the same: I went straight to Laing's shop and bought a tupenny pencil with blue lead at one end and red at the other, then a penny ice cream; and walked up the street to the hobby horses. I trembled as I mounted the steps, and when the horses started and the organ blared, I felt that the end had come. The sickly smell of hot oil did not tend to make me happier. I had a terrible phobia that the machinery would break down and the horses carry me round for ever and ever. My terror and delight were so great that I sat on and had another pennyworth—a pennyworth I could ill afford. I never had the nerve to try the swing boats, but got some vicarious thrill out of watching drunken plowmen try to swing themselves over the top. I always turned away disappointed in the end, as I did after every thunderstorm, because no one was killed.

What a great day! Even after all one's money vanished, Market Day was still exciting. I soon got a sharp nose for potential trouble, and when a fight started, with bloody noses and black eyes, I often managed to squirm into the front rank of lookers-on.

At the Cross, a public square, there were always one or two cheapjacks selling eighteen-carat gold watches for "any price you like, gentlemen." Their technique was always the same: "I didn't come here to make money. I came here to do you a favor. Will any gentleman give me a penny for this half crown?" Now the half crown was always genuine, yet these slow-wits stood and gazed at him with open mouths. In the end, he practically had to force someone to buy the coin for a penny. The next stage of building confidence was to sell a set of genuine gold studs for two shillings—"But don't go away, sir: each and every man will have his reward"—and sure enough, the buyer got his studs and his money back. I spent a long time each Market Day studying the technique. The difficulty was to know the exact point at which the real business of fleecing the yokels began. The first few got their money back; the next lot got the gold watch, plus a beautiful set of gold dress studs; and for the rest of the day, the buyers merely got dud watches in exchange for their pound notes.

One Market Day, I had half a crown saved up. Brushing aside the temptation to invest in my usual red-and-blue pencil, I went straight to the Cross. This time the man was selling purses, not watches, and held one up when I approached. "Half a crown for this beautiful purse. No offers? Good, then watch me make it more valuable." And he proceeded to drop shillings into the purse. "Still half a crown," he cried; "Who will have it?" I went nearly mad with excitement and had my half crown in a very sweaty hand, but my pluck failed me; I simply couldn't risk it. A plowman bought the purse while I watched with mad chagrin as he counted out the coins in it. There were about ten shillings in all. But already the cheapjack was dropping silver into another purse, and I pushed forward and held out my sticky half crown. He gave me the purse but admonished me not to look at it until he told me to. Gripping the bulging purse tightly, I made for the outskirts of the crowd, where I finally opened it. There were threepence in coppers! Only then did I absorb that the man was not ever trying to be kind to the people of Forfar. Presently Clunie found me in tears and gave me half of the money she had left, while unkindly reminding me of her warning about these men the night before. Though I swore Clunie to secrecy, she gave me away, and I had to undergo a second humiliation, the mocking laughter of my brothers.

About the age of thirteen, I decided that my genius lay in invention. By this time, I had a secondhand cycle with cushion tires, which I spent much time taking to pieces, carefully putting the balls in a saucer that my dog Boulot always managed to upset. At one period, I was riding with only four balls in the front axle. My dismantling mania had a grim purpose; I was studying the cycle to see how it could be improved. For many years, I believed that I had invented the rim brake, but I think now that that was sheer fantasy. What I did create was a rim brake with caliper action. When I described it to a patent agent, he wrote back that it was a fine invention, and if I would forward him my check for fourteen pounds . . . I had to consider other ways and means.

My brother Willie, just returned from summer teaching in a prep school at Bexley Heath, happened to mention one of the boys called Bowden. I pricked up my ears. "The Bowden Brake man?" I asked.

Yes, Willie was sure that the boy's father was the Bowden Brake man. I said nothing but sat down and wrote to Mr. Bowden of Bexley Heath, enclosing a sketch of my invention. After a week, a reply came. I could scarcely open the envelope for the trembling of my hands. It was a nice letter— so nice, I failed to grasp at first that it was not the kind of letter I had hoped for. He had only replied because he was curious to know how I had got his address. Moreover, he was not the "Bowden Brake" Bowden at all, but a distant relative, and knew nothing about mechanics. About a year later, I found a caliper brake in a cycle catalogue.

Cast down I was, but not beaten. I next turned my inventive skills toward power as applied to cycles. I had read about levers and concluded that if the pedal cranks were about three feet long, the power of driving would be enormous. The difficulty of getting two long cranks to revolve without touching the ground would be overcome by a mechanism that made them fold up telescopically as they reached the bottom of their strokes. After an engineer had laughed heartily at this idea and had explained its impossibility, I gave it up.

But power still held my imagination. When a semi-relative, versed in mechanics, hinted that the cycle of the future would be driven by compressed air, the idea set me going. I saw the whole thing in a flash. I would invent a cycle whose tubes formed an air chamber. On the back wheel would be an air pump, and when going down hill, this pump would fill the air chamber. Then, as the cycle climbed the next hill, a lever would open the air port, and the compressed air would work a small motor to drive the machine bravely up the brae. But again a tiresome and interfering practical engineer blew my invention sky-high by demonstrating that you can't get more out of a machine than you put in; as for pumping air into a cylinder going down hill, the pumping would bring the damn machine to a standstill. I think that was the last invention I attempted.

What I was going to miss in giving up invention, were the bulky catalogues that came by post, especially a thumping one like Gamage's. I began to read advertisements, favoring those with coupons for free samples. I wrote to all sorts of firms for prospectuses, especially those that offered to train you by correspondence for thousand-pounds-a-year jobs. There was nothing of the plodder about me: my motto was simple: GET RICH QUICK.

About this time, Neilie had a spell of body-building. Every morning he did strenuous exercises with Sandow's dumb-bells and developer, and his muscles grew big and strong. I wrote a friendly letter to Sandow saying that I could not afford to take his advertised course at six guineas, but if he would let me have the course for nothing, I should be eternally grateful. The body-builder did not reply—much to my surprise, for in spite of swindling cheapjacks, I still retained my belief that men were good, loving, and always willing to help the poor and deserving.

I still have fleeting fantasies that a millionaire will step in and build me a new school after I have written him a nice, friendly letter. The fact that I don't write the letter, and never will write it, only proves the sad truth that age robs one of anticipations. Think of the interest with which I should look for the post if I were expecting a reply from a millionaire!

The letter to Sandow made me uneasy, however, after a boy told me how Sandow, when attacked by two toughs in America, had thrown them over a wall and broken their backs. I wondered dimly if there was any probability of his coming five hundred miles north to chuck me over a wall for my impertinence.

About this time, I also had considerable anxiety over a firm who offered to teach you How To Write Advertisements. I had sent for its prospectus, only to learn the usual grim fact that the fee was about as much as two months of my father's salary. The firm kept sending me stiff letters, demanding to know why I was not replying. I saw myself in a lawcourt being mulcted for untold damages. When I told Willie, he took the matter in hand and wrote them a snorting letter. That was the end of my attempts to get rich quick.

Looking back on the boy that I was, I can fully appreciate my father's irritation. What could Latin verbs matter to a boy whose name was going to be known the world over as the inventor of a new cycle or a new trouser button? "Mary," Father said again and again, "the boy will come to nothing," and my mother seemed to agree. Yet on one occasion I became a scholar. Kingsmuir school had a special annual prize for arithmetic—the Angus Club—which I made up my mind to win, although my chum, Frank Craik, was better at sums than I. It was a long, grim fight, but in the end I won. I still have the prize, a gilt-edged volume entitled *Ferdinand and Isabella,* but have never succeeded in getting past the first chapter.

When a boy, I seldom read a book. I can't remember Neilie reading much then either. To this day I read but little and would rather potter about in my workshop. Any book I did read as a boy was one recommended by Willie or Clunie. Willie read everything he could find, and at an early age had a fine taste in books. Clunie also was an omnivorous reader, and although a year younger than I, read Dickens and Thackeray and *Jane Eyre* when my level was the penny horrible. It was through them that I discovered H. G. Wells, W. W. Jacobs, Anthony Hope—the *Prisoner of Zenda* delighted me —and Rider Haggard. After reading *She,* I knew that my future lay in Central Africa. I also read Marie Corelli. Clunie and I agreed that she was the greatest writer who ever lived; and together, we wrote her a letter to this effect. If she would only send us her signature, we should cherish it until death. She never replied, and soon we grew critical of her work.

Today, when I get letters telling me that I am easily the greatest man alive, I always answer them, hypocritically disclaiming the compliment but wishing the senders all luck in their own futures. Marie Corelli lost two earnest admirers by not answering them; I have so few that I dare not lose any. If any youth thinks that I am greater than Shakespeare and Shaw rolled into one, it would be brutally unkind for me to contradict him. The heroes of my youth often let me down, but perhaps my tactics were all wrong. Had I written: "Dear Miss Corelli, you can't write for nuts, and your characters are dead sticks, and your philosophy is tripe," I am sure I should have had an answer. I always answer critical letters by the next post, while fan mail lies around for weeks, sometimes getting lost.

I indulged much in hero worship as a boy. Willie was my demigod for many years, and my identification with him had much to do with the line my life took. At school I always had a protective hero—usually a stupid lad. I helped him with his sums, and he repaid me by beating up any boy who attacked me. All the best fighters seemed to be dunces. They hadn't the brains to argue, and the easiest reply for them was "a scone on the lug"—what we'd call today, a cuff on the ear.

My heroes were the waggish plowmen who used to congregate evenings at the bridge. Indeed, I used to imitate their typical rolling walk; and, to me, it was always a matter of infinite regret that when my mother made my breeches, she would never sew on the front pockets all the plowmen had. To my mother, such pockets were "common" and slightly vulgar. I remember her once saying that she considered the flies on male trousers indecent, and that her father had always worn

trousers whose flies were hidden by a flap. We called flies
spavers.

At that time, Killacky was a national wonder, winning
most of the prizes in cycle racing; and when a rider passed
the bridge, these local wits would shout after him: "Go on,
Killac," or "Yer wheel's gaein' roond!" I never seemed to tire
of the latter remark, nor its companion to a pedestrian: "Hi,
loon, ye've missed a step!" But it was an ordeal for me to
pass the bridge when the plowmen sat on the dyke. Perhaps
I dreaded a witty line about my enormous feet or my hen toes.

I was feeble at games and, at football, always had the
dishonor of being the last chosen when sides were tossed for.
Yet I cannot recall ever making an athlete my hero. It must
have been about the age of fourteen that I began to seek
importance as a wag, and I have a faint recollection of making
my schoolmates laugh easily. Their standard was not high;
in geography, the River Po—*po* was toilet slang to us—kept
them sniggling guiltily for the whole lesson.

Like most children, we did not appear to be conscious of
the changing seasons. My haziest memories are of the winters,
when there seemed more snow than now, and we made slides
on the roads, skating clumsily as frogs. Sometimes when
the frost was good, we tried to skate on a local pond, but never
efficiently. Our skates were partly to blame, being so blunted
by cart tracks that they would not grip the ice. We hated the
old men and women who put salt on our slides overnight.

To us—first of all—spring meant dust, blowing with the
March winds, and then the joy of bird-nesting. We all had
egg collections, but harried every nest we came across, no
matter how many specimens we already possessed. This search
for nests was exciting, because it led us into forbidden areas
where gamekeepers were savage and terrifying in voice. I still
can feel the agony—as I prepared to climb a tree—of hearing
a voice cry: "What the hell are you doing there?" We had all

heard tales of gamekeepers beating boys up, but these tales must have been legends, for these men never touched us. As a timid lad, I often had to stand guard for the others; that was far worse than actually taking part in a raid.

In late summer, we also came up against the gamekeepers when we went gathering raspberries. Here we were slightly fortified by the knowledge that we were poaching with parental approval. It was an economic necessity for my mother to make as many pots of raspberry jam as possible, and there were berries in the woods for the taking. The local squires did not prohibit the gathering of berries out of arrogance; their defense was that pickers disturbed the pheasants and partridges.

These raspberry expeditions were pleasant. To hold the fruit, we took milk flagons and baskets lined with cabbage leaves. I never ate the berries, and used to despise Eck Fraser for nibbling at his on the way home. Often when he had an almost empty flagon to show his indignant mother, he told her that the gamekeeper had emptied it out.

My mother slaved during the berry season. The jam pot was seldom off the fire, and we loved the delicious smell of the skimmings. She was really a wonderful housekeeper; how she managed to make just the right amount of jam to supply us for the whole year makes me marvel, even now. She was proud of all her jam-making, especially that she was the only woman in the village who could get her strawberry jam firm. Equally satisfying to her was her washing and ironing. She slaved at the washtub and ironing board, using a charcoal iron, and I fear her criterion of whiteness in linen has made me consider most steam laundries inferior ever since.

During the years when I was a boy, she suffered extreme pain—often agony—from gallstones, but she never made her illness an excuse for shirking her housework. I think her proudest moments were on Sunday mornings when she stood at the garden gate and watched us troop off to the kirk: my father in his chimney hat and starched shirt; the boys in their well-brushed clothes and stiff collars, with their snow-white hankies showing from their pockets; the girls with their well-ironed dresses. She had become stout, and seldom made the long walk to town herself, only on special occasions like the Sacrament Days.

Boyhood

Not long after we had moved out to Kingsmuir, the Auld Kirk was completely renovated. An old Forfarian had presented a marvelous four-manual organ, and the whole interior of the kirk had been changed. With a pew in the front seat of the gallery, going to church seemed more pleasant for us children than it had been in the days of the woman with the internal gurgles. Ours was easily the best vantage point in the kirk, and it was fun to look down and watch folks during the sermon; how they nodded, or couldn't find the place when the reading was from Amos or Daniel, or dropped their pennies for the collection. On Sacrament Day, we watched eagerly to see if anyone would drop the communion chalice and we knew who took just a sip or who emptied nearly half the cup. The loud blare of the organ fascinated us. I got into the way of sitting until the final voluntary was ended in the empty church, and whatever musical taste I have dates from that time. The organist became my Sunday hero; my ambition was to sing in the choir.

I shall have much to say about religion in my youth, but somehow it is not connected with going to the kirk. That was a social function, associated with showing off clothes and making contact with people. The sermons meant nothing to me: Dr. Caie read all his prayers, but without much conviction.

To me, his prayers were words, stereotyped phrases about the pitcher broken at the fountain, or the silver cord being unloosed. Looking back, I wonder if anyone felt any religious emotion in that kirk. In my teens, it certainly became a place of worship, for the girl in the front seat of the opposite gallery was my goddess—cold, lovely, unattainable. My chief impressions of the kirk were sex and death. My most outstanding color memories are the pretty faces and hats of the girls in the choir, and the black weeds of bereaved families when they were "kirket" after funerals. The whole family sat in a black row, the widow wearing a heavy veil.

Our chief desire was to see how they reacted when the minister made his remarks at the end of his sermon: "I cannot conclude today without alluding to the tragic loss we have sustained through the death of one of our best-known townsmen. John Brown was . . ." With emotions that had no connection with grief, we children watched the hankies coming out. The younger members of the bereaved family generally seemed to enjoy the publicity, but to the elders it must have been painful. After church, the family wended their way to the cemetery. Some families never seemed to get out of mourning blacks, especially those like the Craiks, who had all their uncles and cousins living—or, it seemed, dying—in the town.

Sundays were rather dull, for we were not allowed to play games, and the only permissible recreation was a staid walk in kirk clothes and tight boots that blistered my toes. But, negatively, Sunday was desirable for its respite from Allen's *Latin Grammar*. We enjoyed another respite on Wednesday nights, when my father, an elder of the kirk, had to attend a meeting. He usually assigned us some pages of Allen or Caesar to do, but no sooner had he gone down the road a hundred yards than we were out with the boys. My mother often threatened to report us, yet she never did. I cannot remember what my father said or did when he found that we hadn't prepared our homework. Clunie stood up to him, at this period, and my second sister, May, positively bossed him. We believed that she was his favorite because she was named after his mother. May knew what she wanted and usually got it. Mother, who constantly was having trouble with her—"the strong-willed hussy"—tried to "break her will" when she was quite small. I cannot exactly recollect how, but I have a faint memory of May sitting very red and defiant in the parlor, while my irate mother yelled: "You *will* do it!" and May screaming back: "I tell you I won't." And she didn't.

Willie and May prospered, simply because they went their own ways, whereas we timid ones, fearful of discipline, did what we were told. I was obedience personified, although in the long run, my passive obedience backfired. Obedience made me stare at Allen's *Grammar,* but something inside me negatived my passive response by refusing to allow me to learn anything.

I am trying consciously to be objective about my parents, trying to look back at them without sentimentality. As a boy I loved my mother deeply—loved her too much—but at that age, I could not love my father. He was too stern, too far away from me. As a model for us children, he used to hold up a frail little chap with glasses, who never played a game in his life but was an earnest student, actually weeping if he weren't at the top of the class. We hated that lad; he became a railway porter.

Many years later, I came to love the old man. His ambitions for us had long since gone, and he accepted us as we were. But in the times of which I speak, he held himself aloof from us boys and would never talk about his childhood. It was only before his death at the age of eighty-four (a fortnight from eighty-five) that he told me of his first great tragedy, his mother's death of cholera when he was a boy. "I grat [grieved] for weeks," he said, as the tears came to his eyes and my own.

I do not know why he was so strained and unhappy when we were young. True enough, he was trying to do all he could for his family with very inadequate means. I am convinced, however, that economic circumstances never go deep enough to affect individuals fundamentally. I am sure, for instance, that no man ever killed himself because of loss of fortune, the reason given so often in the newspapers. For many, money comes too late in life to have any deep significance. My father's youngest brother, who never had a bean, was always cheerful. Father's pessimism must have sprung from an abnormal fear of life, and a sense of its disappointment. But how his fear arose cannot be known. Certainly his ambitions for us must have been a transfer of his own.

He was the soul of honesty, and I do not think he could tell a lie easily. Absolutely conscientious in his work, he must have felt keenly that he did not get his due recompense. His salary depended on inspection reports, and Her Majesty's Inspector at that time was a sour, unfriendly man who begrudged my father any praise for his work. This man would give glowing reports of the neighboring school of Inverarity—a school in which my father had his first appointment as assistant—but Elder of Inverarity was no better a teacher than Father.

Inspection Day was an agony for my father. I see him yet, his white strained face looking out of the window to watch the H.M.I. and his assistant come down from the station in the morning. Father's obvious fear infected us, and we also trembled before the mighty authorities. The inspector was a bad examiner, who attempted to find out what we did not know, rather than draw out from us what we did know. He kept writing notes in a pocket diary, and all of us, including my father, believed them to be notes of damnation.

Afterward, the stern inspector softened a little when he came over for lunch at the schoolhouse. Mother was a good cook, and on Inspection Day she always gave the guest his favorite pudding. We children were never at table. To this day I cannot meet an H.M.I. easily, although I realize that the modern ones are different from the old, and much less powerful.

Inspectors had special arithmetical test cards on pink cardboard, and the only piece of dishonesty I can ever remember in my father occurred when test cards were once purloined from Dominie Deas's inspection the week before ours. Father worked out the tests on our blackboard, but dishonesty had its own reward, for the inspector brought a new edition when he came to us. I conjecture that he missed a few cards when he left the Dominie's school and was taking no risks.

Later on, Hunter Craig came on the scene as a new assistant inspector. He had been an elementary-school teacher himself, and not, like the usual senior inspector, an Oxford graduate who had never taught in his life. Craig was a genial fellow who inspired neither fear nor respect. You could argue with him as an equal, and we all liked him.

I never knew how much my father suffered from his school-board governors. They were mostly farmers, and I recall the chairman coming to sign the register and writing at the bottom "Number present, 98." An odd custom called "The Examination" always followed the H.M.I. inspection. This was the last day before summer holidays, when prizes were given out. The farmers' wives brought bunches of flowers, and school-board members sat in state behind the book-laden table. My father saw to it that every child got a prize. He used to scratch his head when he came to Jake Hanton, and finally would give him a small book with the inscription: "John Hanton, for Reading."

The board chairman began in a businesslike fashion: "James Young, First Prize for geography—that's fine, Jeemy, I'm glad to see you stick to your learning." But after a few books had been given out, the chairman gave up trying to make helpful comments, and simply called out the winner's name when handing out the prize. Examination Day was one of the brightest of the year to us. It meant the prelude to weeks of freedom when we could catch minnows all day long in the Back Ditch, or go farther afield to the Vinney where we tried to "guddle", to catch trout with our hands—but never got any. We never attempted to use a line and hook, no doubt because they were too expensive.

Many years later when cycling Vinney way as a student, I looked over the bridge and saw my youngest brother Percy with rod and line. I asked him how long he had been standing there. "Two hours," he said, "and not even a nibble."

"I'll show you how to fish," I said, with all the superiority of an elder brother, while casting the line. A trout jumped at it, and I whisked it out.

"That's how to catch fish," I said, and left him. It was the only fish I ever caught in my life, but to this day I am sure Percy considered me an expert angler.

We were continually catching minnows with the kitchen drainer. We shoved them into jam jars, and by the time we got home most of them were dead. We knew that the fun was in the catching, so I don't know why we didn't throw them back in the water. To see a large stickleback (or red gabbie) struggle in the drainer, would still give me a thrill, only nowadays I'd throw it back.

In our summer excursions, we always took the shortest way. When crossing fields, we fearfully watched the cattle to see if there was a bull among them. None of us had any illusions about bulls; we knew them as dangerous brutes, not to be trusted even when quiet. Farm dogs, too, gave dangerous spice to our adventures, and we grew accustomed to the friendly farmer's wife who stood at her garden gate and cried: "He winna touch you!" when an evil collie was showing us all his teeth. I learned early in life that a dog never forgets. When

Fraser's collie was a puppy, I hit it playfully with a half-brick. The collie never forgot, and years later I could not go up to Fraser's door.

When we first moved to Kingsmuir we had a Newfoundland bitch called Myrtle; that is, my father bought her as a Newfoundland, only to find she was a mongrel. When she was in heat, we had great sport collecting piles of stones and gleefully pelting the suitors who came from neighboring farms—some as far as two miles. We threw lots of stones as boys, but I cannot recollect our ever hitting anything.

We must have displayed more than a little cruelty, yet we never went so far as one or two pathological specimens, who cut off the heads of young birds and blew up toads by sticking straws up their anus. Nor did we ever kick hedgehogs to death as other boys did. Our limit was chasing Bell Eggie's cat with the Skye Terrier Boulot. We also followed the cattle drovers' custom of hitting stots (castrated bulls) with sticks. Cattle had a poor time then: at the Forfar mart, the drovers used to twist their tails cruelly, a practice later stopped by law.

We were very unconscious of the reasons for things. Though we saw cattle around us all the time, we never connected them with moneymaking. They were good for rounding up with a collie dog; a stick sounded lustily against their dung-caked haunches. To us, in fact, they seemed like toys, playthings. Pigs were different. We all knew that Martha Ramsay kept a pig for the bacon and hams, and we were there at first frost when the animal was led out to its death.

The tub of boiling water steamed in the morning frost. The ladder to which the carcass would be strung was against the wall. Ay, and Geordie Marshall stood there with the knife in his hand. Then the screeching began when many hands dragged the beast from its sty. If it was a large pig, some time and energy were needed to get the animal tumbled on its back, ready for the knife at its throat. The holders sprang away at the first spurt of blood, and the brute struggled to its feet, taking a few grunting steps. After the gore rushed out in a strong stream, the pig collapsed and all was over, so far as we were concerned. Seeing Marshall rip open the carcass was a secondary excitement. We must have been a morbid lot.

Seeing a hen's neck wrung was almost a daily occurrence. When I was about fourteen, my mother asked me to kill a hen. I had just seen experts kill thousands after the Forfar Christmas sale, and it all seemed too easy. They simply took the fowl by the head, gave it a slight twist, and threw the fluttering thing down. But when I caught the hen, took it by the head, and gave a slight twist—at least so intended—the body went flying over the cabbage patch. I stared at a bloody head left in my hand, and suddenly felt rather sick.

Most country people can kill an animal without any feeling; I never acquired the indifference necessary to do the thing well and cleanly. When Boulot the Skye was old and half blind, my mother asked me to kill him with chloroform. I got a bottle from the chemist's, put the dog in an old trunk, and shoved a soaked hankie beside it. I heard the poor brute struggle against the fumes, and in my excitement upset the bottle on the floor. I knew that I could not kill the dog by chloroform. Luckily there had been enough on the hankie to send him to sleep, so I held his head in a pail of water till the bubbles stopped gurgling up. It was a ghastly experience. I buried him "darkly at dead of night" with the wind and rain driving down, and finally crept into the house, feeling more like a murderer than I have ever felt in my life. It was the utter helplessness of animals about to be killed that shattered me.

Recently, I had to kill a kitten because it was obviously in great pain with some internal inflammation. I used the gas oven as the only painless method I had within reach, but although I knew that death was necessary and a kindness, I had that uncanny sense of guilt that comes from knowing that you have complete power over something weaker than your-self.

We really do attribute humanity to our own animals. They seem different from ordinary beasts, because they have our per-sonalities. When my sister Hilda's pet lamb grew up and had to go away with a flock to the slaughterhouse, I felt—as the whole family did—that it would feel the knife much more than the other sheep. This I truly believed, even though I hated the spoiled brute. Of all animals, a pet lamb seems most objec-tionable. Within its native stupidity is a queer, demanding sort of arrogance beyond description. Big animals should never be made pets. I have known pet horses; they are always self-willed and unreliable. Pet bulls can be highly dangerous when they grow up. I have never seen a pet pig so don't know what its evil characteristics are.

We had the usual pets as boys, generally rabbits. Like all children, we fed them for a few days and then neglected them. That was to be expected, for a rabbit is the dullest of all pets. Only their sex life really interested us. Now and again we had guinea pigs, and later, homing pigeons. Neilie specialized in "homers," and he and I got much joy from flying them. We learned, however, that their homing instinct is exaggerated. A homer has to be trained, and the usual method is to send it in one direction by rail, beginning with a near station and gen-erally increasing the distances. One can easily train a homer to fly from Carlisle to Land's End, but the chances are that if you send the bird north instead of south, it will not be able to find its way back to Carlisle from Edinburgh. Perhaps sight helps them more than instinct—a guess only, for I am no authority.

Dove-keeping afforded some excitement in raiding other dovecotes. Occasionally, in the wall-dovecote of Findlay the joiner, we would see among all the mongrels a lovely dove with a ring on its leg. Then we would go to Findlay, tell him that one of our doves had got in among his, and could we catch it?

Because he had no interest in doves and no idea of the number he kept, he would give us permission. Later, at dead of night, we would climb up and steal the bird. It was usually a stray, lost in a race, and therefore worthless, but to us it was a thoroughbred. Would a mongrel have a silver ring on its leg? So we'd carry the dove home triumphantly; but the first time we let it out, back to Findlay's dovecote it would fly. Findlay must have got rather tired of our nightly retrievings.

Some of the happiest days of our childhood were spent at the seaside. We were taken by train to Arbroath and then on to Easthaven. We never knew where Easthaven was when we were young; to us it was heaven, to be accepted without thought of criticism. We had rooms in the row of fishermen's cottages, very cheap and very primitive with their old boxed-in beds. To this day I always visit "The Ha'en" when I go north. It is a small bay, and in those days there were many fishing boats on the sand.

This was an ideal spot for children, one of those beaches where low tide shows long stretches of rock pools, whelks and shells, and farther out, lobsters in holes. We bathed—my mother with us in a long gown. She loved the water but never learned to swim. Because her own father had been drowned accidentally, she kept warning us not to go out too far, and in this way gave us a complex about water. None of us learned to swim till much later in life; and although I can swim, I never have that feeling of confidence that the good swimmer has. My fears were attached to my mother. I used to stand on the beach, a miserable little lad of seven or eight, and scream: "Come back, Ma, you'll be drowned!" My father never bathed; he disliked the water and seldom even waded. Willie also disliked bathing, but the rest of us enjoyed it.

Easthaven must have been dull for Father. His one recreation was searching for agate-type pebbles as the tide went out, and many a beauty he found. Later on, after the rock-pool stage, I also took to pebble-finding, and went a step farther than father in grinding and polishing the best ones.

Clunie and I had ambitions. Our first hope was to find a human body in the pools, preferably one that had been long enough in the sea to be half eaten away by sharks. We were indeed a morbid couple. The body did not materialize, and we fell back on a second-best wish: to find a treasure trove washed ashore from some noble galleon. We selected our exact burial spot in the sand where we were to keep our booty a secret from the others until we could dispose of it with great profit. Our imaginations did not go to the length of spending the money.

Searching for buried treasure played a big part in my young life. I remember reading a story in *Chatterbox* about a boy hero who happened to find a secret panel in a room. With his sister, he went down a flight of stairs to find skeletons and treasure in plenty. Clunie and I were not fools enough to imagine there could be any secret passages in our newly built schoolhouse, though we knew of old castles not far away and one day we might . . . But we were never quite sure what we would do or find. The changing sea at Easthaven was never final; tomorrow a high tide might wash in the treasure or, better still, the drowned corpse. We tried to get the fishermen to tell us thrilling tales of wrecks and sharks, but they were a dull crowd and had no adventures to relate. One old man told us a few tall tales about wrecks and pirates, and then we learned that he had never been to sea in his life.

Time did not exist in Easthaven. There, a week or fortnight was a million years. Time hardly existed anywhere when we were young, and a year seemed a long, long time because we lived every moment of it. Our life was drawn in blacks and whites; there were no grays. We were either up or down, joying or sorrowing.

My mother's constant illness gave me many black days. I

was much attached to her, and when she was ill I could not play. Her bilious attacks were generally heralded by severe vomiting. Her face turned a jaundiced yellow, and pain showed in her weary eyes. Only when she got very bad did we call in the doctor. To poor people, this was the last resort, and my mother nursed us all through the usual epidemics without having the doctor to see us. This time, however, it was often my sad task to go to Forfar for Dr. Wedderburn, a stately old man who drove out with a groom in his spanking gig. He had ushered us all into the world, and apparently at each birth told my mother that her baby was the finest he had ever seen. Mother adored him.

My fear was that my mother would die. Her dreadful stories about stepmothers made me believe a stepmother was a fiend incarnate. Which of the most hateful women in the village, I wondered, would my father marry if he became a widower? It never struck me that he might choose one of the nice ones; and if he did, I knew that even the best of women leather their stepsons. So when I sat by Mother's bed and held her clammy hand, wetting it with my tears, I was vaguely aware that my grief was not wholly disinterested. I kept torturing the poor sufferer with my despairing cry: "Will you die, Ma?"

Sometimes I dried my eyes and stared into the thought of death. One day I said to her: "Won't it be awful for Pa and you when you are both in heaven and we are all in hell?"

"No," she said simply, "for God will change our hearts so that we won't care."

This answer disturbed me greatly, but it did not alter in any way my firm conviction that we children were booked for hell with a single ticket. I never had any doubt about the destination of my parents, although I had grave doubts about the salvation of other adults. When Jake Wilson died, Clunie and I discussed his chances in hushed whispers. Said Clunie:

"I'm sure he's gone to heaven, 'cause he always went to the Sacrament and sometimes to the kirk services."

"But Clunie," I cried, "he swore!"

She considered this for a bit. "Yes, I know he swore, but he didn't mean it."

That comforted me; I was sure that Jake had gone to heaven. But then Clunie frightened me again by bringing forth her accustomed argument that there wasn't a heaven anyway, and maybe no God. I always edged away from her in horror when she began to utter such blasphemies.

Sex and Hellfire

The Scots religion of my boyhood was a modified Calvinism. I cannot remember ever being taught that the doctrine of predestination separated us forever as sheep and goats, without our having any say in the matter at all. No, we had free will. We could choose heaven or hell, but might reach heaven only after praying to God or Jesus and getting sanction. The road to hell was easy enough. You had only to be a sinner to go there.

I got my emotional religion from the home, not from the kirk. Dr. Caie did not preach heaven and hell. True, he read the lessons, and in the kirk I heard about the place where the worm dieth not and the fire is not quenched, but old Caie never drew any moral from that. His Christianity was basically a department of social status. Caie was a gentleman who looked it, and his religion was gentlemanly: conventional, skimming the surface, avoiding the grim realities of sin and damnation.

It was Granny, I think now, who kept my parents up to the mark in religion. To her, everything was so simple. Since God's word was inspired—true from first to last—you had only to "believe" and you were safe for heaven. My mother and father stuck to this religion until mellowed by age. Then they lapsed for many years, finding their salvation at last in spiritualism.

We were not specifically taught religion; it was in the air,

73

an atmosphere of negation of life. My father said grace before each meal, but only when my mother was there. It was she who paused after she had served us all with soup. "Now, George," she would say, and he would thank the Lord for His mercies. I can still hear her voice change when she said: "Now, George." It makes me think of the BBC announcer who, after cheerfully telling us about floods in China, suddenly hushes his voice to report: "It is with great regret that we announce the death of . . ."

On Sunday nights, just before bedtime, we had family worship. We all sat around on chairs while my father read a chapter from Scripture. Then, after singing a psalm or a paraphrase, we went down on our knees as he thanked God for sparing and taking care of us, asking him to bless us in all our doings. It was always difficult to restrain our laughter then. Neilie would pinch me, or I would pinch Clunie, and we rammed our mouths hard against the seats to keep from spluttering aloud.

Sunday was a holy day; only necessary work could be done. Our reading was censored, and we had to read our penny bloods within the protective pages of a "good" book. Granny, with her sharp nose for deception, sometimes caught us. All games were taboo; our walks were not much joy. Village boys played football with tin cans on the road, but even these heathens did not play an organized game with a real ball.

Without being told, we knew precisely the milestones on the broad road "that leadeth to destruction." They were sex, stealing, lying, swearing, and profaning God's day. (The last-named included nearly everything that was enjoyable.) I cannot remember that such virtues as obedience and respect were milestones on the other way—the straight and narrow path that "leadeth unto life." At any rate, disobedience did not come into our line of vision; we were too well trained to attempt it.

When I was thirteen, two itinerant preachers came to Kingsmuir, pilgrims from the Faith Mission. They were breezy, hand-slapping optimists, always bright and merry. Indeed, you almost forgot that these were *saved* men until they interjected a "save the Lord" into their ordinary conversation. The pilgrims became unpaying lodgers in our home, and we must have resented their presence, for when Boulot took a chunk out of the leg of the more cheerful one, we were decidedly pleased.

The whole family trooped to their meetings in the school. The Mission's gospel was simplicity itself: We were born in sin and doomed to eternal torment. *But*—there was a way to escape it—the only way. All we had to do was stand up in the meeting and say fervently: "Lord, I believe," and we would be washed automatically in the blood of the lamb. My father stood up, then my mother, and the pilgrims praised the Lord. Clunie was also saved, but I couldn't bring myself to stand up, though I tried hard. Lying in bed after the meeting, I would say over and over again with fearsome passion: "Oh Lord, help me to believe."

Someone had told me that the human heart was like a fiddle with millions of strings, many as thin as a spider's web, and if one string were to break, death would be instantaneous. When I felt I could not believe, I suddenly thought of this, and terror seized me in its icy grip: I may die before morning, before I can stand up and give my testimony that I am saved. Yet even in subsequent meetings, I could never do so. Clunie very soon lapsed from salvation and was highly sarcastic about the whole affair. She and I tittered when village reprobates stood up and told how they had been washed in the blood. Within a week of the pilgrims' departure, the whole village had reverted to its sinful ways, and old Dave went on singing his drunken way home every Saturday night.

But Father was a changed man. He bought up all the old books of sermons he could find in the penny trays at the secondhand bookshops, and announced that he would carry on the salvation meetings at the school every Sunday. We had to attend, but we realized that he had not the fire and the quick repartee of the original pilgrims. He did not give up his elder-ship of the old kirk, although he shook his head sadly over the deadness of what passed for religion there. This phase lasted perhaps a year, then the meetings stopped, and ap-parently my father was no longer saved. His father's death may have had something to do with it.

Old William MacNeill was no religious man—I knew that because he once had honed his razor on a Sunday—and when he died, I was a little perturbed about his future. I timidly mentioned this to my father as we walked to evening service.

"Will grandpa go to heaven?" I asked. "He was a good man but he wasn't saved, was he?"

"Maybe—" answered my father in an embarrassed sort of way, "maybe there are lots of things we don't know. Your grandfather was an upright, sober man, a man who never spoke an ill word against anyone." It was clear to me then that he had begun to doubt the efficacy of being saved.

Death cast a dark shadow over our lives. In a small vil-lage of many funerals, each was an event, a form of grim en-tertainment. The plumed hearse, with carriages behind it, drew up before the bereaved home. The minister read a short, tear-compelling service in the parlor while the coffin was being carried out to the hearse. In small cottages, a window had to be taken out, for it was impossible to get a coffin through the door. The women of the family did not go to the burial, but stood at the gate wiping their eyes until the last carriage had disappeared over Bunker Brae. Every blind in the village was drawn, and women stood at their doors and sighed, say-ing, "Ay, but he was a guid body." They said that even when the most hated person in the village was buried.

The first funeral I recall attending was that of my younger brother George. His illness had been diagnosed as water on the brain. I cannot recollect having any special emotion about George, but wept in sympathy with others I saw weeping at his funeral. When the first spadeful of earth sounded hollowly on the little coffin, I shuddered. Granny Sinclair's burial at Rosebank Cemetery in Leith was a more pleasant affair, for it meant a trip by train to Edinburgh. My Uncle Neil, her grief-stricken youngest son, was a teetotaler, so could not join the subsequent pub crawl, in which some of the mourners got exceeding merry. Although allowed only lemonade as a boy, I became infected with their gaiety. As mentioned earlier, a relieved feeling resembling pleasure always came over me after family funerals. It began as we left the graveyard, and was intensified when I returned to the room where the coffin had stood on two dining chairs.

Death, to us, was more than the ugliness of the grave. It meant the great judgment, a kind of grand "school inspection" which I, for one, expected to fail, for my copybook was all blots. Knowing that I would roast in the burning fire for eternity, I tried to figure how long eternity might be. It was appalling to think that I would go on burning for millions of years.

In my early teens, I began to have a phobia about disease. I pored over medical books and, like Jerome K. Jerome, the playwright and humorist, had every disease in the books. A pimple on my face spelled smallpox. A student we knew had just died of inflammation of the bowels—appendicitis, it must have been, but that disease was not known then. At once, I felt a pain in my belly, and was certain that God would deal me a similar death.

Feverishly seeking some of Granny's religious books for salvation, I had the dire misfortune to come across the story of a bad man who suffered paroxysms on his deathbed.

"It will soon be over," he said, groaning.

"Nay," said the stern minister who stood at his deathbed, "the agony is just beginning."

I have often wondered why each of us was affected in a different way by the unholy beast we knew as religion. It did not seem to have any effect on Willie. He entered the church later, not because he was ever religious—but because it offered a job. He had no fears of death and hell that I ever saw. My next brother, Neilie, seemed also to escape religion's dire influence, and Clunie, as already mentioned, was frankly skeptical. I alone appeared to have taken as my burden the sins of the whole family.

Mingled with my fear of death was a strange, contradictory element of taking risks. We boys had competitions to see who could run over the Black Box, a viaduct spanning the deep ravine of the railway. A fall would have meant death or serious injury; yet, with the others, I went over again and again, running or attempting to run on the edge of a two-inch plank. We took risks on the railway itself, bragging about how long we could stay on the ties when the train was approaching. We put pins on the tracks and barely sprang to safety. We climbed trees without any fear, but fear became associated with trees when Eck Hutcheon broke his neck raiding Findlay's gean (wild cherry) tree. Frank Craik and I debated solemnly about Eck's destination; Frank thought he had gone to heaven because he was a nice loon, but I was not so sure. A fearful thunderstorm came on as his funeral procession went down the road, and Frank told me I had been right after all, for the thunderstorm was clear proof that God was sending Eck to the burning fire.

Thunderstorms terrified me as a boy. Granny told me very early in my youth that thunder was God's voice in wrath, and knowing well that it was me he was angry with, I fled from thunderstorms like a frightened rabbit. My parents must have been afraid also, for during a storm there was always a hushed atmosphere in the house and my father had a violent headache. I was always scared, yet disappointed after the storm that no one had been killed. Clunie shared this morbid desire with me, and we sometimes made a list of the people we'd like to be struck down by lightning.

Old Nanzy Tam, the sweetshop wifie, told us she had once seen a baby killed by lightning that had come down the chimney. "It was like wadding [cotton wool], soft like butter: ye could put yer finger on its belly and it went in just like that," and she demonstrated on a cushion. We liked that story, and wondered how far we could press our finger into the belly of the fattest woman in the village if she were killed by a flash. We feared death but we jested at it.

One of my worries was the danger of sudden death, the most frightful of all, because there would be no time to repent. Consumption seemed an ideal death, with months to repent in, but poor Eck Hutcheon had had to go to his Maker without one second to cry: "Oh, God, forgive me my sins."

Softening our fear of death was a half-formed scheme to play with the devil until the last moment, and then, by a rapid repentance, slink through the Golden Gate before God could change his mind about pardon. In this respect, the thief on the Cross was an example to us. But the insinuating thought of sudden death could not be got rid of, and our playing with the devil was never a soul-free enjoyment.

The devil was sex.

My earliest memory of sex is a nursery incident when I was six and Clunie only five. We had stripped and were examining each other with great interest and considerable sexual excitement. The door opened, and Mother caught us. She gave us both a severe beating, then made us kneel down to ask God's forgiveness. Later, when Father came home, he took up the cudgels and spanked us again. I was then locked in the big dark dining room. So I learned that of all sins, sex was the most heinous.

This incident affected my life for many years, not only forcing me to associate sex with sin but also giving me a fixation on Clunie, who was connected with the forbidden fruit. There were later sexual adventures with Clunie, but she always had a bad conscience afterward and told Mother, and I got thrashed every time. Only once did I escape a thrashing after Clunie's tale-telling, when Willie was in on it, too—indeed, had suggested our wrongdoing. As the oldest, Willie got all the blame. Being the favorite, however, he was never punished for anything.

A few years later, I went through a period of having hidden adventures with girls behind school doors. We were never discovered, though most of the other boys knew; in fact, they were jealous, because the girls said that I tickled them best. Another memory is my unsuccessful attempt at intercourse with a very sexy girl when I was about eleven.

Naturally, we never had any sexual instruction at home. My mother went on having babies, and we took it for granted that the doctor was bringing them, for Mother could not tell us lies. Other boys told us the truth, or rather, many half-truths; and by keeping rabbits and seeing farm animals, we knew that the young came out of their mothers. But we never applied this knowledge to Mother. I must have been about eight when I saw Father go into the water closet one day. At first, I stared at him in surprise; I knew he couldn't do dirty things; and finally concluded that he must be going to clean it out. So when we heard the man's part in making a baby, I simply did not believe that, either. My parents were pure and holy; they could never, never do a thing like that.

Willie went off to school in Edinburgh, and when he came home for holidays he regaled us with dirty stories of all kinds. We thought ourselves very sophisticated but still dared not face the application of sex to our own parents. They were overmodest always; nakedness was awful. Except for Clunie, I never saw my sisters naked; and if anyone came into my bedroom when I was dressing, I hastily covered my body with anything I could seize. Later, as a twenty-five-year-old student in Edinburgh, I got into the habit of having a cold bath each morning. On holidays, I got my mother to throw a bucket of cold water over me while I sat in a tub, because our home had no bathroom. Mother did this cheerfully but Clunie told me that my father strongly disapproved.

For any sexual offense in school, my father always gave a savage punishment. I remember his giving Jock Ross six with the cane, on his hand held down on the desk, for pretending to drop his slate pencil while taking the occasion to put his hand up a girl's petticoats.

I cannot recollect our ever mentioning masturbation, or for that matter, practicing it. There are a few score slang terms for masturbation, but we did not know one of them. I know enough about psychology to realize that there may be some sort of repressive forgetting here, but to the best of my memory we did not masturbate either singly or mutually.

We did have a habit that we called "looking" each other. We would lay a smaller boy on his back and open his fly, but that was always a collective practical joke. From the age of seven and a half, I slept in a bed with Willie and Neilie, who resented my presence strongly. This arrangement came about after my ejection from the bed I shared with Clunie, by an irate mother who again had discovered us doing things we shouldn't have. My brothers never let me forget my unwelcome intrusion or the circumstances which led to it.

Masturbation must have been known to me all the same, for I was chided one day by my father for making the dog Boulot jump on my arm. I also have a vague memory of Neilie and me being in a locked room, and Uncle Neil demanding entrance. When we let him in, he looked at us in a leering way and said: "Aha, showing birdies!" We were most indignant, a circumstance that to any self-respecting psychoanalyst would have denoted our guilt.

Castration of sheep and cattle and horses was, of course, known to us all in a farming environment. The farmers called this "libbing," and a threat to "lib" us was a favorite joke of some of the plowmen. To us, the laugh behind the threat possibly made it a pleasurable thrill, though I remember that Jeemie Barclay, the village softie, used to go into extreme panic at the threat of libbing.

I don't think that my schoolfellows suffered much from sexual repressions. Some came from homes where the parental language was obscene. The illegitimate ones did not seem to mind, for the bastard was no inferior in Kingsmuir. Fornication was common between plowmen and servant lassies, and getting in the family way seemed just as common. But the most moral, condemning women in the village were always those who had had bastards themselves.

We all knew juicy verses of that delightfully obscene ballad *The Ball o' Kirriemuir,* which told of an occasion when some wag doped the liquor with an aphrodisiac. It was a strong ballad, Elizabethan in its honest bawdiness, redolent of the sex that springs from the soil. Obscene it may have been, but its ribaldry was of much higher essence than that of the sophisticated commercial-traveler story.

My position was a most difficult one. When I spoke dialect outside the house, I shared the villagers' open view of sex; when I spoke English and became respectable upon crossing the threshold of the schoolhouse, I had to put away all openness of mind concerning sex language and practice. At one and the same time, I strove to serve the God of the home and the Devil of the village. It simply could not be done. I fled from raw sex into the realm of idealistic sex.

Earning a Living

When I was fourteen, my father decided to send Neilie and me out to work. Neilie was doing no good at the Academy, and I had been learning nothing at Kingsmuir School. When Father asked us what we wanted to be in life, Neilie replied, "A sheep farmer," and I, "an engine driver." "Ugh," said my father in disgust, "you'll both go into offices."

Father was what my mother called a "flee about." He had changing enthusiasms about jobs, and his advice was nearly always bad. When Pat Craik came home on holiday from London, he was doing well in wholesale drapery. "Trade is the thing," said my father, and planned to make us drapers. But a week later, Willie Adam came home on holiday, and he was flourishing in the Civil Service. Thereupon, Father forgot about the merits of trade and ordered us to prepare for the Boy Clerks' entrance examination. We always hated Willie Adam's visits, for they meant weeks of dull work, doing sums, reading unreadable manuscripts, and cramming geography. The Civil Service exams were competitive, and Father knew in his heart that Neilie and I could never get in. So he returned to the idea of our becoming trade clerks.

At that time, we did not know who or what lay behind Father's eagerness to get us out working. It was Willie throwing away money at St. Andrews University—Willie dancing in hard-boiled shirts, going to special dinners, carousing with the other divinity students. Ever and again came wires saying simply: "Send more tin—Willie," and as more tin vanished, my parents got grumpier and grumpier, working out their ill tempers on us.

I recall a Saturday when they took a cheap trip to St. Andrews. Not expecting anyone, and with many things under foot, Willie spoke to them only a minute before rushing off. They came home in a tearing rage, and my mother gave Clunie a hiding for something of no importance. Since we understood the reason for the bad atmosphere, we hated Willie. Clunie, especially, was bitter about his extravagance: she saw things more incisively than the rest of us.

It now became evident that Neilie and I had to go away and earn a living. Neilie got a job as a clerk in a Leith flour mill; three months later, I received a reply to one of my many letters replying to advertisements in *The Scotsman.* My handwriting was good at that time, and I had penned my applications in a slow hand that attempted to be copperplate. To this day I can write beautifully when I try to—an accomplishment that is sneered at by more recent generations.

Copperplate has often been condemned on the ground that it does not show character, but why should it? I have in my possession a postcard from Bernard Shaw and two letters from Barrie; if handwriting betrays character, then Shaw was a cross between a hidebound schoolmaster and a stupid boy of ten, while Barrie was a congenital idiot. Good handwriting is something handsome to look at, and much of the criticism leveled against it comes from a realization that it is too difficult an art for the critic to attempt.

The letter in answer to my application informed me that I had been appointed a very junior clerk in the office of W. & B. Cowan, Ltd., gas-meter manufacturers in Edinburgh. My feelings were mixed. I was now to be freed forever from

studying Latin grammar, but against that weighed the knowledge that I also was to be freed from play and bird-nesting and
catching minnows. However, I set off boldly enough. I was to
lodge with Neilie in Leith. Neilie earned fifteen shillings a
week, and I was to earn six. The landlady's son, a young man
with a pessimistic view of life, shared our bedroom.

Cowan's works were two miles away—mostly uphill—in
Buccleuch Street, on the other side of Edinburgh. I had to
start off early in the morning, and was always late, so frequently had to take the tram. In those days, the trams were all
drawn by horses. My difficulty was financial. I could afford
threepence for lunch, but if I took the tram, that left me with
only a penny for food. For a time, I solved the question by
strategy. When the car left Pilrig, I noticed that the conductor went on top. If I jumped on while he was up there, I almost always got halfway up Leith Walk before the sight of his
boots on the stair signaled me to leave the car. When I was too
slow, I asked for a ticket to Leith. "Wrong direction," he
would say, and I would give a surprised: "Oh," hurriedly
jump off, and wait for the next car with a conductor on top.
Unfortunately, the conductors got to know me, and I had to
give up this easy mode of travel.

Cowan's was one long misery to me. I did not labor in
the central office, but in a dark evil-smelling hole of an office
in the middle of the works. There I lived in a stink of solder
and paint and gas. My happiest moments were those in which
I was sent to find someone in the works. I loitered with the
workmen, and then got sworn at when I returned to the office.
The only redeeming feature about it all was status: I was addressed as mister. The clerks always addressed each other as
Mr. So-and-So, and they all wore bowler hats. I wore a cap but
it was disapproved of.

For the first time in my life, I experienced homesickness.
I kept writing miserable letters to the family until finally my

mother came to see me for two days. I clung to her in bitter tears and implored her to take me home with her. She told me that that was impossible, and when she left, my homesickness was almost unbearable; I addressed business envelopes and wet them with my tears. My senior clerk, a man called Wilson, was very sympathetic and kind to me, and on that occasion, took over the addressing chore for me.

Neilie lost his job. It proved too difficult for a boy of sixteen, and he went home, leaving me alone. After being in Edinburgh three months, I was allowed to go home at New Year's for four days. I could not enjoy a minute, however, because my thoughts kept turning to the misery that would lie before me when I got back to Edinburgh. After seven months, I was allowed to return home permanently. I still remember the embarrassment of that homecoming, a shame at not having been able to stick it out. When one farmer remarked in company that "thae Neills canna bide at nithing," Neilie and I blushed.

Why was I taken back? I do not know. No doubt my parents had tired of my despairing letters, though there might have been another reason, too. I had written to my father, telling him that the chances of promotion were very poor in Cowan's, and that my future would be much brighter if I came home and studied hard for the Civil Service. From the hell that was Edinburgh, sitting in Kingsmuir schoolhouse all day long seemed like paradise. And I think I truly believed that once home, I should study all the time.

Neilie and I were set down again to study for the Civil Service—Men Clerks this time. But history repeated itself: we could not concentrate. One night in despair, my father threw our textbooks at us and said he gave up. "They're just fit for nothing, Mary."

But Johnston the chemist needed an apprentice, and my father fixed things up that I should begin work there on the following Monday. During the week, however, another local firm advertised for an apprentice—Anderson and Sturrock, drapers—and my father's plans rapidly altered: Neilie would be the chemist, and I the draper. So early on the Monday morning we walked to Forfar to our new jobs.

My duty each morning was to get the shop key at the proprietor's house, and be down in time to open up at eight. Then, with another apprentice, I had to sweep the shop. We sprinkled it with a watering can to keep down the dust, and I learned that a broom sweeps cleanest if the bristles are reversed. Most of my work was delivering parcels. One day, I had to walk a mile with a penny packet of pins that one of the upper-class ladies of the town would not carry. I learned never to expect a tip from the rich, but the poor always gave me a penny or tuppence for delivering their parcels. One of my jobs, to stand in the windows and clean them with whiting, touched the snobbish aspect of my upbringing. I really was ashamed of being in retail trade, and used to hide behind the whitened part of the windowpane if any of the better people were passing.

Snobbery also had its way in my idealization of women, which commenced at this period. I did not idealize common girls; I aimed higher. The girl I loved was always quite unattainable, always in a rank of society far above mine. Forfar, like every other town in the world, had its social structure, with very definite lines of demarcation between classes. If a girl went to Miss Smith's private school she was a superior being, and naturally, at my stage of lowly occupation, I found my objects of worship among the Miss Smith clientele. I say *objects,* for the admired one was never a constant. Today it might be Cis Craik; tomorrow, Jean Gray.

There was nothing consciously sexual about this. Even in imagination, I never thought of kissing them. I was satisfied to have seen them pass in the street; and if the adored one happened to glance in my direction, my joy was complete. Sometimes I made detours round by the Lour Road when delivering my parcels, hoping to get one glance at Jean Gray. One day when I met her, she looked absolutely beautiful in a large sun hat, with her little tilted nose and her bright eyes. My face must have paled with excitement.

Of course, this idealization was the result of the beatings I had received for what might be called sex in the raw; but even at this period, I was having quite earthly adventures with village girls whose feet did not turn the daisies into roses. The two interests never met; they existed in separate compartments, or rather, they were parallel lines that never met.

I hated the drapery business. I was on my feet from seven-thirty in the morning to eight in the evening, and then had the two-mile walk home. Since I wore heavy boots, my big-toe joints got inflamed and gradually stiffened—their condition to this day. My toes got so bad in fact that I had to give up the job. This I did gladly, vowing to my father that now I had acquired sense, I would slave at the Civil-Service exam. Poor Neilie had no excuse for giving up his chemist's apprenticeship; and for four long years he went back and forth, hating it all the time.

The old problem had arisen again. My concentration was no better than it had ever been, and for the third time my father despaired of me. This time he really gave me up, he said, and I stared gloomily into the future, seeing myself as a good-for-nothing tramp, wondering whether I would fail as an ordinary plowman. My one ambition was to be a minister like Willie. I pictured myself in the pulpit delivering wonderful sermons in a kirk that was crowded to the doors, but preaching to only one: to Jean Gray of the great sun hat, which shaded the eyes fixed in holy admiration upon the handsome young minister. Violet Jacob's *Tam i' the Kirk* is a pure joy to me, because it so passionately sums up the Scots religion-sex constellation. The dream was there and the reality did not disturb it—the reality that the ministry could only be reached through long, hard study.

"The boy's just hopeless," said my father gloomily.

"He might be a teacher," ventured my mother.

"It's about all he's fit for," said my father grimly, and without a smile.

Now that Father had given me up, Mother stepped in. She pointed out that no other teacher had as many classes as he had, and "Really, George, you need a pupil teacher." I knew that my father wasn't keen about it, but somehow she got him to broach the subject to the school-board clerk, and in due time I was appointed P. T., a student teacher, in Kingsmuir School. There I served an apprenticeship of four years. Though it is hard to recall my days in the school, I must have taken classes to relieve my father, for I do remember teaching small boys and girls to read by the look-and-say method. I found that the best way to learn anything is to teach it, and soon I could string off nearly every town, cape and river in the whole world, as well as the exports of Peru or the imports of China. I think I learned my profession well, for I copied my father, and he was a good teacher—good in the sense that he could draw out rather than stuff in. Father still disliked me apparently, and was inclined to treat me more like a pupil than a student teacher. Though he never ticked me off in front of my pupils, I was still afraid of him.

After his second year, according to student-teacher rules, the apprentice sat for his first examination—a small affair set by the school inspector. Then, at the end of his fourth year, came the King's Scholarship, or normal exam, that decided whether he would become a normal student or not. Passing with a First Class automatically made him a normal student, to be trained for two years in Glasgow or Edinburgh. If there were enough vacancies, a Second Class might get a student in;

a Third completely disqualified him.

My exam by the inspector at the end of my second year was not encouraging. "This candidate," said the report, "is warned that his work all round is weak." My father seemed more ashamed than angry with me.

When I took the normal exam at the end of my apprenticeship, I came out Third Class, nearly bottom of the list. I was about nineteen then, and recall sitting in our conspicuous pew the next Sunday wondering if the congregation knew what a dunce I was. My father rather thoughtlessly nudged me and remarked that Nora Stewart was in the choir; Nora had taken the same exam and passed First Class.

In all my adversities Clunie comforted me, and on this occasion, gave me a list of great men who had failed in examinations. She herself, clever in learning as she was, failed the normal exam a year later. When anyone failed to get into the Normal Training College, he became an "ex-Pupil Teacher," but by passing two other exams, could get a teacher's certificate —again a class affair, First, Second, or Third. Then one became an authorized teacher but untrained, and therefore much inferior to a teacher who had gone through the Normal College. A man who managed to procure only a Third Class in the certificate exam ranked as the lowest worm in the educational garden; he had no chance of getting promotion, and was likely to remain an underpaid assistant all his days.

My student-teacher days are mostly a blank to me now, though photographs of school groups show me standing stiffly with a very high choker collar. I look back on my position as a difficult one, for I had to be on the side of authority before my own desire to play had been lived out. It was the role of a boy pretending to be a man.

Pursuing Society and Culture

When I was about seventeen, my social ambitions began to seek a tangible outlet. As children of a teacher, our social status was very poor, and the best families in Forfar did not "know" us. Furthermore, we had no money and could not entertain or attend social functions. We realized we were outsiders. Willie and Neilie did not care, for they weren't snobs, and besides, Willie had his own society at the university. I aimed high. Neilie and I joined a small group calling itself the Graphic Arts Club, which suited Neilie, because he was a real artist, and me, as a possible door to society. I drew a little, mostly copies of Charles Dana Gibson women, but was never an artist, then or later. We drew in charcoal on brown paper, using models who generally came from the poorhouse. One club lady took an interest in me, and she and her sisters were very kind, inviting me to their house for croquet or supper. I was very ignorant of social behavior, and had some difficult moments with, what seemed to me, an abnormal number of knives and forks. I hastily bought a book on etiquette, which hardly helped, for it concentrated too much on how to address bishops and princes. For many years after, an elaborate dinner table made me nervous. My first acquaintance with a finger bowl was touch and go, but luckily I did not drink the water. A separate crescent plate for the salad proved another stumbling block. I thought it was for my bread and treated it accordingly; then discovered its true function, and sat very, very red throughout dinner.

Drawing-room behavior meant nothing to me. I was unaware that one stood up when a lady entered or left a room; had no idea that during afternoon tea, you held your tiny bit of cake in your saucer and not on your knee. I learned my lessons well, however, and in a short time murmured a conventional thank-you after a lady had played a Chopin waltz on the piano.

Behind this social maneuvering of mine there was a subtle plan: one day I might meet a girl I worshiped. Her name varied from time to time, but her class did not. Tennyson's *Maud,* which I read and reread at this time, became a symbol embracing the several ideals of beauty in the upper circles of the town. Unfortunately, the Mauds were not interested in books and music, and I did not meet them. But I did get myself introduced to the lovely Jean Gray. That was a sad happening, because our proximity deprived her of her golden glory, and I had to seek another, really unattainable object.

I must have been a most objectionable prig and humbug during this period of my life. Still, something was gained from it. I heard good music for the first time in that pre-record, pre-radio era. In the beginning, I listened to Chopin and Schumann because it was the correct thing to do, but the time came when I listened because the music itself brought me joy. I cannot recall learning much of other cultural matters. When books were touched upon in conversation, I sat silent lest I should betray my ignorance. One day when someone asked me who my favorite author was, I answered "Dumas," pronouncing the final "s." "You mean 'Dumah,'" said a superior man present, and I reddened and inwardly kicked myself because I had never read a word of Dumas anyway. Even so, I was slowly developing a certain literary taste at home. Willie brought us books of poetry—*modern* poetry, as we called it then. He introduced me to the majestic beauty of "The Hound of Heaven" by Francis Thompson, and the queer, haunting rhythm of Meredith's "Love in the Valley."

Willie himself was a lad of varied talents, and had a great influence on my development. His style in drawing was original if somewhat stiff, and for years the St. Andrews University magazine used his design with his pseudonym "Nil" on its cover. He wrote neat triplets and sonnets, and his prose was good. But while he read voluminously, he never seemed to assimilate ideas. He showed no interest in politics or science, and avoided discussion and argument. I cannot remember his having a sense of humor. Yet I imitated Willie for years. If he was a minister, I would become a minister. If he edited his university magazine at St. Andrews, I would edit mine in Edinburgh. If he drew with pen and ink, I drew with pen and ink. Willie's only interest I didn't copy was writing poetry, for I never wrote a line of verse in my life.

My efforts to become a pianist reached their peak at the age of seventeen. All the other children had been sent to study music—Willie, the fiddle; the rest, piano. Neilie took piano lessons for about four years, and when they were ended, forsook the piano forever. Why I alone received no music teaching, I do not know. Every now and again, however, I would decide to learn by myself. For a few days, with the aid of something called *Hemy's Tutor,* which I bought or borrowed, my fingers would laboriously pick out the scale with one finger— "Every Good Boy Deserves Favor." By seventeen, I had beaten all my previous records; it took a whole week to convince me that anything more was hopeless. I have often wished halfheartedly that I had been taught to play, knowing that if music had been strong in me, I would have learned in spite of all difficulties; but knowing, too, that I could never have been anything more than a mediocre musician.

During my student-teaching days, I met a man who made mathematics live for me. He was Ben Thomson, the maths master at the Academy, and later its rector. When I went to him for private tuition, he gave me a genuine love for the subject, which explains why I belong to that rare breed of people able to while away a railway journey doing algebraic and geometrical problems. Ben was a staunch friend. He gave me most of the lessons free of charge, and years later would help me by post when I had difficulties with the subject. I regret that he never wrote a textbook, for his way of presenting maths was unique. I kept telling him he should do this, and my last request reached him shortly before his sudden death. Forfar Academy in his time turned out many brilliant mathematicians.

I have said that I was not a reader. Nevertheless, I must have read quite a lot in the practice-teaching period, and recall borrowing many books from the Meffan Library, mostly fiction. I reveled in the whimsical sentimentality of Barrie's novels, identifying myself with his Sentimental Tommy. Again and again I cycled to his Thrums (Kirriemuir, seven miles away), and sitting in the den, tried, not very successfully, to people it with his characters. Kirriemuir was on the way to Memus where the Craig family lived in the Free Kirk Manse. The Craig girls were an original, unconventional lot, gaily flirting but always keeping just out of reach. They kept sentiment at arm's length with a laugh, and were good companions rather than love objects. The oldest became a household word: every British housewife knows Elizabeth Craig as an authority on cooking. I haven't met her since those days.

Willie had taught us that there were two kinds of girls: the kind you had to be introduced to, and the kind you picked up. According to Willie, the latter were easily the more interesting. During the summer season, they could be seen in pairs, parading the beach at Carnoustie or the streets of Kirriemuir.

Much experience was needed to know which pairs were pick-upable and which were not. If our "Good Evening," met no response except a haughty, withering glance, we concluded there was nothing doing; although we recognized a type who used the withering tactics to increase our effort. Almost invariably, one girl was pretty and the other plain. Whichever elder brother I was with, he naturally took it for granted that I should go off with the plain one, an assumption that did not appeal to me. Sometimes I would get in first, make off with the beauty, and then spend the cycling way home having bitter arguments about sportsmanship.

These flirtations were mostly superficial affairs, sitting on a bench in the dusk hugging and kissing. The truth is that we had very little success with our pick-ups, either because we looked poor and country bumpkinish, or, more likely, because the really attractive girls had plenty of followers and did not need to go looking for strays. Living two miles out of town and not being recognized by the town's social sets, we knew no girls, and our picking-up was as much the result of needing female companionship as it was of starving for sex.

About this time, I read an upsetting little book by Richard Le Gallienne—*The Quest of the Golden Girl*—whose heroine was a prostitute. The girls I picked up were never golden; they were not even base metal. They simply played at love, and most of them feared that things would go too far. The average pick-up led one on for a certain length, then hastily said it was time she went home, and ran away. I suppose she was looking for a Golden Boy and was as disappointed with the reality as we were. We took our failures lightly, and rode home late at night feeling healthy and happy. Tomorrow was a new day. Tomorrow we'd try Montrose or Arbroath for a new romance. I was talking to Neilie about these days years later, and we agreed that the happiest memory of that period was the long ride up the hill to the Jubilee Arms at Cortachy, with the thirsty vision of the bottle of Bass we were to have at the top. We did not smoke in those days. Where we got the money to buy even a bottle of beer, I cannot remember, though it was cheap in those days—threepence, I think. Whiskey cost three shillings a bottle; and Gold Flake cigarettes, sixpence for twenty.

My ambitions seem to have been latent at this time. The future did not exist for me, possibly because I dared not contemplate a future as an unsuccessful teacher with no hope of promotion. What I daydreamed about is long forgotten. By this time, religion had become an empty, outside thing, and my churchgoing had only one object: to see the girls. I sang in the choir, but although I had a good ear and could sing anything in tune, my voice lacked strength, and I never became a permanent member. I enjoyed choir practice once a week and sang lustily the bass of the anthems, but always timidly, a tenth of a tone behind the leader: one of my phobias was to be singing an anthem to a full congregation and coming in at the wrong time. Excellent orchestral performers have told me that this is a frequent nightmare.

A Young Dominie

When my apprenticeship ended, I applied for jobs, and finally got one in Bonnyrigg near Edinburgh at fifty pounds a year. The school was run by an old lady called Miss Mac-Kinley, who looked like an eagle and was a very stern disciplinarian. After the laxity of my father's school, it was a great shock to find myself suddenly in a school where the children were not allowed to talk in class. I was ordered to thrash any child who even whispered, and did so because I was really scared of the old woman. I stood it for two months and then got a better job at sixty pounds a year in Kingskettle in Fife.

If anything, the discipline of Kettle school was worse than that of Bonnyrigg. For three years, I had to be the sternest of taskmasters. The room used by Calder, the headmaster, was separated from mine by a glass partition, and his sharp eye could see everything that went on. For three years, I did my work with fear in my heart. Calder never relaxed: he kept me at arm's length, and all my attempts to approach the human side of him were frozen by his stony stare. Yet, in a queer sort of way, I felt that he liked me; and also in a queer sort of way, I liked him in spite of my fear. Calder's teaching methods were surprising to me. When he gave his class a test in arithmetic, he slowly worked out every problem on the blackboard first; then the children worked out the same problems in their books. Only the very stupid ones got the answers wrong under such a system, and God help them when they did, for the headmaster wielded a fierce strap and laid on heavily. The H.M.I. gave Calder excellent reports—because he kept excellent whiskey, the cynics said.

Kingskettle remained a horror to me. There must have been times during those three years when I was happy, but the main memory is one of fear: fear of being late in the mornings, fear of having my class examined by Calder, fear of him when he leathered the poor ones who could not learn. I realized that if I had been his pupil, I would have been strapped every day. My father had never been that strict. True, he had strapped often and sometimes hard, but there was in his school a certain freedom, freedom to laugh and chat and carve your name on the desk. We never had to march in or out like soldiers.

Kettle school was like a new world to me. There was no laughter in the school save when Calder made one of his oft-repeated jokes at the expense of a pupil. All pupils moved in military style; and everyone, including myself, was insincere, inhuman, fearful. Calder was my first contact with a real army disciplinarian. I had heard of the type—a few notorious ones existed in Forfar—and they all had a common characteristic: they were all men of small stature. One interesting point about Calder was his habit of always writing very slowly in copperplate. Even if he made a pencil note, it was beautifully written. Practically every pupil in the school could write well, too.

Once I took Calder's senior drawing class in his room, while he stood doing his registers at the desk. The lesson was given in dead silence, but when he went over to his house, hell broke loose, and I could hardly keep even the pretense of discipline. But I never reported the ringleaders to Calder when he returned. I tried to teach designing, with flowers and leaves as bases, and some pupils brought forth rather good, balanced patterns of the wallpaper type. These designs were the only original work ever allowed in school, for even an essay was first written on the blackboard by Calder and then copied by the class.

Calder was unhealthy, kept having painful boils on the back of his neck, and was quite unable to carry on his work for weeks at a time. During such periods, I was in complete charge of the school. I enjoyed these times, even though it was not an easy matter to keep order; not that I tried very much, knowing well that the moment Calder came back, his army discipline would grip the pupils automatically.

My farm lodging cost me fourteen shillings a week, and the wife of the farmer, Mrs. Tod, gave me more than my money's worth. The food was excellent—I can still remember the cream, so thick that it had to be raked out with a teaspoon. I was treated like a member of the family, which included a daughter and two sons. Will, the elder, had been to sea; at that time, indeed, was an unemployed ship's engineer. I called him Sir Oracle, for he laid down the law about everything and everybody. He believed that no conversation was of any value unless it contained a sequence of what he called "smart things," and I thought him a witty lad. Will made me feel like a very unsophisticated person when he talked about what he had seen on his voyages, and what sins he had committed in foreign ports. Looking back now, I am inclined to think he exaggerated more than a little.

He had a lovely bass voice, and I liked to hear him sing "Out on the Deep" while his sister Aggie, who also had a fine voice, accompanied him on the piano. But he always broke down with coughing after the first verse, for he had been thrown down by an express train when a schoolboy, and his heart had been affected. He did not live long, nor did his younger brother Walter, who was a simpler soul than man-of-the-world Will. I liked Wattie. He tried to sing in a small

croaky voice, but always broke off and laughed at himself. He
was a dear laddie, and when he died not long after I left
Kettle, I suffered genuine grief.

Wattie belonged to the volunteers and persuaded me to
join. That was good fun. Once a week we put on our khaki
uniforms and were driven in a wagonette to headquarters some
miles away, or to the rifle range up on the Falkland Hills. Our
usual driver, Geordie Henderson, was landlord of the local
hotel and a real character. We laughed at his efforts to talk
like an educated man. When Kettle Farm caught fire and
Geordie had to take charge as captain of the fire brigade, he
wanted volunteers to come and man the pump. "Come away,
Gentlemen," he cried, "come away and call the pimp."

My first visit to the rifle range was thrilling. When I lay
down at a hundred yards, never having fired a rifle in my life,
and I had four bull's-eyes in succession, the officer in charge
got much excited. "At last," he cried, "I've got a marksman
in my company. Come back to the five-hundred-yards and have
a shot there." Proud as Punch, I went to the five-hundred-
yards' stance—or was it *butt?*—and took a long and steady
aim. I missed the target completely, and went on missing it
completely, till the disappointed captain gruffly told me not to
waste any more good ammunition.

Volunteering was a picnic until we went to camp for a
fortnight in August. Then they put us through the paces with
a will, and at night we turned into our tents dead beat. Camp
was a social kind of life for us, a jolly lot who did not take
our military duties too seriously. Some of the more independent Fifers in our battalion refused to salute officers, and once
I saw our colonel, Sir Ralph Anstruther, stop a miner, demanding to know why he did not salute. "Can't you see I'm an
officer?" he said sharply. The miner shrugged his shoulders
and spat. "I doan't give a dawm what ye are," he said. "I
never saluted anybody in my life." So speaking, he walked

leisurely away while the impotent colonel stood and fumed. The officer got his own back, however, by ordering a special saluting drill after supper, and we had to march up and down saluting a lamppost when we should have been swaggering along the streets of Carnoustie with the girls.

Eager to be a soldier, I got the infantry training manual—a new edition had been issued after the Boer War—and studied it well. But I never won my sergeant's stripes, though passing the exam with flying colors, because of my departure from Kettle and resignation from the corps. While with the volunteers, I won a prize—for shooting, *mirabile dictu.* When asked what I wanted, I chose books: one of them *The Right Line and Circle,* and the other a trigonometry text. The captain's sister made me very proud when she raised her eyebrows in presenting them, and said: "Ah, a student!" God knows my reasons for selecting these books; I certainly never used them.

Another great memory of that period is King Edward VII's review of forty thousand volunteers in the Queen's Park in Edinburgh. What a day! We left Kettle at two in the morning, marched to the park, and stood about for hours. As we marched by the king, he was heard to say: "And a damn fine regiment, too." We were proud of this until learning that the remark had been meant for the regiment that had passed before ours. All I recollect about the king was his yellowish face and how unhappy he looked.

It was during my stay in Kettle that I became ambitious, again, to enter the ministry. The man who encouraged this desire was the local minister, Reverend Aeneas Gunn Gordon. He was a Canadian, tall, straight, distinguished, with a strong beard and a nose like an eagle's beak. He took me under his wing, and I told him of my wish. "You need Greek," he said. "Come down to the manse every morning at eight and I'll teach you."

He knew his Homer, almost by heart, and taught me so well that I could read the first two books of the *Odyssey* and a part of Herodotus. (Today I cannot read a word of Greek.) Gordon had one failing—which never affected my admiration; sometimes he drank too much, and I recall seeing him of a morning holding Homer upside down, while quoting it correctly. He was a man who read everything but appeared to absorb little and gave out less. Though liberal in the way of charity and human kindness, he delivered dull sermons, and his conversation seemed commonplace. Yet he gave me a certain interest in literature. He used to read aloud from *Paradise Lost,* and I learned to appreciate "the organ music of Milton." On his advice I read Dante and Tasso, and then the essays of Macaulay. The latter gripped me, making me conscious of literary style for the first time in my life; I was then in love with a girl in Glasgow, and used our correspondence to improve my own style. How far beyond her those purple passages and that noble diction must have been. My present attitude toward style, with few exceptions, can be stated simply: the important thing is *what* is said, not *how.*

When Gordon got married, I was his best man. It had been arranged that I should wear my father's frock coat and striped trousers, which fitted me well. But getting ready for the morning train—my holiday had been spent at Kingsmuir— I could not find my black shoes. I searched in vain, keeping one eye on the clock; Sister Ada had taken them to be repaired. My only other boots were yellow as a dandelion. There was no way out: I set off in my frock coat and tall hat and those dreadful boots. In Dundee, as I crossed from station to station, I met all the Newport folks coming off their train; their amused stares still haunt me. In the southbound train, I tried to hide my feet under the seat.

My functions as best man worried me. I knew that my chief job would be to scatter sweets and pennies to the children around the kirk, but all I had in my pocket was ninepence. After the wedding, when I had to send an announcement of the ceremony to *The Scotsman,* I was obliged to do so without payment, and of course it did not appear next morning. The bride was furious with me, scorning my explanation. She never liked me after that, which made me resentful, because I really felt responsible for the match. Certainly I had been the go-between during the courting days. Looking back now, I think she disliked me because Gordon liked me so much. Thirteen years later, she gave me quite a cool reception when I dropped in to see them on my motorcycle. After the wedding, I believe, Gordon never touched drink again.

It was in Kettle that I began, briefly, to shoot rabbits and crows with Tod's gun. One Saturday morning, I killed a few crows. Walking through the field the following night, I heard a faint squawk and saw on the ground a poor bird with half its guts blown away. Almost sick, I killed it with my heel, and from that day in 1903 to this, have never shot another bird or beast.

I never got to know the people of Kingskettle. East Fife people have a difficult reserve that will not break down: they never allow anyone to enter their private lives. The people of East Suffolk, where I now live, seem very similar. The people of Glasgow are much friendlier than those farther east in Edinburgh. But why there should be this difference between east and west, I cannot say. The breeziness of the west may be only superficial and meaningless, but it is easier to live with. In Kettle, I always remained an outsider. It was a village with much musical talent; as a singer, I might have been more welcome, but my only accomplishment was reciting, and they did not care much for that.

My elocution days were a painful, ludicrous interlude. I must have been about eighteen when they started. It was usual then for people to contribute something to the common entertainment when invited out; some sang, some played piano, one man did card tricks. My line casually became known as reciting. I began with an American fragment called *Oh, My!* but soon progressed to more ambitious stuff. Books on public speaking always gave extracts for recitation, and a common one was *Rubinstein's Playing* as described by a backwoodsman or cowboy. Once memorized, this was a gem for the amateur who fancied his histrionic powers. I can still look back with shame to an evening when I "did" Rubinstein, tearing my hair and letting my fingers run up and down an imaginary piano. The audience was rural, had never heard of Rubinstein, and had seldom, if ever, heard a piano played; naturally they wondered what this was all about. Resolving to stick to the obviously comic, I had some success with a *Strand Magazine* story called *The Presentation to Lamb,* in which I was supposed to make up a speech for the bashful Lamb when his club gave him a wedding present. Lamb got drunk and muddled my speech in glorious fashion.

My first political efforts occurred in Kingskettle. My landlord Mr. Tod, a Tory, was thick in the fight against Asquith, whose constituency included East Fife. Tod used to read me A. J. Balfour's speeches from *The Scotsman,* and I was full of zeal for the Tory Party. When Asquith came round, arrogant and rather bored, I joined in the hooting against him. On election day, I sailed about with a blue ribbon on my lapel, which delighted Gordon, another Tory sympathizer.

At this time, too, I recall going to the theater. I had seen my first play, *A Night of Pleasure,* at the age of twelve in Edinburgh's Theatre Royal. For me it certainly was a night of bliss, for I had never seen such visions of radiant loveliness in my life. I had never imagined any woman could be so beautiful as the heroine. What the story was about I do not remember, save that the lovely damsel was wronged in some way. But it all came right in the end.

My next visit to the theater occurred during Neilie's medical studies in Edinburgh. We waited for two hours in the gallery queue before the doors opened, then scrambled for a front seat and got one. After another half-hour's wait—at nineteen I fidgeted like a small boy—we saw the great Sir Henry Irving in *The Bells* and *Waterloo*. I sat through these performances in open-mouthed ecstasy. But now, after all these years, I see Irving as an actor in the worst sense of the word. He strutted, made wild gestures, and overplayed both the false passion of Matthias in *The Bells* and the sentimentality of dotage in *Waterloo*. Of course, I may be blaming the actor for the faults of the dramatists. In either event, I had no criticism in my soul during the first years of the century: life had not tarnished my boyish wonder.

Having reached by stages a teaching salary of seventy-five pounds a year, I applied for a job in Newport at a hundred pounds. About four o'clock one day, two strange men called at the Kettle school to take me to tea. One of them was H. M. Willsher, the Newport headmaster. They offered me the job, and I packed my little trunk. Willsher could not have been more unlike Calder. His discipline was easygoing—he did not care how much the children talked—and from the first day I loved the school. My two years in that southern suburb of Dundee were perhaps the happiest of my life thus far.

Newport can be reached via the Tay Bridge or the Tay Ferries. It was residential, and the only proletariat consisted of people who did the necessary work in the suburb—tradesmen, street cleaners, etc. So the pupils were socially mixed. The highest class sent their boys to the public schools and their daughters to other private schools. Our school got the lower-middle and working classes.

For me, Newport was an opportunity to realize my more snobbish dreams. In Forfar and elsewhere, my class status had been fixed; but here in Newport, I saw that Willsher and the other teachers were hail-fellow-well-met with the goodly citizens and, even as an ex-student teacher without a university degree, I also might be in good society. Actually, I had passed my final exam and was now the possessor of an Acting Teacher's Certificate. That, of course, explains why I now earned a hundred pounds a year.

Anyway, I was determined to go to the university by hook or by crook. During my time in Kettle, I had worked hard, and one morning cycled over to St. Andrews for the first part of my preliminary exams—two subjects, English and Maths. I made a bad mess of the first maths paper: it was far too difficult for me, even though Ben Thomson had been coaching me by post. I came out in despair, half thinking that I should give the whole thing up without attempting the second paper in the afternoon. At lunch I ran into a lecturer, an old pal of Willie's, and told him of my failure. He patted me on the back cheerfully. "What you want is a brandy and soda," he said, and led me to the Cross Keys. I had never tasted brandy before but liked the taste and had another double. If not singing as I entered the exam hall, no doubt I felt like it. My memory of the paper is nil, but I did pass in both subjects. Thus, when I went to Newport, I was already a semi-matriculated student. Now I studied Latin and Physics for the second portion of the exam.

The first thing that happened to me in Newport was romantic; I fell violently in love with a pupil. Margaret was about sixteen; I, twenty-four. Her voice struck me as the essence of sweetness. To me, she was all that was lovely. Her long lashes almost hid her beautiful eyes, and I found that I could not look at her when she looked at me. She personified the whole school for me: if she happened to be absent, the day was dark, long, and dreary; when she was present, the day was always far too short. Years later, when I told her how much she had meant to me, she seemed much surprised. Wiser now in human motive and behavior, however, I think she must have known, and no doubt used her dangerous eyes to torment the bashful, half-baked youth who trembled at her glance. Her beauty was not real to me, but something on which to build fantasies. So, of course, I made no advances. Wooing her did not seem to be so important as worshiping her.

The remarkable thing about Margaret was her persistence in my mind. While other girls faded from memory, she continued to haunt my dreams for years. I have found other grown men whose dream-Margarets ever and again came back into their lives as dream-pictures, and I have known women who had their dream-men. This puzzles me still. I have had long periods of psychoanalysis with different specialists, but the Margaret image baffled them all. They guessed she was my mother as I first knew her, young and desirable; then they said she must be a substitute for Clunie. Neither explanation gave me any emotional response. I do have a strong feeling that her indifference was her chief attraction. She obviously did not admire me; yet, on the evening before I left the school, she suddenly threw her arms round my neck and said: "Mr. Neill, you are a dear." Damn the girl. That should have broken the spell. But it only made her more desirable than ever.

For years I heard nothing more of Margaret. Then, when she was a widow past seventy, I wrote her and later went to see her. The beautiful eyes were dim, the long eyelashes had gone. I often wrote and phoned her thereafter; she was lonely living by herself, also lame and in pain. She had had a slight stroke and dreaded another. All her life, the lass had remained lower-middle-class, outside the mainstream of new ideas. I laughed at her shock when I used a four-letter word. As time went on, however, the aging Margaret began to change. "You have opened up a new world for me," she would say. And she was a sweet old woman, though too set in her ways to accept modern ideas. One Sunday night, when I phoned her, there was no reply. Neighbors found her in a coma.

Poor Margaret. We agreed that marriage between us would have been a mistake, and I doubt if she ever could have overcome her conventional life in a Scottish suburb. But what is the use of guessing anyway? She was a youthful dream. A young man's fantasy assumes that if a girl is pretty, she has a pretty nature as well. And Margaret was doubly blessed. She had true manners, being considerate of others and hating to offend.

Adoration of Margaret did not prevent my having decided interests in other girls, and I gradually achieved a socially satisfying life through the Leng family. Sir John Leng had founded the big newspaper industry in Dundee. Mrs. Leng was a kind old lady, and I became tutor to one of the young Leng boys. I was invited to a dance they gave. Thus, at last, I had reached my long-wished-for ambition—to move in the best society.

Alas, I had never learned dancing and had no evening clothes. With only a hundred pounds a year, I could not afford to go to a good tailor. So I went to the Kingsmuir tailor and asked him if he could make me an evening suit. He scratched his head doubtfully, but thought he might have a try if he could find an illustration in *The Tailor*. I got my suit by post, and stupidly enough did not try it on. When entering the ballroom for my first dance, I found the trousers had been cut about two inches too long.

The cloth my tailor suggested was far too heavy; and for years I sweated much more than I should have done at dances, which were mostly waltzes then. Stoutish men had to take three collars with them. I would guess that the eightsome reel accounted for turning one collar into a soaking rag, and the waltzes and lancers accounted for the other two.

But even before the problem of costume was solved, I

had to learn to dance. A young teacher in Dundee gave me three lessons in waltzing—one, two, three—turn—four, five, six—and I picked up the step easily. Quickly, too, I learned the intricacies of the eightsome reel and lancers, soon being able to take my position at the head of a lancer set.

In the fashion of that era, the girls stood with programs in hand, while the men moved among them like farmers buying cattle at the mart. One youth would pretend not to see Mary because she had almost broken his arm in the waltz, and looked the other way when he saw Jean, who had no rhythm at all. This tactic could backfire, however; frequently all the best girls had booked up their programs in advance. One entire evening, disgusted by the whole custom, I danced only with plain wallflowers. At the time it seemed the most heroic thing I had ever done; now I am inclined to question my motive.

Socially, I was fairly well pleased with my life. But culturally I had progressed, too. Harry Willsher, the school's headmaster, became my musical mentor. Apart from his personal talents, he was music critic for the Dundee paper. One evening, hearing me remark that I liked Elgar's "Salut d'Amour," he sat down and played it. Then, without a word, he repeated the composition. "Shall I play it again?" he asked, but I said no. He smiled. "The lesson is this, Neill. Good music you can hear again and again: inferior music bores you stiff if you get it more than once." I was much impressed; yet today, if I had to listen ten times in succession, to something I really like—the trio from *Der Rosenkavalier,* for instance— I should feel like drawing a gun on the singers.

For the first time in my life, I was within distance of drama and opera. It wasn't first-class opera, but good enough for someone who was not a first-class appraiser of music. I heard *Faust, Tannhäuser, Lohengrin, Carmen.* Because of someone's organizing genius, I also heard Saturday concerts for a shilling, thus coming to know the artistry of Pachmann, Paderewski, Siloti, Elman, and our own Scottish Lamond. I was more impressed by their names than by their music, and feel certain today that if someone put three famous pianists behind a screen and had each play a Chopin polonaise I could not tell which one was playing. That may be an over-statement: I can tell when a waltz is played by Pachmann, but that is only because he had so individual a style. Of orchestral music I was equally ignorant, and still question whether any-one lacking a musical education senses the real difference be-tween one conductor and another; though a nonmusical person may be able to distinguish between a good and a bad render-ing of a favorite piece. I like the polonaise from *Eugene Onegin,* for instance, but have heard it played well only once or twice; loving it, I can detect a bad performance.

In those days, Dundee had a theater. Touring companies came every week, and I had the joy of becoming a regular theatergoer. Musical-comedy successes came from London, and we saw Martin Harvey, a popular actor of the period, in *The Only Way, The Breed of the Treshams,* even *Hamlet.* His *Hamlet* played one week; that of Sir Johnston Forbes-Robertson the next. To me, both were surpassing fine. My cultural standards those days may be better understood, too, if I say that *The Only Way* seemed a much better play than *Hamlet.*

During this period, I discovered my dislike of seeing or hearing anything alone. The same desire to share with others comes over me today when I listen by myself to a good concert or opera on the radio. Sometimes, in Dundee, I took Clunie to my favorite plays. She was just as ignorant of the theater as I, but my slight advancement made me laugh in a very su-perior way when the curtain fell on the first act of *The Only Way,* and she, with memories of local shows in the village school, remarked: "Martin Harvey will be helping to shift the furniture, won't he?"

Newport was well off then, but Dundee was mostly a dirty slum. Yet I remained incredibly unaware of social disparities, with no feelings at all about riches and poverty. Indeed, there were no signs of my being a potential rebel. When Winston Churchill came to contest Dundee as a Liberal, I rejoiced at a Tory handbill: "What is the Use of a W. C. without a seat?" and threw things at young Winston when he spoke at an open-air meeting, mainly because a girl called Ella Robertson dared me to.

My brother Neilie, about to qualify as a doctor, did his obstetrical cases in Dundee. He would be called out at dead of night, and I sometimes gave him company through the long streets. We entered houses that were hovels, where women labored in beds swarming with lice. Sometimes a woman would be having a baby in a room full of sleeping children. Such sights should have made me conscious of social evils, but apparently they didn't. I must have been emotionally and intellectually asleep.

Newport is one of the few places I still return to with strong feelings. It gave me peace, and helped me to carry on my teaching work without fear. I shall always have a tender spot in my heart for Harry Willsher, who was a companion rather than a master.

In Newport, as mentioned earlier, I came into contact with a higher class of society. There I learned how to behave like a gentleman, picking up all the futile little tricks comprising the term *good manners*. My frock coat and tall hat saw me through evening affairs; on Sundays, I went to church all dressed up, with white slip showing bravely under my waistcoat to indicate a nonexistent one beneath. But here an eccentricity began to edge its way in. I recall finding a highly colored waistcoat that had belonged to my maternal grandfather, and wearing it with my frock coat. I have always had a definite complex about dress, and wore open-necked colored shirts long before they became fashionable. Unusual dress is one means of drawing attention to oneself, and in the beginning no doubt that was the reason for my perversity in dress. But now, when I have other ways of being an exhibitionist—lecturing, for example—I still dress unconventionally. There is a protest in the habit, a sort of "why the hell should I be limited because everyone else wears this or that?" Fashion has always made me resentful; uniformity pains me. I associate proper dress with social usage, and never wear collar and tie to go to London except when I have to meet diehard prospective Summerhill parents.

But in Newport days, my dress reform was timid and hardly perceptible. I was too much afraid of alienating the little circle I had entered, for status was the one thing that mattered to me then. I was interested in society only as an external thing, rather than as a means toward gaining artistic or intellectual culture. I enjoyed hearing Willsher and his friends talk about books or music, but I did not expect men and women in society to do so. They talked of tennis and dances, as healthy young people ought to. Possibly, in my superior way, I tried to educate some of them. I remember lending H. G. Wells's *Marriage* to a girl of sixteen. Her father read it, wrote me a note calling me a dangerous seducer of innocence, and said I should never darken his door again. That, no doubt, put a stop to my attempts to uplift.

Meanwhile I had gone to St. Andrews and passed the second half of my entrance exam, feeling very much pleased with myself. The door to the university was now open, and I said a sad farewell to Newport in the summer of 1908. Since the university did not open until October, I went back to Kingsmuir. I had saved enough to carry me over a year, or maybe two—heaven knows how. My main difficulty was choosing a profession. I had long given up any wish to enter the church, and had no definite ambition to enter anything else.

The return of an old pupil to see my father settled the matter. He had worked toward a B.Sc. in Agriculture and spoke of big jobs in the colonies. "The very career for you," said my father with enthusiasm, and I accepted the suggestion.

It was because of this degree, ostensibly, that I went to Edinburgh instead of St. Andrews. My dreams of a university had always attached themselves to St. Andrews. In visits to Willie, I had been enraptured by the romance of the "gray city" with the scarlet gowns of the students and the happy atmosphere of Willie's tales. The social life there appealed to me strongly. It had a happy, family air about it; almost dangerous in a way, because St. Andrews men had a backward longing for their Alma Mater resembling the maudlin drunkard's rhapsodical desire to weep on the village pump. I chose Edinburgh because it was easier to get a degree in agriculture there, really because it seemed likely I should get a more cosmopolitan education. In St. Andrews, I knew I should meet men from Perth and Stirling, whereas in Edinburgh, I might meet men from all over the world. My acceptance of the plan to study agriculture shows how much of a drifter I was. I had no interest in agriculture, and knew that I never could have. For me, accepting it as a career meant as much as accepting an invitation to play tennis because I had no wish to do anything else at the moment.

University Life

Neilie was in his final year of medical study, and I went
to lodge with him. It was a cheap place off Clerk Street. The
better-off students all lived over Marchmont way. Mrs. Sutherland, our landlady, was a gem; a dear, kind woman who looked
after me for four years. I was now really hard up and had to
look twice at every penny spent, for there was no means of
earning more. Luckily, I came under the Carnegie Trust and
had my university fees paid by that grant, although matricula-
tion and exam payments were not included. Neilie and I could
only allow ourselves threepence a day for lunch. The Students'
Union had a restaurant; also a lunch counter, where every day
we each had a glass of milk and two penny buns. Other students had the same but they dined well at night. We could
only afford high tea in our lodgings, and our only good meal
of the week was the Sunday midday dinner. We always quar-
reled about the division of it until we evolved a sound plan:
Neilie divided the main dish between two plates, and then I
chose one.

Though my approach to higher. education may have been
casual, I took seriously my first-year classes in chemistry and
natural philosophy—at least in the beginning. Every morning
we had a lecture by Sir James Walker, the chemistry professor,
and I took voluminous notes. I thought it a waste of talent,

however, for Walker to spend his precious time teaching raw students the elements of this subject; and in 1936, when I dined with the principal of Johannesburg University, I made such a remark at table. The professors present were up in arms at once. They defended the lecture system by saying that this very contact with a man like Walker was the best education a student could have. I still don't believe it. Any assistant could teach a class what happens if you put sulphuric acid on zinc, and why should a good chemist like Walker not spend all his time doing research at the expense of the university or state? I liked chemistry with its practical lab work and passed it easily. But my work must have cost the university something, for I used up all the chloroform cleaning my pipes.

Natural philosophy was double Dutch to me. Professor MacGregor was the worst lecturer I ever encountered, mumbling into his beard as he wrote mysterious formulae on the blackboard, while we passed the time cat-calling and tramping tunes with our feet. MacGregor never seemed to mind: I wonder if he ever heard us. Our greatest day occurred when the lab assistant, Lindsay, had to turn the handle of an instrument to show the workings of sound waves. Then we all threw pennies at him; but like his master, he stood there quite unperturbed. He had had many years of this, and possibly his only interest was the amount of the collection he would sweep up when class was over.

Lab work in Nat. Phil. was a farce to me. I remember being given some apparatus concerning an inclined plane, and repeatedly timing something, so I could write down each result. After getting about fifty of these results, I added them up and took the average. I disliked the dullness of this work and hated my inability to do it quickly. Another man would finish his experiment in about half an hour, and looked to be the class medalist. One day I asked him how he managed to get through his experiments so quickly. "Take three readings and fake the rest," he said shortly. After that, my experiments took about twenty minutes each.

I can honestly say that I hardly understood anything about sound, light, and heat—not to mention electricity. When the final exam came round, I stared at a paper that was far beyond my comprehension, and went home for the summer vacation feeling depressed. I passed. Still wondering how and why, I can only conclude that old MacGregor was as absentminded in correcting papers as he was in the lecture hall, and muddled my paper with someone else's. For all I know, he mixed up mine with that of his medalist, whom he may have flunked.

By the end of the first year, I had discovered that science was not my line, and made up my mind to take a degree in Honors English. Probably one of my father's old pupils had come home and was doing well as an M.A. in Hon. Eng. Honors English meant that, with the exception of history, I could spend all of my time taking English classes. I duly entered for history and first-year English.

We had Sir Richard Lodge for English History, and I enjoyed his lectures thoroughly. There was no cat-calling in *his* room; one look from him and we all became diligent little boys and girls who were seen and not heard. One youth tried cat-calling one day. He sat behind me, and I looked round in annoyance. Suddenly I heard Lodge shout: "You, sir!" He was looking, I thought, at the bad man behind me. "You, you, you, sir," came the persistent, hard voice of the professor, and he pointed at me. I rose from my seat and silently asked a vital question by indicating myself with my forefinger. "Yes, you," thundered Lodge. "Get out of this classroom, sir."

Very white, I marched from the room with my head up. After class, I knocked at the door of his private room. "I thought you would come to apologize," he said. "I didn't, sir. I came to tell you I had nothing to do with the noise."

He eyed me with some suspicion. "Of course, if you say

so . . ." He shrugged his shoulders as if to show he didn't believe me.

Then suddenly I lost all my fear of authority and my temper as well. "Look here, sir," I said. "I had to work for years to save up enough money to come to the university. I am years older than the average student. Do you think, in these circumstances, I came to Edinburgh to behave like a raw schoolboy?"

His eyebrows went up in surprise. Then he smiled, held out his hand, and apologized. My honor was satisfied, but I could have sunk through the floor next day when Lodge began his lecture by offering a public apology, for it wasn't so much an apology as a panegyric. His word-portrait made me not only a scholar but a super-gentleman—and a prig.

My English professor was George Saintsbury, the renowned English author and critic. I sat under him for three years, but he did not know my name or know me by sight except on one occasion. His lectures were soliloquies; he spoke them like a parrot, and did not seem to care whether we listened or not. That suited us all right, for we did not listen. At least I personally did not, knowing that I could find it all in his voluminous writings a week before the exam. He had a high, squeaky voice, and amused us by his gentlemanly attitude toward his contemporaries: "Er—I do not quite agree with my friend—er—(then quickly) Mr. Bridges when he says—but I must be just and take into consideration what Professor Raleigh, who by the way in his attitude toward Dryden . . ." We had great sport trying to stick to the main road through all his parentheses.

Our course of study was not a creative one. We were supposed to "know" literature from Beowulf to Pater. We had to learn Anglo-Saxon and Middle English. We used set books and studied set periods—my final exam covered Elizabethan drama. In effect, we read books about books. For an exam, it was necessary to know what Coleridge and Hazlitt had said about Shakespeare; in any question on style, we were supposed to know exactly what Longinus had said about the subject. By that time I had discovered Ibsen and was full of enthusiasm for his plays. When my classwork demanded from me an essay on *Much Ado,* I quite foolishly wrote a damning criticism of the play, comparing its theater with the contemporary theater of Ibsen. That is, I criticized Shakespeare for not writing a realistic play—a stupid thing to do, but putting forward the point of view I held then. Saintsbury was very angry with me— the one time he must have recognized my name.

I held then, and do now, that it is better to write a bad limerick than be able to recite *Paradise Lost.* That is a fundamental thing in education. But the university never asked us to compose even a limerick; it did not ask from us any original opinions about Shakespeare or about anyone else. In those years, I read Spenser, Chaucer, Pope, Dryden, most of Shakespeare and much of his contemporaries; practically all of the Restoration Drama, Coleridge, Tennyson, Dr. Johnson, Keats. . . . But why go on? I was compelled to concentrate on whether a blank-verse line had elision or not, or whether one could trace the rhythm of "Christabel" in "The Lotus Eaters." It was all piddling stuff, like taking Milan Cathedral to pieces stone by stone to discover where the beauty lay. I had to read so glorious a thing as *The Tempest* with annotations, painfully looking up the etymological meaning of some phrase that did not matter a scrap.

Saintsbury gave me a feeling for prose style, and that's about all. He knew the beauty of literature, but he could not get it across to us. I spent three years with him in dreary swamps of prose rhythm and poetic diction, seeing the trees but never the woods beyond. He held that his work had to deal with manner and not matter; else, he said, English Literature would bring in every study under the sun. I can see that, but it simply isn't possible to treat Macaulay's *Essay on Clive* as a piece of literature without giving—or having any opinion on—the historical and political aspects of Clive's life. Saintsbury found it so easy to separate subject from style that he praised Blake as a great technical poet, and Nietzsche as one of the greatest German prose writers, while dismissing the subject matter of both with the words: "They were, of course, mad."

Whatever I actually gained from Saintsbury, it was certainly not an appreciation of literature. To this day I cannot read poetry for pleasure, cannot touch the classics. One year I went over to Norway—an M.A. in Honors English—and my literature for reading on the voyage was a bundle of *Black Mask* magazines—American crook yarns. True they were shoved into my hand by a friend as I left, but if I'd had Keats and Shelley in my bag, I still would have read the *Black Masks.* I hasten to add that it would be grossly unfair to blame Edinburgh University for any bad taste acquired: I am merely suggesting that if my years there had been spent in studying matter instead of manner, I might have had a better taste in literature today. I know that anything I could say today about Chaucer and Keats would be unimportant and uninformed.

When Professor Chrystal, the celebrated mathematician, died, I went to see Saintsbury about giving me an obituary on the Professor for our university magazine, *The Student.*

"I am just going into my Honors Class," he said. "If you are quick at taking notes, I shall allow you to come in, for I mean to say something about my old friend."

"But, sir, I have been in your Honors Class for three years."

He looked up quickly and asked my name. When I replied, he said, "Good heavens, how you have grown."

I had been six feet years before I entered the university, and there weren't a dozen of us in that class. Saintsbury recognized books but not students. Lecturing to a bunch of raw undergraduates must have been hell for him.

On the whole, social life at Edinburgh was pleasant. Being a member of the Union, I always had a meeting place and an armchair of an evening. The difficulty was the shortage of cash. Most of my friends were well off. They wore the same sort of golfing jacket and flannel bags as I did, but they had money to spend; and when drinks went round it was awkward, because I never had more than a few coppers in my pockets.

I could not afford to play any games or even go to see matches. I had to pretend I hated music halls in order to avoid joining parties going to the Kings or the Empire. Nowadays I should tell them the truth, that I was poor. Mainly from my mother, who feared that we might revert to her working-class mother's status, I had got the Shavian idea that poverty was a crime, a thing to be ashamed of, to hide as skillfully as one could. I must have played my part well, for years afterward a fellow-student, who had been a pal, remarked: "Yes, it was all very well for you, Neill. You had money and I hadn't."

During my second year I had a stroke of fortune. My landlady gave me her paper to read one Sunday, and I idly tried a competition therein. A week later, seeing a placard on Nicolson Street: EDINBURGH MAN WINS FORTY POUNDS, I did not make a connection. Only later, back at my digs, did I learn of my luck from the excited landlady. "You've won first prize!"

A pal of mine at that time received a similar amount from an uncle; and though just as hard up, he gave a champagne supper, blowing his money in one night. I put mine in the bank and lived on it for a very long time, drawing it sparingly for necessities only. I mention the other man, not because I considered him a damned fool then, but because humanity is roughly divided into two classes, represented by him and by me. In my own family, Willie would have squan-

dered his forty pounds at once; Neilie would have kept it as
I did. I never saw the pleasure in eating all your cake at one
bite, because temperamentally I am not entirely forgetful of
the morrow. Or to put it in the fashionable way, I like to lay
up treasure in heaven. But apart from that, I still think the
other man was a fool. We argued the point later, when he was
lunching on fourpence but kept persisting that the fun he got
out of his champagne splash had been worth a year of four-
penny lunches. It would not have been so for me.

This diversity of character makes me think of the
prodigal son story. Ask yourself: What side am I on—the son
who went away and had a good time, or the dull brother who
stayed at home? Most men say they are with the Prodigal Son.
I never do, and I know why: I think of Willie getting all the
jam when he went away, while the brothers who stayed at
home got the dry bread. And I never admired the Prodigal
Son for having his champagne supper and then in cowardly
manner coming back to beg for forgiveness and a meal.

The whole question of my attitude toward money is important. Because of the poverty suffered in my young years, I
have a queer meanness about money. I grudge paying out
small sums, yet can sign a check for a large amount without
a moment's hesitation. Many other men regard checks in a
similar way: to us, a check isn't real money. It is fantasy
money, and therefore of no emotional value. When motoring,
I pay for petrol without quibbling; but if I have to take a
taxi, I sit and watch the meter painfully whenever there is a
traffic snarl in the street. If I suddenly became a millionaire,
I should still travel third-class and buy a secondhand car. I
dislike borrowing money and dislike more lending it. Only
once was a lent fiver paid back to me—by a Scot, of course.

In still another way, money was a problem on occasion.
My editorship of *The Student* gave me free dress-circle tickets
to all the city theaters on Monday nights, and luckily, evening

dress was not obligatory. But there was a whole week of opera once—*Die Meistersinger, Orpheus, Elektra,* some others—and I went every night to these more formal events. Toward the end of the week, I had to doctor my one dress shirt meticulously with white chalk to make it look decent.

Of all the week's opera, *Die Meistersinger* knocked me over. I had never heard such music. To me, it was the purest of gold; but instead of inspiring me to noble thoughts and deeds, it made me a swindler. Another performance was scheduled during the week, and of course there were no more press tickets. Determined to hear the opera again, however, I dressed myself in my chalked boiled shirt and went down to the theater just before the end of the first act. During the interval I sneaked in, pretending I had lost my pass-out check, and with good luck found a fine, empty seat.

As editor of *The Student,* I also had the privilege of being invited *ex officio* to an inter-university conference in St. Andrews. It was a great affair. Champagne flowed like water, and most of us got canned, gloriously canned. We all thought Walter Elliott, one of the delegates from Glasgow, the most brilliant speaker of the conference. But why so good and likable a man ever became a Conservative, and cabinet minister in such a government, is a riddle to me.

I was allowed a small grant from the S.R.C. (Students' Representative Council) toward my expenses at the Conference. It was not enough, and I drew about a pound more. But Walker, the secretary, stood me on the mat and gave me a thorough dressing down. "No other editor ever used more than the allotted amount," he said, and I stood silent, ashamed of my poverty, hating the man. He was comfortably off, and looked at me as if I were something the cat had dragged into the house. My predecessors in the editorial chair had been gentlemen; that seemed to be what he was trying to tell me. I felt both angry and guilty.

As an editor without money, I had to spend more than I could afford. I was invited to all university dinners, and although these cost me nothing, the small outlays on cloakroom tips, dress-shirt laundry, etc., were beyond me. Matters became easier when an ex-editor told me I should sell the books sent in for review. I did so, getting half the published price; but there again there were difficulties, because my medical student friends kept asking for the privilege of reviewing costly books. Often I put them off and wrote the reviews myself; by studying the indexes, I managed to write passable reviews, though knowing nothing of medicine. When a book came out that I wanted, I wrote to the publishers, telling them tall stories about the circulation and influence of *The Student,* and in nine cases out of ten they sent the book.

I cannot recall exactly when I began to write, but it must have been some time before becoming editor. I began by submitting drawings and cartoons—awful things that make me blush to remember; my drawing, then as now, was atrocious. At that time, a student advised me to try a comic literary sketch for the *Glasgow Herald.* I sent one in, and a few mornings later found it in the paper. Possibly that was one of the most ecstatic moments of my life, the first time in print. It seemed incredible, wonderful, glorious; I trod on air all that day. Later, I sent in other sketches and received fourteen shillings for each one that was published.

About then, I became friendly with a girl in my English class. It was a platonic friendship that lasted a long time. During long walks, May and I talked mainly about ourselves; in vacations, we wrote long letters to each other—again, I fear, mostly on the same subjects. She was a clever lassie, who encouraged me to write prose and helped me to gain a self-confidence that was lacking. I see now that I abused her friendship, using it to flatter my own ego, for her belief in me supplied much that I needed. I look back on that friendship now with a feeling of tenderness.

We were both snobs, but strangely enough, it was our snobbery that ultimately parted us. She had friends among the aristocracy and used to stay at their country houses. To me she brought some of the glamour of the best people; yet at the same time, I found my resentment against them growing. May had strong opinions about what was "done" and what wasn't; and I rebelled when she expected me to have manners like her rich friends. Fundamentally, she was what we might call fascist today, while I was fundamentally socialist. She remained a positive snob, while I became a negative one. She was critical of individuals but accepted society without question: I was critical of society and apt to accept individuals for what they were. I liked her humor, and we laughed at the same things (manners excluded). We made no pretense about the fact that she was my Lady Bountiful, patronizing a very raw youth who, with some encouragement, might do something in life. I was slightly afraid of her, I remember, but she was a good scout and someone I could meet again with real pleasure.

It might be interesting here to contrast my growth with Willie's, since he had been so strong an influence on my early life. Later he veered to the right, while I gradually assumed a more leftist attitude toward politics and other matters. There was one great difference between us as boys. He developed very young, reading the Bible at three, and entered the university when sixteen. My own advancement seemed incredibly slow. Though I was twenty-eight when editing *The Student,* my editorials might have been written by a boy of fourteen. Their puerility is lamentable and their arrogance—*comical* is perhaps the best term. As editor, I suffered badly from being the sole authority. There was no need to ask anyone's opinion, and I published my own geese, believing they were swans. Some of my friends called certain articles tripe; alas, that happened after their publication. But editing the magazine was a liberal education in its way. I got to know about spacing, proofreading, and technical production matters. My position gave me a certain standing among students, and I met interesting men at public functions. After one big dinner, I half-carried home one of Edinburgh's best surgeons. On his doorstep, he drew himself up and said thickly, "Young man, I'm tight, absolutely bunged up, but if someone came now and told me I had to go to the operating theater, I'd cut out an appendix with a hand as steady as a rock." I never had any doubt that he spoke the truth.

During one of the summer vacations, I fell in love with Beatrice. We went through heaven and then hell, and I know now that the hell was on account of Clunie. Unconsciously, I compared every girl with Clunie; unconsciously, she hated every girl I loved. While praising them, she subtly made me see their shortcomings. I lost Beatrice, warm and dear as she was, because—without knowing it—I was looking for the ideal that my mother's sinful notion of sex had compelled me to form. There was, of course, more to it than that. Half of me wanted to marry Beatrice on the spot; the other half cried: "Wait, don't tie yourself up before you have made your career." There was a definite pull—women versus ambition— that may have come from hearing my mother say: "Marriage hinders a man, because it forces him to think of bread and butter." While I thought and hesitated, the practical Beatrice went off and married someone else.

I cannot honestly say that my four years in Edinburgh were very happy. I always return to the city unwillingly and without any interest. It is beautiful—more beautiful perhaps than any other city I have seen—but for me, Edinburgh remains a dead city, parochial and pompous. Its university life had little or no group spirit. We all lived in digs. The only meeting place was the Union, and thousands were not even members of that. A man could take a degree in Edinburgh without speaking to a single student during the time he was there. And some students seemed to do just that, too.

Union life itself was narrow. Many students were medicals from the Colonies, bringing with them their beastly colonial attitude toward the "nigger." Many colored students studied at Edinburgh; and because of the colonial men, they were all classified thus. One day when I lunched with an Egyptian—supposed to be a prince—two South Africans hastily moved away from the table. When the exploited native populations finally rise to smash their chains, not a few of their leaders will have received their impetus from the abominable treatment of the "nigger" in the English and Scottish universities.

My finals were at hand. During my last year, I had given up my time and interest to editing *The Student,* and anticipated a very poor degree—in fact, the poorest possible, a Third-Class pass. But in the finals I did not do as badly as expected; indeed, at the end of the week, I almost dared hope for a First in spite of my frankly bad Anglo-Saxon and Middle English. I got a Second and was quite pleased. In due course, I was capped M.A.; but by then, sad to recall, I did not feel unduly proud or pleased. Everything in life comes too late, we hear. Whether that is so or not, it was certainly true of my degree. As Robert Louis Stevenson said, "To travel hopefully is a better thing than to arrive." The degree, once a glittering peak, had become a minor hill, from the top of which I could look far out and see distant peaks, high and perhaps inaccessible—work, fame, perhaps death. More bluntly stated: I had got my degree and didn't know how to use it. All I knew was that *I didn't want to teach:* to think of going on all my life as English master in some provincial secondary school or academy, made me shiver. No, teaching would be the last resort, if every other line failed.

London

Journalism was my future, and I studied the ads in the papers. I applied for a few jobs but got no answers. Then R. Scott Stevenson, later an ear, nose and throat man in the West End, said he could get me some work at T.C. & E.C. Jacks, the Edinburgh publishers. The job was subediting a one-volume encyclopedia planned to contain something more perhaps than the Britannica. Its chief editor was H. C. O'Neill. It turned out to be a lousy job. Half the contributions came from clergymen with unreadable penmanship. When the copy *was* readable, it ran too long. We often had to throw the stuff into the waste-paper basket and rewrite it ourselves. I recall writing up the Panama Canal in this way, cribbing of course from other encyclopedias. The work was extremely useful in one way: it gave me a dread of superfluous words.

I had been about a year at this work when O'Neill persuaded the firm to transfer its editorial office to London. Having reached the age of twenty-nine without crossing the border, I found the idea of going to London both wonderful and inevitable; had not Barrie and lesser Scots writers gone south to find wealth and a name? I counted the days before I should set off, but as so often occurs in life, something happened to dampen my enthusiasm and hopes at the last moment; my mother became very ill. Now having a small but regular income, I arranged for her to go to a nursing home and have the offending gallstones removed. My hopes went south; my fears stayed behind in that nursing home. I stayed just long enough to see her after the operation—she was down but not out—and then set off with definite relief.

I don't recall how I looked, arriving in King's Cross station on a Sunday morning late in 1912, but I felt much as Keats's baffled Cortez: "Silent, upon a peak in Darien." Here was London, the center of life and everything valuable to life. I made for The Strand and Fleet Street. With a thrill I looked round, trying hard to keep from realizing a slight disappointment. They were meaner streets than I had pictured, less picturesque than the Strand that appeared so colorfully on the jacket of *Strand Magazine*. Still, these were but names; wait till I saw the great men who ran the British press. During the next few weeks, I would wander at lunch time from Long Acre to Fleet Street to look at the great men. But never did I see anyone who looked more important than a messenger boy, and this made me wonder.

Dorothy, an actress friend I had met in Edinburgh, lived in Hammersmith, where I went to find lodgings. Dorothy was the only soul I knew in London, but even she left in a week's time, to go on tour again, so living in Hammersmith did not help me much, although her mother was good to me. For the first time in my life, I learned the truth of the platitude that a man can be loneliest in a crowd. When my work was over, I had no one to speak to. Weekends were the worst. Visiting places like Harrow and Windsor, I saw cheerful groups playing tennis on inviting lawns, and heard pianos played in the evenings within suburban houses, while I stood on the road feeling lonely. Sometimes I had the mad impulse to walk up to a group on a lawn and say: "Let me sit and watch you play. I'm as lonely as hell," but was inhibited by Scots caution. I got into the habit of hiring a skiff at Richmond and rowing upstream. Never having handled an oar in my life, I learned painfully, blushing at the insults hurled at me by occupants of nicely varnished boats I scratched. Many a time on a gray and windy day, mine was the only skiff on the river. But I wasn't afraid, though unable to swim—except for one occasion, when Neilie, visiting in town, came with me and did the rowing. While nervous sometimes when sitting beside certain drivers—what motorist isn't!—I had never been afraid while driving a car myself. Fear, converted into action, ceases to be fear. On sunny days up the river, I hated myself for coming; the sight of merry boatloads of parties, of punts with pretty girls lying under parasols while young men poled them along, these made my loneliness almost unbearable. Sometimes I went for long walks, hoping for something to happen—a miracle of some kind—but always returned to my lodgings disappointed. God, they were dull, too!

One Sunday night in Uxbridge, while feeling especially miserable, I saw an attractive-looking girl sitting on a bench reading a novel. Quite nervously I sat down beside her, knowing that I would speak to her and dreading a rebuff. For some time, I remained there, glancing sideways at her. She seemed to bury herself more deeply in her book. "Let's talk," I said suddenly. "I'm damn lonely."

She gave me a cold glance of fear, murmured something about not knowing me, and buried herself still more deeply in the novel. Suddenly, I felt a wave of anger come over me. "Christ, woman," I shouted, "you sit here reading a foolish story and when a chance for real romance comes along, you escape it with a look that says, 'We haven't been introduced!' " She stared at me for a moment or two and then began to cry.

"It's the way I was brought up," she answered wretchedly. I didn't know what to say next, for I saw then that the poor kid must have been just as lonely as I. We talked a little in an awkward way, but she hadn't much to say and was, I thought, not well-educated. Our "romance" lasted about five minutes, and then she said she had to go.

There were pleasant interludes, however, in this lonely time. When Dorothy came home from her tour, her boyfriend took us out in his car—oh, wasn't he proud of its being able to touch forty on the Windsor road! Sometimes we boated up river, and they always wanted me around, as the welcome third gooseberry. We made a jolly party. I can still hear Dorothy's silvery laugh when I overbalanced with the pole and nearly fell in. Sometimes she would bring one of her musical-comedy friends. I learned that a touring company consisted mainly of very conventional, ambitious middle-class girls, many of whom sent money home to help the family. They were easy folk to get on with, but so narrow in their interests—"the show," and what Bert said, and how wild the stage manager was. Dorothy, in her waggish way, kept telling her friends that I was a very clever fellow—an M.A. I don't know what lay behind her joke, possibly delight in seeing them stare at me as if I were inhuman. The magic letters did seem to scare them, however. They began to apologize to me for their lack of education.

During the working day, I divided my time between Long Acre and the British Museum. The encyclopedia having been finished and published, I had been asked to write the English Language-and-Literature portion of a Popular-Educator reference work that Jacks were then preparing. After completing it, and fearful of losing my job, I took on the Mathematics section. Then I did Drawing, with my illustrations that fortunately never saw the light of a bookseller's shop, for O'Neill wisely decided to cut out that subject. At last, nothing remained for me to write, and I found myself unemployed. I was worried. The one thing I did not want to do was to return to Scotland and—the only possible job there —teaching.

By this time, Neilie had come to town, and we set up house with J. B. Salmond, later editor of *Scots Magazine*. He worked in Fleetway House then, and our studio flat was always full of carefree lads from the Northcliffe Press. They kept telling me that if I could write a washerwoman's weekly serial, they could guarantee me five hundred pounds a year. Unfortunately, all my attempts to write such a serial ended in obscene laughter when Salmond read the results aloud.

When our lease of the studio ended, Neilie and I tried several lodgings and hated them all. Meanwhile, my health had gone bad and I was far from fit. Poor feeding at the university, followed by bad feeding in London digs with ill-nourishing lunches outside, and, finally, the sardine and tinned-salmon lazy table of our studio flat—all these affected me, and lack of exercise didn't help. Also, I was very much worried over the threat of being summoned as correspondent in a divorce case. This I escaped, possibly because the irate husband, a well known musician, knew that I hadn't got a bean.

One night, I woke up with a sharp pain in my leg. Neilie, being a doctor, diagnosed it as phlebitis—inflammation of a vein. I was alarmed because I knew that such inflammation caused a clot, and if even a tiny fragment of this clot broke away, there was a chance of very sudden death. Neilie exaggerated this danger, I fancy, in order to keep me from going out to work next day. I went to King Edward Hospital in Windsor, where an old university pal of mine named D. G. Watson was house surgeon. I had been out there often and knew the staff well. The surgeon ligatured my vein, so that the clot could not move, and I lay in bed for about a fortnight, having the time of my life.

After my recovery I returned to town and answered various ads. One ran: "Art Editor wanted for new magazine in Fleet Street," and gave a box number for reply. Obviously, this was no job for me, but having nothing to lose, I sat down and wrote an application letter, frivolous in tone. My surprise a few mornings later, when I got a reply asking me to come and see the editor of *Piccadilly Magazine,* 40 Fleet Street, was mixed with trepidation; I knew nothing about art. I went, however, and was interviewed.

Vincent, the editor, took up two letters. "That one," he said, "is from a man who has been on —— Magazine for ten years as art editor. This one is from the art editor of —— Magazine where he has been for twelve years."

I swallowed hard.

"I am going to offer you the job," he went on.

I gasped and said, "In God's name, why?"

"Because," he said, "your letter was the only one that amused me. When can you start?"

I accepted his offer of a hundred fifty pounds a year.

I really liked working on that newly formed magazine, even though, because of my leg, I spent my weekly salary on taxis. My job was to read short stories and hand on my choices to Vincent. If he approved, I had to find the right illustrator for the story: Balliol Salmond, if it was a yarn about a girl in a boat; someone else for a story with shooting; Harry Rountree for animals. When returning a serial to H. G. Wells's agent as unsuitable, I felt myself grow inches higher.

As part of my duties, I also interviewed people. Once, when we were running an article on the human behavior of horses, I went to the great jockey, Steve Donaghue, to get his opinions. He gave them in a friendly way, and as I was going, offered me a tip for the next big race. When I got back to No. 40, the whole staff was on the doorstep. "Did he give you a tip?" somebody asked. I thought for a moment, and passed along the horse's name—whatever it was. They all rushed out to bet their shirts on it. This amused me, for I knew nothing about betting or horses. The horse came in either last or second to last.

My interview with a fighter known as Bombardier Wells
was difficult. For the magazine's first issue, a symposium had
been planned on the question: *Should the knockout be
abolished?* I set out cheerfully enough to ask Billy Wells what
he thought about it, but suddenly, on the street, I realized
that Billy himself had been knocked out the previous night.
Finally, when a man in a dirty sweater led me into his presence, I never felt so small in my life—literally. Billy towered
above me, and his hand crushed mine so tightly that I almost
squeaked. Asking the embarrassing question made me tremble,
but he took it quite well and we had an interesting chat.

World War I

The *Piccadilly Magazine's* first issue had been scheduled
for the end of August, 1914. One of the articles, well illustrated with photographs, was entitled "The Real German
Danger—The Crown Prince." But the shot at Sarajevo killed,
among other things, the budding *Piccadilly Magazine.* It never
appeared.

I was staying with Watson, my doctor friend in Windsor,
when war was declared, and still remember how the two of
us—both Socialists—sat up talking about it while the Life
Guards nearby cheered all night long. He said tensely: "Oh,
the fools, the bloody damn fools. Can't they see it means
their death and the death of most things we love?"

During that period, I had joined the Westminster Labour
Party, which met in a small room somewhere in St. James's,
to talk and plan a new world. Among the speakers who stood
on a soapbox in the Park, along with me, were two men I had
known at the university. One later became a metropolitan
police surgeon, and the other a Harley Street doctor—both
probably lifelong Tories.

There are moments in every man's life which he looks
back on with sudden embarrassment, saying to himself: "What
a bloody fool I was then!" Today I feel like that about my
soapbox oratory. My ignorance of politics and economics was

profound, so I can only conjecture that my self-confidence was robust. On one occasion, I foolishly mentioned the General Post Office as an example of socialism. A postman knocked me down, propped me up again, and then beat me into political impotence and death—his battering ram a thorough, shattering knowledge of the inner workings of the post office.

Neither Watson nor I had any grasp of the realities behind the war. In our previous meetings, we had sometimes talked about the chances of war being stopped at the start by the refusal of international labor to load a ship or move a shell. Like most other people, we were quite vague about the whole question, and the only thing we strongly agreed upon was that Germany had asked for it and was going to get it, too. We talked about what we should do. He would volunteer at once as a doctor, and I said, unenthusiastically, that with my university degree I could easily get a commission. "No go," said Watson. "They wouldn't have you with your leg as it is at present. You need six months' rest, old man, and of course the war will be over by then."

Watson went to a base hospital in France but got tired of the monotony, volunteered to serve with a regiment, and died of wounds. He was one of the nicest fellows I have ever known—bright, keen, with a jolly sense of humor. We had been friends for a long time before discovering that our fathers had taught in the same school as apprentice teachers.

I went home to Kingsmuir perturbed in mind. I felt that I really should join up, preferring the artillery because of my bad feet. On the other hand, supporting my cowardice, was the statement of Watson and another doctor that I wasn't fit. After a few weeks, I applied for and got the job of temporary headmaster at Gretna Green school. When I arrived there, I found that the permanent head, a hefty he-man, was serving with the K.O.S.B. (King's Own Scottish Borderers), but I did not feel too bad about the situation. My bad leg was swollen and numb, rather than painful, and I think now that the condition must have been, in modern parlance, psychological— my protection against joining the army.

The story of my stay in Gretna Green was told more or less truly in my first book *A Dominie's Log*. But its sequel, *A Dominie Dismissed*, was pure fiction, written during my army service later.

Coming from Fleet Street to a slow village required some adaptation. I had lodgings in a small cottage, and when my landlady brought in the paraffin lamp of an evening and drew the blind of the small window, I felt that I was separated from the whole world. It was characteristic of this gulf separating Gretna from London that she frowned on the use of typewriters on Sundays. I think I began to write books to keep myself from going balmy.

It seems ludicrous that a man who is known as an educational heretic should have taken to this profession merely because journalism and his military courage failed him. Yet I began to think about education for the first time in Gretna. My predecessor had been a disciplinarian, and I arrived to find a silent, obedient school; but I knew that the bigger lads were watching me carefully to see how far they could go. I put on my severest look and glared at them; and on the second day, when the biggest of them tried me out with a semi-insolent answer, I gave him a leathering with the strap. I was still governed by the old dictum of the teaching profession: show you are master at once.

To say I could have gone on as a disciplinarian if I had tried, would be a silly thing to say, for I couldn't will myself to do that. Gradually, the children discovered that my discipline was a bluff, that I really didn't care if they learned or not. The silent school became a beer garden, full of noise and laughter. But we carried on the usual lessons, and I suppose they learned as much as they would have if afraid of me.

Either way, it seemed to me such futile waste to teach the geography of India to children who were going out to the farms.

The school board did not care very much what I was doing. Some of its members, as individuals, became friends of mine; Stafford the minister, Dick MacDougall the board clerk, and their wives, were kind to me. According to general opinion among the villagers, I was quite a nice chap but, of course, half-daft. To my horror, I found myself fast becoming countrified—narrow, interested in local gossip, craning my neck to see where the doctor was going. I tried to keep in touch with larger affairs by having the *Nation* and *The New Age* sent weekly by post.

One sunny May morning, a terrible troop-train disaster took place a field's breadth from my lodgings. When my landlady woke me and told me there had been a smash, I jumped on my cycle and went off. The scene resembled a silent film. The only sounds were the hissing of engines and the pops of cartridges as fire crept along the wreckage. Men were lying dead or dying; one soldier with both legs torn off asked me for a cigarette, and he grinned as I lit it for him. "May as weel lose them here as in France," he said lightly. He died before the cigarette was half smoked.

To me, the whole affair seemed unreal, like a dream. I joined a party that was trying to free a man from under an engine. As we worked, another man said to me: "They expect the engine to explode any second." But after an uneasy glance at the hissing steam, I thought no more about it. The quietness of that morning was unbelievable. Hardly a man groaned, and when the dying men called aloud, it was always for their mothers. Women and children were among the injured, but no cries or sobbing seemed to come from them. It was said that the officers shot some of the men who were hopelessly pinned under the blazing wreckage. I never knew if the story was true, but hoped it was.

What impressed me so strongly that morning was my lack of any emotion at all, even pity. To be fair to myself, of course, I was busy all the time doing things for the wounded. I felt uncomfortable about this, however, and late at night, sitting in the manse, I said to the minister: "I must be the greatest egoist God ever made: nothing to give anyone, selfish to the core. This morning in that field I had not the tiniest suspicion of any feeling. I was just a stone of indifference."

Stafford stared at me with open eyes. "I was just about to say the same thing to you. I thought I was a monster because I felt nothing." We apparently had assumed the attitude that doctors and nurses have. Just as a person's fear changes into positive energy when rowing a boat in a bad swell, so he can absorb terror and pity while assisting others in pain. And one cannot feel deeply for complete strangers.

Contrariwise, I recall how one of my pupils—a boy— was killed that morning, run down by a motorcycle on his way to the disaster. His mother asked me to go and see his body that night, and I felt a real grief. I also felt keenly the plight of the signalman whose mistake had caused the accident: I had his sons in school and liked them, as well as their father. To me, imprisoning him was only one of the many signs of barbarity in our legal code.

I went off one Saturday to Dumfries to join the army. I know that I had no real wish to be a soldier, but something must have influenced me; either a bad conscience after a friend had been killed or, just as likely, an order that all men should be examined under the Derby Scheme. I was rejected because of my leg, and given a certificate stating that I was permanently unfit for service. Just as I left the building, however, a sergeant asked me if I had joined the Derby Scheme. I told him that I did not need to, because I had been rejected. "But," he said, "you get half a crown if you join." When I asked him how, he took me to an officer, before whom I swore that I would serve "my King and Country" when called upon to do so. The sergeant got a half crown from me for his pains. Later, when all rejected men were ordered to be re-examined and I was passed as fit, I should have had the disgrace of being drafted, if that sergeant hadn't had a thirst on him and an eye to the main chance.

It is difficult to return even in fantasy to my Gretna days. I have motored through the village at least once a year but have stopped there only once—and regretted it. Going back is nearly always a mistake; old threads refuse to be taken up. Dimly I recall pleasant tea parties with my assistants, May and Christine and Bell; the bustle and chaos of the building of the great munition works, and the transformation of a dull hamlet into a township with cinema and shops. There was also a love story—wrecked again on the Clunie fixation.

Later, in the army, I made a good friend, and we were always together. A year after the war, we ran into each other in the Strand, delighted to see each other. We made a date to have dinner, and for half an hour we talked about old times: "Remember Tubby? That morning when he hadn't shaved and the sergeant . . ." We laughed a bit. Then the conversation ceased, and we both realized that we had nothing more to say to each other. Army life had drawn us together because we had to concentrate on military things; in civilian life we hadn't an interest in common. It was a sad dinner party, and although we tried to make an artificial cheerfulness, and promised to meet again, we both knew in our hearts that we never could. I know now that if someone long dead—someone I loved (say Clunie) came back to me, we could not pick up where we left off.

In the early spring of 1917, all medically rejected men were ordered to report for re-examination. I was passed A-1 by a doctor I had known at the university. This was in Dumfries, and the recruits were sent off the same night to Berwick upon Tweed. There we were asked what regiment we wanted to go into. Thinking of my feet, I said the artillery. The sergeant gave me a look.

"Artillery"—he laughed nastily—"hi, youse blokes, here's a guy as wants to join the artillery!" Then, to me, he snapped: "You have two choices, King's Own Scottish Borderers or the Royal Scots Fusiliers."

I asked where the training camps were situated.

"K.O.S.B., Catterick; R.S.F., Greenock."

I chose the R.S.F. simply because Glasgow was nearer to the people I knew. I was given a pass and set off for Ayr, the R.S.F. recruiting base. One other recruit had chosen the R.S.F., and he advised me to take two days' French leave before I reported. I was afraid to, but when I got to the barracks in Ayr and found that no one expected me—the sergeant in fact was annoyed at my turning up on a Saturday night—I much regretted not having taken the man's advice. By this time, my heart was in my boots: I was a walking misery. The incivility and arrogance of the NCO's with whom I had come in contact, together with the prison appearance of the barracks, gave me a hate of the army that has never left me. I was given a mattress, told to fill it with straw, and then, with other recruits, had to do some fatigue—carrying beds. Next day I got my uniform, along with my first instruction from an absent-minded corporal whose interests were apparently elsewhere. In a few days we left by train for the training camp at Fort Matilda, between Greenock and Gourock. After vaccination and inoculation—a sickening business to me—our training began in earnest.

My chief associations with the R.S.F. are two: feet and fear. My feet have always been tender, and even today, when I have my shoes specially made, my toes blister if I walk far on a hot day. For years I had worn only shoes, and after an hour's drill in army boots, my ankles were raw flesh. I reported sick again and again, and usually had some dressing put on, but the doctors never seemed to think rest was necessary. I had to go on parade again every time. One lance corporal said to me: "Hi you, big fellow, if you don't be careful you'll be up for swinging the lead (malingering). You've reported sick for three mornings and got M.D. each time." M.D. meant Medicine on Duty.

I cannot recollect any fear of going to France. I knew that we were supposed to have a few months' training and then go out automatically in drafts, to replace casualties. Strangely enough, that didn't worry me; my fear was attached to the lance corporal who made my life a hell for weeks. For some reason, he disliked me at sight; and after parades, when there was any fatigue to do, he always chose me, usually addressing me as "youse big bastard." He was a cab driver in civilian life, they said.

One day, while giving out our letters, he stopped and peered at an envelope. "Jesus Christ, who the hell's this?" he asked. "A. S. Neill, Esq., M.A., author of *A Dominie's Log*. What the hell . . .?" I modestly held up my hand. His mouth opened. "You an M.A.?" He gasped. "My Christ!" The sequel was astonishing. He never gave me fatigue again, never bullied me. On the contrary, he treated me as if I were the colonel himself. Later, I was to find other NCO's who confessed to a great feeling of inferiority when I was in their squads: they were ashamed of their lack of grammar.

We slept twenty men and an NCO to an army hut. Many of the men, who came mostly from Glasgow, were Glesgakeelies, rough diamonds of the slums. They were fine, friendly lads, always kind to each other, usually cheerful. To them, the army food I found almost uneatable was the best food they had ever had; to them, army discipline seemed not much worse than the discipline of the factory. Their language was almost completely sexual, everything—food, parades, sergeants—described as "fucking." They discussed openly the most intimate details of the anatomies of their wives and sweethearts. They told very dirty stories, mostly without any point, and looked a little nervously at me while doing so. They knew I was a teacher and always addressed me as mister.

One night, when the stories were particularly lurid, every man had told one except myself.

"What aboot a story from you, Mester Neill?" said one.

I smiled.

"All right, boys. A sparrow was sitting on a treetop one morning. A horse went by and left some droppings. The sparrow flew down and made an excellent breakfast, and then it flew back to its treetop and opened its throat and sang to its maker in joy. A hawk came along. It seized that sparrow in its talons and bore it off."

"But here," said one, "what's the point o' the story?"

"That," I said, "is a story without a point. But it is a story with a moral, and the moral is: If you've eaten shit, don't make a song about it."

Dead silence followed, and I realized that I had told the wrong story. They were taking it as censure, feeling themselves to be reproved by teacher. Hastily I told them a dirty story that outclassed anything they had told, and their loud laughter showed me that they accepted me as one of themselves.

Life in the army seemed like one continuous rush: we never had time to do anything properly, even shaving. Worst of all was the duty of mess orderly for the day. One waited in a queue for meals to be carried to the huts. Then one had to wash up after the meal and be spotless for the next parade, with rifle clean, buttons and boots shining. Behind all this rush was the dread of being late for parade; that was a crime. But one could be "crimed" for many things—being unshaved, having dirty buttons, unpolished buckles, unwhitened braid.

To be crimed was to be given pack drill with full equipment, doubling up and down the square till exhausted.

I managed to avoid being crimed except once. My rifle, a modern one that I cared for as tenderly as a child, had been taken from me; and I was given an old-fashioned Lee Enfield instead. At rifle inspection, the officer crimed me for having a dirty rifle. I went to my sergeant and told him I had spent a hour trying to clean the thing, but the dirt was ingrained. He took me to see the sergeant in charge of musketry, who examined the rifle. "Nobody can ever clean the thing," he pronounced. I don't know what went on behind the scenes, but my name was taken off the crime list.

This incident was exceptional. Generally, one had no redress, and it was this feeling of absolute powerlessness that kept me in the depths. Any corporal could crime you, and you dared not say a word. Theoretically you could, but we all knew that any complaint about a superior officer made you a marked man, and you would get it in the neck ever after. Old soldiers always pleaded guilty without defense, whether justly charged or not.

Hated duties could not be evaded. As a system, the discipline was mistake-proof. You had to be somewhere. If you went sick, your name appeared on the sick list; if you were doing fatigues, your squad sergeant had a note of it. The only man I knew who dodged the system effectively for six weeks was a youth who had been transferred from one squad to another. When he joined his new squad, he found that his name wasn't on the roll; they had forgotten to transfer it. He gave up going on parade. Every morning, he walked out of camp with belt and cane, a large envelope in his hand marked O.H.M.S. (On His Majesty's Service), When he was finally found out, nothing happened to him, because the NCO's who had left his name off the roll knew that they were "for it" if they reported him.

My feet were giving me hell. Every night I soaked them in cold water, and every morning I soaped my socks, but the blisters came as before. I was limping during square drill when a major came along. He told me to fall out and asked what was wrong. I told him. He said I should report sick, and I told him it was useless, for they would only send me on parade again. He then ordered me to take off my boots and show him my feet. "You go back to your hut and rest," he said. "By the way, what are you in civil life?"

Two nights later, while I sat tending my feet in the hut as usual, the orderly sergeant came round.

"Neill here? Wanted at the Company bunk."

I trembled. Wanted at Company headquarters generally meant being put on the mat. I thought of all my crimes— dodging church parade every Sunday, overstaying my leave— there were enough of them—and reported in trepidation. The major who had ordered me to rest sat writing at a table. I saluted and waited at attention. By this time, I was certain that because of my bad feet he would offer me a job clerking in the office. Finally he looked up.

"Know anything about mathematics?" he barked.

"Yes, sir, I wrote a book on mathematics."

"Oh! You seem to be the very man we want." He lifted a document. "I have here a form from the War Office saying they need men of mathematical knowledge as officers in the artillery. I shall put your name forward."

I was then transferred to the Cadet Corps. All sixteen of us had special drill. We were supposed to show the regiment how the best soldiers perform, and our training was modeled on that of the Guards. When slapping our rifle butts in presenting arms, we almost made our hands bleed. We had lectures in huts and out on the hill, and my feet now got a chance to recover. My pet aversion was bayonet fighting. We were told to regard the sacks as Huns who had just raped our sisters, and were instructed to stab them with fitting fierceness. Unsuccessfully, I thought of ways and means to get out of a form of fighting that would be useless to me in the artillery. But fate again found a way. I had gone to visit Clunie and found that her landlord knew our gym sergeant major; they had been pals in the Scots Greys. The landlord told me to give him his regards when I got back.

The sergeant major looked forbidding, but I pulled myself together and went up to him. "Well?" he demanded. When I gingerly gave him the message from his old pal, he thawed at once, insisting on taking me into his hut for a drink. When he asked what I was doing, I told him of the artillery commission in the offing. Next morning, while I was stabbing clumsily at a Hun sack, he came up. "Here," he said, "this is to be no good to you. Buzz off. You don't need to come to bayonet fighting or, for that matter, early-morning p.t." (physical training).

I was delighted. Luck had rid me not only of the hated bayonet drill but of the almost hated gymnastics besides. There was another danger, however, when I stopped going on first parade. At any moment, an officer might buttonhole me and ask why I wasn't there. And I knew that on no account must I ever give away the kind gym sergeant major. Also, if I were caught "dodging parades," I might lose my chance for the commission. I solved the question by joining the signalers. Signaling would be useful to me as an artillery officer, I thought, but what appealed to me more was the fact that signalers had little footwork to do. I learned to like reading Morse by telegraphy or light flashes, but never became proficient enough to read the lamp messages that passed between vessels of the fleet in the Clyde every night.

By this time, I had become a good soldier—that is, I knew my way about, and knew how to get on with my immediate superiors. Bribery could be hazardous, but without it weekend leave wasn't always easy to get. It could be highly dangerous to offer money to a sergeant major, yet there were ways and means. At one time, our sergeant major was most sparing with weekend passes, and for three weekends in succession, he refused to give me one. So I sat down and wrote to Walter Martin, the cigar merchant in Piccadilly (his wife had admired my *Dominie's Log,* and Martin had sent me cigarettes at times): "For God's sake, make me a present of a barrel of panatellas."

The cigars came. I sauntered out and saw the sergeant major tending his little garden. I lit a cigar, took up a position with my back to his garden fence, and waited as if expecting someone. I puffed hard, and with the tail of my eye, saw him sniff.

"Evening, sir," I said with deference.

"Evening. That cigar smells good," he said.

I took out the small case that went with the barrel. "Try one, sir."

He invited me into his hut for a drink, and we had a few whiskeys. As I was going, I said, "Look here, sir, I'm in a difficulty."

"If I can help . . ." he began.

"It's like this, sir. A friend has sent me a box of cigars and really they are useless to me, for I don't like cigars (this was and is true). I thought of giving them to the lads in the hut, but . . ."

"Nonsense," he interrupted hastily, "that would be waste."

"I'll bring them round to you, sir," I said, and duly did so. Though weekend passes came easily after that, I felt rather mean and small; the other poor devils had no rich friends to help them.

Shortly afterward, however, I did a real Boy Scout deed. In the train compartment, while off to Glasgow on a weekend pass, I saw Pat, an Irishman graded C3, whose job was to clean out latrines. Sick of the army, he was running away.

"But, Pat," I said, "at Glasgow station the military police will look at all passes, and they'll pinch you for being without one." He was cast down at this, but I cheered him up by saying I thought I had a plan. When we got out at the Central Station, I saw two redcaps approaching us. I gave them one scared look and legged it down the platform as hard as I could, ignoring their cries to stop. When they caught me at the barrier, I handed them my pass, trying to explain that my haste was to catch my train at Buchanan Street. I looked round and saw that Pat had got off safely. He must have returned to Ireland, for I never heard of his being captured.

One day, in company orders there arrived a command that 32703 Private Neill report to Trowbridge Cadet School, Wiltshire.

After Fort Matilda, Trowbridge seemed like heaven. Discipline was easy, and polished buttons did not seem to matter much. The whole section, including the officer in charge, burst into laughter when I marched with the Guards' swing-of-arm, up to the shoulder; and I was ordered to cut out that swank stuff. Then the section laughed at my cleaning my boots before afternoon parade. Tut, tut, I thought, a pleasant place, but, oh, what soldiers!

For the first time in my army career, the work was interesting to me. We studied map-reading, maths, laying out lines of fire, and had gun drill with six-inch howitzers. We did much with an instrument called a No. 5 Director, and all of us used the prismatic compass. The other fellows were nearer my level than those of the R.S.F., many having been clerks and teachers, and we had some jolly times together.

Sometimes our study excursions would be made on army bicycles. For some queer reason, we were always about half a dozen cycles short, and six unfortunates had to go on foot, perhaps six miles. The lucky ones knew that the pedestrians would make sure of getting a cycle home, so they took out their tire valves and hid their saddles and pumps; one man took his front wheel off and carried it about all day. I was one of the outward walkers once, but sneaked off early to the cycle park and found, as I expected, an assortment of valveless, saddleless, handlebarless bikes. All I had to do was to collect several items from several bikes and make a finished article—easily done, because they were all standard makes and their parts interchangeable.

One of these excursions was utilized as our exam in map-reading. We all received a map and a small table, and were placed at different points. I stood alone in the middle of a large field. While bending over my map, I heard a sniff, and thinking it was the inspecting officer, I tried to look as busy as I should. On hearing a second, louder sniff, I looked round into the face of an enormous bull with a ring through his nose. Edging round the table, I wondered if a jab of the map on his horns would blind the animal long enough for me to leg it to the distant fence. I spoke to the bull in a friendly way, hoping to convince him that I knew I had no right to be there in his field. After a time, he quietly began to eat grass. Probably because of the bull incident, I missed the carping criticism the other fellows had taken from the inspecting officer that day.

I had one degrading experience at Trowbridge, involving a major who lectured on bracketing, a most complicated study of range distances in firing practice. He was not a good lecturer, and his voice must have put me on the verge of sleep. Suddenly I started, for he was looking at me and, in an angry voice, was ordering me to the blackboard to explain what bracketing was. I had not the faintest idea but of course could not say so, proving my complete ignorance by standing there like an ass with a bit of chalk in my hand. By this time he was livid and red.

"Why brainless idiots like you get to cadet schools is more than I can understand. I don't blame you—you can't help your stupidity; I blame the system that sends you up here. Have you had no education?"

I hung my head.

"Answer me. Where were you educated?"

"Edinburgh University," I said humbly. A titter round the room was nipped off by the glare of the officer. He never spoke to me again.

Our term ended, we passed our exit exams, and in front of us was Lydd—the real thing, the nightmare lying ahead of a pleasant dream. Trowbridge had been like a university, easy and academic. But Lydd was officered by men just back from the front with no sympathy for the academic in anything. Our three weeks in Lydd were one continuous grind, and we discovered that everything we had learned at Trowbridge was of no value there. Laying out a line of fire no longer suggested a leisurely problem in maths; it was a thing to be done in ten seconds with a slide rule. The men at Lydd knew their jobs and put the wind up us all, for failure meant not only the disgrace of being returned to Trowbridge for a month or two, but also being put into a section of new men. No, that probability we dared not face, so we slaved.

The major at Lydd who taught the bracketing was a fearful man, and we had been warned about him long before we came up. When we were using real shells for the first time, he took us one by one to the observation post. There we all watched the burst of a shell, and had to know at once which directions to telephone to the gunner for his next shot. The major kept firing questions at us, and when we made mistakes— as we did, mainly through fear of him—he called us everything he knew.

We all passed, however, and were duly notified that we had received commissions in the Royal Regiment of Artillery.

After our ten days' leave to collect uniforms and kits, I was posted to an officers' "pool" in Aldershot, saddened to find that most of my pals had been posted to Farnborough. Our pool consisted of about sixty officers waiting to be sent to France. The life was pleasant enough. I remember clearly the night I arrived and being saluted by the sergeant major. How hard to believe that I would never again fear an NCO! I had a bitter feeling when I thought of our good food and comforts, and compared them with the food and lack of privacy I had as a noncom. Officers and privates lived poles apart in every way; the old distinction was still there—Eton at one end, the slums at the other. The officer planned; the private had no need to think, only to clean with spit and polish.

I had a batman, an independent sort of fellow from Lancashire. He was an active socialist, he said, and to hell with it anyway—what was a bloody officer but the servant of capitalism? So my orderly lay on my bed, smoking my cigarettes, while I polished my leggings and boots for the morrow. He kept assuring me that he bore me no personal grudge because I was an officer. He seemed a nice chap but a born pessimist, who swore that every league football match was faked—sold to the highest bidder—and offered to bring me written evidence if I liked.

Aldershot was a lazy life. We had lectures and sometimes slow exercises, but we all felt that these were just to keep us from getting too discontented. Every few days, a list of officers for the next draft would go up, but my name never appeared among them. Instead, I was told to attach myself to a training battery where my duties included lectures on lines of fire.

One day, I saw a gunner obviously paying no attention as I laboriously, and badly, tried to explain the mathematics of laying out a line of fire. To me, he seemed a stupid sort of a fellow.

"Here you," I said, "you don't seem to be taking any interest in what I am teaching. What are you in civil life?"

"I am maths master at —— Secondary School," he said.

Rising to the occasion, I held out my chalk. "For the Lord's sake then, show them how this damn thing is done."

And he showed them.

I kept hoping to be sent to France on a draft; not because I had miraculously acquired more courage, but simply because the other men were all out, or going out, and I felt left behind, like the lame boy in the Pied Piper story. Then an epidemic of influenza ran through the camp, and I went down with it. Mine was a bad attack, ending in neurasthenia. At Gretna Green, I had once been off work for a month with the same trouble, but this became worse—a complete nervous breakdown, with insomnia, and nightmares when I did fall asleep. In short, I was a dud as a soldier or anything else. The M.O. worried about me—probably suspected me of being a mental case—and said he would send me up to a nerve specialist in town when I was fit to travel.

The specialist turned out to be Dr. William H. Rivers, the famous anthropologist. I did not know anything about him, nor did I know anything about psychology. I recall being mildly surprised when he asked me to tell him a dream, and being more and more surprised at his evident interest while I told it. It was a dream about a snake I had killed that kept coming to life again. I had never heard of Freud then, but apparently Rivers had. Finally, he said to me: "If you go to France, you will either win the V.C. or be shot for running away. We won't risk it. I'll recommend that you give up your commission on grounds of ill health."

So ended my inglorious career as a soldier. I must have cost the nation quite a lot of money, giving back little in duty or work. I realize now that my nervous breakdown was the method used by my unconscious to keep me from danger. On a conscious level, I seemed ready to go to the fighting front without any abnormal fear. In fact, I felt that as an officer it would be easier because I would be leading men and would have to show them how to face danger.

Years after the war, Walter Martin, my cigar-king friend, said something to me that was unbelievable.

"Neill, I saved your life."

"How?"

"I had a pull at the War Office and arranged that you would not be sent to the front."

I can scarcely believe this, but if it *were* so, it would explain why my name never appeared on the draft notices in the officers' pool. Walter died before I could ask him to tell me more, and I still doubt very much if any such influence could have exempted an individual soldier.

After a long convalescence, I began to think of a job. Back in the Gretna Green period, a lady who was much involved with King Alfred School in Hampstead had written me, after having read my *Dominie's Log,* and when I went to see her she told me about Homer Lane, who founded the unique Little Commonwealth reform camp for juvenile delinquents. She gave me a report of one of his lectures. She had also introduced me to John Russell, the headmaster of King Alfred.

While at the cadet school, I learned that Lane's Little Commonwealth was in Dorset, not very far from Trowbridge. I wrote him asking if I could come to see him, and, when he said I could, got weekend leave. Homer Lane was easily the most impressive personality I had met up to then. He told of his cases as I listened, entranced. His young delinquents charmed me, and I got Lane to promise to let me work at Little Commonwealth when I had finished army service.

My first act when I felt fit enough, was to write Lane, saying I could come. I got a reply telling me that the Commonwealth had been closed, and that Lane himself was in bad health in London. Disappointed, I thought I should try second-best. I wrote to John Russell about a job, got one, and joined the staff of K.A.S.

J.R., as we all called Russell, was a dear old man. I liked him from the first moment I saw him, and he liked me. Since Russell's beginning as a pioneer thirty years before, K.A.S. had been regarded as the most advanced school of its kind. While perhaps not the first to practice coeducation, it did more to force the issue upon English opinion than any other school. Long before my time, it had done away with prizes and marks and corporal punishment.

I entered this famous school rather timidly with my very Scottish accent. My reputation as a mad Scots dominie had preceded me, and some of the pupils later told me that they had stared at me the first day, wondering if I were really mad or only a crank.

I liked the *Stimmung* of the school at once; its free and easy discipline took my heart. But I disliked the staffroom, and often have wondered why it was not a happier place than it was. It did not have the congenial atmosphere of the classrooms; and although the staff members were friendly as individuals, they were collectively—what I called them then— bloody. J.R. got me to ask Homer Lane to come and give the staff a few talks on psychology. Lane sat with a face like vinegar, and after the first talk, said to me; "My God, Neill, what is wrong with that staff? It gives me the absolute jimjams. It's full of hate." In a way, I think that I may have been a fly in the ointment—the young whippersnapper who had come to tell them how to run their school. Very properly, they put me in my place.

Fundamentally, the problem was J.R. himself. He was God, a lovable old God, but nevertheless, God—and a moralist of great force. I first realized this when Patrick, aged eight, kissed Clare, aged seven. J.R. had a "call over" about it and spoke for nearly an hour. I came away feeling that kissing must be the main sin against the Holy Ghost.

There was something dead about the pupils; they lacked an interest in life. This seemed most obvious at meetings of former Alfredians, when the "old boys" sat at the feet of J.R. or George Earle, an English master who served as second-in-command, and listened as if their one-time teachers had all the wisdom in the world. Their attitudes toward the old school resembled a St. Andrews student's toward his old alma mater— a regressive looking-back to Elysium. They were not quite of this world.

I learned with mixed feelings that some of the big lads in the school had never heard the word *shit,* and did not know the ordinary swear words, but that one or two of the girls knew them all. Dimly, I began to sense that I had come to a school whose life attitudes were fundamentally and essentially those which had damned my own life in Scotland—moral standards from without. K.A.S. was far from being free, and very soon I found myself "agin the government."

I had begun to be analyzed by Lane and became a frequent visitor to his home. What he said about freedom was the gospel I had been looking for; a scientific foundation for the vague yearnings shown forth in my *Dominie's Log.* Thus it came about that I began to try to "improve" K.A.S. in staff meetings. The school wasn't moving with the times, I complained. It should have self-government. Dear old J.R. spread his hands and said, with his usual smile: "Go on, Neill. Try it. Try it."

I tried it. The classes changed from one room to another at the ringing of the lessons bell. Thus the Betas would have maths the first period, say, and then come to me for geography when the bell rang. Naturally, all self-government meant to them was a chance to let off steam in my room for an hour. They made a hell of a row, and the teachers in neighboring rooms got annoyed. At the next staff meeting, they all said it was obvious, of course, that self-government didn't work. It didn't, but it certainly "played." The day came when J.R. came to me very perplexed and very sad, and said: "One of us has to resign, Neill." Once more I was unemployed.

The Death of Clunie

It was while I was at K.A.S. that Clunie died. A wire from home sent me north to find her ill with pneumonia. For years, she had had some obscure disease of the throat; and for years, she had been treated by x-rays. I think I knew that she would not recover. I sat by her bedside for hours, trying to appear hopeful and cheerful. God, it was a week of the kind of hell that I had never known before and have not known since. I did not dream, but woke up each morning feeling that I had been in the deepest pit of Dante's Inferno and feeling I had been there for a thousand years. Most men know what it is to have someone who will always understand, someone you naturally turn to in joy or sorrow. To me, Clunie was that one: I knew exactly what her reactions would be to anything I said; knew what would make her laugh, what would pain her. I knew also that she was always on my side; I was her hero, and I could do no wrong. The Peter Pan in me loved Clunie because she appreciated me. When something amusing happened, my first thought had always been: "I must tell Clunie this. How she'll laugh!" At her funeral, some small thing happened—I forget what, maybe only a top hat falling off some dignified mourner—and my first thought was: "Clunie will laugh at this when I tell her."

My grief was made more harrowing by remorse—the re-

morse that is always a component of grief. I remembered the
times when I had neglected her. She had wanted me to come
home for the previous Easter holiday, but I went to Dorset. To
me, in my despair, that seemed unforgivable. I kept remembering what I did not want to remember. My mother, on the
other hand, kept forgetting what she did not want to remember. As her wet eyes followed the coffin to the hearse, she said:
"Clunie was the perfect daughter. I never had to lift my
hand to her in all her life." It struck me then that that was
one of the things I should have liked to tell Clunie, for
Mother had given her many a spanking. Clunie had often
laughed at our mother for her extrovert's trick of trying to
deceive herself; and, although my father was an introvert, he
had a similar ability. At one time, Clunie and I called them
"the ostriches."

Nearly all children go through a stage during which they
become very critical of their parents. This happens with the
strengthening of a psychological urge to break free from the
apron strings. I went through such a stage from about eighteen
to twenty-four. At one time, I was ashamed of both my parents. My father embarrassed me because he had no "manners";
if we had a guest to dinner, Clunie and I implored Mother
not to have soup because of Father's loud method of supping
it. I was ashamed of Mother because she talked too much,
often irrelevantly. She was really a very bad listener, and always tried to edge in a word, even when the conversation
dealt with subjects she knew nothing about. I recall one occasion when this infuriated me. A visitor was telling us about
his adventures in China, and she kept interrupting him with
silly remarks about her brother Sandy once having known a
man there. I was impatient, arrogant; my father, on the contrary, had the patience of Job. He read his *Scotsman* every
morning, while my mother always took up the paper about
bedtime. "Listen to this, George," she would say and proceed

to read out a whole column of news that he had already seen. Not once did he dare say: "I've read it, Mary."

My rather hateful, critical attitude toward my parents seemed to disappear after Clunie's death. Only then did I begin to have tender feelings about my father. No longer was I the Cinderella of the family; by this time, Father had accepted me as a son to be proud of—someone who had made good—though he still tried to look out for good jobs for me. When an old friend of Mother's came on a visit from Australia, where he had made good, my father spoke to him about my prospects out there. He said that he was a bosom friend of the Prime Minister, and would get me a job as inspector of schools if I said the word. I didn't say the word, but have sometimes wondered what would have become of me if I had gone out to Australia.

I was ashamed of my mother's garrulity, for she liked to make conversation a monologue. But all the time I hated myself for criticizing her. My parents gave up so much for us; they were so concerned about our health and happiness and future. They were really grand folk, but so very remote from us in every way that was of inherent moment.

As a grown man, I used to write home once a fortnight. Every letter took a long time. I sat and chewed my pen and wondered what to say. Most of the letters were about the weather. And when I went home as a young man, I found it difficult to talk to my parents. We had no common interests. Poor souls, they were so naive about us. When I was nineteen, on occasion I would come home late. Father asked where I had been, and I could not tell him I had been out with Liz Macdonald because one did not tell parents such things in the early days of the century. I did what all other sons and daughters did then—and may do now—I lied. I always got away with my lies, but my brother Willie made a bloomer when he said he had been having a chat with old Geordie

Cable. Geordie had been dead for five years.

I am sure that most people carry throughout their lives a guilt feeling about their parents. My mother used to lecture us on our ingratitude. "We have done everything for you, fed you and clothed you, and what do we get? No gratitude. Mrs. Smith who half starved her children and treated them harshly, her children adore her now and would do anything for her." The sad feature was that the statement was true.

The gulf between Victorian parents and their children was unbridgeable. It is too often the same today. The fear a child acquires from angry adult voices and spankings in babyhood lives on for a lifetime. It was fear of our parents that made us strangers to them.

At the university, I knew only one student who could share a risque story with his father. When I was over thirty, a visiting teacher once began to tell my father and me some sex stories. I was much distressed and embarrassed, and I think my father was, too. I could get into some kind of a human relationship with my mother, but never with my father. My sisters did not fear him and used to be pert with him sometimes, and in my innocence, I wondered why he seemed to like their pertness. He mellowed when he grew old; but as a young father, he was stern and heavy.

Freudians have told me that my zeal for educational pioneering arose as a reaction against my father. How they explain the fact that my brothers who also feared him did not go in for pioneering, I do not know. There must be at least more than a grain of truth in the assertion, nevertheless.

I have long given up theorizing about the origins of behavior. It is so pointless, for even if my life work has only been a protest against what began over seventy years ago, what can be done about it? Who cares? I do not.

In his notorious statement that history is bunk, Henry Ford was not so far from the truth, if we consider history from the individual angle of any human being. I attach tremendous importance to environment. My school testifies to that. Yet there is something beyond environment that we cannot get hold of. Saying that a great composer was born into a musical family does not explain him. On the dark side, failing as a house-painter does not explain Hitler. I really wonder if my fear of my father had much to do with my career.

Looking back on my own experience as a teacher, I can say without boasting that I was a good one, although not ideal from the point of view of preparing pupils for States examinations. My teaching stressed imagination. When I set a subject for an essay, it was never *"How I Spent My Holidays"* but rather, *"What Happened when my False Teeth Fell Out on my Plate,"* or *"A Snail's Description of its Journey from the Front Door to the School Gate."*

Nearly fifty years ago, I said to a class: "I am going to give you the first sentence of a story: 'Hell and Buggery!' said the Bishop. Now, boys, you carry on."

A boy of thirteen wrote: "The bishop leaned over his pulpit. 'Brethren,' he said solemnly, 'as I entered the cathedral this morning, I heard one of you use these dreadful words. I shall take them as my text.' " I certainly could not have risen to that standard; I'd have made the bishop flub an eight-inch putt on the green.

I had to give up teaching older pupils because they protested that my methods would be of no help to them in passing outside examinations—a true criticism that condemned the deadly officials who set up the English papers—not their teacher. I could determine a child's standard in English within a half-hour's talk, plus a look at his notebook that contained his writing on any topic he liked.

Granted that one cannot teach anything of importance: to love, to be honest, to be charitable. But there are skills that *have* to be taught; hence the good old apprenticeships, even if the first year consisted of making tea for the qualified journeymen. My contention is that schools, by and large, deal with things that do not matter, and that teachers become as narrow as their subjects. Bacon, if he lived today, might say that specialization maketh a narrow man. This applies not only to teachers but to other professionals, including doctors. Seldom have I met a doctor who had a wide interest or a wide area of conversation.

The older generation of teachers may have had a broader outlook than today's crop. My father, I recall, had interesting discussions with neighboring village dominies. In those far-off days, the dominie was the oracle, for he, apart from the minister, was the only educated man in his village. Since Kingsmuir was too small to have a kirk, my father served as advisor, materially and spiritually.

Like the schoolmaster in Goldsmith's *Deserted Village,* Father had a fund of information:

> *And still they gaz'd, and still the wonder grew,*
> *That one small head could carry all he knew.*

Though not a man of good judgment so far as his own family was concerned, he seemed to give good advice to the villagers. True, the matters may have been minor ones, but not to the one asking: "Should I send Wullie tae the Academy, or let him work as a loon on the farm?"

Sometimes pupils at a higher school brought him intricate problems to solve—the kind in which a man rows up a river at three miles an hour against a current flowing at one mile an hour; he stops for lunch for half an hour and meanwhile the current has changed—problems beyond me, but my father never failed once.

I know that my ability as a teacher came from watching my father's methods. Long before modern devices were used for teaching geography (the method consisted mainly of lists of names), he made his pupils ask questions: "Why is Glasgow where it is? Why London? Why is there more rain on the West Coast of Scotland than on the East?"

Somehow I knew all the rivers of Britain; the cotton, pottery, iron, and coal towns. Snippets still remain—Hexham famous for hats and gloves, Redditch for needles, Axminster for carpets. And even now, I feel that motoring to Scotland means going uphill, because it was uphill on the hanging map.

He had no way of knowing how foreign names were pronounced. For him, the capital of Iceland was *Reeky-a-veek;* Bucharest was *Boo-carest;* Arkansas was pronounced with the final "s." He followed his own pronunciation for common English words: pencil was *pincil,* a lantern was a *lantren,* a physician was a *physecian.* Yet he always knew the meanings of even the most uncommon words. If crossword puzzles had existed in his days, he would have been a whiz.

Father failed to make some things clear, and I never understood ratio and proportion until I had lessons from Ben Thomson, the maths teacher in Forfar Academy. Father and I did square roots, but I never knew the reason for the method. And I still don't know. Maths to Father was a mechanical process.

In a word class, we formed a half-circle; if the boy or girl at the top of the line did not give the right answer, the one who did took that pupil's place. On one occasion I reached the top. The word was *evident,* and I offered, *easily seen.* But I had a very bad conscience later, for I had just learned the word from a line my brother Willie used: "That's quite evident, said the monkey after he shat on the tablecloth." I had a vague, frightening notion that the word *evident* was associated with shit and that my father knew that.

Father's method certainly gave us a vocabulary. And he offered us a sound training in grammar, so that even today I feel a mild shock when someone says: "He spoke to Jim and

I," or "These sort of things are useless." In teaching us Latin, Father showed us how that language helped in spelling; we knew that *committee* had two "m's" because it came from *con* (with) and *mitto* (I send).

I had just begun to appreciate the lines of Virgil when I had to face an examination. After passing that test, I never opened a Latin book again. And that is the absurd feature about learning classic languages. One spends dreary years over the grammar; but unless one continues to take Classics at a university, the whole subject disappears from memory.

I am convinced that my father showed me how to be a good teacher. Though he had little humor, he had some imagination, and he could make history live for his pupils.

Origin of Summerhill

When I had to leave K.A.S. early in 1920, I was genuinely anxious, for I saw no future. True, I might get a job as English teacher in a Scots school, but London had gripped me, and I didn't want to leave it. Mrs. Beatrice Ensor stepped in and offered me the job of jointly editing *The New Era* with her. I took up my duties in Tavistock Square, sharing a room with her husband, a nonsmoker who hated my smoking all day at work. The Ensors were Theosophists, and the paper was owned, I believe, by The Theosophical Society. Some people found Mrs. Ensor a forbidding person, but I liked her and teased her most of the time. She was the only adherent I ever met who could laugh at Theosophy and at herself.

It was good fun having a paper to edit. Mrs. Ensor gave me a free hand to say anything I liked; and I soon saw that the more outrageously I attacked pedants and schools, the more delighted she was. She was a born organizer, and through her, I went to Holland that same year to meet some Austrian children who were coming to England after the war. This was my first trip to the Continent, and those ten days in Holland were full of interest. Everything was exciting, and today I would give all I possess to recover the special sense of adventure that accompanies a first trip abroad. Today I go reluctantly, hating the waits at customs offices, the examination

167

of passports, the monotony of hotels and porters, and, worst of all, the long train journeys. Experience always dies; it can never live again. I drive a car automatically, but when I was learning, every mile was a delightful mastering of a difficult challenge. In truth, though it sounds like a platitude, the surmounting of difficulties is the dearest part of life.

Pleasant as my work could be, *The New Era* was no abiding place; I knew that I must move on. Luck brought me an invitation to take part in a New Educational Fellowship Conference in Calais, and another invitation to go on to Salzburg to lecture to an international conference of women. Salzburg's beauty and warmth bowled me over and made me want to stay there always. Though I still have vague longings to go back, I know that I never shall.

From Salzburg, I went on to Hellerau, a suburb of Dresden, to stay with and visit my friends Karl Baer, and Christine, his American wife; the architect, Dr. Otto Neustätter, and his wife, Frau Doktor; and there, in 1921, under the pedagogical eye of the German Ministry of Education, we founded an international school.

Germany gave me much that I could not get at home. For one thing, I lived there nearly three years in an atmosphere of rhythm and dance, of great opera and orchestral music. I met nationals of nearly every European country, and each day learned something new. My stay in Hellerau turned out to be the most exciting period of my life thus far. Only the German educational system could teach me nothing. To me ·it seemed barren and hollow—pedantry masquerading as progress. Recalling it now, there comes to my mind in metaphor, the German meistersingers with their rules and foot measures, hating and fearing the new young Walther with his *Preislied* of freedom. The Germans did not really want freedom. They were afraid of it, and their more. honest and enlightened teachers confessed to this.

At first, I knew not a word of German. When I brought over my first English pupil—Derrick, aged eight—I was trying to learn German with *Hugo's Tutor;* but in three weeks, Derrick was not only talking German—he was speaking Saxon dialect. (In Summerhill my German pupils speak English in a few weeks, and, oddly enough, answer in English when I talk to them in German.)

Our International School had three divisions: eurythmics (rhythm and dance), the German school, and my own Ausländer (foreign) department. I won't discuss here the deep-seated differences between my division and the German one. The important thing was what my stay in Hellerau did for me. It gave me weltanschauung—a world view—and in killing my nationalism, made me an internationalist forever. The experience humbled me. There I was with my M.A. in English, having to sit silent while others talked of art, music, and philosophy. I felt uneducated, and do so today when these subjects are discussed. For me, a university education had been no education at all.

How blind I was then—how blind we all were—not to see that the postwar poverty of Germany would lead to Hitler. Personally, I lived like a millionaire; much of our tuition was paid in pounds. I traveled first class from Munich to Vienna for three shillings, the exchange rate was that good; Benedictine and Curacao fifths were eightpence each. On the other hand, I recall changing ten pounds in a Dresden bank when a telegram arrived asking me to come to Vienna. I was away for ten days, taking my marks with me. On my return, they were not enough to pay my tram fare to Hellerau.

Every day at school was stimulating, some days more than others. I gave psychological talks to the girls studying eurythmics. One day, a Russian girl came into my office. She threw her arms round me and said: *"Herr Neill, ich liebe Sie."* I did not know her name, and it was a shock to get a declaration of love from someone I had never spoken to. My shock became alarm when she continued: "I have told my husband, and he is coming Saturday to shoot you." In spite of my alarm, I felt slightly amused at the idea of being shot for a woman whose name I didn't know. On Saturday morning, as I walked to school, I saw her approaching with a man about six feet three. I thought of fleeing, but we met and she introduced us. Her husband shook my hand warmly, if painfully. The woman had transferred her desires to me and had built a fantasy around the two of us.

During the early twenties, a more frightening situation arose when the French put black soldiers in the occupied Ruhr. The Germans were furious. One day, while I was in a Dresden tram, four tough-looking youths entered. I saw them eyeing me, and heard one say: "He's a Frenchman." They rose and came toward me. I hastily took out my passport. They smiled. "Ach, an Englishman!" "No," I said, "Scotsman." Then they insisted I get out with them at the next stop and have a drink. I did and discovered that they were filled with pity for me, because to them Scotland was a slave state held down by the bullying English.

As already noted in this book, I was never a particularly brave man. But more than a decade later, about 1936, I had my moment while idling in Hanover between trains. It was a fine Sunday morning for walking through the town. Suddenly, I heard music, and round the corner came a troop of SS men. Everyone on the sidewalk stopped to give the Hitler salute. But I could not bring myself to do it, and just stood and looked. At a signal from the leader, two troopers came toward me. I trembled, for not long before, when my friend Geoffrey Cox (now Sir Geoffrey) had had a similar experience in Berlin, his British passport did not protect him from a beating. Still I could not raise my hand in salute. Hastily, I showed my passport. They hesitated and then handed it back to me, after which I sought the safety of the Bahnhof waiting room.

Since the Germans did not allow me to teach Germans, my school division consisted of English, Norwegians, Belgians, and Yugoslavs only. I was forbidden to teach English to the German division because I had not taken my degree in a German university. For such instruction, I had to appoint a German woman whose pronunciation was terrible. She kept arguing with me about accent, and when an Irish visitor appeared whose brogue could be cut with a knife, she cried: "*Wunderbar—das* is the proper Oxford accent."

Our staff of teachers was a mixed lot. The Communists among them demanded that the school be ruled communally. For about a million marks (fifteen shillings English), I bought a bicycle; but it was never there when I wanted it. "It should be common to the whole staff," I was told. How earnest these Germans were! I made a gift of a cinema projector to the whole school, and a program committee was elected to choose the films. When I gave priority to Charlie Chaplin, they were shocked. "That is not education." So we had the children sit and watch boring films about travel and shellfish. If a film did not have a pedagogic message, it was considered useless. The leader of the German department began his speech to parents with the words: "Here we work," and was annoyed when I asked him why his opening words were not: "Here we play." He and I shared the hostel, the *Schulheim,* with me taking the upper story and he the lower one. Of an evening, my group would dance to records, while below he was reading aloud Goethe or Nietzsche. One by one, his pupils would sneak up the back stairs to join in the dance; there were bad feelings about that.

Many of our pupils were Jewish, and I am sure they all ended up in Belsen or Dachau. Even in 1921, Dresden shops had notices saying that no Jews would be served. Once I pulled a futile trick on a bookseller's shop. I asked to see editions of Ibsen, Strindberg, Nietzsche, and the counter was soon covered with beautiful volumes as the staff fussed around the "rich Engländer." Then I told them there was a book in the window I wanted to see. Whereupon I went out, came back, and said: "I see you don't serve Jews."

"But, mein Herr, you aren't a Jew."

"No," I said, "I am no Jew, but in my country we do not bar Jews from shops." I had had no intention of buying anything.

Later, I saw that such tactics would most likely add Anglophobia to anti-Semitism.

I cannot go into all the arguments and difficulties we had in the school; our fights with the State authorities, our internal differences about policy. I had an early encounter with German prolixity when the board of governors asked me to translate a printed syllabus into English, so that we could get English and American pupils. It was about ten pages long; my translation ran to a page. There was annoyance. "But," I replied, "that's all you said." Brevity is not a strong feature of German writing.

My co-governors (and founders) of the school were good people, all of them, and we weathered the interminable difficulties well. Dr. Otto Neustätter appeared as a dear old man in my *Dominie Abroad*. Neustatter's wife, Frau Doktor, whom I later married, was a sister of the brilliant, once-famous Australian novelist, Henrietta Richardson Robertson, who wrote under the name of Henry Handel Richardson. One of the pleasures of those long-ago days was the presence of Edwin and Willa Muir. Willa taught in our school; Edwin wrote poems and prose.

We took a lease on the school building; but Gurdjieff, who was looking for a house for his philosophical school of thought, fell in love with our *Anstalt*, and persuaded Harold

Dohrn, the owner, to hand it over to him. When we said we would fight the case in court, the owner suddenly came over to our side. Later, I heard that Gurdjieff had made a case of it, and Dohrn said in court that Gurdjieff had hypnotized him. In any event, Gurdjieff lost the case, and later, with Ouspensky, set up his school in Fontainebleau. I could not read Gurdjieff after that incident; somehow I never got over his remark: "They don't matter; my work is infinitely more important." He and all my Hellerau associates are long dead—Baer and Dohrn shot by the Russians.

Here I should say that most of the people mentioned in this book are no longer living. Every autobiography is, if not a lie, an evasion of the truth. Suppose one of my brothers had been a criminal, or one of my sisters a prostitute, I could not tell of them, for their children would most probably be alive. Indeed, I wonder what value an autobiography has. To know that J. M. Barrie, Ruskin and Carlyle were impotent, to know that Freud when catching a train had to be in the station an hour beforehand, to know that Reich was overjealous or that Wilde was a homosexual—I cannot see how such knowledge affects our judgment of their work. Luckily, we know almost nothing of Shakespeare. Wagner was a nasty man, anti-Semitic, mean to his friends, mean about money; but knowing this does not take away from the delight I have when listening to *Die Meistersinger* or *Tristan und Isolde*.

In 1923, revolution broke out in Saxony. Shots were fired on the Dresden streets. Our school was emptying. The dance division went to Schloss Laxenberg near Vienna, and I took my division to a mountaintop at the edge of the Tyrol, four hours' train time from Vienna. We were housed in an old monastery, and beside it stood a *Wahlfahrtskirche,* or pilgrimage church. According to hearsay, such pilgrimage docked off four hundred years from purgatory.

This church had stone saints all around, and when the

pilgrims came from all over Catholic Europe, our English pupils placed haloes on the sculptures by shining broken mirrors on them. There was much crossing themselves by visitors, and when the trick was discovered, I wondered why we were not lynched, for the local peasants were among the most hateful people I ever met. Few had ever seen a foreigner; and the fact that we were "heathens" was enough to kindle, and keep alight, their hatred of us. A German girl of nine sunbathed in a swimsuit. We had a policeman up next day saying the village was shocked and angry. Farmers and their wives threw broken bottles into the pond we bathed in. The climax came when I was summoned to the education ministry in Vienna.

"Herr Neill, do you teach religion?"

"No."

The official took down a hefty volume and read out the law: every Austrian school must teach religion. I explained that I had no Austrian children, but that was no excuse to him; the law must be obeyed. So it happened that I took my little group to England.

But we had fun, too. When we arrived in Austria, the snow was deep and we had to buy skis. (We pronounced the word in the Norwegian and German way—*shees*.) Our postman took nearly an hour to climb the mountain, but only about ten minutes to return. None of us, however, reached that stage of skiing proficiency. We danced a lot—foxtrots and tangos— which I loved. Today I cannot dance, not because of age—I could still do a tango—but because the new rhythms are too quick for me, and I can see no skill or grace in wagging knees and bottoms.

I had a sentimental attachment to anything Austrian. The first German book I ever read was *Das Tagebuch eines halb-wuchigen Mädchens,* which was translated later into English as *A Young Girl's Diary.* This diary of a middle-class girl from the age of eleven to fourteen was written, of course, in a child's

language and was therefore easy for me to read. Indeed, I
learned from it a great number of Viennese words that many
Germans do not know. Freud wrote a short preface for this book,
calling it a jewel, and in a way, it does explain much of his theory
about sex, for he must have been influenced by the ignorant sex
repression of the late nineties. In fact, he could have found
his whole sexual philosophy within its pages. The diary gave
me a glamorous, really romantic view of Viennese society with
its afterglow of Strauss waltzes and *Rosenkavalier,* along with
the city's gaiety and *Gemutlichkeit.*

In late 1924, when my pupils came with me to England, I
rented a house in Lyme Regis, Dorset. It was called Summerhill
and stood on the hill going to Charmouth. Lyme was, and is, a
class-conscious little town made up mostly of retired people.
My wife and I (by this time I had married Frau Doktor
Neustatter) were outsiders; upper-class noses looked down on
our dirty little youngsters—till one day a crested Rolls Royce
drove up. The Earl of Sandwich, one of the founders of the Little
Commonwealth, had come to visit us for a few days. After that,
people bowed to us.

This reminds me of Bertrand Russell's story in his autobiography. During an antiwar protest, he was being roughly
handled by a policeman. A woman shouted: "That is Bertrand
Russell, the writer and philosopher." The cop paid no attention
and went on hustling Russell. "He is the brother of an earl,"
cried the woman.

"What!"

The hustling stopped. Good old English snobbery. We
had only five pupils, three paying half fees, two paying nothing.
My first wife and I stood looking at an ironmongers window
wondering if we could afford a spade. Because Lyme was a
holiday resort, we turned the school into a boarding house in
the vacations and managed to make ends meet. Then we got
too many problem children, misfits that other schools did not

want. Fifty years later, we have the same trouble. In fact, the school's whole life has been handicapped by too large a proportion of such pupils. An American father will write: "My boy is a normal kid but he hates lessons." The pupil arrives, his face full of hate; he bullies, steals, destroys. Obviously, the father knows he is dumping his failure onto us. It is interesting to note that none of our academic successes—our professors, doctors, lawyers, scientists—came as problem children.

Our staff was small in Lyme. George Corkhill taught science—good old George, who was with us for nearly thirty years; "Jonesie," who had joined us in Austria, taught maths; my wife acted as matron. It was a stirring time; and because they were so interesting, the problem children then gave us more joy than sorrow. One girl, who later became golf champion of half a dozen countries, had been accustomed to making her parents and teachers angry at her defiance. She decided to take me on. She kicked me for an hour but, in spite of the pain, I refused to react. Finally, she burst into tears, and learned the hard way, I expect, that her attempts to take the micky out of adults did not always succeed. At that stage, I was a proper fool. I thought that psychology could cure everything, barring a broken leg. I took on children injured at birth, cases of sleeping-sickness, and mentally deficient boys and girls. Of course, I soon found that I could do nothing to cure them.

When our three-year lease was up, we had twenty-seven pupils and could not house them. I bought an old Morris Car and set off along the south coast to find a larger place. There I saw some beauties at 50,000 pounds each. Then I went up the east coast, the last house on my list being Newhaven in the small town of Leiston, Suffolk. It was only 2,250 pounds, a sum I did not have but could handle on a mortgage. I brought the name Summerhill with me; yet in forty-four years, not a single visitor has asked me what it means, despite the fact that the place is dead flat.

When World War II broke out, we remained in Summerhill during the "phony" period. After Dunkirk, however, when invasion was expected, we had to move. In North Wales, we found a big dilapidated house whose lavatories and most of its windows had been smashed by local boys. There we stayed for five years, the longest years of my adult life. It rained continually. I had to give up my car, queueing up for buses. All around us were Welsh-speaking people, of course; and some of the aged knew no English.

The atmosphere of Festiniog made me feel as though I had returned to my native Scottish village. Chapel services and hymns, with their usual hypocrisy, were everywhere. One shopkeeper said to me: "I don't believe in any God; but if I didn't go to the bloody chapel every Sunday, I wouldn't get any custom." The villagers were shocked by our pagan behavior, yet, one by one, they began to sneak into our Sunday-night dances.

Wales was hell for me. Shortly after we arrived, one of our brightest boys accidentally drowned; and later, after my wife Lilly had a stroke, she lost her speech and became confused mentally. No wonder Festiniog was a misery to me. We lived in gorgeous scenery, as on our Austrian mountain; but after a week, I never really saw it.

During this period, the school was not really Summerhill. Many parents sent their children there to be safe rather than free; and when peace came, such children were withdrawn. Before vacations, our pupils made the long, weary journey to London. But we were lucky; not once did they get blitzed.

We suffered from overcrowding. Food was rationed, and tobacco became difficult to buy. The pubs closed at 9:00 P.M. as against 10:30 in England. Our boys perpetually warred with the village boys, who were very aggressive in spite of—or because of—all the chapel-going.

I discovered that I had returned to the joys of the Scottish Sabbath. In Festiniog, one dared not even dig the garden on that holy day. Once, after a spell of rain had flattened the corn, we had a bright, windy Sunday; but not a farmer would reap.

Even so, with its deep resentment against England and the war laws, Wales had certain advantages. Our school was registered with a coal merchant for fuel, stiffly rationed then. When a competitor asked if I needed coal, I said yes but explained that I could not deal with him because of being registered with Jones Brothers.

He laughed and said: "That's okay. How many tons do you want?"

"But," I replied, "what about the law?"

"Bugger the law!" he said. "In any case, I have just supplied two tons of coke to the leading magistrate, and he also is registered with Jones Brothers."

After that, we never ran out of coal or coke.

Though we heard Welsh spoken during those five years, I never learned a phrase. In another period of my life, while spending a year in Norway, I never learned to speak a word of Norwegian. On both occasions, there was no motive to learn; my residence was temporary.

Those years in Wales have few memories for me. My wretchedness there seems to corroborate the Freudian theory that we forget what we want to forget. I cannot even recall the rooms in our house, nor remember the names of most of the staff there.

I visited the Leiston Summerhill once a year during the war, staying with Watson, who was most kind about chauffeuring me around. It annoyed me to see soldiers at every window, and to be ticked off by young officers.

"Sir, what are you doing on government property? Who are you anyway?" I would be asked.

"Nobody of any importance; I just happen to own the house."

"Can you prove that?"

"Oh," I said wearily, "arrest me and take me out to the road and ask the first passerby who I am."

But when the Scottish Fusiliers were occupying the school, and I told them it was my old regiment, they let me go anywhere I liked. Only once did I have the courage to say to a blustering subaltern: "I want your name, to report you to your commander for insolence." But then, when the power-struck young officer climbed down, I felt sorry for him.

Perhaps the most joyous day of my life was the one in 1945 when I set off on my return to Leiston with my second wife Ena and a cat. In the five years the Army used the school, it had done more damage to the premises than my kids had done in twenty-five. But nothing seemed to matter; we had come home to dear old Summerhill. Until our furniture began arriving from Wales at least ten days later, we gladly sat and slept on floor mattresses. For me, all problems were forgotten in the quiet happiness of being back at last in the place I loved. Never have I felt that same emotional attachment to a school. I never revisited my schools in Germany and Austria, or went back to Wales to see our house there; nor have I ever had any wish to do so. Perhaps because Summerhill is my own—something I bought and improved—the place has become an extension of my own personality.

I have already written so much about Summerhill that I have no desire to describe it now. Today, in 1972, it is still not well-known in Britain. Many Americans say to me: "We talked of Summerhill to people in London, and they had never heard of it; whereas in New York or Los Angeles, many know of it." Not claiming to be a seer, I hesitate to quote the Biblical adage that "a prophet is not without honour, save in his own country." Maybe the answer lies in Britain's class system. Most of the landed families have had to sell their old castles and mansions —partly because domestics are few and far between—but the gentry tradition lingers, with its Eton and Harrow for the upper class, its grammar schools for the middle class, and its secondary modern schools for those who will never work in white collars. But I suppose the same system exists in all countries, even in the communistic ones.

Summerhill was never patronized by the elite—the rich, the stage and TV folk. I doubt if Princess Anne would have fitted in—not after her first vacation, when Buckingham Palace might have heard a few four-letter words. Ethel Mannin, the popular novelist, sent her daughter; Professor Bernal, his two sons. Generally, however, famous parents have eschewed us. Of course we get many Americans, and I know not which are scions of celebrated parents there. Two years ago, I met a woman in New York who runs a day school and charges 3,000 dollars a year; but I am sure that none of her parents would send their kids to a school like Summerhill.

Interestingly enough, children have no class feeling at all. If one of our pupils were driven to school in a Rolls Royce, the others would have no reaction whatever. So it is with color. When we get black pupils, even the smallest child does not notice their color. We have Jewish pupils, and no one knows or cares. I had one staunch Roman Catholic forty years ago, who had to tell his beads every morning, and wrote home saying he had lost them. His father drove up in a chauffeur-driven Rolls, said nothing to me, but took his boy by the collar, shoved him into the car, and drove off. I was not concerned, for he had paid a term's fees. So with another Catholic boy I finally had to send home. The poor kid was living most of the year in a school that did not believe in sin, yet during vacations he had to go to a priest and confess his transgressions. The conflict was more than any child could bear. I don't know what would happen if we had a Jewish child from an orthodox home.

I never regretted coming to Leiston. The air is bracing, and the eleven acres are a paradise for kids. When often asked what the town thinks of us, I never have an answer. I don't think the town understands what the school is all about, but all the people are friendly. My staff and I frequent the local pubs, yet I have never seen a State teacher there, or for that matter, a doctor or a lawyer. Summerhill, having no class, belongs to all classes. One youth of about seventeen hung about our gates for a time, and when I asked him what he wanted, he replied: "A free fuck." I don't say he was typical of Leiston inhabitants.

I am "Neill," without the mister, to some of the workmen, as I am to staff, domestics, pupils. No one touches his hat to me, and some locals may wonder what the crowds of world visitors come to see. I was a member of a local golf club for twenty-five years, but I think that only one member knew who I was—my school doctor.

I have always had the ability to laugh at myself, even when being capped for an honorary degree. Years ago, when a friend wanted a copy of my first book, written in 1915, I went into a bookseller's shop in Ipswich.

"Have you ever heard of a book called *A Dominie's Log* by A. S. Neill?"

"Heard of it? Why, I've got it, saw it on the shelf the other day." He could not find it. "That's the worst of insignificant writers; their books go astray," he said. "If you leave your name and address . . . "

"Thanks, I'll look in again."

Some years ago, while walking in the woods above Oslo, I lost my way. Suddenly, I saw a man coming up through the trees, and not knowing any Norwegian, simply pointed and said: "Oslo?"

"I'm buggered if I ken," he said.

We talked for a bit about Scotland.

"Now that we have met," he said, "we may as well exchange names. My name is McDonald."

"My name is Neill."

He looked up at me quickly. "You aren't *the* Neill?"

I made a fitting gesture of modesty. "What do you mean by *the* Neill?"

"Bobby Neill, the footballer."

I think Stalin and Hitler's problems were caused by an inability to laugh at themselves, and maybe that is Nixon's trouble, too. The first requirement of any man is to recognize what a little guy he really is. There are few great men but too many great names—or at least popular names. Who will remember the pop singers of today in ten years' time? One day, some history of education will have a footnote about a man called S. A. O'Neill, an Irishman who ran a school called Summerville, and I won't be there to have a laugh.

Homer Lane and Wilhelm Reich

Though American by birth, Homer Lane is much more widely known in England. After working in that well-known American reform school, the George Junior Republic, he was invited by a few well-known social reformers—the Earl of Sandwich and Lord Lytton among them—to open a home for delinquent children in Dorset: the Little Commonwealth. It was that remarkable experiment I had tried unsuccessfully to join after leaving the army. Lane never wrote about it, but after his death in 1925, pupils who had taken notes at his lectures allowed an editor to make a book of them: *Talks to Parents and Teachers.* The man who did most of the work was John Layard. Three years ago, Schocken published an American edition in paperback, for which I wrote the preface. W. David Wills wrote Lane's biography, and the matron of the home also published a book called *The Little Commonwealth.* Lane could not write, for he was not an "educated" man. His correspondence, written on post-cards, abounds in misspellings.

Without describing Lane's philosophy of education here, I would like to explain what he did for me, for he exerted the greatest influence on my life. After the Commonwealth had been closed, Lane set up in London as an analyst. In the early twenties, I knew nothing about analysis, and had hardly heard of Freud. So, naturally, I had no thought of being analyzed myself until Lane told me that every teacher should be. He offered to take me on for free daily sessions. It was not a Freudian style of analysis, and I did not lie on a couch; we just sat and talked. Like my later analysis by Stekel, it did not touch my emotions, and I wonder if I got anything positive from it. Indeed, I feel certain now that Lane's chief contribution to my life lay outside the field of analysis altogether—in his treatment of children. His immortal phrase was: "You must be on the side of the child."

Lane told me of his charges, the toughest he could get from the juvenile courts. The whole thing was incredible—thieves and robbers cured by freedom and self-government—no, surely not. When finally I mixed with the youths, I knew that Lane had not exaggerated a bit.

Lane was a wonderful personality; I do not want to call him a genius because the word is too often abused. Lane had great gifts; he had an uncanny instinct for seeing in a flash the motive behind some unusual behavior.

If Lane did not cure my complexes, he managed to give me a new one. Interpreting a dream one day, he said: "This shows a fear of heights."

I laughed. "Good heavens, Lane, in my student days I used to climb a tower and sit with my legs dangling over the side while I read a book."

"Dreams don't lie," he countered.

"Okay, Lane, I'll prove you are wrong," I said, and next day climbed the Wren Monument, which stands two hundred feet high. Looking down, I was terrified. The usual explanation of a height phobia is an unconscious wish to jump—and that may be—but what puzzled me then was the fact that I could easily look down a deep well. Once also, on the top of a mountain in Bavaria, I had a sudden attack of fear. Yet there was no temptation to jump, for it was a gradual slope downward. The real import of Lane's role lay in his dealing with wayward children, not with neurotic adults.

Lane's humor pleased me. I recall how he once took up a word from one of my dreams—*lime*.

"Lime, the stuff that binds," said Lane. "I am the lime. I am helping you to rebuild yourself—*lime-Lane*—see the connection?"

"But, Lane, I dreamed about a line, a railway line."

He roared with laughter. Dream analysis seemed just a game to him, a sort of crossword puzzle.

Lane was charming, always immaculately dressed, genial— and a dreadful romancer. He told us stories of his youth: how he had run away to the Indians, how he had knocked out a gang leader and taken his place as foreman on the job. His biographer David Wills discovered that he had done neither.

Lane was a great admirer of Barrie and hated Shaw. He loved *Peter Pan* and *Dear Brutus*. Like Barrie, he never really grew up; and all the stupid things he did in his life were infantile things.

Yet it was this Peter Panism that made Lane the creator of a new treatment for sick people. Once he built a wall along with his Commonwealth boys. When they saw that his structure looked perfect while theirs was bad, the boys began to knock it all down. And Lane joined in. He rationalized this by saying that he had to show them that children were more important than bricks; but I have an idea that he enjoyed the destruction because he also was a mischievous little boy. Every Sunday night, while Lane was "analyzing" me, I supped with his family—his wife, children, and a few ex-delinquents from the Commonwealth. Often he was the merry soul of this quiet group; often he sat silent in deep gloom.

Lane's influence was limited. Since his death in 1925, the state institutions for problem children have not been changed in favor of freedom and understanding. They treat young delinquents with all the evils that made them so—punishment, strict requirements of obedience, hard discipline, moral talks. I wonder how many teachers in Britain today have heard of Lane.

I recall my first visit to the Little Commonwealth, arriving in the middle of a stormy self-government meeting. Lane and I sat up into the wee hours talking—no, he talked while I listened. I had never heard of child psychology, or dynamic psychology of any sort, for that matter. I had written two books before meeting Lane—books groping for freedom. Lane showed me the way, and I have always acknowledged it. To me, he was a revelation.

I don't think I am being smug when I say that many who have been influenced by Summerhill have not acknowledged it in books and articles. This is always so. Recently an English doctor published an article on the connection between neurosis and the stiffening of the muscles—Reich's discovery—but the article did not mention Reich. I grant that such things do not matter in the long run, but I believe that honesty should admit sources.

We, his disciples, accepted Lane as the oracle. We never queried his dicta. When he would say something like "every footballer has a castration complex," we nodded our heads in agreement. We never questioned how he came to that conclusion, and we were not all young fools; his group included Lord Lytton (already mentioned), later Viceroy of India; Dr. David, the Rugby headmaster who became Bishop of Liverpool; doctors, teachers, and students. David Wills, in his biography of Lane, says that of all his disciples Neill was the only one who could view him objectively later on. That may be because I am a hardheaded Scot, or more likely, that my transference was not so strong that time could not break it.

I had a quarrel with Lane in the middle of my analysis. He accused me of misrepresenting his ideas when I went lecturing. We had a proper set-to, and I stopped going to his sessions. For a few months, I went to Maurice Nicoll, a London doctor who was the leading Jungian there, but again I got no reaction emotionally. I cannot recall anything about the analysis save that when I dreamed of a black dog, the analyst said it represented free, floating libido—whatever that meant. One Sunday night in Lane's home, he asked how my London analysis was going and I told him. "You come back to me," he said, and back I went again to listen to his elaborate breakdown of my dreams.

In perspective, I can see he was not a good analyst. He was brilliant in interpreting the symbolism in dreams, but what he said never touched my emotions.

I've said that on my discharge from the army I wired Lane COMING, NEILL. and got a reply from London saying the Commonwealth had been closed by the Home Office. The story was that a delinquent girl had stolen money, and had run away. Caught by the police, she said that Lane had tried to seduce her. The Home Office sent down an unsympathetic K.C. to investigate. He had to report that there was no evidence against Lane, but the Home Office nevertheless ordered the Committee to appoint another superintendent. The Committee, of which the Earl of Sandwich, Lord Lytton, and Lady Betty Balfour were members, refused to remove Lane, saying they would rather close the Commonwealth.

I have never had any doubts about Lane's innocence. His taste in women was too aesthetic to allow him to seduce a problem girl. Every man who has dealt with difficult adolescent girls knows how far their dreams will carry them. I myself have dealt with them for years, but never have any accusations been made against me. This was partly due to the fact that at the first sign of a dangerous fantasy, I would at once get in touch with the doctor or teacher who had sent the girl to me.

In 1925, Lane was tried on a technicality—for being an alien who had not registered with the police. In reality, he was being tried for the same misdemeanor he had previously been accused of; in this instance, for seducing a woman patient. He was deported, went to Paris, caught pneumonia and died.

I don't know whether these accusations were justified, but I have never thought that it mattered if he did sleep with a patient. After Lane's death, the late Lord Lytton was much upset; he seemed to be lost. When he invited me to sup with him at his club, I had the feeling that Lytton was endeavoring to find a substitute for Lane. If he were, he must have found me sadly lacking.

I said to him: "Lytton, suppose you had complete proof that Lane had been guilty of sleeping with a patient, how would you feel about it?"

The question seemed to shock him for the moment. "I don't think," he said slowly, "that it would alter in any way my love and admiration for the man."

Lane, by the way, had an unpleasant habit of telling one patient all about the one who had just left the room, an unpardonable habit in any therapist.

I never believed the stories of Lane's seducing delinquent girls in the Commonwealth. Later, when the law accused him of seducing patients on the analytical couch, I had some doubts, but even then, never once had any shock about it. Maybe some of his female patients got more out of seduction than I got out of dream analysis. Professionally, of course, it is wrong, for when a woman becomes the analyst's lover, the analysis stops dead. Professor Jack Flugel, an old friend and well-known Freudian, once quoted a New York analyst to me: "Flugel, I am not one of those analysts who fuck every patient." Jack was one of the few analysts I met who could laugh at himself and others. The tragedy of Lane's life was his being associated with social scandal, rather than being renowned for the great work he did with problem children. Scandal cannot kill a man's work forever, but it can ruin his life.

I have called Lane a romancer, and took with a pinch of salt his story of a dinner party where he sat next to Barrie. "When I asked Barrie if he knew the symbolism of Peter Pan, he gave me a look of alarm. 'Good God, no,' he said, and then turned to the lady on his other hand, and never spoke to me again."

When I read of Lane's death in the papers, I found myself smiling. At first, this seemed like hardheartedness, but later I got the true explanation: I was free at last. Up to then, I had relied entirely on him—what would Homer say? Now I had to stand on my own feet.

Later, in Vienna, I became a patient of Dr. Wilhelm Stekel, a member of the Freudian school who broke away, like Jung and Adler. I had reviewed a book of Stekel's that claimed that analysis was too expensive and too long. He said that an analysis should not take longer than three months, a statement that appealed to my Scottish thrift. Stekel was a brilliant symbolist. He hardly ever asked for an association to a dream. "Ach, Neill, this dream shows that you are still in lof with your sister." His words touched my head but never my emotions. I don't think I got a transference to him, maybe because he was so boyish in some ways.

"Neill, your dream shows that you are in lof with my wife."

"Stekel, I like your wife, but she has no sexual attraction for me."

He flared up angrily.

"Vot, you do not admire my vife? That is to her an insult. She is admired by many men."

Another time I asked him if I could use his W.C. When I returned, he looked at me in an arch fashion and pointed a finger. "Ach so! Der Neill wants to be Wilhelm Stekel, the king; he vants to sit on his throne! Naughty Neill."

He brushed aside with a laugh my explanation that I had

diarrhea. One of his favorite sayings regarding Freud was: "A dwarf sitting on a tall man's shoulder sees farther than he does"—a doubtful assertion.

I have no intention of describing Reich's work, but simply his effect and influence on me. We first met in 1937, when I was lecturing at Oslo University. After my lecture, the chairman said, "You had a distinguished man in your audience tonight—Wilhelm Reich."

"Good God," I replied, "I was reading his *Mass Psychology of Fascism* on the ship coming over."

I phoned Reich, and he invited me to dinner. We sat talking till late. I was fascinated.

"Reich," I said, "you are the man for whom I have been searching for years, the man to link the soma with the psyche. Can I come and study under you?"

So for two years, I went to Oslo for the length of my three yearly vacations. He said I could learn only by undergoing his Vegetotherapy, which meant lying naked on a sofa while he attacked my stiff muscles. He refused to touch dreams. It was a hard therapy, and often a painful one, but I got more emotional release in a few weeks than I had ever had with Lane, Nicoll, or Stekel. It seemed to me then the best kind of therapy, and I still think so, even after seeing that some Reichian patients apparently remain neurotic following their treatment.

Reich often said: "Bend the tree when it is a twig, and it will be bent when it is fully grown." But I doubt if any therapy ever gets down to the roots of neurosis. In the early twenties, we were all searching for the famous trauma that caused the sickness. We never found it because there was no trauma, only a plethora of traumatic experiences from the moment of birth. Reich came to realize that only prophylaxis was the real answer, rather than therapy, but kept up his practice mainly to raise money for scientific studies.

When war came in 1939, I trembled about Reich's fate,

for he was a Jew on the Nazi destruction list. An American
patient, Dr. Theodore Wolfe, who later became the translator
of his books, managed to get him into the United States. His
history there is well known up to his death in prison.* His
widow Ilse's book, *Wilhelm Reich: A Personal Biography,* is
a brave and sincere description of a brilliant and complicated
man.

Reich, as Ilse points out, was deficient in humor, and my
friendship with him was marred by the fact that we could not
laugh at the same things. No one would have dared to tell a
sex story in his presence. The word *fuck* infuriated him: "The
sick sex—the aggressive male—fucks; but women do not fuck.
The word is *embrace.*"

He had no liking for ordinary conversation about cars or
books. Gossip was anathema to him. His talk was always about
work; later, in the U.S., he relaxed when he made his weekly
visit to the movies in Rangeley, Maine, near the locale of
his school and clinic. He was completely uncritical of films.
Once, when I described a film as kitsch, he was angry with me.
"I enjoyed every minute of it," he said.

I stood in a special relation to Reich. Around him were
all his disciples, his doctor trainees, and all was formal. I appeared to be the only one who addressed him as Reich. True,
I had also been his patient, his trainee, but maybe owing to
my age, I was in a category by myself, along with Dr. Ola
Raknes from Oslo. We had seminars. Reich filled the blackboard with hieroglyphics, equations that meant nothing to me,
and I doubt if they meant anything to the others present. His
orgone theory was Greek to me. Reich said orgone energy was

---

*Reich was jailed because of his failure to answer the accusation of a U. S. Gov't.
bureau that he had been fraudulently advertising his orgone box. This bureau
believed that alleged claims that the accumulator might cure certain ailments were
unfounded; Reich, while unable scientifically to prove his representations in court,
refused to withdraw his box from circulation.

visible, but I had a blind eye to it. Reich had a small motor which was charged by a small orgone accumulator. It ran slowly; but when gingered up by volts from a battery, it seemed to revolve at great speed. Reich was in ecstasies. "The motive force of the future!" He exclaimed. I never heard of its being developed.

I do not know enough about his "rainmaking" to form an opinion. What one might call psychic orgone energy cannot be used in any way I can imagine. But here I admit my ignorance of science of any kind. I was never interested in Reich's later work. To me he was the great man of *The Mass Psychology of Fascism*, *Sexual Revolution*, *Character Analysis* and *The Function of the Orgasm*. I still think *The Mass Psychology of Fascism* is a masterpiece of crowd analysis.

I wish our conversations in Maine could have been taped. We talked and talked, and consumed a lot of Scotch and rye, but oddly enough, had no hangovers. Though Reich scarcely relaxed, as I have said, his lower jaw was so loose that it worked as a well-oiled joint. on a machine. His muscles could relax, but his brain never did.

Often he tried to persuade me to bring Summerhill to Maine. "No, Reich," I would reply. "I once had my school in a foreign country, and would never do it again. I don't know the customs or the habits of the U.S.A.; and anyway, my school would come to be regarded as a Reich school, and that I could never have."

Reich was an all-or-nothing man, impossible to work with: any dissenter had to go his way, or out on his neck he went. I knew I could never work with him.

He was not a fearful man—not for himself anyway—but when being driven in a car, he sat on edge, just as I do if the driver is not good. He was anxious for others. When Ilse drove their small son Peter to school, it was always: "Be careful, Ilse. Don't drive fast." When he was having his observatory

built, I climbed a high ladder to get a view from the top.
(What had happened to my height phobia then?) He stood at
the bottom with much concern. "Be careful, Neill. Look out.
Come down."

Reich and I loved each other. In 1948, when we parted
in Maine for the last time, he threw his arms around me.
"Neill, I wish you could stay. You are the only one I can talk
to. The others are all patients or disciples." Then I knew how
lonely he was.

Once I said to him: "Why are you so formal? Why do
you address Wolfe as Dr. Wolfe? Why aren't you just Reich
to them all?"

"Because they would use the familiarity to destroy me,
as they did in Norway when I was Willy to them all."

"But, Reich, I am Neill to my staff, pupils, domestics,
and no one ever takes advantage of the familiarity."

"Yes, but you aren't dealing with dynamite as I am," was
his cryptic answer.

Reich had no effect on my school. I had been running it
for twenty-six years before I met him. But he had a strong effect on me personally. He widened my perspective, my knowledge of self; he uprooted remnants of my Scots Calvinism
about sex matters, showing that my approval of children's sex
play had been intellectual, not emotional.

It is obvious from Ilse's biography that Reich lost his
reason in the end. That never worried me. Many great men
have gone mad—Swift, Nietzsche, Schumann, Ruskin, lots of
others. And the fact that I haven't gone mad is proof perhaps
that I am not a genius. It is an odd world indeed, in which
a Reich is mad while a Reagan, a Nixon, a Wallace are sane.

Ilse has told about Reich's jealousies, his tempers. I saw
the tempers often when he would fly off the handle about
seeming trifles. One morning at the breakfast table when he
had been raging at Ilse, he turned to me. "Neill, why do I do it?"

"Because of the reconciliation," I said. "You want a second honeymoon." And he burst into laughter, crying out: "That is a profound and true explanation."

I wish I could recall his sayings. One I do remember: "The trouble with psychoanalysis is that it deals with words, while all the damage is done to a child before it can speak."

From the time Reich went to America until he went to prison, we corresponded. Ilse tells of the only time he rejected me, when he was being tried. I was in Oslo then, and Ola Raknes and a few of his old friends sent him a telegram of sympathy. The reply came back: DON'T TRUST NEILL.

I knew why. His boy Peter had visited me in Summerhill; and when American planes flew over, he said that they had been sent to protect him. I knew he was quoting his father. I told him this was nonsense, and when he went home, he must have told Reich. But we made up after that, and no break occurred in our friendship.

Reich gave me the German manuscript of *Listen, Little Man* to read, and asked my opinion about publishing it in English. "No, Reich," I wrote, "It will make your enemies attack you as a conceited fellow who sees all others as inferior or sick." He agreed with me, but shortly afterward, when a woman wrote a poisonous article about him, he rushed the book into print as a counterblast. I often told him he was a fool to react to every ignorant or spiteful journalist. "Ignore them as I do," I said. But no, he had to fight.

Like other men, Reich had the qualities of a little man; but unlike most men, he was conscious of the fact. Not that he had humor enough to laugh at himself; but I am sure he was aware of his extreme jealousies and suspicions. Yet, as Ilse said, he had no *Menschenkenntis*—knowledge of people. More than once, I saw him taken in by people I suspected as phonies. He trusted people, and when they turned out to be fakes, his fury was terrible. But it generally subsided as quickly as it arose.

Unconsciously, he was seeking martyrdom, I am sure. The *Murder of Christ* is almost autobiographical. Again and again, I heard him say: "They will kill me." He had been a martyr before I met him. When fleeing Hitler, he was thrown out of Denmark and Sweden; and his enemies were scheming to have him thrown out of Norway, a plot killed by the war.

Ilse tells of a shattering thing that happened to Reich when he was a boy. He found his mother in bed with his tutor, and told his father. His mother killed herself. This incident accounts for his life-long jealousy, his distrust of all his womenfolk—his suspicion that they would betray him.

I felt his death more acutely than I felt the death of Lane. A bright light had gone out; a great man had died in vile captivity. I think that Reich will not come into his own as a genius until at least three generations from now. I was most lucky to know him, and learn from him, and love him.

Love and Marriage and Zoë

I call myself normal sexually, even though I fancy I have sub-limated sex to ambition. In my student days, I had the usual unedifying adventures with girls. As mentioned earlier, the nice girls were taboo: "Who touches me, marries me." So we students picked up shopgirls—girls from the working classes. I never once went to a prostitute, maybe because so many enthusiastic amateurs were around. But it was all wrong, all degrading. Once, after intercourse with a shopgirl on Blackford Hill, she began to cry. I asked her why. "It isn't fair," she sobbed. "You students take us out and we like your manners and educated speech, but you never marry us. I'll have to marry some workman who can only talk about football and beer." That was the end of my picking up shopgirls.

Twice I nearly got married. Both girls, like myself, were of the lower middle class. I hesitated. I was in love, but reason crept in: you want to do something important in life; will she be able to keep up with you? Stupidly, I tried in both cases to educate these girls, gave them books, talked of Shaw and Wells and Chesterton, of Hardy and Meredith. I think it was the old snob complex my mother had given me, now transformed from social to cultural climbing.

Also, there was the economic factor. I did not earn enough to support a wife and family, which would have meant settling down for a lifetime as a country headmaster, far from an urban intellectual life and a career in literature. Emotionally I was wrong, but I could not act in any other way, not with my grandiose plans.

At the time, I had no definite idea what kind of success I was after. I knew I had to write, but did not know what. Plays, novels, essays? I had no notion that my life work would be children rather than books. In the end, of course, it meant children *and* books, but the books were not literary creations; they were records of my work with children.

My sex life was subsidiary to my work life. I got little pleasure from hole-and-corner affairs; these adventures were sex without love, without tenderness. My Calvinistic conscience that made them even dirtier must have more than once made me impotent. Indeed, I sometimes wonder how anyone reared as a Roman Catholic or a Calvinist can ever get away from the sex guilt inculcated in early life.

Looking back now, I wonder if the handicap in my love life came from Calvinism or from the fact that I could never arrange a sex life with girls of my own social level. In my youth, contraceptives were just coming in and were not considered safe. Also, in a Scottish small town, virginity was priceless to the middle and upper classes; an illegitimate child was an eternal disgrace and precluded any chance of a girl's getting married. Only plowmen and farm lasses fornicated. (They often had two of their bairns at their wedding later on.) As a son of the village schoolmaster, I could not make love to dairymaids. Social snobbery and sex fear put middle-class girls beyond any contact other than golf or tennis. The lower class had very little guilt about sex; but everywhere else, sex outside marriage was the main sin against the Holy Ghost. This applied to women folk, of course. In my native town, quite a few married men fooled around; but then, there was one law for men and another law for women. Women had to be "pure."

Earlier on, I told of the time when my sister Clunie and
I were beaten for sex play. Just as Reich's guilt about his
mother colored his entire life, so I fancy did this beating have
a most sinister effect on my own sex life. It bound me psychologically to Clunie till she died in 1919. It made the genitals
the center of the greatest wickedness.

I never had any symptoms of homosexuality. But I wonder if some homos could date their condition to an early incident that made a certain girl, and therefore all girls, taboo.

In our schoolhouse home, nakedness was shunned like the
plague. But there are worse customs. An American Rabbi told
me of a Jewish sect that will not allow a boy or man to touch
his penis when urinating. Incidentally, the Kinsey Report listed
Judaism as the most sex-suppressive of all religions.

There is a Scottish story about a man of eighty who got
married and visited his physician. "Doctor, the lassie is young
and I want to have a family. Do you think that at my age I
can . . . ."

"Why not," said the doctor, "but if I were you I'd take
in a lodger."

A year later, the old man met the doctor on the street.
"Doctor, I have graun news today; the wife is to have a bairn."

"Oh," said the doctor rather cynically, "that's fine. What
does the lodger say about it?"

"Delighted. She's pregnant, too."

Composed, I guess, by some old wishful thinker.

At my age, sex is academic. As my doctor brother said just
before he died at the age of eighty: "We end where we began.
When we were babies, our penises were only for peeing with;
and at eighty, they are just the same."

I am slightly worried about the sex of today. So much of
it is sick sex. What man with a healthy sex appetite could
watch a striptease or a play in which sexual intercourse was

shown? It may be my Calvinism speaking, but I cannot think of any of my old pupils who would seek vicarious sex excitement in such ways. Free children, in general, have a healthy attitude toward sex.

In Hellerau, I danced with many a pretty girl but remained fancy-free. Violent passion was not for me, and that is why I came to marry a woman older than myself. Walter Neustätter, one of my pupils in King Alfred School in London, was the son of Dr. Otto Neustätter. The boy's mother was an Australian who had been a music student in Leipzig. Becoming friendly with Frau Neustätter, I discovered that we had similar views on education, and that Lil was a well-traveled, cultured woman. She and her son Walter came to stay with her husband, Otto, in Hellerau—I've told about that period earlier. Lil (some complex kept me from ever addressing her so) became matron of my department when we moved to the mountains at Sonntagberg. Later, she occupied the same position in Lyme Regis. Lil divorced Otto when we were in Lyme Regis. I married her because of my school, but there was another motive besides respectability. As an alien, Lil had to register with the British police; and being an outsider, she was full of misery and resentment. Marriage to me made her a British subject.

Otto, Lil, and I all remained the best of friends, and we went holidaying together, along with Otto's second wife. I loved Otto and he loved me. He was Jewish but not orthodox. Otto escaped Hitler in time to get to the United States where he later died.

My wife worked hard, and "Mrs. Lins," as the old pupils christened her, from Lilly Lindesay Neustatter, became just as important to the school as I was; just as my wife Ena is today. I have been lucky with both wives, wonderfully competent and understanding women.

My work filled my life. Mrs. Lins and I got along splendidly. She loved travel, so we went on trips to Germany, Italy,

France. Sometimes we took cruises. I was always slightly annoyed at these expenditures, preferring to spend the money
on a precision lathe or a shaping machine; yet all that travel
must have enlarged my outlook.

But to get back to sex; some place along in my first marriage, the obvious thing happened, I fell in love with a pretty
young Austrian who worked in England. Then a miserable
hole-and-corner business began. I had to lie, inventing trips
to town to see my publisher or my agent. We stayed in out-
of-the-way hotels, scared that someone we knew would enter
the dining room. On country walks, we hid our faces when
motor headlights shone on us. We registered at hotels under
false names. It was hell and damnation.

Then Lil discovered the affair; weeks of wretched argument and cruel statements followed. I thought of walking out
and living with my new love. I didn't. Again the conflict arose
between love and job: to have gone with Helga would have
wrecked the school. And now, I think that at fifty my emotion
then was what is often called the middle-age climacteric, a final
attempt to renew youth and romance and passion. I loved
Helga, but not enough to sacrifice my work. She married a man
of her own age. I believe she would not have been satisfied
with a father-substitute.

I have said that I will not write about people now living—
Helga's name wasn't Helga—so I will say nothing about my
second wife Ena, except that ours was a love match and produced a love child, our daughter Zoe.

I cannot recall my emotion when Zoe was born, only my
natural and general feeling of the unfairness that makes the
mother have all the pain. I don't think I have ever had a feeling
of possession about my daughter, never had the thought she
was made of a clay that had a smoother texture than that of
the child next door.

In a way, my married life in a community set up has been

easy compared with the life of a couple who lives in complete privacy. Many marriages are wrecked because of propinquity; husbands and wives are too much together. In the best of families, characters clash. In a school, there is no time for clashing; the common task binds the spouses together.

Many men in Britain complain about women entering pubs, for the pub is about the only place where a man can get away from his family. Homes are full of ambivalence—love and hate—but a community is comparatively free from character conflict.

I now break my earlier resolve not to write about folks now living to speak about daughter Zoe. I have written of her in more than one of my books, and her name must be familiar to millions. Many have asked me about her and her life. Some have wondered if she typifies the old Scots saying that the shoemaker's bairns are the worst shod. My brief answer must be that Zoe, at twenty-four, is as good a product of a free home and school as I could wish to see. Thus far, she does not seem an academic; from earliest infancy, she has had a great interest in horses. She is a qualified riding mistress, and has a large stable on the schoolgrounds. She laughs at my own view of riding acquired more than twenty years ago by seeing a rodeo in Madison Square Garden. "Cowboys can't ride," she says. "They simply sit on horses."

Zoe's schooldays were difficult. When she lived in our cottage, she was an outsider to the children who boarded in the main school. But when we made her a school boarder along with the other children, she felt she hadn't a home. And she suffered much from the jealousy of others.

Ena and I have long been convinced that boarding-school teachers should never have their own children in their schools. So when Zoe was eleven, we sent her to a foreign boarding-school. "Daddy, you are a swindle," she wrote. "You give freedom to other kids, but not to your own daughter. I hate my school; its freedom is fake, and it offers no real self-government." I visited the school, and brought her home. Incidentally, two other Summerhill girls later attended that school; both had the same criticism.

At the back of my mind, I suppose, was the wish that Zoe would choose my own work and interest, and run Summerhill after me. Many parents have indulged such wishful thinking, especially fathers with big businesses. We are all wrong; luckily, we have no control over our children. In time, I came to realize that horses were Zoe's life. Her happiness was all that mattered.

Today, Zoe is a recognized horse expert, known for kind and gentle methods. Her prize-winning stallion Karthage did not need to be broken; when she first jumped on his back, he took it as a natural show of kindness. "My stable is a horsey Summerhill," she says.

In September of 1971, Zoe married a young farmer and now they own a farm, a few hundred yards from the school. At their wedding, I had to propose the health of Tony and Zoe Readhead (pronounced Redhead), and although I can lecture for hours without any nervousness, I was a little anxious about making a short speech on so emotional an occasion. Having a vague memory of a fitting passage from one of my books, *The Free Child,* I quoted:

> *Yesterday was my birthday. My Zoe, who will be six next month, said, "Daddy, you are old, aren't you? You'll die before me, won't you? I'll cry when you die."*
>
> *"Hie, wait," I said, "I will maybe wait to see you married."*
>
> *"In that case," she said, "I won't need to cry, will I?"*

I did not read further but added: "It strikes me that if

a small child can take for granted that she won't need her father when she grows up, she has automatically solved the dear old Oedipus Complex."

A Matter of Identity

I really did not want to write this autobiography. Others bullied me into it. To me, my life is not important. Only what I have done seems cogent, and what have I done anyway? Unlike the Freuds, the Einsteins, who made great discoveries, I unearthed nothing new, but built upon an existent, dynamic psychology. This psychology showed that emotions—not intellect—are the driving force in life, and I founded a school in which the emotions would come first.

I ask myself: what sort of guy am I? Folks call me amiable, and it may be so, for I *am* pretty equable and placid, never flying off the handle as Reich used to do. I don't see myself as a Pharisee thanking God that I am not like other men, yet aren't we all in some way? Every criticism of another is Pharisaical.

I have no idea how I look, since I can't recall looking into a mirror since I took to an electric razor some years ago. It takes one a long time to realize that nobody else cares a damn. The lovelorn swain of twenty really thinks that the desired one will be impressed by his having socks and tie that match in color, just as the simple fellow believes that if a girl is beautiful, she has a beautiful character. I have often wondered why beauty in a girl's face is so important, why graceful carriage or lovely figure takes second place. But most questions in life are never answered. H. G. Wells said that one just begins to understand a little about life when Nurse Death comes along and tells us to put away our toys, because it is time to go to bed. At eighty-eight, I understand what he meant.

I have had fame—or maybe it should be called publicity—with two thousand visitors coming to Summerhill each year. My heavy fan mail is pleasing even if it means hours of answering folks I do not know.

I never expect to be recognized on a street, and would be surprised, even pleased, if a stranger identified me as A. S. Neill. This may be the result of my youthful experience of being the dunce of the family—"Mary, that boy will come to nothing." Perhaps I came to something as a compensation for my early inferiority.

Along with humility goes the opposite. If a new book on progressive education contains no reference to me, I am annoyed —but not very strongly. When one is old, praise is sweet to be sure, but blame has no special emotional impact, either. A bitchy article in a Sunday paper about the Summerhill fiftieth anniversary party did not make me angry or even concerned; I have not been accustomed to enmity. I know of no one who is my open enemy, but there must be a few thousand parents in the United States, in Germany, in Brazil, etc., who hate my guts. Some of their children write: "When I quote *Summerhill* to my parents, they go haywire. Daddy has forbidden me to read the book."

I sometimes wonder what other writers think about their own books. I have written twenty; and if I had to read them again, it would be torture. The only work of mine I still can read and enjoy is *The Last Man Alive,* a story I wrote for some of my pupils in 1937. This was the only book completely written in the spirit of fun, and it took the form of pure fiction, while most of my others have been full of opinions, some proved wrong by time and experience.

It is possible to write one's life and make the environment

of more importance than the private life of the writer, but here one comes up against snags. What is of importance to the general reader? Is it of interest to anyone that I stole apples as a boy? Some years ago, when I intended to write the life of George Douglas Brown, the author of *The House with the Green Shutters*, I went to his birthplace to interview old men and women who had known him. "Tell me," I said, "about Geordie Broon."

"Man," said a very old native, "I mind the time when Geordie and me went poaching rabbits and the gamekeeper cam and . . . ."

I failed to learn anything of moment about Brown and never wrote the book, but passed on a sheaf of correspondence about him to James Veitch who did. Now that I sit down to write my own life, I feel very chary about boring readers with commonplace reminiscences of a Scottish village. Still, I cannot explain myself without bringing in the environment that formed me.

Many, many times I have been asked how I became a reformer in education. Was it rebellion against my village dominie father with his tawse? I have never been able to answer. Environment does not account for a Churchill, a Charlie Chaplin, a Horatio Bottomley. In my own experience, my brothers and sisters did not become rebels, though I must own that my doctor brother Neil, three years older than myself, created anatomical paintings for many years. Granted that no two children in a family have the same environment, there is a general environment common to the whole family; but in the words of Carlyle; "Mighty events turn on a straw; the crossing of a book decides the conquest of the world."

I have often thought of that quotation. In one mail, I was offered two jobs, the headmastership of Gretna Green School, and English master of Tain Academy. I chose Gretna Green because I would be my own boss. Had I chosen Tain, my life would have been completely altered. I might never have met Homer Lane; certainly I would not have gone to Germany and Austria. "The fault, dear Brutus, is not in our stars, but in ourselves, that we are underlings." Or is it? Had I accepted the invitation to become an Australian school inspector in 1912, would I ever have had a pioneer school? My star would have been a bureaucratic job of watching others run their schools. I think of the one or two bright lads in my father's village school who could have had brilliant academic careers, according to my father, but became slow-witted plowmen instead.

My philosophy is rather like old Omar's: everything by chance without plan or justice. I recall a near thing once, when I moved away from a railway Left Luggage office and an I.R.A. bomb exploded, killing two passersby. Poor Leslie Howard was shot down in a plane because the Nazis thought Churchill was on it. So how much do we control our fate?

I like to fantasize about what might have been. Had I chosen Tain, I could have ended up as a teacher of English in a State school until I retired at sixty-five. But what would have become of the compulsion within me to challenge? Would environment have killed the spark? If his environment had been different, Hitler might have remained a mute, inglorious agitator in his home town. The Second World War made Churchill, a man of many mistakes, the savior of Britain. A death made Lyndon Johnson president, so I guess that even his enemies are praying that no one assassinates Nixon.

It is a world "where Destiny with men for pieces plays." There is no logical reason why I should live to be well up in my eighties when so many died young—Chopin, Keats, Shelley, Lipatti, and Chatterton among them. Scores of young potential geniuses must have died in the two great wars; they were not captains of their souls.

This brings up the question of free will. In small matters possibly, the will is free. I can decide whether to order whiskey or beer in a pub. In larger matters, I cannot see any free will. How can a man, indoctrinated by Catholicism in infancy, ever get away from the feeling that he is a sinner? A Calvinist may get away from the guilt of sin as I did. There can be no free will as long as conditioning of the young obtains. It is true that a small minority becomes free to choose—challengers of the status quo—but the huge majority, accepting establishment molding, has no will to challenge anything. I am one of those who challenged, yet my will is not free. I can choose to be a pioneer in education; I can choose not to be a Communist or a Catholic or a football fan or an admirer of TV kitsch. I don't alas have the free will to stop smoking when I know that my heart would be better without tobacco.

So what is the answer? John Smith is a blend of his innate character and his environment. I run my school in the belief that environment is the primary necessity, but have to concede that even this can fail if a child has had no love as a baby. Yet environment is the only thing I can deal with; it is concrete and not abstract.

Environment alone can negative any free will. Summerhill and Eton pupils do not become crooks later on, but I grant that Eton has produced many a cabinet minister. Middle-class morality inhibits the personal: dress alike, think alike, behave alike. At the other end of the scale, what chance is there for free will in a boy born in a slum, a Negro in a ghetto? Maybe the chief result of therapy is that it convinces the patient that he has no free will, that his behavior has been conditioned all the way from birth.

Then comes the dilemma. I was conditioned by religion, authority, middle-class morality, social mores, and broke away from them. Other members of the family did not. Determinism is not an answer either; under it, I would have remained a conventional Scottish dominie in a village school, possibly an elder of the kirk.

In German, *ich will* does not mean *I will*; it means *I want to*. A nasty word is the word *will*; a man with a strong will is usually a selfish bully, bossing other people. Funny thought: here am I, a weak-willed man, doing a job that required oceans of will but without bullying anyone. I give up, but still think that we have no free will in emotional affairs. Maybe it is all a matter of semantics.

I read recently that a coward is always an introvert, a solitary person. The hero is brave because he is one of a crowd, unconsciously feeling its strength and courage behind him. An interesting theory. It may be that while the brave extrovert is physically courageous, the introvert is morally brave.

But, then, who is wholly introverted or extroverted. We go in both directions, but I fancy that most people lean toward the extrovert side. They are the ones who are influenced by public opinion, by speeches, by TV advertisements.

Here I am, gropingly trying to say that I am a split personality: both a pioneer educator and a child still bound emotionally to my parents, to my early environment.

II

THOUGHTS ON SUMMERHILL

Summerhill's Inspectors

Britain is the freest country in the world. Nowhere else could I have had the Summerhill school. All schools in this country are under the control of the Ministry of Education; and all schools, public and private, are examined.

The report of our first big inspection, in 1949, was printed in *Summerhill*. After a gap of ten years, there came another inspection and another report. I have never been badgered by the Ministry, and His (or Her) Majesty's Inspectors have always been civil and friendly and helpful in their own ways, if not mine. Their chief job has been to investigate the school's domestic arrangements, the quality of the teaching, and the course of study.

John Blackie, the first H.M.I. we had, was a broad-minded man. I told him he could inspect progress in maths and French, but would be unable to inspect happiness, sincerity, balance, or tolerance. "I'll have a try," said John, and he made a good one.

As to what school inspectors will be in the future, I am no prophet; I can only make guesses founded on the trends of today. The Education Ministry's attitude toward Summerhill has been one of sufferance rather than favor. The school owes its continued existence to the presence there of a few enlightened officials, as well as fear on the part of others that closing Summerhill would brand the Ministry as reactionary. Over the years, few of the visiting inspectors have had any understanding of what we were doing. Most measured us with a yardstick that did not consider our products—sincerity, balance, tolerance, happiness. They were men and women who, if they had ever heard of child psychology, did not betray any sign of it. Their standards were achievement, and methods of teaching relevant to the State schools they inspected.

A boy of twelve appeared unwashed with filthy clothes. Out came an official notebook. I thought it useless to explain that he had come to us as a bad problem with a deep grouse against society expressed as defiance of society's mores. Really, I could see little difference between that inspector and the dreaded, stiff disciplinarians who inspected my father's village school eighty years earlier.

To be fair to the inspectors, they are doing the jobs their government demands of them, treating education as a matter of learning and not of living. Both parliamentary parties agree about education in essentials; both see schools as factories to produce citizens who know school subjects. The fact that possibly only three in a football crowd of 80,000 could do a square root or list the exports of Peru does not seem to concern the Establishment.

The Ministry is—*must be*—the Establishment. It represents education as generally accepted by the majority of parents and teachers. If a Minister of Education were to forbid corporal punishment by decree, the outcry from many parents and teachers would be terrific. If the Minister ruled that religious instruction be prohibited in schools, there would be public meetings of protest all over the country—the majority of attendants, I fancy, being those who make no attempt to live as Christians. To most folks, a child's playing is a waste of time. It is impossible for some people to consider play more important than work. The Ministry tolerates schools like Summerhill, but could not officially approve of them.

In England, every private school is registered; but to be "recognised as efficient" it must apply for recognition. Recognition follows, or is refused, after an inspection. I have never applied, partly because recognition to me means something bestowed. I didn't apply for my three Honorary Degrees; nor does one apply for a baronetcy. I have a notion that Summerhill would not qualify for recognition because of its failure to meet the normal standards for book learning. Indeed, the fact that every new pupil when told that lessons are optional immediately drops all school subjects—except the creative ones like art and woodworking—proves to me that lessons are forced on children against their wishes. Summerhill pupils often bloom late from an academic point of view. One old boy, an engineer, seldom attended any lessons. Today, he has half a dozen earned degrees. To a visiting inspector, that boy would have probably been classed as a failure.

To my way of thinking, the very word *inspector* is an insult. Adviser would be a better name, especially since that is what an inspector actually is today, even if his advice is limited to irrelevancies like methods of teaching.

Inspection makes Summerhill insincere. The kids tidy up, rub out the *shits* and *fucks* on the walls; they feel self-conscious and unhappy. Some time ago when an H.M.I. inspected the school, he got a hostile reception from the pupils and was troubled. So was I. But I knew what lay behind it. A sensational daily paper had published an article alleging that the Ministry was gunning for Summerhill, and the kids looked on the harmless inspector as a dangerous spy who might close the school. The Ministry, of course, can close an independent school; but I fancy that this seldom happens except where a headmaster is a practicing homosexual or an alcoholic.

Some time ago in a newspaper, there appeared an excellent example of the hypocritical Puritanism of the British Establishment. A training college expelled a female student who had been found with a man in her room. Her appeal to the High Court was dismissed. The seventy-two-year-old presiding judge sternly told her she was not a proper person to teach children. Her sin had been the breaking of the eleventh commandment: *Thou shalt not be found out.* How unjust is such a verdict, when thousands of such girl students who lodge extramurally in cities are permitted a sex life.

Tories are always more moral than socialists; our present Tory Government in Britain is inspiring all the sex-haters, life-haters, and Mrs. Grundys to have a sort of orgiastic bean-feast of self-righteousness. The most vehement seem to be the Roman Catholics, and also the members of Moral Re-Armament. I mention these dangerous people because they are the social equivalents of the inspectors of my apprentice days. They are the anti-lifers par excellence.

Why does the teaching profession tolerate inspection? Doctors and lawyers, with their powerful professional lobbies, do not tolerate inspection. True, they are not State servants as teachers are; but since National Health began, most doctors are paid by the State, and I am sure they would fight any attempt to make the practitioners of medicine an inspected body.

I should reject inspection on the ground that my old pupils are nearly all successful in life. I should say to the Ministry: "For fifty years, educated and intelligent parents have sent their children to Summerhill, believing in its system, pleased with its results. Why should my school be judged by an official standard that is not mine? Summerhill is primarily for living, and it refuses to be judged by a body of people who think only of teaching methods and discipline. Let the inspectors rule about the number of water closets, and baths, and fire extinguishers. Summerhill accepts that ruling. But leave our education to us."

Alas, I am not brave enough to defy the powers above, so I compromise. I employ eight teachers for sixty children—

some the wrong teachers from my viewpoint—those who teach the exam subjects, subjects which I find most pupils regard as necessary dull grinds.

England is the land of independent schools; there are few on the Continent. Until the new school rage proliferated in the United States, I think that the private school in the U.S. was usually a military academy. Scotland never had the tradition of private institutions; there are four so-called public schools there, but they are English schools with the English tradition of Eton and Harrow, and at a venture I should say, English speech. John M. Aitkenhead's Kilquhanity is the only "free" boarding school I know of in Scotland; it also has had its troubles with the inspectorate.

Ah, well, I should not complain. The Ministry has very much let me alone, and will do so until I die. What will happen then I cannot guess. Some Minister may say: "We tolerated that school until the old man died, but we cannot go on allowing a school in which children can play all day without learning lessons." I shall look forward to reading about it in the *Paradise Post,* or more likely the *Hades Herald.*

The Summerhill Staff

Sometimes I think that I have had more trouble with staff than with pupils. Among the odd bods of my time was the science man who let a boy of eight handle a bottle of cyanide, and a girl of the same age pour fuming nitric acid into a test tube so that she burned herself.

There are no set duties for the Summerhill staff, except their being in classrooms at teaching periods. And many of the teachers have reacted to freedom like unfree children. Some neurotic types have taught classes all morning, and slept or read the rest of the day; whereas the really good teachers have always used their free time mixing with the kids.

New teachers are hard to find, and in spite of Summerhill's fame, it is not easy to get a good staff. Advertisements draw letters saying: "I am not a teacher, I am a bank clerk (or a librarian or whatnot), but I know I can teach." Since many people think that teaching is an unskilled employment, I do not know why so few apply. It may be a question of money, yet we pay close to the State standard—eight hundred pounds a year, plus board, lodging, and laundry. It may be that teachers fear to teach in a school where lessons are voluntary. Under such circumstances, only a good teacher can have a well-attended class, and my worst job is to say to a poor teacher: "The kids say your lessons are so dull that they won't go to them; you'll have to leave." If such a system obtained in State schools, our city streets would be full of unemployed teachers.

By law, I must have qualified teachers. Not that an academic background makes much difference, for I have had both trained and untrained teachers with varying results. Obviously, teaching is an art, not a science; a teacher is born, not made. But the law is there, and Picasso could not get a job as an art teacher in England because he has no certificate. Of course, I want a teacher to put across his or her lessons, but that is not the main consideration in Summerhill. I look for teachers with humor rather than dignity; they must not inspire fear, and they must not be moralists. I am inclined to acquire more introverts than extroverts, but I do not want he-men with strong personalities. Free children reject such. When we had an ex-scoutmaster with his: "Come on, lads, we'll build a boat;" they turned away in scorn.

One sort has appeared again and again: the teacher who seeks popularity by being on the side of the child for the wrong reason. Children soon see through that type. Too many new teachers and housemothers have trouble discriminating between freedom and license. One housemother let her group smash a lot of furniture because "I thought I wasn't ever supposed to say no." But there have been some excellent teachers—community-minded people. I have already mentioned George Corkhill, our science master for nearly thirty years—stolid, never ruffled, always the center of a group of little ones. Corkie followed *their* interests; his idea of chemistry was making lemonade and fireworks. His retirement meant a great loss to the school.

Since this book is about me, I must tell of my own reactions to the staff, and its reactions to me. Never once have I told a teacher what to do or how to teach; one or two complained that I did not come to their classrooms often enough. My chief difficulty has been handling disagreements between teachers and pupils. A boy once wanted to make a banjo, but the woodworking teacher refused to let him, saying that it was too difficult a task. Both came to me for arbitration. I said: "If he wants to make a banjo, that is his wish; if he makes a mess of it, that also is his affair. Give him the wood." The teacher was furious, accused me of siding with a pupil against the staff, and resigned on the spot. I realized too late that this should have been a matter for our general meeting to decide.

I have an almost morbid complex about being a boss. I hate telling anyone what to do, in the belief perhaps that if he does it only because I ask him to, he isn't being original enough. I hate playing God; when I have to send a pupil away for terrifying small kids, I always feel miserable and slightly guilty. But I never feel guilty when telling an unsuccessful teacher to leave—just embarrassed. I may be demanding too much from my staff. Balanced people full of fun, active in school life, are what I want. I get a few, but not as many as I should like.

Once a big stone, knocked off a wall by some kids, lay on the path below. I stooped to lift it and then paused, deciding to leave it and see what happened. Staff and pupils walked around it for six weeks before I lifted it back to its place. But one must take a certain factor into account: I have a feeling of possession about the house and grounds that my staff does not share. I understand. When I used to help my brother plant his potatoes, it was not a work of joy; they were his spuds, and he would eat them.

Generally speaking, the Summerhill staff has been a contented lot with little of the bickering and jealousy so often found in staffrooms: "Jones has six periods for English, while I have only four for maths."

Now and again we have had a crisis within the staff. One young man who thought he could run the school better than I, agitated among the staff and made some converts, so that the atmosphere was strained. When such a challenge appeared years

ago in Dresden, I got rid of the rebels as soon as possible—
but reluctantly, for they were good teachers. Psychologically
speaking, one might say that instead of challenging Father at
fourteen, they waited until they found a father-substitute, even
a nonauthoritarian one. As a mother-figure, my wife gets much
more hate than I do. Through my work with children, I can
understand this.

Once, in the days when I used such treatment, I got our
needlework teacher to make dolls for play therapy. These appeared as father, mother, son, daughter, all with sexual organs,
of course. Children up to the age of twelve played with them.
In six weeks, poor mother was kicked to bits, but father remained untouched. This made me wonder if Freud's Oedipus
Complex was all wrong. Father is out all day; Mother has to
live with the children, feed them, say no to them. Because she
is the real authoritarian figure in the home, resentment against
the mother looms greater than that against the father. Such hate
becomes most evident when Ena is serving meals and the "me
first" element springs forth.

My staffmen and I seem to get less hate from disturbed
pupils than women teachers do. In my own case, the obvious
explanation is my neutrality. The English teacher can complain
at a general meeting about the savagery of a problem boy, but
I dare not; I cannot be an accuser and a therapist.

It is sad that former pupils do not become teachers and return to Summerhill as members of the staff. I have had ex-
pupils as housemothers, and they did this work well, partly
because they did not require a period of living out their complexes when coming into a non-authoritarian atmosphere. Contrariwise, when I offered one of my girls, age nineteen, a job
as housemother, she said: "I'd love to, but no; I'd feel I was
making Summerhill an escape hatch instead of facing the outer
world."

New American Schools

When *Summerhill* was published in New York in 1960, my publisher, Harold H. Hart, founded the Summerhill Society, whose aim was to set up a Summerhill type of school in the United States. He subsequently resigned from the organization; but since then, dozens of new schools have sprung up, all claiming the freedom of Summerhill. While this has been heartening to me, it has also been a bit disturbing.

Through the New York press, I have asked schools not to call themselves "Summerhills", for a number of these schools do not really follow Summerhill principles. For example, I was told of one school, claiming to be run on Summerhill lines, that had half an hour's compulsory religion every morning. In that school, if a boy swore, his mouth was washed out with soap and water. On the other hand, some of these so-called Summerhills mistake freedom for license. I hear that some of these new schools have failed; perhaps because the founders had freedom in their heads instead of in their guts; but more likely, because most of them are day schools, and it is almost impossible in any single community to find enough parents who believe in freedom. My pupils come from the United States, Germany, France, Denmark, and England; none of the parents could find an adequate free school in their home towns.

I regard Summerhill as part of a wide challenge to Establishment education. Certain educational writers inspire as much as Summerhill does—Carl Rogers, John Holt, George Dennison, Bruno Bettelheim, George Leonard, Goodwin Watson, Paul Goodman, and many more. Freedom is not a one-man show. It is a new *Weltanschauung,* a great hope in this mad world.

The London Summerhill Society was founded over a dozen years ago. Its function was utilitarian: to raise funds for a school deficit. True, the London Society made good propaganda with its magazine *Id;* but its main concern was to raise money—an aim that had its difficulties, for most of the few who believed in Summerhill were comparatively poor.

The London Society and its magazine are now defunct, but I look back with warm gratitude to what the Society did. When, after the American invasion, we began to get out of the red, the necessity for adjunct supporting funds ceased. But in its time, the Society was not only a financial support: it was a token of love for the school by old pupils, parents, and sympathizers. The Society's biggest "do" was the school's fiftieth anniversary party held in London. More than 250 guests attended. It gave the school stoves, a refrigerator, and some electrical equipment. When it offered us a TV set, I put the proposal to a general meeting, and the offer was refused by a large majority. I asked a girl of fourteen why. "Because it would ruin the social life of the school," she replied. The school has a TV set now, but its use is limited by the community.

I cannot mention by name the members of the London Summerhill Society, but I must pay tribute to David Caryll, a musician and a fellow Scot. He wanted to turn my farcical novel *The Booming of Bunkie* into a musical, and he sent me the first act; but he was killed by a car when crossing a London street. He was one of the most loyal parents Summerhill ever had.

Child Psychology

After coming back from the psychoanalytic atmosphere of Vienna in the early twenties, I thought that analysis was the answer to the problem child. I spent years analyzing the dreams of such children, and I was proud when a boy who had been chucked out of Eton for stealing graduated from my school cured.

But another boy and girl, who had also been expelled for stealing but refused to come to me for analysis, *also left Summerhill cured.* It took me a long time to realize that it was not my therapy but rather the freedom to be themselves that cured the offenders. A most satisfactory belief, for if therapy *were* the answer, millions of kids in the world could not afford cure.

I think I have had more success with the kind of psychology that is not found in textbooks. When I rewarded a bad thief by paying him a shilling for every theft, I was not acting on theory. The theory came later, and may have been inadequate, if not wrong. The unloved thief was stealing love symbolically. So I gave him a token of love in the form of a coin. The point is that the method worked again and again, but I know the situation was more complicated than that. How much did his new freedom in Summerhill help to cure the boy? How eager was he to be accepted by his peers as a good guy?

When a new boy broke windows and I joined in the fun,

I was not reasoning. The explanation came later: Billy wasn't breaking windows but protesting adult authority. My joining in put him on the spot: authority breaking windows? Looking back, I think it was a bit unfair to spoil his wrecking fun. The simple rationale of my methods may be that I thought of the wrong way to treat a kid, and did the opposite. In conventional schools, stealing means the cane, or at least a moral talk. I made stealing nonmoral.

One boy ran away from three schools. On his arrival, I said to him: "Here is your fare home. I'll put it on the mantelpiece, and when you want to run away, come and get it." He never ran away from Summerhill. But was it my attitude, or the pleasure he had in being free for the first time in his life? There is no final answer.

I have had successes but also failures. In Dresden I told a Yugoslavian girl that she was using too many nails making a box. She lashed out at me: "You are just like all the bossy teachers I have had." I couldn't make real contact with her again.

Once, while giving out pocket money, I said to Raymond, aged nine, "You were fined sixpence for stealing the front door," and he burst into tears. I should have known that he was a mental case.

Telling the nine-year-olds a story that involved them in adventures, I made Martin the character who stole the gold we had found. Later, he came to me weeping. "I never stole that gold." From then on, I made none of them baddies, even in fiction.

In the early days, when Summerhill had so many crooks, I was not always the winner. One boy asked me for my autograph, and I did not notice that the paper I wrote it on was folded, until a local shopkeeper showed the whole of it to me: "Please give bearer fifty Players Cigarettes—A. S. Neill."

For a week, Dick kept selling me stamps; only the acci-

dent of my having stained one with green ink made me aware
that he had been robbing my stamp drawer. I gave him five
shillings' reward for his cleverness, childishly showing him that
he couldn't take the old man in. Old man? I was in my forties
then.

Today, I doubt if I could use the reward trick with a
thieving pupil. There is a new, intangible sophistication among
the current youth. This fresh orientation may stem from the
spread of knowledge about psychology. Some of my older pupils, Americans especially, juggle terms like inferiority complex, mother fixation, etc. Nowadays, if a boy was charged with
destroying books in the library, and I made the proposal at one
of our self-government meetings that he be appointed chief
librarian, I am sure there would rise a cry: "One of Neill's
psychological tricks again." No child would have said that
forty-five years ago.

In Summerhill, we do not seem to have the usual generation gap. Visitors ask: "Who are the teachers and who are the
pupils?" In general, such a gap can be avoided only if parents
grow with their children. This is not easy; for it seems that as
people grow older, they become more conservative. I find this
true in myself. I cannot join in the modern enthusiasm for
showing sexual intercourse on stage, because my whole background has conditioned me to think that this is sick sex. After
two thousand years of repression, I cannot get away from the
notion that sex is a private affair, and I wonder how an actor
can get an erection with an audience looking on. I do not like
to see men with long hair or even beards. Here I am conservative; but on the other hand, I like youth's freedom of dress
and language.

Our Old Pupils

Sometimes I have been asked if I am prouder of our Summerhill graduates who have proved to be academic successes than of those graduates who went into arts or technical work. The answer is no, although I have often mentioned our two professors, (one in maths and the other in history) and our two university lecturers. We've turned out a few good doctors (one a lung specialist and another a surgeon) and two lawyers. I mention scholars, because the usual criticism of Summerhill is that children will not be able to pass exams when free to attend or stay away from lessons. But I am as proud of our furniture maker, our potter, our artists who show in Bond Street, and our old boy who is making a name for himself with his illustrated children's books. I know of only one old pupil who cannot hold down a job. Not a bad record for fifty years. Naturally, I am not in touch with all past pupils, so I cannot be aware of what everyone is doing. I speak only of those who spent at least four years in the school.

I am not primarily interested in whether former students are professors or bricklayers; I am interested in their character, their sincerity, their tolerance. I like to think that they have a better chance of being pro-life than disciplined, molded children have. Our boys and girls are not rebels; they don't take part in violent meetings and marches. They know that spouting freedom from a soapbox is no answer.

One former pupil said: "All I can do is bring up my own kids in freedom, hoping that our neighbors will learn something from their behavior." Another parent, who married a Summerhill boy, made a wise and arresting remark: "The effects of a Summerhill education are not felt until the second generation. We know how to avoid the restrictions and suppressions of our upbringing."

Many of my old pupils are fine men and women, hardworking, tolerant, pro-life; some, of course, have been disappointments. For them, Summerhill did not sink in far enough. True, I think that most of them treat their own children in a free way; but of course, one must remember that most of the children who came to my school were greatly influenced by unfree homes and unfree schools.

Summerhill has often been criticized because its graduates do not seem to be crusading to make this sick world better. This may be true. I am sure that most of my students share my distrust of politics and politicians, people who find it almost impossible to be honest. A British prime minister might consider the Vietnam war a barbaric crime against humanity, but because of arms and trade and dollars, he must publicly support the policy of the United States. If his constituency is made up mainly of Roman Catholics, he dare not vote for a bill to legalize abortion or homosexuality.

I have written half jokingly that a Summerhill pupil owes any success he might have to the school, but can pin his failure on his parents. This is nearly true. Our successful graduates came mostly from homes with some freedom and family affection, while many of our "semi-successes" came from unhappy homes. More than once have I said that freedom alone will not cure a child who had no love as a baby; it can ameliorate his condition, but too often the chip on the shoulder abides. My vision of a Summerhill full of children from self-regulated homes remains a daydream.

I have often criticized universities and schools because they develop the intellect to the neglect of the emotions. Summerhill attempts the opposite. Nevertheless, Summerhill fails in those instances when a child grasps freedom emotionally without the intellectual capacity to amalgamate head and heart. I am sure, however, that the majority of old pupils have synthesized both factors easily and naturally.

I still cannot be sure whether Summerhill freedom is better for the bright ones than for those with lesser intelligence. Bill, who happens to be a doctor, reads the weekend literary journals. Paul, now a farmer, reads the tabloids. Well, if both are happy, what the hell?

Above everything else, I must record one characteristic common to all former pupils. Their loyalty to Summerhill is both sincere and heartwarming. Two years ago, at the school's fiftieth anniversary party, the warmth and enthusiasm of those who attended was tremendous.

III

THOUGHTS
AT THE END
OF A LIFE

Changes I Have Seen

Time, you old gypsy man,
Will you not stay,
Put up your caravan
Just for one day?

RALPH HODGSON

Everyone, I fancy, sometimes wishes to return to pleasures long dead. But nostalgia is not one of my virtues or vices. I can return to the haunts of my boyhood with no emotion whatever. So with tomorrow; it gives me no thrill to imagine that one day in my native town of Forfar, some town council may put up a brass plate on the house in which I was born, 16 East High Street. Posterity means nothing to me.

But to get back to that caravan and time's refusal to stay; I have seen many changes in my long life. These are not only material things like motors, films, radio, TV, but what one might call cultural things, changes in human outlook. Years ago, we had to be well-covered when bathing. Free sex and swearing were taboo. When Shaw's play *Pygmalion* was produced with Eliza Doolittle's "not bloody likely," every paper printed the word b——y. Today, even some highbrow papers will print the four-letter words. But why good old Anglo-Saxon words were ever thought obscene, I never knew.

235

I have lived to see a great sex release in women. In my early days, a woman was not supposed to have any pleasure in sex, a belief sponsored by many women without orgiastic life because of the ignorance or selfishness of their men. Today, women openly acknowledge their demand for as much sexual freedom as men enjoy. It was not a woman who coined the phrase: "A fate worse than death"; virginity has lost its air of sanctity. I am glad that I have lived long enough to see this new freedom for women, even though we have a long way to go before seeing equal numbers of men and women in parliaments, senates, and businesses.

I have seen the gradual change in attitudes toward war. Half a century ago, the hero was one who died for his country, but now among many young people the hero is he who lives for his country. The university campuses show this difference. But it has not gone far enough yet. Most young men, conditioned to obey authority from cradle days, become soldiers without challenging the forces that lead nations into wars. But many are realizing that war, or prison punishment, never solved anything. A cynic, comparing the economic strength of Britain and Germany today, might claim that it is better to lose a war.

Things have moved, but not always in a forward direction. Sixty years ago, Britain had no color question. Today, in 1972, our racial problems are threatening to make Britain another America with irrational hate in every town, in every street. Racialism is the most sinister promise of the future, more dangerous than pollution, because racialism comes of human weakness and hate. Myself, I could never understand it. I have no feelings about Negroes or Jews or Chinamen or Indians; to me, they are fellow travelers on a long, difficult road.

I first met racialism at Edinburgh University, between 1908 and 1912, as already mentioned. I met it again in South Africa twenty-four years later, and was not too surprised, but still recall my own somewhat cowardly behavior. When someone at a lecture asked me my opinions on color segregation, I said that I had come to talk about education, not racialism. Looking back, however, I think this was wise; to attack the segregation policy would have kept many from my lectures, and the newspapers would have blown it up. Bernard Shaw was braver; one report of his visit to South Africa said that he had shocked the country by predicting that, one day, it would become a light-brown nation through mixed marriage.

In my lifetime, the world has become more sinister, more dangerous; and here, I am not thinking of hate and conquest wars. I am thinking of the lessening power of the people and the growing power of big businesses and combines, the dehumanization of industry. At the beginning of the century, small businesses were common. The boss was Bill Smith, who knew his employees and their families. Today, workmen have no Bill Smith to approach with any difficulties they may have; they have the great bureaucratic, inhuman company.

In Leiston, I can go to a small factory and ask for the manager; but what American can seek an interview with the head of a large industry? The class war has become centralized, workers against a great international corporation. Recently in England, the postal and electrical strikes angered this nation of householders. George Orwell's 1984 is only a few years ahead of us.

Changes in education have been too slow for me. Freedom in schools has grown, but not as fast as belief in book-learning and examinations; the old patriarchal demand for obedience and discipline is as strong as ever in all state systems.

I have seen a change in children since Summerhill began, a change so subtle that it is intangible. My pupils seem to me to be less communal, less able to grasp and practice self-government. Some get too much money from their parents, so that saving for a rainy day is something unknown to them.

Today, I don't see the young, even those in their twenties,

saving money. It burns a hole in their pockets. Partly, this may be the result of the insecurity of modern life with its wars, crimes, and hatreds, and the threat of ultimate nuclear destruction, which could come, because so much of our diplomacy is of the nineteenth-century kind. In a war between Israel and Egypt, with Egypt backed by Russia, the United States could be dragged into a war that might destroy humanity and all life. Fundamentally, the change in youth must be blamed on its loss of faith in those in authority.

I have lived to see the decline of the Protestant religion, in the orthodox sense. Churches in England are not full; too often, they are empty. Youth does not believe in sin, nor in heaven, nor in hell. The gods of the youth are more or less harmless—pop stars, disk jockeys, football heroes. One might call these the apostles of a new religion, a religion which has one characteristic in common with the old religion: the hate and violence between the supporters of football teams compares easily with the hate and violence of religious Ulster whose Roman Catholic and Protestant teams want to murder each other.

A few words about today's pornography. Pornography has been with us always. In 1900, shabby men asked us to buy dirty postcards. Few do today; the sexy weeklies handle the job for them. The only cure for pornography is freedom from an antisex education. My old pupils would see nothing exciting in a leg show, a strip tease, or even a show with intercourse on stage. The ultimate cure for all pornography would be—climate allowing—a civilization in which we all walk about naked, and in which sex had no connection with guilt.

I am reasoning from the fact that the Catholic Church is shocked by nakedness. Oh, you should have heard the Dublin priest who had seen a Summerhill film on TV with boys and girls bathing naked; you should have heard what they said to me about it in the TV bar where, by the way, they exhibited no inhibitions about imbibing large whiskies and brandies. I saw more drunks on Dublin streets that weekend than I had seen since my Scotland days when whiskey was two shillings and sixpence a bottle. On Saturday night the town was full of drunks. According to the Irish, God approves of drink but not of sex.

Vanity

I sometimes think that the sickness of the world is due to human vanity. For generations, women have bedecked themselves with furs, indifferent to the agony of trapped animals. More money is spent on cosmetics and dress than on books and music. Men, too, have showy vanities; they are proud of their houses, their gardens, their cars. Primarily, men like to be esteemed for their activities, their success in business or in academics or in sports.

What is common to both sexes is the longing for approval. A large part of our lives consists of this desire to be seen, to be heard, to be appreciated, to be admired. Fear of death is fear of the end of one's ego. When all our egos are combined, we get nationalism and the Establishment. I am the center of the universe—therefore "My country! Right or wrong!" This can result in "Heil Hitler!" or "Heil Nixon!"

The race for money is fundamentally a race for recognition; so is the race for power. Rich people, not content to leave their money in the bank, must show they are wealthy by their standards of living. The poor have little to be vain about. "My Bobby has passed the eleven-plus exam, but Willie next door failed." "We are the only ones in the street who have a color television set."

Vanity gives us a blind eye for the miseries of the world.

It is expressed by the slogan: "I'm all right, Jack," with the emphasis on the *I*. We read of tortures in dictator countries and then placidly turn the page to read the football news. We see Chicago cops beating with clubs, and we switch the TV to look at a show for ten-year-olds by Andy Williams. We are all guilty. Nowadays, many youths from rich American homes are scorning wealth and safety, and subduing their vanities, to seek free, untrammeled lives of their own. These members of the new generation have no desire to seek the fleshpots of Egypt, bless them.

It is interesting to guess who in history has been without vanity—possibly Christ, Gandhi, and Einstein; Dr. Livingstone, too, though many missionaries thought they were spreading Christianity when all they did was to bring a sense of guilt to innocent people. The Bible tells us that there are no marriages in heaven, but our local bigwigs are pretty sure that people going there are divided into classes at least. Reich, who showed no signs of vanity in life, willed that he have an elaborate tomb in Orgonon, Maine.

My vanity may lie in the thought that after I am dead my books will keep my memory alive. But this thought brings no comfort; I cannot lay the flattering unction to my soul that my books will endure as long as the tombstones in Forfar Cemetery. Yet Shakespeare wrote in a sonnet:

> *Not marble, nor the gilded monuments*
> *Of princes, shall outlive this powerful rime.*

Was he right?

Politics

The politician's stance, "I speak for the people who elected me," often suggests a man of no principles and no guts. If one of my old pupils became a prime minister, I should feel that Summerhill had failed him. Politics means compromise, and free people are very bad compromisers.

The mystery is why folks are Right or Left or in the middle. Of course, it is a case of early conditioning. For many years, I have been distinctly Left in politics, education, and life. Perhaps I'm as perverse as the Irishman washed up on a foreign shore whose first words were: "Is there a government here? If there is, I'm agin it."

I believe most humane reforms have come from the Left. In Britain today, it is the Tories who seek to clamp down on moral issues. It is usually a Tory who reports to the public prosecutor on allegedly pornographic books. The very word *conservative* means standing still or looking backward. It refers to all who have anything to conserve or preserve: money, property, or position. In Britain, most shopkeepers, farmers, and lawyers vote Conservative.

My interest is in the origins of Right and Left. I have known politicians who were Socialists at twenty and Tories at fifty. Time tends to move one toward conservatism, but I like to think that I have remained a challenger in my old age. The basis is probably emotional, not rational. Originally, my politics were mixed up with emotion. When I threw a tomato at Winston Churchill and missed, I was prompted by the bonny daughter of the local Tory chairman. Winston was then a Liberal candidate.

In 1913, when I first went to live in London, I joined the Labour Party and spoke ignorant rubbish in Hyde Park. After the Russian Revolution when reports told of new sexual and educational freedom, I fondly imagined that Utopia had suddenly arrived for good. But as a canny Scot, I did not join the Communist Party. Still, for years, I had a blind spot; I simply would not accept the stories of Stalin's mass murder by starvation of a million or more peasants who would not fit into his collective farming scheme. But I *did* wonder why Bolsheviks of the old brigade were confessing to crimes they had never committed—before they were shot in the back of the neck.

The truth is I wanted to believe in the new order; I wanted to think that the new education in Russia was wonderful. My disillusionment took years to surface. In 1937 I applied for a visa to visit Russia. It was refused, no reason being given. By that time, I had given up my hope that Communism was a cure for world sickness. I ceased to be interested in politics of any kind, but voted the Labor party in the belief that it was more pro-life than the Conservative party. In spite of my disappointment with Labor rule, I still hold to that belief.

I was not conscious of politics again until 1950, when I applied to the American Embassy for a visa. I had already lectured in the U.S.A. in 1947 and in 1948 and my 1950 tour had been arranged by the Reich people. After being kept waiting for an hour at the Embassy, I suspected that something was wrong. Then I was called before an official.

"Are you a Communist?"

"No, I am not."

"Have you ever written anything in favor of communism?"

I guessed he had phoned the Home Office and asked for my dossier.

"I have written about eighteen books, but have never read them since, and have little idea today of what is in them. But I have a vague feeling that I praised Russian education as it was after the Revolution. Then Russian education was for freedom; but today, it is like your education and our education, both against freedom."

My application was refused, and my lecture tour canceled. Those were the McCarthy days, of course.

I recall saying to the consul: "I am a communist in the way Jesus Christ was one—communist with a small 'c.' " He gave me a look of shock; I guessed he was a Catholic, and I found out later he was. The sequel came in December, 1969, when Orson Bean invited me to come to the States to take part in the Johnny Carson show. Once again, I went to the Embassy.

"It won't take more than twenty minutes, Mr. Neill. Please fill in this form."

Question: "Have you ever been refused a visa by the American Government?" I signed and wrote, *"Yes, in 1950."* Which meant that the twenty minutes would be more like two hours. I was asked to fill in the complete form. Then more waits, and more interviews. Finally, I was given a visa for four years. The annoying thing was that the consul said: "We have no record of your being refused a visa." I felt like kicking myself for my useless honesty.

I suddenly realize that I am quite proud of having been refused a visa by both the U.S.S.R. and the U.S.A. This may be my claim to immortality.

But this is gossip, not politics. I know that someone has to deal with government, finance, foreign policy. I know that democracy is phony; our last election in Britain gave the Tories a majority, though Labour and Liberal combined got more votes than those cast for the Tories. But since the alternative to democracy is dictatorship, we cannot give it up.

It is all so sinister. When I watch, on TV, the national party conventions in the U.S.A. with their infantile parades and bands and flags, I feel dejected and hopeless. Behind these silly facades, I see the self-seeking lobbyists and the rat race of capitalism. When a President makes some gesture—Nixon to China, for example—who knows what the motive is? Some Americans say he is thinking of the next presidential election. Certain Englishmen say that the U. S. Government soft-pedals its support of Israel because it is worried about repercussions among the suppliers of Arab oil.

International politics is a dirty game; home politics can be likewise. The Tory government is thriving off industries that the previous Labour government nationalized, paying ones like Cook's Tours. *Trade follows the flag* goes the old saying. But trade often seems to control politics. The three political parties in Britain are against apartheid; yet if any party tried to stop diplomatic relations with South Africa, the trade lobbies would kill any such parliamentary bill.

A few years ago an American writer wrote that if the Vietnam war were suddenly stopped, forty per cent of American industry would collapse.

Nay, my politics are confined to our school democracy, which is as near real democracy as it can be. We meet in a big room and make our laws by a general show of hands. But I know that the mass of voters cannot meet in a room. The democracy in which one man is supposed to represent the opinions of 30,000 is somewhat specious; yet I do not know the answer. I am aware that many politicians do much good work; I grant many have made humane rules. But politicians who concern themselves with social ills are rare.

In Britain, our prison system is a disgrace. Men are treated with scant humaneness, are deprived of sex, of culture, of everything that makes life, life. According to reports, some prisons in the U.S.A. are much worse. The barbarous prison system is accepted not only by politicians but by the clergy, the doctors, the lawyers—indeed, by most people in general. It is because politics does not deal with crying evils that I cannot arouse any enthusiasm for politics. Schools beat kids and the politicians turn a blind eye. Our government will build a new school with modern appliances, and then leave its administration to some headmaster to run with the cane—if he is that sort of criminal. When parents in Britain complain about their kids' being beaten in school, the magistrate usually sides with the caning teacher. In a sick world, politics must be sick.

The politicians tell us that the laws they make apply to all—whatever their class. Yes, that is true! A tramp can sleep on the Thames Embankment, and so can a duke.

I am constantly being asked why Summerhill does not teach politics. A democracy is supposed to be governed by the electorate. But the electorate is composed of millions of individuals who were character-formed in their cradles, in their homes, and in their schools. They were taught to obey authority, to repress sex, to fear a God of fear. In short, they were castrated, so that in later life they have become sheep seeking a leader. Hence a nation's following Hitler against all its interests. Hence, in Britain, where the majority of voters are wage earners, the electorate puts in a Tory government whose interests are almost entirely the opposite of workers.

Summerhill aims at a new democracy of free citizens who will not follow any leader. Until children are no longer molded into castrated sheep, democracy remains a fake and a danger. This is no theory; it is founded on long observation of children who have self-government. No child in my school holds up his hand because he sees me doing so when we vote.

I grant that our little school parliament could never fit a large democracy. That is why I have never been willing to have more than seventy pupils at most. With 200 boys and girls, it would mean electing representatives; all real interest would be gone. I grant our system is impractical; we cannot have millions of voters raise their hands at a public meeting to vote for or against the Common Market. But a day may come when voters will be free enough to see through all the tricks and oppose lobbying and the self-interest of many politicians; in short, a day may dawn when voters will not be overgrown school kids conditioned from birth to follow leaders mechanically.

Spiritualism and other Religions

I have already told how my parents gave up their Calvinism for spiritualism. When my sister Clunie died in 1919, they asked me if I could get in touch with a medium. I was then in London. With great difficulty, I arranged to have an interview with Mrs. Leonard, Sir Oliver Lodge's medium. She went into a trance and said things that astonished me: that Clunie had been a teacher, and that she had died of lung trouble—both correct. I began to wonder if there was something in spiritualism after all.

Then: "Have you any questions for your sister?"

"Yes, ask her if she ever thinks of Spott."

"She says, yes; she loved Spot. But then, she loved all animals."

Alas, my question had referred to Spott, the village where Clunie had taught. I did not tell my parents about that part of the interview.

I doubt we shall get far with the esoteric until we grasp what our conjurers do. I spent three nights trying to discover where the great magician David Devant got the dozens of eggs he was clutching from the air. I never learnt. A friend who belongs to the *Magic Circle* tells me that such tricks are simple; but because of his oath, he cannot tell me how they are done. Another conjurer with less scruple explained to me how the levitation act is performed.

I simply cannot become interested in a life after death. Billions have died, but where are they? The metempsychosis folks make the matter easy. The soul of the dead is parked; and when a babe is born, some power selects a soul to put into the new body.

I have doubts about psychic manifestations in haunted houses, but am puzzled about poltergeists who seem to throw furniture about the room. My first wife's sister believes that her house in Lyme Regis was haunted. She and her husband, Professor George Robertson, went to the cinema one night. She had been knitting before they left. George, an unbeliever, said to me: "When we got back, Ett's wool had been draped all over a picture frame. I couldn't reach the wool, and had to borrow a ladder from next door."

I often heard knocks in her house; but only when a certain German girl—said to be a medium—was present. Long after the death of the Robertsons, I knocked at the door and said to the new occupant: "Do you ever hear knocks in the house?" She stared at me blankly, and said of course she didn't. The poltergeist had apparently moved elsewhere.

About forty years ago, I experimented with table-rapping; Eric Dingwall, an investigator of psychic research, was present at the time. Eric was a sceptic about anything psychic, yet he told me that on more than one occasion he had received answers that no one taking part at the table could have known.

My lack of interest in things psychic may be associated with my indifference to the spiritual in life. I am not one of Wordsworth's little ones who came to the world trailing clouds of glory. I am an earthy guy, even if my head is sometimes in the clouds.

Reich once told me that religion is sex removed as far as possible from the genitals. I did not understand that statement then, and still do not.

Why did Reich see religion as displaced sex? He believed that sex energy is the mainspring of life. Religion, in relegating pleasure to a world after death, sublimated this energy. It lifted sex to the head, and made it something to be thought about, not practiced. Whatever the motive, millions of children have carried through life a sex guilt given them through orthodox religion. Therein lies the danger. The world will never be happy while such religious belief lives.

I say this in spite of the fact that the death of religion under communism does not seem to have given us anything better than a police state. Any argument with a devout Communist will convince one that communism is no longer a creed of freedom from exploitation; what began as a Marxist analysis of society has now become a new, emotional religion. To some party members, blasphemy against Lenin or other leaders is the sin against the Holy Ghost. Still, communism will change; I am told that Russian youth can't be bothered reading Karl Marx. In any event, when I speak of the abolition of religion, I refer not only to Christianity, Islam, and Buddhism but to all the emotional isms including nationalism, politics, and the Brazilian worship of football.

Here I express my fear that Summerhill itself may become a religion. Many schools are claiming to go our way, some even calling themselves Summerhills. It scares me. My motto has always been: TAKE FROM OTHERS WHAT YOU WANT, BUT NEVER BE A DISCIPLE OF ANYONE. That was the main reason for my refusing Reich's invitation to transfer my school to his estate in Maine. I knew I'd be classed as a Reichian.

The Christian God, the great Father, is like the average earthly father in his strictures on sex. The Christian church, especially the Roman version, has made sex the dirtiest thing in the world. Today, in England, Roman Catholics and Moral Re-Armament puritans are nosing out pornographic books and getting the law to prosecute authors and publishers.

When a man spends his time ferreting out what he thinks are obscene books, as Alfred Lord Douglas did in his later days, I make the guess that he has a latent sick interest in sex and pornography; so when the church makes sex the super sin, I can only suppose that its unconscious fixation is on sex.

In Christian Spain, a bullfight is infinitely more of a pornographic show than any staged in a theater, more than any erotic writings in a bookshop. But the Church approves of bullfighting. And in England some parsons follow the foxhounds. In our British church schools teachers beat boys. Why is sex attacked while cruelty is accepted. Perhaps because sex affords the greatest pleasure in the world, and religion is against pleasure. In Macaulay's words:

> The Puritan hated bear-baiting, not because it gave pain to the bear, but because it gave pleasure to the spectators.

In my young days, cards and theater and whistling on the Sabbath were regarded as sins. Only recently has Scotland allowed tennis or golf on Sunday. In my native town, you cannot play golf until after the morning service.

I am not a strong hater, but my greatest aversion is the Roman Catholic Church. I hate—as violently as H. G. Wells did—an authority that gives five hundred million a guilt about sex—a guilt that makes them all underlings. To me, this church is anti-life, paternalism writ large. How comic, were it not tragic, that a pope, who has never had a sex life, orders millions of women not to use the Pill. I cannot associate the Roman Catholic Church with Christianity. The savage beatings that go on in Catholic schools in Eire must be expressions of bottled-up sex coming out as sadism. Christ did not say: "Suffer the little children to come unto me and get beaten up."

Protestantism is dying rapidly because it has dealt mainly with the head through long sermons and intellectual arguments. The Roman Catholic church grips a child's feelings in its cradle, and what one acquires emotionally can seldom be overcome. Like many a Scot, I broke with hellfire Calvinism, which never touched any emotion except fear of hell. It was truly a "head" religion—I am told that a Glasgow public library contains sixty thousand books of sermons. Protestantism reasoned; Catholicism molded. But why organized religion degenerated into hate of life, I cannot guess. All I know is that Nietzsche was right when he said that the first and last Christian died on the Cross.

To me, it is a perversion of Freud to say that a violent dislike for something or someone betrays an unconscious desire for that something or someone. Utter bosh! Hence, I cannot believe that my hatred of Catholicism indicates an unconscious desire to fall into the arms of Mother Church. Organized orthodox religion is the most virulent epidemic in the world. For many of its followers, God is not in Heaven; he is in the Vatican and in Canterbury, the abodes of all that is anti-life.

Maybe the world will not find happiness until the last religion is dead—and among religions I include those ugly sisters, capitalism and communism.

Lecturing

In my student days, I played with the idea of becoming an actor. I knew that I had little chance of success; for one thing, I could not have got rid of my Scottish accent, and few Scots are required in plays. I had some talent but not enough to make me reach the stars, and I am sure that I would have jibbed at being told how to act by a director.

Looking back many years, it occurs to me that I might have felt that acting was not creative enough; it was like working out a geometrical problem that someone else had set, or playing music composed by another. Oddly enough, a fictional character might outlive the real virtuoso, like Dick Martin in *Young Man with a Horn* by Dorothy Baker. This was a vivid characterization of a trumpeter whose life was said to be founded on that of Bix Beiderbeck. The author almost makes us hear him playing his horn. I have read the book four times.

Whatever the cause, I renounced my ambition to go on the stage and have never regretted it. In a way, I did become an actor, lecturing to thousands of students and parents and teachers. At first I had stage fright and a phobia of not being able to go on, hence I used notes; but for many years, I have never needed them. I think we tend to depreciate a lecturer who relies on notes or reads his talk. Lecturing is an art, a trick if you like. I had an uncanny knack of summing up audi-

ences. When I got on the platform, I knew if the audience
would approve of me or not. The trick in lecturing is to hold
your audience. If people looked bored, I would tell a funny
story. Once in Scotland I faced a grim crowd of set faces.
What's wrong with you lot?" I said. "You all look dead, so I
take it you are all teachers." Laughter, and immediately they
were with me.

On another occasion, I began: "I feel guilty. When I
knew I was to speak to teachers with all their respectability, I
did a cowardly thing—I put on a tie." Then I took my tie off.
So I did become an actor after all.

I have had some odd lecture chairmen in my time. Once in
Scotland, my chairman was the headmaster of the local academy.
When I sat down, he got up.

"Now the lecturer will be glad to answer questions, but
I warn any of my staff who are here that I won't have them
trying to bring this man's ideas into my school."

There were no questions.

In Johannesburg, in 1936, the professor who took the
chair was notorious for falling asleep on every public occasion.
It was partly because he kept awake all through my lecture
that South Africa treated me as a VIP. It wouldn't today.

I once had a chairman who was vague about my name.
"I am sure that you will join me in welcoming the celebrated
educationist, Mr.—Mr. O'Neill."

The best chairman-host I ever had was a rich man in a
York town who told me: "I am not interested in education, and
won't come to hear you, and I'll be in bed when you return.
You'll find all you need at your bedside." And I did—whiskey,
brandy, beer.

What I liked most about lecturing in South Africa was the
fact that in every town my chairman was the mayor, and behind
every townhall platform was his room with a bar filled with
rows of bottles. What I disliked most was the racialism. Black

teachers were not allowed to attend my lectures, except once in Brakpan, a suburb of Johannesburg that had a broad-minded mayor.

Once, in Stockholm, the hall could not hold half of those who wanted to hear me, so the church opposite was asked if I could speak there. Yes, they replied, but on condition that I did not mention religion or sex. That sure cramped my style.

The worst lecture I ever gave was in Oslo where each sentence had to be translated right away. Of course, I kept losing the thread of my discourse.

I never had the gift of extemporaneous speaking. Even today, if I were asked at a dinner party to propose the health of the ladies, I would be terrified. My father could stand up and make a speech about anything, but I never had his talent; I can only lecture on what I know, my work.

I cannot recall ever responding to interruptions with witty answers. I hadn't the quickness of the suffragette who answered the shouted taunt: "How would you like to be a man?" with the sharp rejoinder:"How would *you* like to be a man?"

I once answered a question in a way that I regretted later. In Kimberley, I think it was that a woman asked: "Should I tell my child who his father is?" "Yes, if you know," I said, and immediately kicked myself for being cruel at a poor woman's expense. With that one exception, I have always answered questions civilly.

Honesty

How much does society depend on honesty between people?
I have just had a visit from a man who wants to found a col-
ony of people who will be absolutely honest and forthright
with each other. Some time ago one of my teachers, against my
advice, started such a group at Summerhill. After the first meeting, an adolescent girl came to me in tears, saying that the others had said beastly things about her character and behavior.
My advice about closing the meetings was then taken. In free-
and-easy group therapy, more faults than virtues are pointed
out; the hate element comes through too often.

In Summerhill, I have always taken the line of letting
new teachers discover their own limitations and talents. It may
be moral cowardice that makes me refrain from saying: "Smith,
you are a lazy sod; your lessons show no imagination. Buck up
or get out." The Smith problem is usually solved by a boycott
of his lessons by pupils, forcing him to leave.

Myself, I could not take part in a group that was intent
on being completely frank. If told that I was a self-centered
poseur who disguised my innate meanness with a smile, I would
be angry; and even if I tried, I could do nothing at my age
about changing my fundamental character. Group criticism
could work in things that do not much matter—Jones being
told that he makes a noise supping soup. Jones might resent

the criticism, but would react to it by being conscious that he was a noisy eater.

Reaction to criticism within a small group can be hell, as the family unit shows. Often have I heard a wife say: "Peter is useless in the house. He can't mend a fuse. He has no hands—nor head, for that matter. Thinks only of cricket." It has been my observation that women, more than men, make such statements about a partner; and I expect that in extreme cases, the Peters of life do some strangling.

I try to visualize a world of honesty, where no one had armor, no one pretended, no one had private secrets. Imagine a typical situation with John and Mary. He is fifty, and she forty-nine. She has lost her looks and makes no attempt to adorn herself. He has an eye for a well-turned ankle at the bus stop. Maybe he is having a hidden affair. John refrains from shouting at his wife, "Damn you, woman, your inane chatter, your persistent nagging, your lack of any pride in how you look—they make me sick of the sight of you." If I were John, my main motive for not revealing my true feelings—for being dishonest—would be my fear of hurting another person. It's all really a matter of good manners; one does not talk about swinging when having tea with the widow of a man who has been hanged.

I acknowledge that society would be healthier if we were all honest with each other and spoke our thoughts aloud. When meeting academic people at some formal function, like getting an honorary degree, I feel a hypocrite. During a "weather" conversation with some professor or his wife, I feel innerly like crying: "We are boring each other; we are not talking the same language." But no, it cannot be done.

Before a mutual honesty group is set up, I would advise its promoters to read Ibsen's *Wild Duck* to see what happens when a fanatic for truth thinks he is bestowing happiness on a family through truth. Yet Ibsen may have been wrong, and

I may be wrong. Maybe honesty all around would make a saner, happier world.

I wonder how truthful I really am. If I am honest, is it because of innate goodness or because of fear of the police? During my days of sojourn in Germany, I hated German tobacco. Every time I came home for a visit to England, I returned to Germany with my pockets stuffed with John Cotton mixture. *"Haben Sie Tabac?"* I would be asked. With an innocent look, I would reply: "Nein." Swindling my countrymen was another matter, and only infrequently dared I travel a railway without a ticket. I think that kind of honesty is induced mainly through fear of being caught.

When dealing with kids, one is forced to be sincere unless one is a disciplinarian. If they have not been conditioned into being hateful little brats, children have a natural sincerity. Let me say unashamedly that I think I am sincere in one of life's larger aspects. On a TV program, I would not claim that a certain soap powder washed whiter than others. My conscience would not allow me to do so, even for a fortune. I could advertise something I believed in—John Cotton tobacco, for instance. Years back, when I worked in Fleet Street, I knew some left-wing journalists who prostituted their talents by working for a Tory paper. I wonder how many of the ad people on TV believe in the goods they are boosting.

Heroes and Half-heroes

Hardly ever have I known great men. I met H.G. Wells, the hero of my youth, when he was quite old; my dream was shattered by a little man with a squeaky voice and an arrogant manner. Later, I sent him one of Wilhelm Reich's books.

His reply:

> *You have sent me an awful gabble of competitive quacks. Reich misuses every other word, and Wolfe* [his translator] *is a solemn ass. There is not a gleam of fresh understanding in the whole bale. Please don't send me any more of this stuff.*

My reply:

> *Dear Wells, I cannot understand why you are so damned unpleasant about it. I considered you the man with the broadest mind in England, and sincerely wanted light on a biological matter I wasn't capable of judging myself. Your black-out letter might have been written by Colonel Blimp himself. I hoped you would give an opinion on bions and orgones, whether they were a new discovery or not, and all I got was a tirade against Wolfe's translation of Reich's German. You apply the word quack to a man whom Freud*

considered brilliant.

I grant that I asked for it. I intruded. I apologise, and being a Scot, refund your postage. Your reputation is that of a man who can't suffer fools gladly. Apparently you can't suffer sincere research gladly either. When a New York Medical School is trying out bions and orgones on cancer patients, your "no fresh understanding in the whole bale" sounds odd. But this is no quarrel, and I won't bother you about Reich or anyone else.

Wells's reply:

Dear Neill: No, I decline your stamps, but this business is quackery. You call me a Blimp. I call you a sucker. Bless you.

Reich was furious with me for approaching Wells. "I don't need the approval of Wells or anyone else," he blasted.

"Then why did you send me a dozen copies of *The Function of the Orgasm* if you didn't want me to distribute them?" I asked.

Reich just grunted.

A hero who did not disappoint was Henry Miller. After someone had sent him one or two of my books, Henry wrote to me, and we kept up a desultory correspondence for some years. Then he came to London, and we had lunch together. I loved Henry; so warm, so humorous, so obviously genuine. I have often sighed to think that thousands of miles separate us. But to be honest, my judgment of Henry may have been more or less conditioned by the fact that he once wrote in a booklet announcing the publication of *Summerhill:* "I know of no educator in the Western world who can compare with A. S. Neill. It seems to me he stands alone. . . . Summerhill is a tiny ray of light in a world of darkness. . . ." But again, to be honest, I loved Henry long before he had written those words.

In my time also, I have met entertainers of the stage, cinema, and TV, with that almost unconscious, yet common feeling that folks who are popular idols must be in themselves enormously interesting. Millions would have been delighted to meet Gary Cooper, for instance, but I make the guess that Gary Cooper off-screen was just an ordinary, amiable guy. My first disillusion with stage people occurred when I was a student. A touring Ibsen company came to Edinburgh, and I wangled an invitation to have supper with the performers. I was seated beside the leading lady, who had played Nora, Hedda Gabler, Rebecca, and this was to be the treat of my playgoing life. But the woman had no interest in Ibsen; I wondered if she even knew he was a Norwegian.

I sometimes wonder what effect fame has on young people; pop singers who become millionaires, footballers who have world acclaim. Maybe they squander it as they do their money. But I reckon it is all a matter of age. When I published my first book, *A Dominie's Log,* in 1915, I subscribed to a press-cutting agency; and when my mail arrived, I always opened their envelope first. Today I usually leave this to the last. Yet the mere fact that I still employ a press-cutting agency shows that I am not indifferent to public opinion. Unfortunately, almost everything in life comes too late. I have three honorary university degrees which I never use; had they come to me fifty years ago, I would have been elated. I think of Wilde's dictum: "In this world there are two tragedies. One is not getting what one wants, and the other is getting it."

Never have I felt natural with the aristocracy—earls, lords, and countesses—the few times we met. When staying in big houses with a butler, I have felt very much out of my element. Manners tire me—jumping up when a woman rises from her chair. And the class distinction: I never have seen a gentleman rise when a maid brought in the tea tray. The poor have no manners—they don't hold doors open for their wives—yet I observe better manners in a village pub than I have ever seen in the Ritz or the Savoy. Luckily, the people I mingle with are too sincere to have artificial manners.

J. M. Barrie was my hero until I came under the spell of Wells, but we never met. Our birthplaces were only eight miles apart. Barrie went to Edinburgh University, and so did I. He was a famous writer; I also would be a famous writer. It was a clear case of identification. I read and reread his *Sentimental Tommy,* his tales of old Kirriemuir, his Thrums. My discipleship came to a sudden end when I read that tremendous counterblast to Scottish sentimentality, *The House with the Green Shutters* by George Douglas Brown. I fancy it was then that I adopted a new definition for sentimentality: giving a swan's emotion to a goose. *The House* became my Bible; I knew it almost by heart. Now I saw Barrie in perspective as a minor writer with flashes of insight and humor. His *Peter Pan* appealed to children because of the pirates, the adventure; it appealed to their parents because it dealt with the boy who never grew up—feeding their illusion that childhood was one long rhapsody of delight. That the author himself never grew up is brilliantly shown in Janet Dunbar's recent biography, *J. M. Barrie: The Man Behind the Image.*

Barrie had his whimsical patches. When an old lady asked him what he was going to be, he answered—an author. She held up her hands. "What, and you an M.A.!" Talent he had, lots of it. His play *Dear Brutus* is a model of construction. But I doubt very much if I would have appreciated meeting him. Of all past writers, the one I would love most to have met would be Oscar Wilde. To listen to his conversation in the Café Royal must have been a marvelous treat.

So much for the great. Less exalted types—teachers, students, parents, the hoi polloi—have been my milieu; and that has been good. So many never know what ordinary people do and think: judges, trying some poor victim of poverty and ignorance; statesmen, who have no idea what life is like for the poor; do-gooders, who visit the slums in their big cars. Since this is not a book on education, I merely mention the tremendous gulf between teachers and pupils, similar to the gulf between privates and colonels. But class systems would take a thick book in themselves.

Biscuit

My Golden Labrador, Biscuit, is at the end of his tether. The aged boy has lost control of his rational functions and will have to be put to sleep. He was an ideal dog for a school. He never bit anyone, and he always allowed the children to pet and play with him. I shall miss him sadly.

The death of a cat does not as a rule produce the same grief as that of a dog. In my opinion, cats seldom show affection, and persons mean little to them. When I was in the hospital recently, Biscuit was miserable. Most of the time he lay on my bed, waiting for me. Dogs flatter one; cats do not. Dogs love, and cannot condemn those they love. I am sure that Herman Goering's dogs loved him as much as if he had been a Gandhi.

Most of us have affection for dogs because they show affection for us. Such a gift is not a matter of their being gregarious animals. Horses and cows are gregarious, but they show little or no love for their masters. Maybe it is an instinct of the species. The dog is a wolf—a pack animal—and in a wild state, dogs have no avenue for showing love, unless to the leader of the pack. Biscuit loves me because I am his pack leader. Being non-gregarious, cats have no leader. In a way they might be rated higher than dogs for they have a natural independence. They never fawn, never curry favor; whereas old Biscuit is always nosing my arm, hoping for a friendly pat.

Sometimes one can teach a dog obedience, though I never could with Biscuit; if intent on some object, he ignored my whistle. One cannot make a cat tractable. Why can one make a horse obedient and not a cow? Or can one? Oxen on the plow, yes. But cattle in a field, no.

One interesting thing about Biscuit; he had a consistent sense about timing. Every day after lunch, he knew it was time for his walk on the beach, and he plagued me until I put him in the car.

When I was a boy, if my father put on his hat and coat to go to town, my Skye Terrier, Boulot, danced around with joy; yet when Father donned his tall hat and frock coat to go to Church on a Sunday, Boulot didn't even look up.

I once asked a shepherd who had won first prize at a sheepdog trial how much his dog understood. "He doesn't understand a bloody thing," he replied. "He just obeys my whistle. There never was a dog you could tell to put three sheep in one pen and five in the other."

Thousands of dog owners have said that they prefer their dogs to human beings, and I understand what they mean; the boundless faithfulness and love one gets from a dog can never be got from any human relationship. A wife, a brother may criticize; a dog never criticizes, never doubts. One might call it the higher animal, for it does not lie or slander, it does not make war, and it does not hate. If it is aggressive, it is because of a bone or a bitch. Much depends on its owner allowing it self-regulation, so to speak. I guess that if I had put Biscuit on a chain he would have been a biter in six weeks.

One day, dogs will be banned from cities. In Britain, there are local laws about messing sidewalks. Biscuit, by the way, never needed a law; he always left the sidewalk and sought the middle of the road or a grass bank. Mannerly dog was old Biscuit, and now I keep putting off the phone call to·the vet, just as I put off the sacking of a teacher. Too old at fourteen.

I am too old to get another dog; but even were I younger, I would not have a dog because its life span is too short, and the parting too poignant.

Entertainments

What do I do with my spare time? For years it was spent in my workshop, but a year or two back I suddenly lost interest in tools and gave mine to the school workshop. My hobby was metal work, hammering trays and bowls out of flat circular brass or copper disks. I was never very good at it, but I know a lot about tools and machines and processes. I once showed an old carpenter how to unscrew a large woodscrew that resisted all attempts with the screwdriver. I held a red-hot poker on the top of it, and the old carpenter said that in fifty years he had never learned that trick. I always had a lathe, but lathe work is dull because you can only make round things. Because of this hobby I have tended to value tools more than books. Like television or watching a football game, reading is passive, inactive. I prefer doing, and so do children. But having little chance for creation in home or school, millions of children today sit for hours with their eyes glued to the screen.

I spend, or should I say waste, a lot of time doing crossword puzzles in the evening, and watching TV; although I think TV is geared to a mental age of ten.

What do I read? Newspapers, of course; I take in four dailies and three Sunday papers. I enjoy the reviews: theater, TV, books—especially books. I am bored stiff with the old films so often presented in Britain, even those of Garbo; yet I put myself out quite a lot to see Charlie Chaplin. Chaplin is the boss in his films; he writes the script and the music, and produces the picture. His most recent films should have been edited; but his greatest films—*The Gold Rush, Shoulder Arms, City Lights,* and *Modern Times* did not require any advisor. Today, I would gladly walk a long way to see *City Lights* or *Modern Times.*

Occasionally our TV gives us a Buster Keaton film and I laugh like hell, just as I laugh over the best Chaplin. In general, Westerns bore me; but every week I watch "The Virginian," mainly because the characters are alive; whereas in "Perry Mason" no one lives—they are all sticks. In my twenties, I was not a popular guest at parties, for a prime activity was whist, and I could not play because I could not concentrate. I have never been a games watcher, and hardly ever saw a football match until the World Cup appeared on TV, and then I began to admire the skill of the players. Cricket has always been Greek to me; it is an English, not a Scottish game.

I took up golf when I was a student, and the irons I used were rusty, the shafts made of hickory, and the balls old floaters. I never was good at the game, and cared little whether or not I beat my partner. I played for the shots; to place a three-iron shot two inches from the pin made my day. I discovered that one of the skills necessary for a golfer is how to avoid the club bore who explains every shot of his last round. I also discovered the tremendous hold of the game on a person; golf stories testify to that.

A man about to drive from the tenth tee sees a funeral approach along the road. He doffs his cap, and lowers his club and then goes on to win the round.

At the nineteenth hole, his partner says to him: "That was a nice gesture you made at the tenth tee."

"Gesture? No gesture; dammit all; we had been married for twenty-five years."

I never became silly about golf myself.

I often wish I had learned to play the piano, my favorite instrument. Not that I could have become a good player; I am not musical enough. Fifty years ago in Germany, I bought a trumpet, thinking that because I had been a bugler in the Volunteers at the beginning of the century, I could master the instrument. Someone stole it, and I never missed it. All I can do now is to make small kids look at me scornfully when I tell them I am the best phonograph player in the school. "Corny Neill!" is the usual reaction.

My attitude toward music is romantic; I have many Chopin records, but no Bach. I have no idea what counterpoint is and my musical knowledge must be like that of a foreign king who was the guest of Queen Victoria. She took him to a concert, and when the band finished tuning up, he rose and clapped his hands.

Games on TV have become an obsession with me. Seeing a crowd of many thousands yell their heads off at a football match makes me feel hopeless about humanity, but I cannot decide which is the worse opium of the people: TV or football.

I was never a gambler. Occasionally, I have bought lottery tickets. In 1922, I won second prize in a state lottery in Germany—possibly 200,000 marks. I had to go to Berlin to collect my prize, but didn't go when I found out that my fare from Dresden to Berlin would amount to more than my win. In Germany, I also speculated, buying coal, iron, and beer shares when the pound was worth a million marks. What became of my shares I never knew; probably the stabilization of the mark wiped them all out.

I am a poor businessman. I keep my money in the bank doing nothing, when it could be invested in shares. I used to say that if I invested money, it would be in Rolls Royce. "Safe as gilt-edged securities," we all thought then. Tut, tut, how wrong can one be?

Betting has never appealed to me. Horse racing wearies me, although I watch show jumping with interest. I abominate performances with animals, and keep wondering what cruelty goes on in the training of animals. Years ago, Jack London's *Michael, Brother of Jerry,* gave me a hatred of animal training which has persisted for life. I cannot believe that a lion will walk along a wire because its trainer is kind. It sickens me to know that leading aristocrat members of the Royal Society for the Prevention of Cruelty to Animals in England hunt foxes and shoot deer. America with its million shotguns must spread infinite pain over the countryside. Guns and Christianity seem to go together.

I know the usual reply of the animal killers. "You eat meat, don't you? You let others kill for you." True, indeed. Even Bernard Shaw did not get his shoe leather from animals that had died naturally. It is a good point and a fair one. The answer that our animals are killed suddenly and painlessly is a rationalization. In protesting against hunting, I am being a bit of a humbug. Possibly, it is the association of killing with pleasure that troubles me. Humbug I may be, but I know I would find a Spanish bullfight revolting.

In spite of hunting and killing, the people of England are, in the main, animal lovers; much more money is raised for animal protection than for child protection. When an Alsatian guard dog nearly killed a child recently, he was shot by a policeman. The child's parents received scores of letters accusing them of not looking after their child, and thus causing the death of a dog.

Reading

I have often wondered how much reading affects formation of character. My parents and my grandmother always tried to get the children to read good books, meaning books that uplifted and led to a path to heaven—books like *Pilgrim's Progress, Robinson Crusoe,* stories of Livingstone and Stanley—all dull reading. My father's favorite, *Samuel Smiles' Self Help,* was enough to smother any budding ambition.

Once when I was lecturing in London, someone asked me at question time what my pupils read. I answered that I was disappointed that they did not take to the books I loved at their age, and gave as examples *Kipps* and *Mr. Polly,* which I considered the best books H. G. Wells had written. I was astounded and, of course, flattered to see Wells sitting in the second row. A parent had brought him.

When she introduced me to him, I said: "But how comes it that a man of your stature has come to hear me?"

He answered: "Our friend here said to me: 'You've been writing about education for years, knowing nothing about it. Come and I'll take you to hear a man who knows a lot about it.'"

I am sure Wells was bored, for my views on education could not possibly be anything like his science-bound viewpoints. The lady told me later that he did not like my reference to *Kipps* and *Mr. Polly* because he thought his later works were much better. I, as a writer of much lesser standard, can appreciate his attitude. To me, my first book, *A Dominie's Log,* is a poor one; but many have said that it is my best.

In a gathering of artists in Oslo, I once asked what they thought of their early works. Most of them said they could look at work they did twenty years ago, but not so easily at work done a year ago. No man can read his own character, and it is just as likely that no artist can judge his own work.

I liked Robert Graves when I met him years ago, but I have never quite forgiven him. Once during a discussion concerning the respect due religion, Graves asked me if I would strop my razor on the family Bible. I answered, "Certainly, if the leather were of the right sort." Then, in a book, he mentioned me as the man who habitually strops his razor on the family Bible—a slander, for I have never owned a family Bible.

I never could appreciate poetry, for never in my life have I written a verse; I am prosaic. Remember Wilde's: "Meredith was a prose Browning, and so was Browning"? I was not a prose anybody. Today, I cannot read poetry. If challenged to write down any poetry I know, I could only write *The Hound of Heaven,* Gray's *Elegy, The Rime of the Ancient Mariner,* and that little gem *Tam i' the Kirk.*

I have also joyed in Shakespeare's word-painting:

> *And look, the gentle day dapples the drowsy*
> *East with spots of grey,*
> *But look, the morn in russet mantle clad,*
> *walks o'er the dew on yon high eastern hill.*

And I like Oscar Wilde's verse in *The Harlot's House:*

> *And down the long and silent street*
> *The dawn with silver-sandalled feet,*
> *Crept like a frightened girl.*

I have never cared for Robert Burns, and Auden, Eliot and company leave me cold. But I do not want to be pitied. Poor fellow! What a lot he has been missing in life! That cry is fatuous. For I am also missing knowledge of architecture, music, metaphysics, astronomy, science.

Although I am no fan, I have a theory about poetry, which I expounded to Auden over a lunch table in New York. I argued that if a Shakespearean sonnet or *La Belle Dame Sans Merci* are poetry, *The Village Blacksmith* and *Lochinvar* are not. I said that there should be a definite line drawn between poetry and verse. Who could draw that line I cannot guess; all I know is that he would get a headache deciding the status of *The Deserted Village* or *The Lady of the Lake*. He probably would have no trouble placing William McGonagall of my native shire, a poor, gentle creature who sold his poems on the streets of Dundee at a penny each. Such an arbiter might choose *The Burial of the Reverend George Gilfillan:*

> *On the Gilfillan burial day,*
> *In the Hill of Balgay,*
>> *It was a most solemn sight to see,*
>> *Not fewer than thirty thousand people as-*
>>> *sembled in Dundee.*
> *All watching the funeral procession of Gilfillan*
> *that day,*
> *That death had suddenly taken away,*
> *And was going to be buried in the Hill o' Balgay.*

That McGonagall was far from normal is evident from his verses; yet they live, and not only as things to laugh at. There was a warm humanity about the man that makes him a poet in spirit. Were I the umpire, I should hesitate before casting him forth from among the true singers.

> *Beautiful Moon, with thy silvery light,*
> *Thou cheerest the poacher in the night:*

> *For thou lettest him see to set his snares*
> *To catch the rabbits and the hares.*

It is not very far below the standard set by *Lucy Gray* or *The Queen of the May.*

I read *The Prisoner of Zenda* without realizing that the hero was a bastard. Clunie and I were forbidden by our parents to read *Tess of the D'Urbervilles,* but of course we read it secretly and could see no reason for the ban. Books that touched sex were taboo, but horror stories never were. *Dracula* kept my bedroom windows shut for weeks.

Today, horror comics are allowed in homes that frown on sex. Sixty years ago, we had no horror comics; we had the clean fun of Tom Browne in *Chips* and *Comic Cuts;* we had the thrilling adventures of *Deadwood Dick* and *Buffalo Bill,* but we did not call the booklets *penny dreadfuls;* to us they were *bloods.* They made a good introduction to Rider Haggard and Anthony Hope.

As in the films, the bad man always lost the battle. The heroines were lifeless puppets, but we were not aware of that fact. All was honorable: even the black-mustached villain refused to fire at a man's back. Yes, it was all clean in the sense that it was simple, straightforward, and without double meaning.

As a graduate in Honors English, I should be reading Keats and Shelley and Milton or Dickens and Thackeray. The books are on my shelves but I shall never read them, although I do dip into Keats once in a while. Detective stories bore me. Many books on education and psychology are sent to me, chiefly from the United States. Too many are written in a stodgy style.

Reich killed any interest I had in reading about psychology, because he went deeper than most writers. All the volumes about psychological cases and their terminology seem to me now of little importance.

I seldom read a novel, but recently I have taken to reading

biographies, wondering if it helps one to understand writers. I have never read a biography that made a man bigger or more noble. The life tells mostly of the little man in all of us. Luckily, we know practically nothing about Shakespeare. In Britain, when writers give us books or articles about royalty, they rhapsodize about the family, the human touches—photo of the Queen making tea at a picnic. To be fair to them, the royal ones try to be honest; the Duke of Edinburgh confesses that he is no intellectual, that he seldom reads.

My preference has always been prose, but I came to dislike the ornate style when it was euphuistic, roseate. I like the style of Mary Johnson in her novel *By Order of the Company,* a tale of the days of James I and the colonization of America. She caught the pictorial language of the period. No one today would write: "Death is not more still than in this Virginian land in the hour when the sun has sunk away, and it is black beneath the trees, and the stars brighten slowly and softly, one by one."

A phrase written by R. L. Mackie, who was a student at St. Andrews some sixty years ago, has always stuck in my mind:" Sometimes I am a grey-hooded monk who has renounced the world with love and music and all its vanities, till one day the scent of roses is blown into my face, and I find myself weeping." It must have been my Calvinist origins that fixed that quotation in my mind for life; that terrible religion saw to it that the scent of roses did not come our way.

Like Winston Churchill, if I were asked what writer in the past I should like to have met, I would reply: Oscar Wilde. But I doubt if the men felt themselves lucky when they sat in the Cafe Royal and listened to his conversations with Whistler and Frank Harris. Oscar's wit, unlike that of Whistler, was never cruel. Perhaps the nearest he came to cruelty was when a man claimed to be an old acquaintance.

"Mr. Wilde, I don't think you remember me,"

Wilde studied his face.

"I'm sorry but I don't. I've changed a lot."

I never could stomach the wit of Gilbert in the Gilbert and Sullivan operas. To me it was shallow and cynical, "based on a superficial view of society," I wrote more than sixty years ago in Jacks' *Self Educator*. Shaw, on the other hand, thought society rotten at the core.

At my age of 29, Shaw and Wells were my favorite writers, and possibly they had more influence on my career than all the later psychologists had. Yet, in hindsight, Wells always disappointed. He labored a theme like the planlessness of the planners, and I kept looking for the solution that never appeared. When one came, it was no solution at all, as in *The Shape of Things to Come* where the world was saved by a group of scientists. I wonder what Wells would have made of the scientists today with their pollution and H-bombs, and the ruin of natural plant and animal life.

Shaw also had no solution. His brilliant analysis of society led to no promise of a new society. It must have been analysis without synthesis that made me lose interest in Shaw and Wells. They dated themselves; neither accepted the dynamic psychology of Freud. I write this acknowledging that I have dated myself, for I cannot accept the psychology of Skinner and Pavlov and Watson. Scientology seems Greek to me, and I suspect it as something phony. I have no idea what the word *existentialism* means. Every man must date himself in one way or another. I like to think that I have not become dated in education.

Like Reich, I dislike small talk and gossip; and that is one reason why kitchen-sink drama leaves me cold. Characters talk and say nothing. *Waiting for Godot* bored me; two tramps talking, just talking. Drama should be movement; yet I grant that much of Ibsen is conversation, but conversation that depicts character. The Godot tramps are simply saying that the world is very sick, but I cannot recall hearing any suggestion for doing anything about it. In *An Enemy of the People,* the doctor tells the little Norwegian world that it is sick, but he acts; he *does* something about it.

One of the regrets of my life is that I never learned French. In books, most French passages are not translated; German ones are, but I don't need them for I can read German. In my youth I learned little Latin and less Greek, which are long forgotten. I learned German simply because my stay in Germany compelled me to. I cannot speak it well, for I have never mastered the articles—*der, die* and *das.*

I meet very few Americans who can speak a foreign language, and the British are not linguists. On TV appear politicians from France, Germany, Holland, speaking perfect English, but I doubt whether any of our cabinet ministers are proficient enough to be interviewed in French or German. Churchill's French was atrocious, yet he persisted in addressing the French in their own tongue.

In my travel days, I always avoided France because I am not very good at sign language. In a Parisian café, I once wanted honey and made a noise like a bee; the waitress fled from an obvious lunatic. I traveled in German-speaking countries. Even that had its difficulties. Once, traveling from Munich to Vienna, I got into conversation with a young man in my compartment—in German. As we neared Vienna's main station, I asked him in German where he came from. "Edinburgh," he said. My hero, Ibsen, knew German because he lived in Munich for a long time, but he confessed to limitations in understanding French and seemed to have hardly any knowledge of English.

Yes, I regret not knowing French. My only foreign languages are German and American.

Writing

Style cannot be taught; it is you.

True, one can learn about punctuation and grammar, but not about what might be called creative writing. I never had any difficulty about spelling; I am sure that it is primarily a visual skill. If I am not sure of the spelling of *niece,* I write down *neice,* and at once see which is correct. But again, this facility can't be acquired; it's inborn. There's a boy of fifteen in the school who reads all day and late into the night; yet cannot write a line without a misspelling.

My American pupils have difficulty with exams in England. Possibly some examiners do not know that in the U.S.A., *traveller* contains but one "l", *Humour* is *humor,* and so on. It takes about two years for an American pupil at Summerhill to take a "bawth" instead of a "beth," but no American changes his or her: "I have bin" into our "been." In the U.S., speakers and writers split infinitives. But what can you expect from a barbarous country.

In the matter of punctuation, I always put a colon before a quotation, and nearly every printer I have had changes the colon into a comma. Shaw was the only writer strong enough to insist on his own punctuation and his own orthography; he wrote *dont* not *don't.* Shaw was keen on simplified spelling; but even now, long after his death, people do not seek any changes, at least not in Britain. In New York I saw signs: "Nite Club." In time I suppose we shall recognize the difficulty a foreigner has with words like *trough, through, cough;* but I shall not live to see *truff, thru, coff.* Change must come, though.

Why does anyone write? Why do I write? I write because I feel I have something to say, something that others might find interesting. And here I voice my grouse against TV. When I appear it is generally at a late hour when most folks are in bed; while all the popular performers who, in my opinion, have nothing to say, are on the air earlier in the evening. They get an audience of ten million, while I get a scant hundred thousand.

Authorship is frustrating, because one cannot know what influence one has had on readers. I once modestly thought that well-known people did not read my books, and suffered a mild shock when reading one of Asquith's letters to a young woman in hospital in which he mentioned sending her a book to cheer her up: *A Dominie's Log.* He was Prime Minister then. Yet I think it would be safe to bet that my books are not in the White House Library.

In fifty years of writing, I have seldom had any opposition or any rude letters. My books have not been banned by any country, even by narrow Catholic Eire or by race-hating South Africa. I did read once that Sydney Public Library in Australia had banned one book, but cannot recall which one.

The books I have written are milestones on a journey, things left behind. That is why I cannot read any of my own published works. Once written, a book illustrates my dead past, and I was never interested in the past. I have sort of a vague appreciation of what Henry Ford meant when he said that history was bunk.

Some authors have a hostile attitude to their publishers; I never had. In 1915, I wrote a series of articles for the *Scot-*

tish Educational News. I sent the articles to a well-known London publisher, and got a reply from Herbert Jenkins who worked there. He said the book was too radical for his respected firm, but that he was setting up his own firm and would gladly publish my *Dominie's Log.* Thereafter, for many years, Jenkins published my books. His most famous author was P. G. Wodehouse, whose books must have been the main support of Jenkins' firm.

I had one big grouse with Jenkins; he would change my style. If I wrote: *"I am tired," said Mary,* he changed that to: *"I am tired," said Mary wearily,* or *bitterly,* or what not.

Jenkins died of cancer comparatively young. He took no exercise, sat in his office seven days a week. There is a story about him that tells that he was so fond of his mother and sister that he would refuse any invitation to dinner if his mother and sister were not also invited. Yet upon his death, he left £60,000 to the Society for the Prevention of Cruelty to Animals and he left nothing to them. I cannot vouch for the authenticity of this story; I got it through hearsay.

I cannot say much about Harold Hart, seeing that he is the publisher of this book. I simply record that he saved Summerhill. In 1960, when he published *Summerhill,* we were down to twenty-five pupils, and I wondered if we could carry on. The publication of the book at that time was a real gamble. Hart believed in the Summerhill idea, and poured loads of money into full-page ads in the Sunday edition of *The New York Times* and in the *Saturday Review of Literature.* The publication of the book brought an invasion of American pupils to the school. Eleven years later, the German translation brought a Teutonic invasion. In Germany, the book was published under the clever title of *Anti-Authoritarian Upbringing,* and the book immediately became a best seller, selling 600,000 copies during its very first year of publication.

When my London publishers, Herbert Jenkins Ltd.,

merged with another firm, I transferred to Victor Gollancz Ltd. and became friends with the new director, Livia Gollancz. Some thirty years after its original publication, both Hart and Gollancz republished my *The Last Man Alive,* a children's novel which Jenkins had issued in 1938.

They say that every comedian wants to play Hamlet, and it may be that every writer wants to be a different kind of writer. My desire to be a novelist or a playwright led nowhere. One can do only one job well in life, and no one has ever been able to analyze talent. Had I practiced golf twelve hours a day for twelve years, I would not have been a Jack Nicklaus. Not all the students who studied philosophy for a lifetime became Bertrand Russells. Gray's *Elegy* tells of the "mute inglorious Miltons" that may be lying in the churchyard, but I think he was overestimating the potentialities of the population. Someone once wrote that talent is conscious while genius is unconscious. True in part, but not true enough. I refer to that hater Wagner with his glorious music. Which element represented his unconscious—his musical genius or his misanthropy?

One of my chores has always been correcting proofs. An author should not correct his own proofs; he has a blind eye for minor points—misspelling, wrong punctuation, etc. Proofreading must be the dullest job on earth. Few proofreaders ever get gems to spot like: "Queen Victoria pissed over Waterloo Bridge on her way to Westminster." In 1913, when I was helping the editor of a washerwoman's weekly to read the proofs of a short story, we had to cut a sentence about a heroine who had been deserted by her unfaithful lover: "Mary knew that she would never find happiness until the sod had covered her."

I once heard an argument in an editorial room in Scotland. One editor said that a typesetter became so downright mechanical that he did not realize what he was setting. The editor claimed he had proved his point by giving a typesetter his own obituary notice to set; the typesetter did not notice that he was being declared dead. But I think my informant was a liar, for no man would miss his own name.

It suddenly strikes me that maybe I use writing as a process of thinking. Certainly I think more clearly when I am typing. It may be that print itself has a certain power; this would account for a million Babbitts accepting opinions from their daily newspapers. Sinclair Lewis's Babbitt never knew what to think until he had read the editorial in his daily newspaper. I guess that applies to most of the voters in our fake democracy. Hence, when I look at what I have typed, I may unconsciously think that what is down on paper may be of importance because it is in print.

Handwriting is inferior to the printed word—useful for letters to relations, or letters ordering coal. Within fifty years from now, all children at school will type, and the art of handwriting will have died out. A pity to someone like me, who can write beautiful copperplate and would hate to see the art die.

In old age I can still write beautifully if I try to, although with the modern ball point pen I cannot use the thin upstroke and the heavy downstroke. Like all dominies, my father's handwriting was beautiful even in his old age. Not a shake in it, and there is none in mine at eighty-eight.

I see every day that handwriting does not seem important; my pupils smile in a superior way when I show off my copperplate. Damn the new generation. It won't give us old 'uns any opportunity to swank in pride.

"Writing maketh an exact man," said Bacon, but I see little proof that it does. Too many say too little in too many words. I like the story of the Scottish boxer who promised to wire his wife the result of his fight. He wired O.K.K.O. and saved a sixpence in the telegram.

My interest in plays began when I first read Ibsen. He is the only dramatist who ever tempted me to travel one hundred miles to London to see a play. I was enthralled with *Hedda Gabler* in which Peggy Ashcroft had the lead, and also with *The Wild Duck* which starred Dorothy Tutin. Both were fine performances. But I could never get interested in Ibsen the man. Friends in Norway often motored me over to his birthplace, Skein—pronounced Shane. I got no thrill out of seeing the room in which he worked. All I've read about him makes me feel that I wouldn't have liked that grumpy remote man, who was so critical of society but was yet so pleased to receive society's titles and honors. Another case of a big man having his little man component. But how great a dramatist that man was. For me, Ibsen's technique is almost beyond criticism.

Strindberg has interested me less than Ibsen. Before I knew a word of German, I was taken to see his *Totentanz* (Dance of Death) in a Berlin theatre. I didn't understand a word, but the play held me by the very intensity of its emotion.

It is because of my early fascination with Scandinavian plays that I cannot find any real satisfaction today in what is called "kitchen sink drama," with its long dialogues between tramps and others who have nothing to say to me.

I hardly ever have seen a play on TV that made me cry. TV drama seems to me to be ephemeral stuff. I see no revivals of Pinero, nor of Barrie (barring *Peter Pan*); even Shaw is seldom produced today; and alas! even Noel Coward and Somerset Maugham seldom get to the TV footlights. I wonder whether a play like Williams' *A Streetcar Named Desire* will last.

I used to write plays, and like to think my dialogue was witty. But my dramatic attempts failed, chiefly because I tried to explain the characters' actions, showing the psychology behind them. Ibsen and Shakespeare explain nothing; they let their characters reveal themselves through their actions.

In my younger days, I could have torn many plays to pieces—the artificial dramas of Arthur Pinero, T. W. Robertson, H. J. Byron, Henry Arthur Jones—for I was completely Ibsenized then. Ibsen was my dramatic god. He killed for me all the banal stuff that struts on the stage and is never played again. It is said that a drama critic is a failed dramatist; there may be some truth in that, for all my attempts to write plays failed.

To sum up, I could not have been a scholar, nor a playwright, nor a novelist. My wish was to deal with the living, the growing, the children of tomorrow. I am content to think that my books have helped parents to think twice before attempting to mold their children's characters.

On Being Scottish

Although out of Scotland for nearly sixty years, I still speak with a Scottish accent. Robbie Burns is no longer Robbie Burrrrrns, but I have never adopted the barbaric English fashion of leaving out the "h" in *wheat, why, wheel.* In the north, I believe, *what* was once spelled *hwat:* hence the Scots' pronunciation of the aspirate. And this reminds me of a story, apocryphal perhaps, about the Labour leader, Jimmy Thomas, who became a member of the British Cabinet. Thomas never lost his Cockney speech.

One day, he said to a lordly colleague: "Birkenhead, I've got an 'ell of an 'ead; what can I do for it?"

"What about a couple of aspirates?" was the reply.

In my boyhood, many snobs had an ambition to speak with an English accent. This was a symptom of the Scots' national inferiority complex. Such a complex makes home Scots suspicious of others like me—rats who left a ship that did not sink. As it happened, I had to leave Scotland because its lingering Calvinism did not provide an atmosphere for a free school. But today, things are better. My good friend, John M. Aitkenhead, runs his Kilquhanity school with freedom and self-government.

Another reason for my leaving: Scotland never had the boarding-school tradition. Its public schools (*private* in the

U.S.A.) are schools with English accents, teachers trained in the tradition of prefects, and an overvaluing of games.

My stay in Germany and Austria killed any tendency of mine to be a nationalist. I never took part in the home-rule-for-Scotland campaign; possibly because I had no more faith in an M.P. sitting in Edinburgh than one sitting in Westminster; possibly because I saw the dear old Scottish shops with their tartans and tweeds in Edinburgh's Princes Street taken over by chain stores. Nationalism and international finance make strange bedfellows.

The Scots are much less starchy and more informal than the English. For example, I was a member of an English golf club for twenty-five years. If I made a remark about the nineteenth-hole greens to two men having a drink while I was ordering mine, their looks said *We don't know you.* For all those years, I scarcely ever addressed a member I didn't know. But when I played in Edinburgh and met a foursome going the other way, a golfer would shout to me: "Hi, man, ye're liftin' yer heid." I was.

The hardiness of the northern people is illustrated by a joke dating from my cradle days. An Englishman in the lavatory of a Scottish golf club sees a notice: "Members are requested not to scrub their balls with the nail brushes." The Englishman's comment: "Hardy race, the Scots."

Their money-making talent is another legend, but though this is the only remaining vice in a Calvinist country where wine, women, and song constitute sin, Scotland seems to have produced only one millionaire—Andrew Carnegie. Our reputation for meanness about money is worldwide. Fifty years ago in a Moscow paper, I saw a cartoon showing a Scottish taxi with about a dozen people crowding it. My carefulness with money, already mentioned, has nothing to do with nationality; it stems from the comparative poverty of my youth, when a penny was a fortune to a boy without pocket funds. In my old age, I travel first class on the railway, but always have a vague feeling that I am wasting money.

Scots and Jews are said to have much the same attitude toward spending money; and both races, by and large, have the blessed ability to laugh at themselves. Not always, however. Once, at the end of a lecture in London, I told this story:

A young Scots farmer, returning from a conference in London, was asked by his brother how he liked the English.

"Verra nice fowks. But, ma Goad, I never saw so many noisy buggers in my life. That hotel I was in—the whole bloody nicht, fowks shouting in the passages and hammering on my door."

His brother replied: "You wudna get much sleep, did ye?"

"Och, to hell wi' sleep; I was ower busy practicing my bagpipes."

When I used to cross the border, motoring north, the friendliness of the Scots became apparent. In a cafe, the serving girl had no deference; she was my equal. "Ye'll be on yer hoaliday?" she'd inquire. If one asked the way in Glasgow, most likely a man would walk down half the street to show him. That could not happen in South England, but it could in Northumberland among the Geordies. I don't say that this friendliness goes very deep; I do not claim that Scots are kinder folks than the English. But I am convinced that they have better manners up north, in the sense that manners mean thoughtfulness of the feelings of others.

Politically, or rather economically, Scotland is badly treated by its much more populous neighbor. Unemployment in Scotland always remains proportionately higher. It is the poor relation of England. Yet when there is a general election, home-rule candidates seldom influence the voters, proving perhaps that the hardheaded Scots have no faith in a nominal democracy that is ruled by big vested interests. The U.S.A., by allowing its people to buy and carry guns, shows its barbarity to the world; but even if the vast majority of citizens wanted to make and enforce a gun prohibition law, I am sure that the gun lobby would successfully oppose them all the way. Among all the lobbies in Britain, the Scottish lobby has a wee muffled voice..

I am too old now to see Scotland again. For many years, I motored north every August and found that nobody knew me. Certainly, those who may have known would never admit it. I cannot recall any Scot's asking me how the school was going, or if I were writing any more books. So far as I know, the local paper never mentioned my name. And being a Forfar loon, I didn't mind a bit; I understood the reaction, which might be summed up this way: "We ken dawn weel that he is the son o' Dominie Neill, that he has a school in England, that he writes books; but to us he is still the laddie we played with, and we'll bedawmed if we let him think he is any better than we are." I am not the first Scot to experience that attitude toward the returning native.

Of course, such behavior implies another element: envy. Once, while visiting Dundee, I was speaking with my old friend, J. B. Salmond, editor of the *Scots Magazine* there. He told me that Norval Srimgeour, the editor of the *Dundee Advertiser,* had expressed a wish to meet me, and should he ask him to come over? Norval came and shook hands with me up to the elbow. "Man, Mester Neill, you are the one man I wanted to meet. Your line is education. Now, as I see the matter, it's like this . . . " And for half an hour, he told me his views while I nodded and dropped a few monosyllables. At the end, he gripped my hand again. "Man, I havena enjoyed a conversation like this for years."

I became aware of a defensive attitude when lecturing in Scotland. A Scots audience was always more aggressive, more argumentative, than an English one. I recall a time in Edinburgh, for instance, when angry headmasters shouted at me as

I condemned corporal punishment. John Knox and John Calvin still live.

Money

As explained earlier, I did not need to worry about money when the school was in Hellerau. During the postwar inflation, I was a millionaire, dining my German friends in restaurants with wine galore, the bill coming to a few English shillings. But when I returned to England in 1924, I was almost broke. I have told in these pages of the financial struggle we had in Lyme Regis. We had one stroke of luck there, however. An Australian called Cooper sent me a liberal check for the New Education Fellowship, to which I belonged. When I replied, saying that I was the wrong guy, and should I forward it to the Fellowship, he said no, keep it. The money was a godsend then, and may have saved us from bankruptcy.

For many years, we had no gifts. Then, in 1950, William K. Elmhirst of Dartington Hall made a Deed of Covenant giving me a thousand pounds annually for seven years. Bill was a retiring, modest lad; and since I felt that he did not want his generosity to be a public matter, I did not broadcast his gift. Some years ago, a law firm sent me a thousand pounds from an anonymous donor. More recently, Joan Baez gave me the proceeds, £1400 from a special concert for Summerhill in London, and sent me an additional £2000 after singing at a pop concert in the Isle of Wight. Dear old Joan. One old pupil has given a lot of money to the school to repair, mend, paint, and change it. He made all our muddy paths into tarred roads. Like all truly generous people, he wants to remain anonymous, bless him.

When Her Majesty's Inspectors advised our scrapping a few buildings we did not have the money to rebuild, so I sent out an appeal—much against the grain. The money poured in to the tune of £1,200, and we used every penny of it erecting new teaching huts and dormitories. For many years, I had poured all my book royalties and article fees into the school. A private institution cannot make much profit; too often Summerhill has been in the red, mainly because of bad debts. Had all the debts been paid up during the last fifty years, I could have lorded it in a chauffeur-driven Rolls. But no, that would have meant wearing a tie.

Money may not buy happiness, but it surely does buy comfort. To roll up to the opera in a private car and have a seat in the stalls is comfort, whereas standing in the gallery queue for two hours is, at the least, uncomfortable. Money can also bring the means for creation, for a good job, for a university career. Summerhill has been unable to do all it wanted to do because of poor financing. My teachers—eight for sixty kids—are mostly to train our children in subjects that have to be passed to get into a university or even a business. We have art and handwork teachers but cannot afford dance or music teachers—much more important to me than maths or history teachers. We long to have a fine library, a well-equipped physics lab, and a chemistry lab, plus a cookery department. State schools can afford all these—luxuries to some parents and teachers, but necessities to us. Yet we cannot. And I wish I could pay my staff more than I do.

In my earlier days, I daydreamed of my school's being supported by a millionaire, and twice have I known men who wanted to finance the school. Both times I asked: "You would want a say in the running, wouldn't you?" And to the an-

swer: "Of course," I said: "Nothing doing." The situation
was different when money came from Henry Miller, Joan Baez,
and many a kind American, for they attached no strings.

Perhaps Summerhill's own concept is responsible for its
lack of funds. Certainly its old pupils do not seem interested
in making money, possibly because this requires one to be
competitive, while competitiveness, outside of games, is unknown at the school.

Often money causes unhappiness because too many valuable things have had to be sacrificed during its pursuit. One
thinks of the banal form of culture among the Babbitts of
America with their superficial breeziness and the back-slapping
greetings: "Hullo, old horse thief!"

I am not mean with money, only careful after a boyhood
minus money. Scots really have a money complex. Like myself,
many overtip, an overcompensation for the alleged Scottish
meanness, but I doubt the story that when Sir Harry Lauder
used to cross to America first class he tipped the dining
steward sixpence. Nor do I give any credit to this story
about the Scottish-American millionaire Andrew Carnegie. A
young man went to ask him how to get rich. Andrew was
sitting in a small room lit by a candle.

"Oh," said Andrew, "then we can speak in the dark?"
And he blew out the candle.

In my own life, I rule out the pursuit of money as an important motive. I am not saying that money does not matter. It
does. I knew the pain of having to buy the cheap article when
the best quality cost but a few shillings more. In later life, I
have hated having to travel second class on ships, and "hard"
on continental trains. Even today, I have a slightly embarrassed
attitude to first class passengers on the railway, even though
reasons tells me that most of them are traveling on expense accounts. Oddly enough, in my third or fourth hand car, I feel
no inferiority to the owners of Rolls Royces and Jaguars, pos-

sibly because cars did not exist in my early youth, while trains with toffs in them did.

I do not think I ever thought of money as the criterion of success, nor regarded money as an open sesame to the society of earls and dukes. No, no, the only key to that door was fame—but fame for having accomplished what?

Dreams

A man's dream life might show him how small he is—but not his daydream life. In the daydream, we are in control and we dream of success, courage, conquest. The night dream is beyond control. I doubt if Freud was right in claiming that every dream expresses a wish, however complicated the symbolism. Having had hundreds of my dreams analyzed in therapy, having analyzed hundreds of children's dreams, I cannot believe that all dreams are wish fulfilments. I don't think that analysis of my dreams helped me one bit. I can never analyze my own dreams or my nightmares, which by the way, seem to disappear as one ages.

Dreams get behind the image a man has made for himself, behind what Reich called his armor. Big men can be little men in their dreams. I knew a high churchman who often dreamt that he stood in his pulpit naked. I once dreamt I was shitting in a pot in a crowded ballroom—an odd kind of wishful thinking. In our dreams, we all do daft things, infantile things, idiotic things—but not, in my own experience, cruel things. This fact supports my belief in original virtue; rather than being a combination of Dr. Jekyll and Mr. Hyde, a man is a combination of an adult and a baby. The irrationality of the dream is that of a baby; its pictorialization is that of the nursery and that of children's books. A professor dreams of flying elephants.

My own dreams have no connection with people I know. I never dream of my family, my school, my early life, though I did when younger. For years after Clunie and Homer Lane died, I dreamt of them again and again. These were unpleasant dreams; the sun did not shine in them. Vaguely, I knew in my dreams that these persons were now dead; the contact with them in fantasy was not a happy one. Twice since Reich died, I have talked with him in dreams; but again, with no happiness. In all these instances, the wish fulfilment was not disguised by symbolism.

Dreams, of course, depend to some extent on the glands. Octogenarians do not have sex dreams or prowess dreams; they don't run races, nor do they drive fast cars—awake or asleep.

My anxiety dreams have gone with the years. I used to dream of standing before a large audience unable to say a word. I had distressing dreams concerning travel. The train was moving out of the platform, but my feet would not take me to it. For many years, I dreamt about traveling to my childhood home in Scotland. My parents were expecting me on a certain day by a certain train. I never got there. Everything seemed to stand in my way. The taxi was late, or the train was late, or I couldn't go because of a forgotten lecture date. It was all misery and frustration.

Some dreams are without much disguise. A man whose wife has just bought a new expensive striped coat will dream of going tiger shooting. A woman with an impotent husband will dream of being in the center of a bevy of he-men film stars. But most dreams are disguised by what Freud called the censor, the moral self that will not face raw instinctive longings. . . . Well, well, it would be most intriguing to know what popes and bishops and diehard puritans dream. Or for that matter murderers.

What is the connection between a waking man and a

sleeping one? Is the dream the language of the Id, the deepest unconscious? I doubt that it is, for presumably, the Id is the pro-life part of man, while so many dreams are neither joyful nor creative. In my young days, a kiss in a dream was infinitely more ecstatic than a kiss in real life; on the other hand, grief in a dream was more painful than a grief in reality.

Often I am confused. Who is the president really? Who the Prime Minister? Is it the dignified gentleman who makes speeches and laws during his waking hours, or is it the poor dreamer who walks down the street naked and ashamed? Who am I? The educator, or the driver who can't see the road? I think such challenging thoughts would even knock the conceit out of a pop star.

Drugs, Tobacco, and Health

My vices these days, are few. I smoke pipe tobacco—have smoked John Cotton for over sixty years—and have always ignored medical warnings that tobacco, with latakia in it, is a danger to the heart.

I have never tried drugs. I know nothing about them, and only wonder why smoking cannabis is a crime while smoking cigarettes is legal, seeing that few die from smoking cannabis while many thousands die of lung cancer.

The drug problem bothers me. Taking drugs is a way to escape from a miserable life, and for some it seems the easy way. I am afraid that instead of seeking freedom through natural life, youth will continue the use of the quick trip. We cannot moralize about this. When I smoke my pipe, when I drink a whiskey, I am using drugs; and TV watching, reading novels, watching films, all represent a flight from reality.

All the evils of humanity could well be described as flights: the flight of the German nation into the fantasy world of Adolf Hitler; the flight of the American people into the dead safety of Nixon's silent majority, fearful of change and of youth; the flight of religious people into the dream of bodily immortality.

I like a drink but haven't been drunk for many years. Malt whiskey is my favorite. When I used to drink rye with

Reich, I liked it; but over here in England, rye doesn't appeal
to me. I always have drink in the house, yet seldom touch it
unless a friend visits me. I could easily give up any drinking,
but all my attempts to stop smoking have failed.

I can recall only one incident in my drinking life that
was unpleasant. In 1936, on my South African lecture tour, I
was a guest in the famous Diamond Club in Kimberley. In the
bar, a merchant stood me a whiskey. Six other diamond merchants joined us, and I suddenly noticed that each was ordering
me a double. I was in a spot. I had often heard of colonial
hospitality, and how pained people were if their cordial gestures were rejected. I drank the lot, and then rushed to the
lavatory and put my finger down my throat. I must have given
a lousy lecture that night. Had I been older, I would have
thanked them, and would have asked them to excuse my passing up the drinks in view of the lecture.

So far as my health has been concerned, I have been very
lucky. Apart from two painful attacks of sciatica, my life has
not been troubled by serious illness. About forty years ago, I
lay for three months with phlebitis, and it was then that I
became interested in Nature Cure. That notion seemed to coin-
cide with my philosophy of education. I used to make an
annual visit to a Nature Cure clinic, and most certainly felt
refreshed and fit after each stay.

Nature Cure asserts that disease is generated from within;
that the body reacts to the poisons in bad feeding by throwing
out these poisons. A skin disease or a cold are self-cleansing
processes. So far that sounds rational. My father and grandfather said that they owed their longevity to their many colds;
and a French doctor once claimed that his longest-lived patients were those with skin disease. The medical profession
scoffed at this "quackery," insisting that disease came from
outside infection—from germs. Long before Vitamin C was
discovered, Nature Cure practitioners were using oranges and

lemons as cures. Some doctors, especially in Germany, used the cold compress method for sprains, but did not go as far as the Naturists did with body compresses for pneumonia.

Emotionally, I was all on the side of Nature Cure. But in the course of time, doubts arose. If diet is so important, why did my father die at eighty-five after eating the "wrong food" all his life? Nature Cure warned against wearing flannel next to the skin; my father wore nothing else, summer and winter.

But I saw a positive side, too. I saw women crippled with rheumatoid arthritis who were scarcely able to move, yet who on my next visit a year later were walking about the grounds, not completely cured but greatly improved.

Both sides in this health controversy have been narrow and dogmatic. Nature Cure will have no truck with inoculations; few adherents accept the fact that tetanus injections have saved thousands of lives in the last two big wars. My doctor brother told me that after penicillin came in, he seldom lost a patient with pneumonia.

On the other hand, medical men have laughed at the idea of fasting, ignoring the fact that an animal does just that when ill. A vet told me that most of the mortality among horses and cattle in this county was caused by farmers forcing food down the throats of their sick animals "to keep up their strength."

When I boarded the ship after my South African tour, I felt like a dying man—too many drinks and no exercise. But I fasted on water for six days and arrived in Southampton the picture of health. The odd thing about fasting is that it makes one feel so bright mentally. During my fast, I felt I was sharp enough to tell even Einstein where he was wrong.

My doubts about Nature Cure increased when people who had lived according to its regimen all their days died of cancer or diabetes. That proved to me that the eating of good food wasn't the sole controlling factor.

I fancy that many naturopaths have been unconscious
moralists: One of the best known cultists claimed in a book he
wrote that many of his cases of ill-health were caused by
masturbation. All Nature Curists have been down on stimu-
lants: tea, coffee, alcohol, tobacco. Also on meat of any kind.
I believed, and at the same time disbelieved. I have main-
tained the same ambivalent and skeptical attitude toward
doctors who prescribe a salve for a skin disease without asking
what was causing it. I have hardly ever seen a doctor who
asked what I ate, if I took exercise, if my sex life was satisfactory. Their solution, it seems to me, was to treat the specific
disease, while the Nature Curist tried to build up the whole
body. A combination of the two systems, Nature Cure and established medicine, might be the answer.

There is one great difference between the two schools.
The Nature Curist says: "You must make an effort to cure yourself. You must take exercise, eat pure food, avoid all stimu-
lants. Your cure is up to you, not to me. I am only an advisor."
The average medical practitioner does not appear to be interested in the way you live. "You have asthma, sciatica, kidney
trouble—take these pills." If asked what the pills contain,
many doctors get annoyed. I have heard so many sinister tales
about cortisone that I do not want to take that drug; but for
all I know, my pills may contain it. As Shaw said, every profession is a conspiracy against the laity.

I have suffered from constipation most of my life. The
analysts kept telling me it was psychological. But I cured this
condition by eating dates every day. When I attended a Nature
Cure clinic, I was never constipated on their diet.

Reich, by the way, paid no attention to food; he seemed
to think that what you ate was unimportant, and that sex
economy was infinitely more important than domestic economy. Churchill smoked and drank all his life; Compton Mackenzie at eighty-eight smoked an ounce of tobacco a day. I

knew two farmers in Scotland who appeared to live on whiskey, and both died past ninety. Oh, it is so hard to make up one's mind about health.

Causes of illness are largely unknown. Why does a man die of cancer, and his brother die of diabetes? Why are my sister and I alive at eighty-three and eighty-eight, while the rest of the family are dead?

Armoring

Reich spoke of armoring—acquiring an outer shell with which to face the world, and hiding the depths of one's personality.

We all armor ourselves. Introspection is limited; and that is why a man cannot psychoanalyze himself; he dare not face his inner conflicts, his repressions. It would not be easy for a prominent evangelist to face his naked soul, to find out that he was selfish, mean, sadistic, and an unconscious womanizer. Rather impossible, I should think. A balanced man is one who is prepared to discover the little man in himself. From that angle, none of us is too well-balanced.

I wonder what form my own armoring takes. I have often been called amiable, kind, tolerant, a pleasant guy to meet. So I ask myself what lies behind this facade. It is difficult for me because during my analyses with Homer Lane, Maurice Nicoll, Stekel, and Reich I must have coughed up oceans of unpleasant material, which I'd rather forget. For one thing I recognize that my altruism in dealing with children covers much selfishness, but I see no harm in that. My altruism is selfish in that it gives me a feeling of self-satisfaction—But, of course, all altruism is ego-fulfilling.

I am selfish about certain material things. I don't like my car to be driven by anyone else; I never lend my typewriter; and many of my things are part of myself. I am comfortably off, but when I get an appeal for money for some home for poor children I do not subscribe, rationalizing that I need all my money for my school. I pass by a beggar in Oxford Street, and two minutes later enter a shop and buy tobacco at more than eight shillings an ounce.

Last night on TV, we were told that three quarters of a million have been killed in the Sudan war in the last three years. I felt no emotion. Distance kills emotion. If a thousand were killed in Suffolk, I would experience a great emotion, for the personal component would enter—"God! It might have been me!" But how selfish am I in other ways? I find it almost impossible to condemn, but that is mainly due to long experience in dealing with psychological motives; I see behind crime a sick person who cannot control his impulses. But suppose one of my little pupils were raped and murdered by a sex maniac, I fancy it would be hard to be objective then.

I am unselfish with my time. I see and listen to thousands of visitors who have as a rule nothing to give me; they come to get *from* me. Yet I see them patiently without, I believe, a deeper anger at being pumped dry. Yet, here again, what is behind my patience? My armor, my facade? Neill cannot destroy his image of being a nice guy who offends not even the rudest visitor. Can he?

I have a "privy fault"—an expression possibly taken from Congreve where a lord remarks to a guest, referring to the pretty maid who brought in the wine: "She hath a privy fault; she farts in her sleep"—a lovely neat way of betraying his relationship with the maid.

I have a privy fault. I hate being opposed, and this is generally called a God-Almighty complex. When I used to lecture, I disliked the wise guy who got up and contradicted what I had said, disliked him intensely when I felt *he was right*. Tin gods don't make mistakes—or at least don't acknowledge them. Oddly enough, I am not much affected by what folks write about me. One book reviewer will call me a genius; and another a stupid fanatic. Neither remark seems to rouse much emotion one way or the other.

I have no dignity in my job. Everyone, including domestic staff, addresses me as Neill. But dignity enters at certain times, when I'm rudely called to task by a cop when I park in the wrong place, when I go walking in the woods with my dog and a shouting gamekeeper bawls me out. In both cases, my dignity is offended mainly because I am in the wrong. On such occasions, I cannot laugh at myself.

Like many others I have always had a complex about my own name. Alexander was contracted into Alec, but Clunie as a small child could not say Alec and called me Allie, which made me ashamed as a kid because a girl in my class, Allison, was also called Allie. "Huch! You've got a lassie's name." More than once I have known married women who hated having lost their maiden names; and quite early in life, I discovered that many a woman was pleased when I called her Mary or Susan. Shakespeare to the contrary, there is something in a name.

When I was made an honorary Doctor of Essex University, I consciously set out to be a gentleman even to the extent of wearing a tie; but my shirt was the only blue one in the crowd. I listened attentively to conversations about things I had no interest in. I adapted myself to academic society in which I never feel at home. We all practice this kind of armoring on the ground that good manners mean thinking of others. As Reich often said: "You have to be a conscious hypocrite on occasion."

I like to think that I am not too heavily armored; that in general, I speak and act sincerely and seldom tell a lie—at least never to a child. Lying is pardonable, but living a lie is a tragedy.

I confess that I have it easy; I am my own boss and have

no need to pretend. Think of the millions who work under bosses, bowing and saying "Sir;" maybe fawning in order not to get the sack. Too often the armor that is worn for the occasion comes to permeate the whole personality. You see it in the subservience of butlers and footmen, a dying race to be sure.

When young, I got most of my best dirty stories from clergymen who, when they preached on Sundays, appeared to be holy men. Many have the knack of being dual personalities, like one of the elders in my childhood kirk who praised the Lord on the Sabbath, and gave short weight with his sugar during the week.

The best way to escape being a dual personality is to be independent, a fortune given to few of us. That is not, of course, the whole story. An independent artist may have a nagging wife, and he hides his murder wishes with a few humble: *Yes, darlings.* A good illustration is *Babbitt* which I am now rereading for the fourth time. Babbitt is the picture of all stupid, money-mad, middle-class men in the U.S.A. Sinclair Lewis wrote *Babbitt* about fifty years ago, but Babbitt still lives. I meet him again and again, in buses, on trains, and on planes, the genial soulless Babbitt who thought that a glade of forest and lake were a waste of good space that might be used for garages, restaurants, and cottages.

Nearly forty years ago, in South Africa, I met a doctor who seemed to have no armoring. If invited to go out to a dinner he didn't look forward to he said simply that he didn't want to accept. He said to me: "Neill, I am not coming to your lecture tonight, because I have no interest in what you're to talk about." A really honest man, but I fear he had few friends. Reich was another who told no lies to evade social invitations. I was never so brave. It is only in my old age that I can say: "Thanks for the invitation, but I'd rather stay at home."

Any official occasion bars laughter, bars the human touch.
Once, while giving evidence at an appeal tribunal on my income tax, I offered a light remark, and the subsequent frowns
made me realize what officialdom means. It means the suppression of the emotional side of life; it means community armoring; it means the dignity of Bumbledom. I see it among local
officials, town councillors, town clerks; they erect a hands-off-
me barrier that excludes any familiarity. It is strong too, in
the police force. A constable once said to me: "If the inspector
heard you address me as Bill, I'd be transferred to another
town immediately."

My idea of hell would be a garden party at Buckingham
Palace. Crowd armor protects against the danger of making
emotional contacts. This may be primarily typical of England;
there is less of it in Scotland where class barriers do not seem
so strong.

My honorary degrees make me think of crowd armoring.
I have had three such ceremonies. They robe you in cap and
gown; you march in procession; and you get your honorary
degree in a crowded big hall. In spite of the presence of a few
friendly professors and dons, I have always felt strained and
unhappy in such an atmosphere. I think the reason is the
blank impersonality of the Establishment. I make a remark to
the man sitting next to me, and the reply is usually mono-
syllabic.

I feel somewhat guilty about receiving honorary degrees,
not because of Establishmental aloofness, but because I do not
value the academic education doled out at universities, and
because I have written so much criticizing them. I never put
my degrees on my school prospectus. I suppose I rationalize
when I say that the only value these degrees have for me is
that they protect me. No Ministry can now say that I am not
qualified to run a school.

I am quite prepared to face the fact that underneath I

may be as proud as Punch of my M.A. degree, for in Scotland
an M.A. is of great moment. I've quoted the incident when
an aunt said to J. M. Barrie: "What do you want to be, James?"
"An author."
"What, and you an M.A.!"
I suppose that conceit is a form of armoring. We are
rarely conceited about what we can do very well. I was never
conceited about my work in Summerhill, but used to be about
my dancing. Fifty years ago, a young lady invited me to go to
Budapest to partner her in a competition of original dancing.
(Poor Nushi died in Belsen.) I was very conceited about that
invitation, knowing all the time that, compared with professional dancers, I was a clumsy clod. Luckily for my self-
approval, I did not go to Budapest.

I used to be conceited about my acting, again realizing
that, compared with a professional, I was a ham. I am convinced that if Yehudi Menuhin's hobby was growing cucum-
bers, and he won a prize at a garden show, he would be more
conceited about that than about his fiddle playing. Conceit is an
armor against admitting to oneself that one is inferior. Such
conceit fades with the years but never quite expires. Reich's
desire to have an elaborate tomb in Orgonon was a kind of
posthumous conceit; in life, he scorned display and honors and
pageantry of all kinds. Myself, I have no feelings about monu-
ments after my death. All I want is a quiet cremation with no
fuss, no flowers, no black clothes, no epitaphs. I should really
like to have my body taken away by the undertaker and have
no funeral ceremony at all; but I fear that my family would
be criticized: "The hard boiled lot, not even giving the old
man the respect of a decent burial."

But sensible burial customs should come, even though in
the U.S.A. the funeral lobby would fight tooth and nail for
their scandalous exploitation of the bereaved, their idiotic em-
balming and face-painting plus maybe many thousand dollars'

worth of good oak that could be better employed in building.

Odd how the word *conceit* has lost its original meaning of a *thought* or *something conceived.* So many words have changed. A matinee is not a morning performance—it is an afternoon one. Manufactured goods (Latin *manu* by hand, *factum* to make) are made by machinery. In my town, a cafe is a *caff,* and a chauffeur is a *shover.*

Death is feared and hated because it destroys the little conceited man in each of us. A modern interpretation of Christianity might run: *A belief that the little man in us will die and be buried, while the big man in us will pass to eternal glory and happiness.* In other words, the little man equals the body and its conceits and frailties; the big man equals his spirit, his soul. All religions are wish-fulfilments.

Thoughts on Death

When Neil my doctor brother died at eighty, I felt no grief. I think that, with age, the emotions get dull; one can neither exult nor deeply grieve. I grieved when Reich died, but not much when Homer Lane died. My good friends Edwin and Willa Muir died and I did not shed a tear.

Distance makes a big difference. If your brother dies in your arms, you grieve painfully; but if he dies in Australia, the grief is less poignant. Grief is diminished by flight. The rich fly to another country, but the poor have to seek flight in humbler ways. After Clunie's death, I found myself doing all sorts of things I was not accustomed to do: washing dishes, mending chairs—anything to take my mind off my misery. But even then, I recognized the selfish element in grief: "I am left alone now."

Possibly one's saddest grief is the loss of a companion in thought. After Edwin's death, Willa Muir said to me: "When I have a sudden thought, I say 'I must tell this to Edwin'." I had the same feeling after Clunie's death. Maybe the loss of a companion is worse than the loss of a loved one. It may be that religion was invented to soften the emotion of grief. Unbelievers like myself do not have that consolation; I, for one, do not want it.

I cannot guess where the expression *Good grief!* came

from. It may have some hidden connection with the unconscious relief so often associated with death. I think of the
Scottish funeral with its tears, and the subsequent feast in the
parlor with much laughter and ale. There is a similarity here
to a military funeral with its dead march; on the return from
the grave, the band is likely to play *The Girls I Left Behind Me.*

I make the guess that the family who harbors the most
hate evinces the strongest show of grief.

At eighty-eight, especially after a bout in hospital with a
heart attack, I cannot help thinking more of death than ever before. Following an injection of I.V.P.—whatever that is—just
before an x-ray examination of my kidneys, I almost passed out.
Vaguely, I heard a doctor call for oxygen. The odd thing was
that I had no fear, only a curiosity; and later, when a doctor
told me I had had a coronary attack, I was not alarmed.

I said to the doctor: "Do you know the story about the
Coronary Club? The oldest member wins £75,000 in the football pools. His wife opens the letter and is afraid to tell him.
She goes to the club chairman, the vicar, and he offers to break
the news. He finds the old man in his garden.

"Well, Mr. Brown, what do you do now that you have
retired?"

"Oh, I just potter about; can't do any heavy work with
this ticker of mine."

"Any other hobbies?"

"No."

"Ever try the pools?"

"I try them sometimes, but they are just a damned waste
of money.

"Mr. Brown, what would you do if you won £75,000?"

"Vicar, I'd give half to your church restoration fund."
And the Vicar drops down dead.

If one lives to be very old, nature seems to make the passing easy. I find that I have gradually lost interest in things,

and to a lesser degree, in people. I see the gardener use the scythe I used to keep so clean and sharp, and it means nothing. I gave all my prized workshop tools to the school workshop. When I get up in the morning, I feel I'm a hundred, and have no interest in anything or anyone; but when I go to bed, I am fifty. The morning mail brings nothing to excite me; the morning papers have little interest. In old age, there is nothing to look forward to. I can think of no promising event that would give me a thrill, not even a check for a million from a rich American, nor an offer of a title—which I would not accept—nor a new honorary degree from a university. Sure I like to see myself praised in the press, but when I do, I leave it to others to preserve the clipping. Nature prepares us for the end. I have not reached the philosophy of Stevenson with his ". . . gladly die, And I lay me down with a will." But I begin to understand why he said it, even though he died long before old age was due.

If the weakness of old age did not come, I wonder how long a man could live happily, how long he could retain his interest in the beauty of flowers and landscapes. Should I say to myself: "Soon you will not see the Summerhill trees and flowers, the happy faces of the kids. Soon you will leave your friends forever. How very sad!" No! I cannot.

My caravansary has rested in many a lovely spot, and I am content not to wish that those experiences be repeated. In youth, everything is permanent. In the old schoolhouse, we children never thought that life would change, that our parents, and our brothers and sisters would die; if anyone had told me then that I would end my life in a small English town that was not on the map, I think I would have laughed at the absurdity of the idea.

Youth is not interested in death unless some evil like Calvinism or Catholicism makes it a terror. My pupils, with no religious fears, think of life, of doing things, of loving, of success. The only function of life is to live; and since I have had a full life with most of my aims reached, I have no regrets that past joys and successes are gone forever.

When a film magnate stood on the sinking *Lusitania,* someone asked him if he weren't afraid. "No," he said, quoting Peter Pan, "death is the greatest adventure in life." To me death is not such a great adventure because I think, with Hamlet, that "the rest is silence." I can't imagine a silent adventure.

One of my old pupils, a radio operator on a ship during the Second World War, told me that underlying his fear of being torpedoed was the thought that he had no children to carry on his name. I am glad to have a daughter to carry on mine; but now married, she is no longer a Neill. I think it wrong that women allow their names to be changed in marriage by a patriarchal society, a device that renders them inferior. I shall leave my Zoe, and in time, she too will die. What I leave is my work, which I hope will live for at least some little time.

In one of my books I wrote about some pioneers who discover new lands. Then the prospectors come with their commercial plans. Soon the virgin land is changed into a hideous mass of saloons, skyscraper hotels, and neon advertisements. I hope my pioneering in education will not lead to an undistinguished mass of pseudo-free schools, which practice a benign molding of young character.

One thing annoys me. Because of my age, my insurance company will not reinsure me for driving unless I show an annual certificate of fitness from my doctor. And even then, the company won't give me comprehensive coverage. Statistics show that drivers past sixty have the least number of accidents; I am constantly avoiding collisions with young speed merchants who get full insurance. The fact that my driving license has been clean for forty-five years makes this inequity especially galling. Still, I should not complain; in Japan and Norway, no one past eighty can drive a car at all.

I have no belief in an afterlife, and if there were one, I am sure it would be dreadfully dull. Since I do not fear death consciously, I think it must be my unconscious that gives me a strange feeling when I drive past the gate of the local crematorium.

My doctor brother's deathbed was perfect. He had no pain. "I have had enough of life," he said, "and I am tired and want to die now. Having no religion, I have no fear of hell and damnation. Good-bye, old man."

But I fear a death with pain; and more than once have I wondered whether I would have the courage to take an overdose, were I dying painfully with cancer.

Most of us are not great poets or great musicians. We do our little jobs and live our little lives as happily as we can. We realize dimly that our deaths will be felt only by a few friends and relatives. The wise Bertrand Russell is now a book reference in a library. My little school is but a flea on the elephant of world education. Millions of Russians and Chinese will never know Summerhill existed; and if they did know, they would not be influenced one iota by it. An atomic war would most likely destroy even Beethoven and Shakespeare. But then again, the majority of people on earth have never heard of these two anyway.

Both Hitler and the Communists declared that the individual did not matter—only the state, the *Volk*. They were wrong because their power aims were wrong. But there was a certain truth in their claim that humanity means the masses— the undying masses. I am not contending that the individual should not try to reach the masses. Most leaders and thinkers cannot lead masses, but solitary figures may spark fires that sweep the world. For example, the attack on slavery came from a somewhat unknown Englishman, William Wilberforce.

I think of names that were prominent in the world of psychoanalysis years ago: Rank, Stekel, Abraham, Bernfeld, in Vienna; Flugel, Jones, Eder, in London. How many know their names today? They did their share of work and crept silently to rest, one by one. So it is in education. Bill Curry of Dartington Hall was a good lad, but is now forgotten. Already, younger men are saying that Summerhill is out of date. Time outmodes many things.

I have what might be described as a grouse against death: it kills the body when the spirit wants to live. I think those people err who say that we will our own deaths, yet perhaps in sickness, one can appear to do so. In my old age, my heart does poorly and may kill me, but my head is alive and my interest in all things living is as keen as it ever was. Someone may think up a new arrangement by which one is parked after death, and allowed to revisit the earth every twenty years for a week. The chances are that after the first visit, most of the departed would call off any further visits.

The perfect death is that of John Keats: "To cease upon the midnight with no pain." It seems as if nature eases death by weakness and resignation. But I cannot accept Freud's theory of a death instinct. Six million Jews wanted to live. The lucky ones who jumped from windows to escape torture were reacting to a pain instinct. As hate so often becomes the reaction to thwarted love—so a longing for death is the reverse of a love of life. I regard the flight into hard drugs which leads to an early death as such a longing.

At the end of a long life, I calmly declare: "I have done a job—a good one, I think. I have helped many a kid to freedom and happiness. My books have reached a few million people—thanks to Harold Hart, my American publisher. I shall die without illusions, without fantasies of grandeur or of fame. And after my demise, I shall be forgotten; the world will not miss me, for the world is of today and tomorrow.

Women

I never understood women. What man can understand them? In some ways, they are a different species. Had I been reared in a pro-sex atmosphere, I might have had a better understanding of female psychology. For me, women were beings apart, protected by a rigid sex armor that deceived the male youth. In my innocence, I thought that when I told a woman she would make a great bedfellow her shocked look was genuine. I did not realize that underneath the reproachful look she took my remark as a wonderful compliment. In my young days, a woman's life consisted of defense; that had to be so in a society that made chastity and modesty the prime virtues. In my student days, some friends censured me because I used the word *shit* in the presence of two women students. Today, I'm quite sure women use the word *fuck* as often as men do.

Women were put on a pedestal, and we did not realize that their feet were of common clay. Having sisters did not help me one bit to understand other women. The family sex taboo blanketed all lassies; they were all untouchable, mysterious, unattainable.

Max Miller, the English comedian, used to tell the story about a girl who went to a shoemaker to have her shoes repaired.

"Do you know what makes shoes wear out?" the cobbler

asked her.

"No," she said.

"That's right," he replied.

Many in the theatre roared with laughter, but it took me two days to figure out that the reluctant maiden had to walk herself home from every date.

At eighteen, I fell for a bonny lassie who did not react to my advances. (I learned later that she was a lesbian.) Her sister was plain. I cultivated the sister, insanely thinking that she would convince her beautiful sister what a fine guy I was. I was blind to the fact that she hated her sister like hell.

I used to think that the way to a girl's heart was paved with compliments. It took me a long time to realize that a rival won my girl's heart by telling her what a nasty bitch she was.

I recall a dance, in old days of dance cards and white gloves, when the women stood around and the swains booked dances with them, each writing down the dance appointment in the little book with its silk string. The university beauty was besieged. I was introduced to her, and didn't ask for a dance. Later, she touched my arm. "Our dance," she said. She had cut another dance. "But," I said, "we didn't—"

"I know, damn you. You are the only one who didn't ask me for a dance."

It was when I first saw Shaw's *Man and Superman* that I began to doubt the time-honored theory that man is the pursuer and woman the pursued. I began to see the bag of female wiles: dropping a handkerchief, borrowing a book, crossing the legs. I did not appreciate that the driving force of sex was as cogent in women as it is in men. At nineteen when I read in some French novel that a woman's main interest was in her vagina, I was shocked. That is not true, yet it is partly true. Cosmetics and fancy pins and dresses mean: I am desirable sexually; feast your eyes on me and take me. And yet many a woman has said that she dresses for other women and not for men. That cannot basically be true.

A man can never understand the enormous importance a woman attaches to dress and appearance. I find this feminine concern with outer appearance slightly depressing.

Does feminine preoccupation with outward show have anything to do with the inferior status of women in a patriarchal society? Maybe. In a man-made world in which women are second-class citizens, there are only a few female J.P.'s. The business executives, doctors, and lawyers are overwhelmingly men; the only department in which women are equal is in teaching and nursing. So to counteract male dominance, women stress their importance by being ornamental. One of the most cheering trends in modern life is the rebellion of many women against this inferior role. On the other hand, it is depressing that the women of Switzerland do not want the vote.

A woman may vote for a handsome film star, but I doubt if many men would vote for a beautiful female star if she stood for election. It is the difference of values that makes it impossible for a man to understand a woman, or for that matter for a woman to understand a man. Sixty years ago, I had an affair with an upper-class woman in London, a woman who always dressed in the height of fashion. When we went dining, she insisted that I come in my frayed Norfolk jacket and my uncreased baggy flannel trousers. "They look at the pair of us," she explained, "and then look again because of the incongruity of the partnership."

"Meaning," said I, "that they look at you."

"Naturally," she smiled.

Men are afraid of women. Every woman, especially a wife, is a mother substitute. Many married men in England address their wives as Mum. The hen-pecked man is more than a music-hall joke. The man rationalizes his fear by pretending that he gives in for peace.

When I was a boy, I knew two village schoolmasters who were not allowed to smoke in the house; they sat out in their sheds on bitter nights. My father was a non-smoker; but had he been a smoker, I fancy my mother would have said: "George, your tobacco gives me a sore throat." Maybe not, but he often gave way for peace.

I sigh regretfully when I see the modern girl with her independence, her frankness about sex, her carelessness in dress with her blue jeans and blouse. I sigh and wish that women had been as sincere and honest in my youth. Real companionship with a woman was almost impossible then. Maybe it was possible between two bluestockings of opposite sex.

Many men fear the intellectual female. I never did. My old platonic friend Willa Muir was a very clever woman, a match for her poet husband Edwin. But she was never un-feminine; and her sense of humor saved her from being an intellectual prig. She was a Scot.

I have found that Scottish women are sharper of tongue, more given to incisive criticism than their English sisters. They seem to want to take men down a peg, to assert their equality, or maybe their superiority. The most aggressive questioners I have met in a life of lecturing were the women of Scotland, mostly teachers, I guess. Scotland has never had the equivalent of that American sentimental abomination—Mothers' Day, a day that suggests that American men have never grown up beyond age ten.

My mother complex always made me have a tender feel-ing for older women, and I have seen a similar attitude among homosexuals. Many who show no interest in young women seem to love fussing around mother figures, thus giving some support to the theory that the male homo has had an unsatis-factory father, and was too attached to his mother. Owing to the incest taboo, his mother is sacrosanct, and so every other woman too, becomes taboo.

So many women seem to prattle about trite things: their neighbors and their doings, their little gardens, their knitting. It is easy to sneer at the emptiness of so much of womanly talk, but I fail to see that men are any more elevated in their conversation. Relativity and psychology are not exactly pub subjects; men will jaw endlessly about football games.

A very clever actor buys his clever wife a necklace, the price of which would support a hundred poor families for weeks. It puzzles me. To stage people, the joy in life should be the creative art, the applause after a part well played. How an actress can value a stone bauble so much I just cannot understand. Surely she does not need so dull a status symbol. This is not meant to be a criticism of a worthy couple of world-wide deserved fame; I use the illustration only to show how ignorant I am of the depth psychology of womankind. I can understand the Hollywood dumb blonde who is said to have had gold faucets in her bathroom. Poor kid, that was her Cinderella idea of success. Yet, in a way, is she any worse than the man who looks on a knighthood as a token of success? All is vanity. If offered a title, I would refuse it without any hesitation. That can be interpreted as inverse snobbery. Woman parades her vanity, but man hides his by pretending he has none.

Woman's tragedy is that she ages more quickly than a man. Her worry about her appearance betrays her frantic attempt to make the most of her sex attraction before the dark night of wrinkles and grey hair descends upon her. I hate to imagine the later life of Hollywood stars who had nothing but their figures and faces to be proud of.

Ah, me! I am old now and cannot recapture the enthusiasms and ecstasies of youth, the dreams of youth, the ambitions of youth. A pretty lass is now an object of academic interest; but I still enjoy looking.

Humor

The greatest insult one can offer a man is to say he has no sense of humor, almost as great an insult as saying he is a bad driver. Such verdicts are unforgivable.

One of the most humorless men I know often sums up other men by saying: "What is wrong with that guy is that he has no sense of humor."

There can be a criterion of good driving, but not one for good humor. Anyway, humor varies with the times. In my boyhood, we all laughed at the funny stories in *Three Men in a Boat;* but today, no young person would see humor in Jacobs or in Jerome. Some of my pupils cannot even laugh at Charlie Chaplin; they prefer Laurel and Hardy or Danny Kaye.

Like all others, I like to think that I have a good sense of humor, which includes a good sense of wit. I have always disliked sadistic humor, like when King Edward VII and Douglas Fairbanks, Senior, played infantile and cruel practical jokes on guests. In my boyhood, McGonagall, the worst poet who ever achieved immortality, was a simple scatter-brained man. The Dundee wits and wags treated him most cruelly, even sending him a letter signed by Queen Victoria making him a Knight of the White Elephant of Burma. The decoration, the letter said, was coming by ship, and the poor man went to the docks daily to meet the ship, until finally he got a

wire from the Queen saying the award had been washed over-
board. That kind of gallows humor is barbaric. Luckily, it is
seldom in evidence these days.

I do not appreciate the humor of the average wisecracker.
A man like Bob Hope leaves me cold. A good comedian does
not need a script written for him. Chaplin did his own scripts,
and I guess so did Buster Keaton.

My favorite story appears in the *Autobiography of Lord
Beresford.* During the first Great War, a distinguished American came over to England. Lord Charles gave a dinner party
in his honor. When the guest's health was proposed, he rose.

"Gentlemen, before I speak about the war situation, I
want to apologize for appearing to-night in morning dress. I
came over on war business, and did not expect to dine out, so
I did not bring my evening clothes. When I got Lord Charles's
invitation, I went to a Savile Row tailor and asked if he could
make me an evening suit.

'Very sorry, sir, but I have no material and my men are
all called up.'

"I tried several tailors and got the same reply. Then someone advised me to go to Willie Clarkson the theatrical cos-
tumier and hire one, so I went to Clarkson. 'Could I hire a
suit of evening dress for tomorrow night?'

"Willie held up his hands. 'Sorry, sir, but it can't be
done; all my suits are out; Lord Charles Beresford is giving a
dinner party.' "

I told this story to a journalist friend in Scotland who
was the chief guest at a Burns Supper. He had not had time
to dress. He told the story, making it local.

"God," he said, "it was received in dead silence, and I
had to conclude that every bloody man had hired his suit."

When Mother told a story, we all sighed. . . . "There
was a man in Glasgow . . . or was it Edinburgh . . . no,
Glasgow. . . ."

My father had a sense of fun rather than a sense of humor. He had to explain the point of a story.

When I first lectured in the U.S.A. in 1947, I discovered that the humor that appealed to Americans was different from the humor that appealed to the English. A joke I made that would have raised laughter in London fell flat in New York; and more than once, laughter arose when I could not see why.

Every nation has its own kind of humor which is therefore apt to become hackneyed, like the typical story of Scottish meanness.

One thing has puzzled me for years—who invents the funny story? I have never once met anyone who claimed to originate a story. Like the border ballads, all jokes are written by anon. "That man writes a lot," said the old lady.

Every man has his own bias. My favorite golf story is the one about the man who rushed into the pro shop.

"Mac, something awful has happened. I sliced my drive on the ninth tee, hit a motorcyclist on the road; he crashed into a car that was just coming round the corner. Mac, what the hell can I do? There are about six people lying dead on the road."

Mac thought for a moment. "Aye," he said, "you've got to get your right hand under the club like this. . . ."

A sense of humor helped me to face life, or was humor sometimes used as an escape from facing raw reality? I do not know, but I do know that humor must have its own special time and environment. A man on his way to the gallows would not relish the best joke ever concocted; yet old Oscar could remark when faced with expensive medical treatment that he was dying beyond his means. Of course, we know that laughter is a release, and that people who cannot relax cannot laugh. Who can imagine Calvin or Knox or Hitler laughing out loud? Maybe what ails the Bible is that there isn't a joke in all its thousands of pages. Maybe politicians are guys who cannot laugh.

Many teachers can laugh but dare not lest their children discover they are human. Too often I have seen sadistic teachers whose humor took the form of tormenting frightened little boys.

It is likely that most schoolboy howlers are invented by teachers. I doubt if any schoolboy ever said that the pope lives in a vacuum (some unconscious truth here), or that a polygon is a dead parrot.

I think that humor has been of great assistance to me in my work. I speak to every child lightly unless he or she seeks my help. Joking with a child connotes to the child friendliness, equality, brotherhood. When someone asked me who would run Summerhill after my death, I replied: "No idea, but if he or she has no humor, the school will go fut." A school that is not a fun fair is a bad school. Alas, the dignity of teachers kills all the fun.

The Future:
Summerhill and the World

I am often asked: "What will happen to Summerhill when you die?" I have no idea. Ena, my wife, will carry on, but because she is not qualified as a teacher, she will need to appoint a headmaster who is. And I doubt that any successor will care to be a slavish follower; he would be a poor specimen, if he were.

No man is indispensable; others will carry the torch. I cannot imagine much more freedom than Summerhill already has given; maybe only in the area of sex. In fifty more years perhaps the freedom schools, with the approval of parents and society, will permit adolescents to have a full love-life.

The Labour Party is against private enterprise in business and in schools; and when again in power, it may well set about abolishing private schools altogether. One result would be the end of pioneering in education. A teacher in a State school can experiment with methods of teaching history or maths, but he cannot experiment with methods of living. A State school head could not abolish religious instruction, nor could he make lessons optional, and I doubt if he could abolish the abominated homework. Can one imagine a Summerhill in Russia or China? Can one see a U.S. Senate voting for free schools as the norm in America?

It is ironic to say that Summerhill is safer under a Tory government than under a Labour government. So, in my own interests, I should really vote Tory; for as long as Eton and Harrow exist, Summerhill is safe. How safe though? The question troubles me. My wife Ena is determined to continue Summerhill without compromise, but how much freedom will a future government allow?

I can hear some future educational officer say: "We tolerated this Bolshy school as long as the old man was alive, but now that he has gone, my Ministry cannot allow a school where children play all day and get no education." It would 'be a waste of breath to answer such a person with the fact that, in fifty years, just about every old pupil we know about has become a success in work and life. Dead officials have deaf ears. I am not boasting when I claim that Summerhill is possibly better known than any other pioneer school, a fact stemming from the accident that I was a teacher who wrote books. The school never has been "recognised as efficient" by the British Ministry, although it is recognized as efficient in a dozen other countries.

I don't want the Summerhill idea to die with me. Movements should not rely on personalities; persons die, but a movement should live and develop. I wonder what the great educators would think of the schools now running in their names—Montessori, Rudolf Steiner, Friedrich Froebel.

Someone has suggested that after my death the old Summerhillians should form a Summerhill trust with a constitution to guard against any fundamental changes from outside. My fear would be a creeping bureaucracy that looked backward: "Neill did it that way, and we must follow." Anyway, committees cannot pioneer, for their pace is that of the reactionary majority.

A recently published article stated that pioneering had now left the private sector and gone over to the State schools. Certainly, many primary schools are showing the new way toward freedom, bless them, but *real* freedom cannot exist in a system whose primary function is to condition children to the established rules and mores. A visitor asked me to explain the difference between Summerhill and a Montessori school. My reply: "A kid can say *fuck* in Summerhill, but not in a Montessori school." As long as parents and teachers insist on forming a child's character, all the free activity in the world will not produce free people.

If Summerhill goes on after me, it must change, just as it has changed in many ways since 1921. The Summerhill pupil of today is different from the pupil of the thirties; his environment has changed. The mass media have brought kitsch to the young. And preoccupation with mindlessness has increased greatly: long hair, pop festivals, the deification of pop and football stars. Mass hysteria is reported in the paper; so is Vietnam, Ulster, the Near East, and the insane armaments race. I don't say that the young are always conscious of this anti-life environment, but the young are unconsciously made to accept the belief that the world is sick and dangerous "so let us have a fine time as long as we can."

I have often said that our schools ignore the emotional life engendered by our commercial, brainless mass media. Millions who have never learned or have long forgotten the names of Milton and Gladstone know and venerate the name of Elvis Presley. The mass media has flourished because the schools have failed in education, just as God is dead because the Church cannot adapt religion to modern thought.

So in thinking of the future of Summerhill, I am wondering what kind of freedom the new world will accept. The most probable outcome will be a compromise, paying lip service to freedom but subtly continuing to worship traditional molds. I would rather have Summerhill die than lose its freedom; but as long as Ena lives, I have confidence that the school will remain true to its own basic principle. I wish I could live for another fifty years to try keeping the freedom flag unsoiled by the life haters and the bureaucrats. The minority is always right, said Ibsen. A half-truth maybe, but in the matter of freedom for children, I know that the majority is always wrong. Long after I am gone, the minority who believe in freedom will be muzzled and hated by that silent majority.

I am greatly encouraged by the fact that my books are read by millions in the U.S.A., in Germany, in Brazil, in Japan, in Israel, and in many other countries. I am gratified by my enormous mail from the young all over the Western world. Only when I sent the German translation of *Summerhill* to a friend in East Germany did it come back stamped *Verboten.*

I visualize the coming world with pessimism. Automation will give millions little or no work to do. The landscape will become more hideous as skyscrapers and neon signs increase; the beautiful countryside will be ruined by electric towers and highways. The handworker will almost certainly disappear. Poverty and homelessness will mark the world for a long time. Even today, the cost of a meal in London's West End far exceeds the weekly pension of the aged. It is a world of kitsch that gets more so every day. Ugliness grows. The dear old town of Frankfurt-am-Main is now a conglomeration of ugly blockhouses. The streets of New York and Washington are not safe after dark, and London is fast becoming a place of fear. Gangsterdom and violence seem to be replacing the crimes of the past.

The snag about optimism is that it can so easily become wishful thinking. Martin Luther King said he had a dream; but since his assassination, the race problem in the United States has become more sinister, more terrifying. Yet when I think of the crooks Summerhill had in its beginning, how freedom and approval changed antisocial boys and girls into good citizens, I feel a certain amount of optimism. I am convinced that if all children were free, crime would be reduced to a minimum. Not abolished perhaps, for a high percentage of criminals are deranged or, at least, subnormal. I like to think that the new generation challenging authority now will someday become the new Establishment. It is they, I hope, who will politically control the elections, even though I am sure that many a challenging youth of eighteen will be a conservative at fifty.

Barring wholesale destruction by nuclear bombs, I feel that life triumphs in the end, though one can argue that history is but the story of evolution from slavery to slums, from the stone age to the pollution age. In my youth, we proudly imagined that mankind had evolved from the primitive savage to homo sapiens, the honest, law-abiding citizen with his humane laws about people and animals. Then we were shocked to find that modern man could be as barbarous as the most savage tribes in history.

For many years, I have preached the gospel of original goodness, a belief strengthened by seeing hateful kids become loving kids when allowed to be free. And now, nearing the end of my long life, I ask questions I cannot answer. If we are born in sin, why are we not all criminals and torturers? Why is the criminal sector always a minority one? But, to be honest, I see the world with a jaundiced eye, for my early world had trees and flowers and comely village pleasures; it was not the vulgar world of today. Our village shoemaker made shoes, the blacksmith shod horses, the mason carved stones. The atmosphere was one of peace. True, there are peaceful villages today, but the cars whizz by, the supermarkets creep in, the young tend to seek life in the cities. My old world is dead, and the new one scares me.

We cannot put the clock back. Most of the young people of today accept this new world without thinking, without criticism. But I have spoken of the challengers among them. My great regret is that I cannot live to see how much these pioneers will triumph in their fight for life. If I were not a pagan, I'd say to them, "Bless you, my children." So I end with the

pious hope that the young will refuse to have Summerhill and
its message squashed by unbelievers.

IV

A PICTURE ALBUM

Mary Sutherland,
mother of A. S. Neill.

Reverse of
the above photograph.

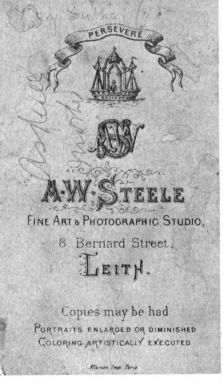

A. S. Neill at age three,
with his mother.

Neill at twenty-five.

Neill at fifty-three.

The Summerhill School
at Lyme Regis, Dorset
(1924-1927).

The Summerhill School
at Leiston.

Neill at fifty-four.

Neill with Miss Potter
at Johannesburg (1936).

Zoe.

Zoe and Neill, 1950.

Sketch of College Church
at St. Andrews
rendered by A. S. Neill
in 1912.

Canongate
Tolbooth

Sketch of Canongate Tolbooth,
Edinburgh,
rendered by A. S. Neill
in 1911.

354

Sketch of St. Andrews Cathedral
rendered by A. S. Neill in 1912.

Sketch of Summerhill School
rendered by A. S. Neill
in 1954

A. S. Neill, 1964.

A.S. Neill.

Isabel McWhirter 1966

Pen sketch
of A. S. Neill
by Ishbel McWhirter, 1966.

Painting of Neill
by Ishbel McWhirter, 1964.

Neill at wedding
of a former pupil.

Neill and Zoe
at Zoe's wedding, 1971.

Neill and Biscuit.

Neill, 1971.

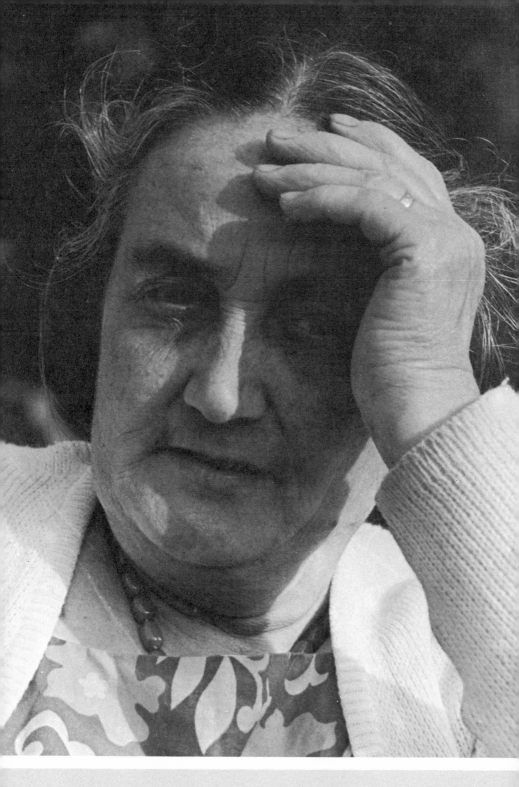

Ena.

Neill.

V

A DOMINIE'S LOG

When A. S. Neill taught school as a young man, the Scottish educational code forbade the entering of personal notes or opinions in the official teacher's logbook. To preserve his sanity, however, Neill began to keep a daily, unofficial record for his eyes only. In 1915, it was published in England as A Dominie's Log. *The following passages from this book foreshadow Neill's later educational theories, and indicate how well formulated they were so many years ago.*

I.

In my private log I shall write down my thoughts on education. I think they will be mostly original; there has been no real authority on education, and I do not know of any book from which I can crib.

To-night after my bairns had gone away, I sat down on a desk and thought, What does it all mean? What am I trying to do? These boys are going out to the field to plough; these girls are going to farms as servants. If I live long enough the new generation will be bringing notes of the plese-excuss-james-as-I-was-washing type . . . and the parents who will write them went out at that door five minutes ago. I can teach them to read, and they will read serials in the drivelling weeklies; I can teach them to write, and they will write pathetic notes to me by and by; I can teach them to count, and they will never count more than the miserable sum they receive as a weekly wage. The "Three R's" spell futility.

But what of the rest? Can I teach them drawing? I cannot. I can help a boy with a natural talent to improve his work, but of what avail is it? In their future homes they will hang up the same old prints—vile things given away with a pound of tea. I can teach them to sing, but what will they sing? The *Tipperary* of their day.

My work is hopeless, for education should aim at bringing up a new generation that will be better than the old. The present system is to produce the same kind of man as we see to-day. And how hopeless he is. When first I saw Houndsditch, I said aloud: "We have had education for generations . . . and yet we have this." Yes, my work is hopeless. What is the use of the Three R's, of Woodwork, of Drawing, of Geography, if Houndsditch is to remain? What is the use of anything? . . .

I am hopeful because I have found a solution. I shall

henceforth try to make my bairns realise. Yes, realise is the word. Realise what? To tell the truth, I have some difficulty in saying. I think I want to make them realise what life means. Yes, I want to give them, or rather help them to find an attitude. Most of the stuff I teach them will be forgotten in a year or two, but an attitude remains with one throughout life. I want these boys and girls to acquire the habit of looking honestly at life.

Ah! I wonder if I look honestly at life myself! Am I not a very one-sided man? Am I not a Socialist, a doubter, a heretic? Am I not biased when I judge men like the Cecils and the Harmsworths? I admit it. I am a partisan, and yet I try to look at life honestly. I try, and that is the main point. I do not think that I have any of the current superstitions about morality and religion and art. I try to forget names; I try to get at essentials, at truth. The fathers of my bairns are, I think, interested in names. I wonder how many of them have sat down saying: "I must examine myself, so that I may find out what manner of man I am." I hold that self-knowledge must come before all things. When one has stripped off all the conventions, and superstitions, and hypocrisies, then one is educated.

These bairns of mine will never know how to find truth; they will merely read the newspapers when they grow up. They will wave their hats to the King, but kingship will be but a word to them; they will shout when a lawyer from the south wins the local seat, but they will not understand the meaning of economics; they will dust their old silk hats and march to the sacrament, but they will not realise what religion means.

I find that I am becoming pessimistic again, and I did feel hopeful when I began to write. I *should* feel hopeful, for I am resolved to find another meaning in education. What was it? Ah, yes, I am to help them to find an attitude.

I have been thinking about discipline overnight. I have

seen a headmaster who insisted on what he called perfect discipline. His bairns sat still all day. A movement foreshadowed the strap. Every child jumped up at the word of command. He had a very quiet life.

I must confess that I am an atrociously bad disciplinarian. Today Violet Brown began to sing *Tipperary* to herself when I was marking the registers. I looked up and said: "Why the happiness this morning, Violet?" and she blushed and grinned. . . .

I find that normally I am very, very slack; I don't mind if they talk or not. Indeed, if the hum of conversation stops, I feel that something has happened and I invariably look towards the door to see whether an Inspector has arrived. . . .

The only discipline I ask for usually is the discipline that interest draws. If a boy whets his pencil while I am describing the events that led to the Great Rebellion, I sidetrack him on the topic of rabbits, and I generally make him sit up. I know that I am teaching badly if the class is loafing, and I am honest enough in my saner moments not to blame the bairns.

I do not like strict discipline, for I do believe that a child should have as much freedom as possible. I want a bairn to be human, and I try to be human myself. I walk to school each morning with my briar between my lips, and if the fill is not smoked, I stand and watch the boys play. I would kiss my wife in my classroom, but I do not have a wife. A wee lassie stopped me on the way to school this morning, and she pushed a very sticky sweetie into my hand. I took my pipe from my mouth and ate the sweetie—and I asked for another; she was highly delighted.

Discipline, to me, means a pose on the part of the teacher. It makes him very remote; it lends him dignity. Dignity is a thing I abominate. I suppose the bishop is dignified because he wants to show that there is a real difference between his salaried self and the underpaid curate. Why should I be dignified be-

fore my bairns? Will they scorn me if I slide with them?
(There was a dandy slide on the road to-day. I gave them half-
an-hour's extra play this morning, and I slid all the time. My
assistants are adept at the game.)

But discipline is necessary; there are men known as Inspectors. And Johnny must be flogged if he does not attend to
the lesson. He must know the rivers of Russia. After all, why
should he? I don't know them, and I don't miss the knowledge.
I couldn't tell you the capital of New Zealand . . . is it
Wellington? or Auckland? I don't know; all I know is that I
could find out if I wanted to.

I do not blame Inspectors. Some of them are men with
what I would call a vision. I had the Chief Inspector of the
district in the other day, and I enjoyed his visit. He has a fine
taste in poetry, and a sense of humour.

The Scotch Education Department is iniquitous because it
is a department; a department cannot have a sense of humour.
And it is humour that makes a man decent and kind and human.

If the Scotch Education Department were to die suddenly,
I should suddenly become a worse disciplinarian than I am now.
If Willie did not like Woodwork, I should say to him: "All
right, Willie. Go and do what you do like, but take my advice
and do some work; you will enjoy your football all the better
for it."

I believe in discipline, but it is self-discipline that I believe in. I think I can say that I never learned anything by
being forced to learn it, but I may be wrong. I was forced to
learn the Shorter Catechism, and to-day I hate the sight of it.
I read the other day in Barrie's *Sentimental Tommy* that its
meaning comes to one long afterwards and at a time when one
is most in need of it. I confess that the time has not come for
me; it will never come, for I don't remember two lines of the
Catechism.

It is a fallacy that the nastiest medicines are the most efficacious; Epsom Salts is not more beneficial than Syrup of Figs.

A thought! If I believe in self-discipline, why not persuade Willie that Woodwork is good for him as a self-discipline? Because it isn't my job. If Willie dislikes chisels he will always dislike them. What I might do is this; tell him to persevere with his chisels so that he might cut himself badly. Then he might discover that his true vocation is bandaging, and straightway go in for medicine.

Would Willie run away and play at horses if I told him to do what he liked best? I do not think so. He likes school, and I think he likes me. I think he would try to please me if he could.

When I speak kindly to a bairn I sometimes ask myself what I mean (for I try to find out my motives). Do I want the child to think kindly of me? Do I try to be popular? Am I after the delightful joy of being loved? Am I merely being humanly brotherly and kind?

I have tried to analyse my motives, and I really think that there is a little of each motive. I want to be loved; I want the bairn to think kindly of me. But in the main I think that my chief desire is to make the bairn happy. No man, no woman, has the right to make the skies cloudy for a bairn; it is the sin against the Holy Ghost.

I once had an experience in teaching. A boy was dour and unlovable and rebellious and disobedient. I tried all ways—I regret to say I tried the tawse. I was inexperienced at the time; yet I hit upon the right way. One day I found he had a decided talent for drawing. I brought down some of my pen-and-ink sketches and showed him them. I gave him pictures to copy, and his interest in art grew. I won him over by interesting myself in him. He discovered that I was only human after all.

I see the fingers of my tawse hanging out of my desk.

They seem to be two accusing fingers. My ideals are all right, but—I whacked Tom Wilkie to-night. At three o'clock he bled Dave Tosh's nose, and because Dave was the smaller, I whacked Tom. Yet I did not feel angry; I regret to say that I whacked Tom because I could see that Dave expected me to do it, and I hate to disappoint a bairn. If Dave had been Tom's size, I know that I should have ignored their battle.

I have not used the strap all this week, and if my liver keeps well, I hope to abolish it altogether.

To-day I have been thinking about punishment. What is the idea of punishment? A few months ago a poor devil of an engine-driver ran his express into a goods [freight train], and half-a-dozen people were killed. He got nine months. Why? Is his punishment meant to act as a deterrent? Will another driver say to himself: "By Jove, I'd better not wreck my train or I'll get nine months." Nine months is not punishment; but the lifelong thought: "I did it," is hell.

I am trying to think why I punished Lizzie Smith for talking last Friday. Bad habit, I expect. Yet it acted as a deterrent; it showed that I was in earnest about what I was saying—I was reading the war news from the *Scotsman.*

I am sorry that I punished her; it was weakness on my part, weakness and irritation. If she had no interest in the war, why should she pretend that she had? But no, I cannot have this. I must inculcate the idea of a community; the bairn must be told that others have rights. I often want to rise up and contradict the minister in kirk, but I don't. The people have rights; they do not come out to listen to me. If I offend against the community, the community will punish me with ostracism or bitterness. We have all a right to live our own lives, but in living them we must live in harmony with the community. Lizzie must be told that all the others like the war news, and that in talking she is annoying them. Yes, I must remember to emphasise continually the idea of a corporate life.

I see that it is only the weak man who requires a strap. Lord Kitchener could rule my school without a strap, but I am not Kitchener. Moreover, I am glad I'm not. I do not want to be what is called a strong man.

II.

. . . I have discovered a girl with a sense of humour. I asked my Qualifying Class to draw a graph of the attendance at a village kirk. "And you must explain away any rise or fall," I said.

Margaret Steel had a huge drop one Sunday, and her explanation was "Special Collection for Missions." Next Sunday the congregation was abnormally large; Margaret wrote "Change of Minister."

Few bairns have a sense of humour; theirs is a sense of fun. Make a noise like a duck and they will scream, but tell them your best joke and they will be bored to tears.

I try hard to cultivate their sense of humour and their imagination. In their composition I give them many autobiographies—a tile hat, a penny, an old boot, a nose, a tooth. To-day I asked them to describe in the first person a snail's journey to the end of the road. Margaret Steel talked of her hundred-mile crawl, and she noted the tall forests on each side of the road. "The grass would be trees to a snail," she explained.

Poor Margaret! When she is fourteen she will go out to the fields, and in three years she will be an ignorant country bumpkin. Our education system is futile because it does not go far enough. The State should see to it that each child has the best of chances. Margaret should be sent to a Secondary School and to a University free of charge. Her food and clothes and books and train fares should be free by right. The lassie has brains—and that is argument enough.

Our rulers do realize to a slight extent the responsibility of the community to the child. It sends a doctor round to look at Margaret's teeth; it may feed her at school if she is starving; it compels her to go to school till she is fourteen. At the age of fourteen she is free to go to the devil—the factory or the herding.

But suppose she did go to a Secondary School. What then? Possibly she would become a Junior Student or a University Student. She would learn much, but would she think? I found that thinking was not encouraged at the university. . . .

Is it possible that I am overdoing the imagination business? Shall I produce men and women with more imagination than intellect? No, I do not think there is danger. The nation suffers from lack of imagination; few of us can imagine a better state of society, a fuller life.

Who are the men with great imagination? Shelley, Blake, Browning, Nietzsche, Ibsen, Tolstoi. These men were not content with life as it was; they had ideals, and ideals are creatures of the imagination.

I once saw a book by, I think, Arnold Forster; a book that was meant to teach children the meaning of citizenship. If I remember aright it dealt with parliament and law, and local government.

Who was Arnold Forster? Why cannot our bairns have the best? Why tell them all the stale lies about democracy, the freedom of the individual, the justice of our laws? Are Forster's ideas of citizenship as great as the ideas of Plato, of More, of Morris, of Wells? I intend to make an abridgement of Plato's *Republic*, More's *Utopia*, William Morris's *News from Nowhere*, Bacon's *A New Atlantis*, H. G. Wells' *A Modern Utopia*, and *New Worlds for Old*.

Arnold Forster was with the majority. Nearly every day

I quote to my bairns Ibsen's words from *An Enemy of the People*—"The Majority *never* has right on its side. *Never* I say." Every lesson book shouts aloud the words: "The majority is always right."

Do I teach my bairns Socialism? I do not think so. Socialism means the owning of a State by the people of that State, and this State is not fit to own anything. For at present the State means the majority in Parliament, and that is composed of mediocre men. A State that takes up Home Rule while the slums of the East End exist is a State run by office boys for office boys . . . to adapt Salisbury's description of a London daily. We could not have Socialism to-day; the nation is not ripe for it.

The Germans used to drink to "The Day"; every teacher in Britain should drink daily to "The Day" when there shall be no poor, when factory lasses will not rise at five and work till six. I know that I shall never see the day, but I shall tell my bairns that it is coming. I know that most of the seed will fall on stony ground, but a sower can but sow.

I am determined to tear all the rags of hypocrisy from the facts of life; I shall lead my bairns to doubt everything. I told how most medicines cost half a farthing to make, and I explained that the manufacturer was spending a good part of the shilling profit in advertising. Then I told of the utter waste of material and energy in advertising, and went on to thunder against the hideous yellow tyre signs on the roadside. . . . Yet I want them to believe in Peter Pan, or is it that I want them to believe in the beauty of beautiful stories? I want them to love the alluring lady Romance, but I think I want them to love her in the knowledge that she is only a Dream Child. Romance means more to the realist than to the romanticist.

I wish I were a musician. If I could play the piano I

should spend each Friday afternoon playing to my bairns. I should give them "Alexander's Ragtime Band" and "Hitchy Coo"; then I should play them a Liszt Rhapsody and a Chopin waltz. Would they understand and appreciate? Who knows what raptures great music might bring to a country child? . . .

III.

I have often wondered at the strain of cruelty that is so often found in boys. The evolutionists must be right: the young always tend to resemble their remote ancestors. In a boy there is much of the brute. I have seen a boy cut off the heads of a nest of young sparrows; I wanted to hit him . . . but he was bigger than I. This morning I was bigger than Peter; hence I do not take any credit to myself for welting him.

I can see that cruelty does not disappear with youth. I confess to a feeling of unholy joy in leathering Peter, but I think that it was caused by a real indignation.

What made Peter hurt the poor wee thing I cannot tell. I am inclined to think that he acted subconsciously; he was being the elemental hunter, and he did not realise that he was giving pain. I ought to have talked to him, to have made him realise. But I became elemental also; I punished with no definite motive . . . and I would do it again.

We have had a return of wintry weather, and the bairns had a glorious slide made on the road this morning. At dinner-time I found them loafing around the door.

"Why aren't you sliding?" I asked. They explained that the village policeman had salted the slide. After marking the registers I took up the theme.

"Why did he salt the slide?" I asked.

"Because the farmers do not want their horses to fall,"

said one.

Then I took them to laws and their makers. "Children have no votes," I said, "farmers have; hence the law is with the farmers. Women have no votes and the law gives them half the salary of a man."

"But," said Margaret Steel, "would you have horses break their legs?" I smiled.

"No," I said, "and I would not object to the policeman's salting the slide if the law was thinking of animals' pain. The law and the farmers are thinking of property.

"Property in Britain comes before everything. I may steal the life and soul from a woman if I employ her at a penny an hour, and I may get a title for doing so. But if I steal Mr. Thomson's turnips I merely get ten days' hard."

"You bairns should draw up a Declaration of Rights," I added, and I think that a few understood my meaning.

I find that my bairns have a genuine love for poetry. To-day I read them Tennyson's *Lady of Shalott;* then I read them *The May Queen.* I asked them which was the better, and most of them preferred *The Lady of Shalott.* I asked for reasons, and Margaret Steel said that the one was strange and mysterious, while the other told of an ordinary death-bed. The whole class seemed to be delighted when I called *The May Queen* a silly mawkish piece of sentimentality. . . .

I have made them learn many pieces from Stevenson's *A Child's Garden of Verses,* and they love the rhythm of such pieces as *The Shadow March.*

Another poem that they love is *Helen of Kirkconnell;* I asked which stanza was the best, and they all agreed on this beautifully simple one:—

> O Helen fair, beyond compare,
> I'll mak a garland o' thy hair;
> Shall bind my heart for evermair,
> Until the day I dee,

I believe in reading out a long poem and then asking them to memorise a few verses. I did this with *The Ancient Mariner.* Long poems are an abomination to children; to ask them to commit to memory a piece like Gray's *Elegy* is unkind.

I have given them the first verse of Francis Thompson's *The Hound of Heaven.* I did not expect them to understand a word of it; my idea was to test their power of appreciating sound. Great music might convey something to rustics, but great poetry cannot convey much. Still, I try to lead them to the greater poetry. I wrote on the board a verse of *Little Jim* and a verse of *La Belle Dame sans Merci,* and I think I managed to give them an inkling of what is good and what is bad verse.

I begin to think that country children should learn ballads. There is a beauty about the old ballads that even children can catch; it is the beauty of a sweet simplicity. When I think of the orchestration of Swinburne, I think of the music of the ballads as of a flute playing. And I know that orchestration would be lost on country folk.

I hate the poems that crowd the average school-book— *Little Jim, We are Seven, Lucy Gray, The Wreck of the Hesperus, The Boy stood on the Burning Deck,* and all the rest of them. I want to select the best of the Cavalier lyricists' works . . . the lyrics from the Elizabethan dramatists. I want to look through moderns like William Watson, Robert Bridges, George Meredith, Thomas Hardy, Henley, Dowson, Abercrombie, William Wilfred Gibson—there must be many charming pieces that bairns would enjoy.

I think that the teaching of history in schools is all wrong. I look through a school-history, and I find that emphasis is laid on incident. Of what earthly use is the information given about Henry VIII's matrimonial vagaries? Does it matter a rap to anyone whether Henry I—or was it Henry II?—ever smiled again or not? By all means let us tell the younger children tales of wicked dukes, but older children ought to be led to think out the meaning of history. The usual school-history is a piece of snobbery; it can't keep away from the topic of kings and queens. They don't matter; history should tell the story of the people and their gradual progress from serfdom to—sweating.

I believe that a boy of eleven can grasp cause and effect. With a little effort he can understand the non-sentimental side of the Mary Stuart-Elizabeth story, the result to Scotland of the Franco-Scottish alliance. He can understand why Philip of Spain, a Roman Catholic, preferred that the Protestant Elizabeth should be Queen of England rather than the Catholic Mary Stuart.

The histories never make bairns think. I have not seen one that mentioned that Magna Charta was signed because all classes in the country happened to be united for the moment. I have not seen one that points out that the main feature in Scots history is the lack of a strong central government. . . .

Again, the school-histories almost always give a wrong impression of men and events. Every Scots schoolboy thinks that Edward I of England was a sort of thief and bully rolled into one, and that the carpet-bagger, Robert Bruce, was a saint from heaven. Edward's greatness as a lawgiver is ignored; at least we ought to give him credit for his statesmanship in making an attempt to unite England, Scotland, and Wales. . . .

I expect that the school-histories of the future will talk of the "scrap of paper" aspect of the present war, and they will anathematise the Kaiser. But the real historians will be searching for deeper causes; they will be analysing the national characteristics, the economical needs, the diplomatic methods, of the nations.

The school-histories will say: "The war came about because the Kaiser wanted to be master of Europe, and the German people had no say in the matter at all."

The historians will say—well, I'm afraid I don't know;

but I think they will relegate the Kaiser to a foot-note. . . .

I find that I am much more interested in humanity than in materials, and I know that the bairns are like me in this.

A West African came to the school the other day, and asked me to allow him to tell (for a consideration) the story of his home life. When I discovered that he did not mean his own private home life I gladly gave him permission. He talked for half-an-hour about the habits of his home, the native schools, the dress of the children (I almost blushed at this part, but I was relieved to find that they do dress after all); then he sang the native version of "Mary had a little Lamb" (great applause). The lecture was first-rate. . . .

IV.

A Junior Inspector called today. His subject was handwriting, and he had theories on the subject. So have I. We had an interesting talk. His view is that handwriting is a practi-- cal science; hence we must teach a child to write in such a way as to carry off the job he applies for when he is fourteen.

My view is that handwriting is an art, like sketching. My view is the better, for it includes his. I am a superior penman to him, and in a contest I could easily beat him. I really failed to see what he was worrying his head about. What does the style matter? It is the art that one puts into a style that makes writing good. . . .

My objection to men and women is that they are too practical. I used to see a notice in Edinburgh: "John Brown, Practical Chimney Sweep." I often used to wonder what a theoretical chimney sweep might be, and I often wished I could meet one. My view is that a teacher should turn out theoretical sweeps, railwaymen, ploughmen, servants. Heaven knows they will get the practical part knocked into them soon enough.

I have been experimenting with Drawing. I have been a passable black-and-white artist for many years, and the subject fascinates me. I see that drawing is of less importance than taste, and I find that I can get infants who cannot draw a line to make artistic pictures.

I commence with far-away objects—a clump of trees on the horizon. The child takes a BB pencil and blocks in the mass of trees. The result is a better picture than the calendar prints the bairns see at home.

Gradually I take nearer objects, and at length I reach what is called drawing. I ignore all vases and cubes and ellipses; my model is a school-bag or a cloak. The drawing does not matter very much; but I want to see the shadows stand out. I find that only a few in a class ever improve in sketching; one is born with the gift.

Designing fascinates many bairns. I asked them to design a kirk window on squared paper to-day. Some of the attempts were good. I got the boys to finish off with red ink, and then I pasted up the designs on the wall.

I seem to recollect an Inspector who told me to give up design a good few years ago. I wouldn't give it up now for anyone. It is a delightful study, and it will bring out an inherent good taste better than any branch of drawing I know. Drawing (or rather, Sketching) to me means an art, not a means to cultivating observation. It belongs solely to Aesthetics. Sketching, Music, and Poetry are surely intended to make a bairn realise the fuller life that must have beauty always with it.

I showed my bairns two sketches of my own to-day—the Tollbooth and the Whitehorse Close in Edinburgh. A few claimed that the Whitehorse Close was the better, because it left more out. "It leaves something to the imagination," said Tom Dixon.

When will some original publisher give us a decent school Reader? I have not seen one that is worth using. Some of them give excerpts from Dickens and Fielding and Borrow (that horrid bore) and Hawthorne (another). I cannot find any interest in these excerpts; they have no beginning and no end. Moreover, a bairn does like the dramatic; prosiness deadens its wee soul at once.

I want to see a Reader especially written for bairns. I want to see many complete stories, filled with bright dialogue. Every yarn should commence with dialogue. I always think kindly of the late Guy Boothby, because he usually began with, "Hands up, or I fire!" or a kindred sentence.

I wish I could lay hands on a Century Reader I used as a boy. It was full of the dramatic. The first story was one about the Burning of Moscow, then came the tale of Captain Dodds and the pirate (from Reade's novel, *Hard Cash,* I admit. An excerpt need not be uninteresting), then a long passage from *The Deerslayer* . . . with a picture of Indians throwing tomahawks at the hero. I loved that book.

Teaching depends on logic. Now Spelling throws logic to the winds. I tell a child that "cough" is "coff," and logic leads him to suppose that rough is "roff" and "through" is "throff." If I tell him that spelling is important because it shows whence a word is derived, I am bound in honesty to tell him that a matinee is not a "morning performance," that manufactured goods are not "made by hand." Hence I leave Spelling alone.

At school I "learned" Spelling, and I could not spell a word until I commenced to read much. Spelling is of the eye mainly. Every boy can spell "truly" and "obliged" when he leaves school, but ten years later he will probably write "truely" and "oblidged." Why? I think that the explanation lies in the fact that he does not read as a growing youth. Anyway, dictionaries are cheap.

To-night I sat down on a desk and lit my pipe. Margaret

Steel and Lizzie Buchan were tidying up the room. Margaret looked at me thoughtfully for a second.

"Please, sir, why do you smoke?" she said.

"I really don't know, Margaret," I said. "Bad habit, I suppose—just like writing notes to boys."

She suddenly became feverishly anxious to pick up the stray papers.

"I wonder," I mused, "whether they do it in the same old way. How do they do it, Margaret?" She dived after a piece of paper.

"I used to write them myself," I said. Margaret looked up quickly.

"You!" she gasped.

"I am not so old," I said hastily.

"Please, sir, I didn't mean that," she explained in confusion.

"You did, you wee bissom," I chuckled.

"Please, sir," she said awkwardly, "why—why are you not —not m—married?" I rose and took up my hat.

"I once kissed a girl behind the school door, Margaret," I said absently. She did not understand—and when I come to think of it I am not surprised.

To-day was prize-giving day. Old Mr. Simpson made a speech.

"Boys," he said, "study hard and you'll maybe be a minister like Mr. Gordon there." He paused. "Or," he continued, "if you don't manage that, you may become a teacher like Mr. Neill here."

Otherwise the affair was very pathetic: the medallist, a girl, had already left school and was hired as a servant on a farm. And old Mr. Simpson did not know it; I thought it better not to tell the kindly soul. He spoke earnestly on success in life.

I hate prizes. To-day, Violet Brown and Margaret Steel, usually the best of friends, are looking daggers at each other. Tomorrow I shall read them the story of the Judgment of Paris. . . .

V.

The more I see of it the more I admire the co-education system. To me it is delightful to see boys and girls playing together. Segregate boys and you destroy their perspective. I used to find at the university that it was generally the English Public School Boy who set up one standard of morals for his sisters and another for the shop-girls.

Co-education is the greatest thing in our State educational system. The bairns learn early the interdependence of the sexes; boys and girls begin early to understand each other. All danger of putting women on a pedestal is taken away; the boys find that the girls are ordinary humans with many failings ("Aw'll tell the mester!"), and many virtues. The girls find that boys— well, I don't exactly know what the girls find.

Seldom is there any over-familiarity. The girls have a natural protective aloofness that awes the boys; the boys generally have strenuous interests that lead them to ignore the girls for long periods. At present the sexes are very friendly, for love-making (always a holy thing with bairns), has come with spring; but in a few weeks the boys will be playing football or "bools," and they will not be seen in the girls' playground.

I can detect no striving after what is called chivalry (thank heaven!) If Maggie and Willie both lay hands on a ruler, they fight it out, but Maggie generally gets it; she can say more. Mr. Henpeck begins life as a chick. I hate the popular idea of chivalry, and I want my boys to hate it. Chivalry to me means rising in the Tube to offer a typist your seat, and then going off to the city to boss a score of waitresses who are paid 6s. a week. As a nation we have no chivalry; we have only etiquette. We hold doors open for nice women, and we tamely suffer or forget about a society that condemns poor women to slave for sixteen hours a day sewing shirts at a penny an hour. We say "Thank you" when the lady of the house stops playing, and we banish the prostitutes of Piccadilly from our minds. Chivalry has been dead for a long time now.

I want to substitute kindness for the word chivalry. I want to tell my bairns that the only sin in the world is cruelty. I do not preach morality for I hardly know what morality is. I have no morals, I am an a-moralist, or should it be a non-moralist? I judge not, and I mean to school my bairns into judging not. Yet I am not being quite consistent. I do judge cruelty and uncharitableness; but I judge not those who do not act up to the accustomed code of morals. A code is always a temptation to a healthy person; it is like a window by a railway siding: it cries out: "Chuck a chunk of coal through me." Codes never make people moral; they merely make them hypocritical. I include the Scotch code.

Until lately I thought that drill was unnecessary for rural bairns. It was the chief inspector of the district who converted me. He pointed out that country children are clumsy and slack. "A countryman can heave a sack of potatoes on his back," he said, "but he has no agility, no grace of movement."

I agree with him now. I find that drill makes my bairns more graceful. But I am far from being pleased with any system that I know. I don't really care tuppence whether they are physically alert or not, but I want them to be graceful, if only from an artistic point of view. The system I really want to know is Eurythmics. . . . The system is drill combined with music. The pupils walk and dance, and I expect, sit to music. . . .

Grace is almost totally absent from rural dances. The

ploughman takes off his jacket, and sweats his roaring way through "The Flowers o' Edinburgh"; but the waltz has no attraction for him. Waltzing is a necessity in a rural scheme of education—and, incidentally, in a Mayfair scheme of education, now that the "Bunny Hug" and the "Turkey Trot" and the "Tango" have come to these isles.

Robert Campbell left the school to-day. He had reached the age limit. He begins work tomorrow morning as a ploughman. . . . Pessimism has hold of me to-night. I have tried to give Robert an ideal. Tomorrow he will be gathered to his fathers. He will take up the attitude of his neighbours: he will go to church, he will vote Radical or Tory, he will elect a farmer to the School Board, he will marry and live in a hovel. His master said to me recently: "Bairns are gettin' ower muckle eddication noo-a-days. What eddication does a laddie need to herd kye?" Yes, I am as pessimistic as any Schopenhauer to-night, I cannot see the sun.

My pessimism has remained with me all day. I feel that I am merely pouring water into a sieve. I almost feel that to meddle with education is to begin at the wrong end. I may have an ideal, but I cannot carry it out because I am up against all the forces of society. Robert Campbell is damned, not because education is so very wrong, but because education is trying to adapt itself to commerce and economics and convention. I think I am right in holding that our Individualist, as opposed to a Socialist, system is to blame. "Every man for himself" is the most cursed saying that was ever said. If we are to allow an idle rich to waste millions yearly, if we are to allow profiteers to amass thousands at the expense of the slaving majority, what chance has poor Robert Campbell? I complete the saying—"and the Deil tak the henmost." Robert is the henmost.

O! the people are poor things. Democracy is the last futility. Yet I should not blame the people; they never get a chance. Our rulers are on the side of the profiteers, and the latter take very good care that Robert Campbell shall leave school when he is fourteen. It isn't that they want more cheap labour; they are afraid that if he is educated until he is nineteen he will be wise enough to say: "Why should I, a man made in the image of God, be forced to slave for gains that you will steal?"

Yet, the only way is to labour on, to strive to convey some idea of my ideal to my bairns. If every teacher in Scotland had the same ideal as I have, I think that the fight would not be a long one. But how do I know that my ideal is the right one? I cannot say; I just *know*. Which, I admit, is a woman's reason.

I was re-reading *An Enemy of the People* last night, and the thought suddenly came to me: "Would my bairns understand it?" This morning I cut out Bible instruction and read them the first act. I then questioned them, and found to my delight that they had grasped the theme. It was peculiarly satisfying to me to find that they recognized Dr. Stockmann as a better man than his grovelling brother Peter. If my bairns could realise the full significance of Ibsen's play, "The Day" would not be so far off as I am in the habit of thinking it is.

I must re-read Shaw's *Widowers' Houses;* I fancy that children might find much thought in it. It is one of his "Unpleasant Plays," but I see no reason for keeping the unlovely things from bairns. I do not believe in frightening them with tales of murder and ghosts. . . . I want to direct this innate desire for gruesome things to the realising of the most gruesome things in the world—the grinding of soul and body in order to gain profits, the misery of poverty and cold, the weariness of toil. If our press really wants to make its readers shudder, why does it not publish long accounts of infant mortality in the slums, of gin-fed bairns, of back-doors used as fuel, of phthisical girls straining their eyes over seams? I know why the press ignores these things, the public does not want to think of them. If the public wanted such stories, every capital-ist owner of a newspaper would supply them—grudgingly, but with a stern resolve to get dividends. To-day the papers are mostly run for the rich and their parasites. The only way in which 'Enery Smith can get his photograph into the papers is by jumping on Mrs. 'Enery Smith until she expires. I wonder that no criminologist has tried to prove that publicity is the greatest incentive to crime.

When I read the daily papers to my bairns I try to tell them what is left out. "Humour at Bow Street," a heading will run. Ye Gods! Humour! I have as much humour as most men, but if anyone can find humour in the stupid remarks of a law-giver he must be a W. W. Jacobs, a Mark Twain, a George A. Birmingham, and a Stephen Leacock rolled into one . . . with the Devil thrown in. Humour at Bow Street. I have been there. I have seen the poor Magdalenes and the pitiable Laza-ruses shuffle in with terror in their eyes. I have seen the in-flexible mighty law condemn them to the cells, I have heard their piteous cries for mercy. And the newspapers talk of the humour of the courts.

I once read that law's primary object is to protect the rich from the poor. The appalling truth of that saying dawned on me in Bow Street. Humour! Yes, there is humour in Bow Street. The grimmest, ugliest joke in the world is this—Covent Gar-den Opera House stands across the street from the court. . . .

VI.

This morning I had a note from a farmer in the neighbourhood.

"DEAR SIR,—I send my son Andrew to get education at the school not Radical politics. . . ."

I called Andrew out.

"Andrew," I said, with a smile, "when you go home to-night tell your father that I hate Radicalism possibly more than he does."

The father came down to-night to apologise. "Aw thocht ye was ane o' they wheezin' Radicals," he explained. Then he added, "And what micht yer politics be?"

"I am a Utopian," I said modestly.

He scratched his head for a moment, then he gave it up and asked my opinion of the weather. We discussed turnips for half-an-hour, at the end of which time I am sure he was wondering how an M.A. could be such an ignoramus. We parted on friendly terms.

I do not think that I have any definite views on the teaching of religion to bairns; indeed, I have the vaguest notion of what religion means. I am just enough of a Nietzschean to protest against teaching children to be meek and lowly. I once shocked a dear old lady by saying that the part of the Bible that appealed to me most was that in which the Pharisee said: "I thank God that I am not as other men." I was young then, I have not the courage to say it now.

I do, however, hold strongly that teaching religion is not my job. The parish minister and the U.F. minister get good stipends for tending their flocks, and I do not see any reason in the world why I should have to look after the lambs. For one thing I am not capable. All I aim at is teaching bairns how to live—possibly that is the true religion; my early training prevents my getting rid of the idea that religion is intended to teach people how to die.

To-day I was talking about the probable formation of the

earth, how it was a ball of flaming gas like the sun, how it cooled gradually, how life came. A girl looked up and said: "Please, sir, what about the Bible?" I explained that in my opinion the creation story was a story told to children, to a people who were children in understanding. [Yet] I pointed out a strange feature, discovered to me by the parish minister, that the first chapter of Genesis follows the order of scientific evolution—the earth is without form, life rises from the sea, then come the birds, then the mammals.

But I am forced to give religious instruction. I confine my efforts to the four gospels; the bairns read them aloud. I seldom make any comment on the passages.

In geography lessons I often take occasion to emphasise the fact that Muhammudans and Buddhists are not necessarily stupid folk who know no better. I cannot lead bairns to a religion, but I can prevent their being stupidly narrow.

No, I fear I have no definite opinions on religion.

I set out to enter the church, but I think that I could not have stayed in it. I fancy that one fine Sunday morning I would have stood up in the pulpit and said: "Friends, I am no follower of Christ. I like fine linen and tobacco, books and comfort. I should be in the slums, but I am not Christlike enough to go there. Goodbye."

I wonder! Why then do I not stand up and say to the School Board: "I do not believe in this system of education at all. I am a hypocrite when I teach subjects that I abominate. Give me my month's screw. Goodbye." I sigh—yet I like to fancy that I could not have stayed in the kirk. One thing I am sure of: a big stipend would not have tempted me to stay. I have no wish for money; at least, I wouldn't go out of my way to get it. I wouldn't edit a popular newspaper for ten thousand a year. Of that I am sure. Quite sure. Quite.

Yet I once applied for a job on a Tory daily. I was hungry then. What if I were hungry now? The flesh is weak—but, I could always go out on tramp. I more than half long for the temptation. Then I should discover whether I am an idealist or a talker. Possibly I am a little of both.

I began to write about religion, and I find myself talking about myself. Can it be that my god is my ego?

I began these log-notes in order to discover my philosophy of education, and I find that I am discovering myself. This discovery of self must come first. Personality goes far in teaching. May it go too far? Is it possible that I am a danger to these bairns? May I not be influencing them too much? I do not think so. Anything I may say will surely be negatived at home; my word, unfortunately, is not so weighty as father's.

In what is called Spelling Reform we cannot have a revolution; all we can hope for is a reform within Spelling, a reform that will abolish existing anomalies. So in education we cannot have a revolution. All we can hope for is a reform wrought within education by the teacher. If every teacher were a sort of Wellsian-Shavian-Nietzschean-Webbian fellow, the children would be directly under two potent influences—the parents and teachers.

"What is Truth?" millions of Pilates have asked. It is because we have no standard of Truth that our education is a failure. Each of us gets hold of a corner of the page of Truth, but the trouble is that so many grasp the same corner. It is a corner dirty with thumb-marks . . . "Humour in Bow Street," "Knighthood for Tooting Philanthropist," "Dastardly Act by Leeds Strikers," "Special Service of Praise in the Parish Kirk" . . . marks do not obliterate the page. My corner is free from thumb-marks, and anyone can read the clear type of "Christlessness in Bow Street," "Jobbery in the Sale of Honours," "Murder of Starving Strikers," "Thanksgiving Service for the Blessing of Whitechapel"—but few will read this corner's story; the majority likes the filthy corner with the beautiful news.

I have discovered my mission. I am the apostle of the clean corner with the dirty news written on it.

I began to read the second act of *An Enemy of the People* this morning, but I had to give it up; the bairns had lost interest. I closed the book. "Suppose," I said, "suppose that this village suddenly became famous as a health-resort. People would build houses and hotels, your fathers would grow richer; and suppose that the doctor discovered that the water supply was poisonous, that the pipes lay through a swamp where fever germs were. What would the men who had built hotels and houses say about the doctor? What would they do about the water supply?"

The unanimous opinion was that the waterpipes would be relaid; the people would not want visitors to come and take fever.

This opinion leads me to conclude that bairns are idealists; childhood takes the Christian view. Barrie says that genius is the power of being a boy again at will; I agree, but Barrie and I are possibly thinking of different aspects. Ibsen was a genius because he became as a little child. Dr. Stockmann (Ibsen) is a simple child; he cannot realise that self-interest can make his own brother a criminal to society.

I told my bairns what the men in the play did.

"But," said one in amazement, "they would not do that in real life?"

"They are doing it every day," I said. "This school is old, badly ventilated, overcrowded. It is a danger to your health and mine. Yet, if I asked for a new school, the whole village would rise up against me. 'More money on the rates!' they would cry, and they would treat me very much as the people in the play treated Dr. Stockmann."

I find it difficult to discuss the causes of the war with the bairns. I refuse to accept the usual tags about going to the assistance of a weak neighbour whom we agreed to protect. We all want to think that we are fighting for Belgium but are we?

I look to Mexico and I find it has been bathed in blood because the American Oil Kings and the British Oil Kings were at war. President Diaz was pro-English, Madero was pro-American, Huerta was pro-English . . . and the United States supported the notorious Villa. Villa's rival, Carranzo, was pro-English. [Pershing's expedition against Villa occurred after President Wilson recognized Carranzo, and Villa turned his wrath on U.S. citizens.] It is an accepted belief that the American Oil Kings financed the first risings in order to drive the British oil interests out of the country. Hence, widows and orphans in Mexico are the victims of a dollar massacre.

Can we trace the present war to the financiers? It is said that the Triple Entente is the result of Russia's receiving loans from France and Britain.

I cannot find a solution. I am inclined to attach little value to what is called national feeling. The workers are the masses, and I cannot imagine a German navvy's having any hatred of a British navvy. A world of workers would not fight, but at present the workers are so badly organised that they fight at the bidding of kings and diplomats and financiers. War comes from the classes above, and by means of their press the upper classes convert the proletariat to their way of thinking.

A more important subject is that of the ending of wars. The idealistic vapourings of the I.L.P. [International Labor Party] with its silly talk of internationalism will do nothing to stop war. Norman Angell's cry that war doesn't pay will not stop war. But a true democracy in each country will stop it. I think of Russia with all its darkness and cruelty, and I am appalled; a true democracy there will be centuries in coming.

For Germany I do not fear; out of her militarism will surely arise a great democratic nation. And out of our own great trial a true democracy is arising. Capitalism has failed; the State now sees that it must control the railways and engineering shops in a crisis.

VII.

To-day I have scrapped somebody's Rural Arithmetic. It is full of sums of the How-much-will-it-take-to-paper-a-room? type. This cursed utilitarianism in education riles me. Who wants to know what it will take to paper a room? Personally I should call in the painter, and take my meals on the parlour piano for a day or two. Anyway, why this suspicion of the poor painter? Is he worse than other tradesmen? If we must have a utilitarian arithmetic then I want to see a book that will tell me if the watchmaker is a liar when he tells me that the mainspring of my watch is broken. I want to see sums like this: How long will a plumber take to lay a ten foot pipe if Father can do it at the rate of a yard in three minutes? (Answer, three days.)

To me Arithmetic is an art not a science. I do not know a single rule; I must always go back to first principles. I love catch questions, questions that will make a bairn think all the time. Inspectors' Tests give but little scope for the Art of Arithmetic; they are usually poor peddling things that smell strongly of materialism. In other words, they appeal to the mechanical part of a bairn's brain instead of to the imagination. I want to see a test that will include a sum like this:—$23.4 \times .065 \times 54.678 \times 0$. The cram will start in to multiply out; the imaginative bairn will glance along and see the nought, and will at once spot that the answer is zero. . . .

I have been re-reading Shaw's remarks on Sex in Education. I cannot see that he has anything very illuminating to say on the subject; for that matter no one has. Most of us realise that something is wrong with our views on sex. The present attitude of education is to ignore sex, and the result is that sex remains a conspiracy of silence. The ideal some of us have is to raise sex to its proper position as a wondrous beautiful thing. To-day we try to convey to bairns that birth is a disgrace to humanity.

The problem before me comes to this: How can I bring my bairns to take a rational elemental view of sex instead of a conventional hypocritical one? How can I convey to them the realisation that our virtue is mostly cowardice, that our sex morality is founded on mere respectability? (It is the easiest thing in the world to be virtuous in Padanarum; it is not so easy to be a saint in Oxford Street. Not because Oxford Street has more temptation, but because nobody knows you there.)

In reality I can do nothing. If I mentioned sex in school I should be dismissed at once. But if a philanthropist would come along and offer me a private school to run as I pleased, then I should introduce sex into my scheme of education. Bairns would be encouraged to believe in the stork theory of birth until they reached the age of nine. At that age they would get the naked truth.

A friend of mine, one of the cleverest men I know, and his wife, a wise woman, resolved to tell their children anything they asked. The eldest, a girl of four, asked one day where she came from. They told her, and she showed no surprise. But I would begin at nine chiefly because the stork story is so delightful that it would be cruel to deprive a bairn of it altogether. Yet, after all, the stork story is all the more charming when you know the bald truth.

Well, at the age of nine my bairns would be taken in hand by a doctor. They would learn that modesty is mainly an accidental result of the invention of clothes. They would gradually come to look upon sex as a normal fact of life; in short, they would recognise it as a healthy thing.

Shaw is right in saying that children must get the truth from a teacher, because parents find a natural shyness in mentioning sex to their children. But I think that the next generation of parents will have a better perspective; shyness will almost disappear. . . .

The great drawback to a frank education on sex matters is the disgusting fact that most grown-up people persist in associating sex with sin. The phrase "born in sin" is still applied to an illegitimate child. When I think of the damnable cruelty of virtuous married women to a girl who has had a child I want to change the phrase into "born into sin."

I have just discovered a section of the Code that deals with the subject of Temperance. I smile sadly when I think that my bairns will never have more than a pound a week to be intemperate on. I suspect that if I had to slave for a week for a pound I should trek for the nearest pub on pay night; I should seek oblivion in some way.

Temperance! Why waste time telling poor bairns to be temperate? When they are fourteen they will learn that to be intemperate means the sack. If we must teach temperance let us begin at Oxford and Cambridge; at Westminster. (I really forget how much wine and beer was consumed there last year; the amount raised a thirst in me at any rate.)

Temperance! The profiteers see to it that the poor cannot afford to be intemperate. Coals are up now, the men who draw a royalty on each ton as it leaves the pit do not know the meaning of temperance.

I want to cry to my bairns: "Be intemperate! Demand more of the fine things of life. Don't waste time in the beer-shops, spend your leisure hours persuading your neighbour to help you impose temperance on your masters."

The Code talks about food. But it does not do so honestly. I would insert the following in the Code: "Teachers in slum districts should point out to the children that most of their food is adulterated. Most of their boots are made of paper. Most of their clothes are made of shoddy."

The best I have found in the Code is the section on the teaching of English. . . .
"No grammar," says the Code, "should be taught until written composition begins." I like that, but I should re-write it thus: "No grammar should be taught this side the Styx."
Grammar is always changing, and the grammar of yester-day is scrapped to-day. [All] a child requires [is] to know how to speak and how to write correctly. . . . Society ladies speak grammatically (I am told), and I'm quite sure that not three people in the Row could tell me whether a word is a verb or an adverb. A middle-class boy of five will know that the sentence "I and nurse is going to the Pictures" is wrong. . . .
I want to abolish the terms Subject, Predicate, Object, Extension, Noun, Verb, &c. . . . Difficulties might arise in learning a foreign tongue. I don't know anything about foreign tongues; all I know is the Greek alphabet and a line of Homer, and the fact that all Gaul is divided into three parts. Yet I imagine that one could learn French or German as a child learns a language.
Good speaking and writing mean the correct use of idiom, and idiom is the best phrasing of the best people—best according to our standards at the present time.
I have heard Parsing and Analysis defended on the ground of their being an exercise in reasoning . . . but I hold that the time would be better spent in Mathematics. . . . Personally, I can find much pleasure in a stiff deduction, but I find nothing but intense weariness in an analysis of sentences. My theories

on education are purely personal; if *I* don't like a thing I presume that my bairns dislike it. And the strange thing is that my presumptions are nearly always right.

Folklore fascinates me. I find that the children of Forfarshire and Dumfriesshire have the same ring song, *The Wind and the Wind and the Wind Blows High*. I once discovered in the British Museum a book on English Folksongs, and in it I found the same song obtaining in Staffordshire. Naturally, variations occur. Did these songs all spring from a common stock? Or did incomers bring them to a district?

When I am sacked—and I half expect to be some day soon—I shall wander round the schools of Scotland collecting the folksongs. I shall take a Punch and Judy show with me, for I know that this is a long-felt want in the country. That reminds me:—a broken-down fellow came to me to-day and told pathetically how he had lost his school—"wrongous dismissal" he called it. I wept and gave him sixpence. To-night I visited the minister. "I had a sad case in today," he began, "a poor fellow who had a kirk in Ross-shire. Poor chap, his wife took to drink, and he lost his kirk."

"Chap with a reddish moustache?" I asked.

"Yes, did you see him?"

I ignored the question.

"Charity," I said, "is foolish. I don't believe in charity of that kind. You gave him something?"

"Er—a shilling."

"You have too much heart," I said, and I took my departure.

If I have to go on tramp I shall try to live by selling sermons after school-hours.

VIII.

To-day I discussed the Women's Movement with my class.

They were all agreed that women should not have votes. I asked for reasons.

"They can't fight like men," said a boy.

I pointed out that they risk their lives more than men do. A woman risks her life so that life may come into the world; a soldier risks his life so that death may come into the world.

"Women speak too much," said Margaret Steel.

"Read the Parliamentary debates," said I.

"Women have not the brains," said a boy. I made no reply, I lifted his last exam paper, and showed the class his 21 per cent, then I showed him Violet Brown's 93 per cent. But I was careful to add that the illustration was not conclusive.

I went on to tell them that the vote was of little use to men, and that I did not consider it worth striving for. But I tried to show them that the Women's Movement was a much bigger thing than a fight for political power. It was a protest against the system that made sons doctors and ministers, and daughters typists and shopgirls, that made girls black their idle brothers' boots, that offered £60 to a lady teacher who was doing as good work as the man in the next room with his £130. I did not take them to the deeper topics of Marriage, Inheritance, the economic dependence of women on men that makes so many marry for a home. But I tried to show that owing to woman's being voteless the laws are on the man's side, and I instanced the Corporation Baths in the neighbouring city. There only one day a week is set aside for women. . . .

I went up to see Lawson of Rinsley School to-night. I talked away gaily about having scrapped my Readers and Rural Arithmetic. He was amused; I know that he considers me a cheerful idiot. But he grew serious when I talked about my Socialism.

"You blooming Socialists," he said, with a dry laugh, "are the most cocky people I have yet struck. You think you are the salt of the earth and that all the others are fatheads."

"Quite right, Lawson," I said with a laugh. And I added seriously: "You see, my boy, that if you have a theory, you've simply *got* to think the other fellow an idiot. I believe in Socialism—the Guild Socialism of *The New Age,* and naturally I think that Lloyd George and Bonar Law and the Cecils, and all that lot, are hopelessly wrong."

"Do you mean to tell me that you are a greater thinker than Arthur James Balfour?" Lawson sat back in his chair and watched the effect of this shot.

I considered for a minute.

"It's like this," I said slowly, "you really cannot compare a duck with a rabbit. You can't say that Shakespeare is greater than Napoleon or Burns than Titian. Balfour is a good man in his own line, and—"

"And you?"

"I sometimes think of great things," I replied modestly. "Balfour has an ideal; he believes, as Lord Roberts believed, in the Public Schools, in Oxford and Cambridge, in the type of Englishman who becomes an Imperialist Cromer. [Evelyn Baring, First Earl of Cromer, was British administrator of Egypt.] He believes in the aristocracy, in land, in heredity of succession. His ideal, so far as I can make out, is to have an aristocracy that behaves kindly and charitably to a deserving working-class—which, after all, is Nietzsche's ideal.

I believe in few of these things. I detest charity of that kind; I hate the type of youth that our Public Schools and Oxfords turn out. I want to see the land belong to the people, I want to see every unit of the State working for the delight that work, as opposed to toil, can bring. The aristocracy has merits that I appreciate. Along with the poor they cheerfully die for the country. . . . I want to see all the excellent material that exists in our aristocracy turned to nobler uses than bossing niggers in India so that millionaires at home may be multimillionaires, than wasting time and wealth in the social rounds of London." . . .

I met Wilkie the mason, on the road to-night. He cannot write his name, and he is the richest man in the village.

"What's this Aw hear aboot you bein' ane o' they Socialists?" he demanded. "Aw didna ken that when Aw voted for ye."

"If you had?"

"Not a vote wud ye hae gotten frae me. Ye'll be layin' yer bombs a' ower the place," he said half jocularly.

"Ye manna put ony o' they ideas in the bairns' heids," he continued anxiously. "Politics have no place in a schule."

I did not pursue the subject: I side-tracked him onto turnips, and by using what I had picked up from Andrew Smith I made a fairly good effort. When we parted Wilkie grasped my hand.

"Ye're no dozzent," he said kindly, "but, tak ma advice, and leave they politics alone. It's a dangerous game for a schulemester to play."

I find that I am becoming obsessed by my creed. I see that I place politics before everything else in education. But I feel that I am doing the best I can for true education. After all it isn't Socialism I am teaching, it is heresy. I am trying to form minds that will question and destroy and rebuild. . . . I travelled to Newcastle on Saturday, and the brick squalor that stretches for miles out Elswick and Blaydon way sickened me. Dirty bairns were playing on muddy patches, dirty women were gossiping at doors, miners were wandering off in twos and threes with whippets at their heels. And smoke was over all. Britain is the workshop of the world. Good old Merrie England!

These are strange entries for a Dominie's Log. I must bring my mind back to Vulgar Fractions and Composition.

There was a Cinema Show in the village hall to-night. My bairns turned out in force. Most of the pictures were drivel—the typist wrongly accused, the seducing employer; the weeping parents at home. . . . Then we had the inevitable Indian chase on horseback, and the hero pardoned after the rope was round his neck. I enjoyed the comic films. . . .

The cinema may have a future as an educational force, but it will deal with what I consider the subsidiary part of education—the facts of life. Pictures of foreign countries are undoubtedly of great use. The cinema can never give us theories and philosophy. [It] . . . can give us humour but not wit. What will happen when the cinema and the phonograph are made to work together perfectly, I do not know. I may yet be able to take my bairns to a performance of *Nan* or *The Wild Duck* or *The Doctor's Dilemma*.

IX.

The word "republican" came up today in a lesson, and I asked what it meant. Four girls told me that their fathers were republicans, but they had no idea of the meaning of the word. One lassie thought that it meant "a man who is always quarrelling with the Tories"—a fairly penetrating definition.

I explained the meaning of the word, and said that a republican in this country was wasting his time and energy. I pointed to America with its Oil Kings, Steel Kings, Meat Kings, and called it a country worse than Russia. I told of the corruption of politics in France.

Then I rambled on to kings and kingship. It is a difficult subject to tackle even with children, but I tried to walk warily. I said that the notion of a king was for people in an elementary stage of development. Intellectual folk have no use for all the pomp and pageantry of kingship. Royalty as it exists to-day is bad for us and for the royal family. The poor princes and princesses are reared in an atmosphere of make-believe. Their individuality and their loves are crushed by a system. And it is really a system of lies. "In the King's name!" Why make all this pretence when everyone knows that it is "In the Cabinet's name"? It is not fair to the king.

I am no republican; I do not want to see monarchy abolished in this land. I recognise that monarchy is necessary to the masses. But I want to bring my bairns to see monarchy stripped of its robes, its pageantry, its remoteness, its circumstance. Loyalty is a name to most of us. People sing the National Anthem in very much the same way as they say Grace before Meat. The Grace-sayer is thinking of his dinner; the singer is wondering if he'll manage to get out in time to collar a taxi.

I do not blame the kings; I blame their advisers. We are kept in the dark by them. We hear of a monarch's good deeds, but we never hear the truth about him. The unwritten law demands that the truth shall be kept secret until a few generations have passed. I know nothing about the king. I don't know what he thinks of Republicanism (in his shoes I should be a red-hot Republican), Socialism, Religion, Morals; and I want to know whether he likes Locke's novels or Galsworthy's drama. In short, I want to know the man who must of necessity be greater than the king. I am tired of processions and functions.

I became a loyalist when first I went to Windsor Castle. Three massed bands were playing in the quadrangle; thousands of visitors wandered around. The king came to the window and bowed. I wanted to go up and take him by the arm and say: "Poor King, you are not allowed to enjoy the sensation of being in a crowd, you are an abstraction, you are behind a barrier of nobility through which no commoner can pass. Come down and have a smoke with me amongst all these typists and clerks." And I expect that every man and woman in that crowd was thinking: "How nice it must be to be a king!"

Yet if a king were to come down from the pedestal on which the courtiers have placed him, I fear that the people would scorn him. They would cry: "He is only a man!" I am forced to the conclusion that pomp and circumstance are necessary after all. The people are to blame. The king is all right; he looks a decent, kindly soul with a good heart. But the people are not interested in good hearts; the fools want gilt coaches and crimson carpets and all the rubbish of show.

A lady asked me to-day whether I taught my children manners. I told her that I did not. She asked why. I replied that manners were sham, and my chief duty was to get rid of sham. Then she asked me why I lifted my hat to her—and naturally I collapsed incontinently. Once again I write the words, "It is a difficult thing to be a theorist—and an honest man at the same time."

On reflection I think that it is a case of personality *versus* the whole community. No man can be consistent. Were I to carry my convictions to their natural conclusion I should be an outcast—and an outcast is of no value to the community. I lift my hat to a lady not because I respect her (I occasionally do—I always doff my hat to the school charwoman, but I am rather afraid of her), but because it is not worth while to protest against the little things of life. Incidentally, the whole case against hat-lifting is this: In the lower and lower middle classes the son does not lift his hat to his mother though he does to the minister's wife.

No, I do not teach manners. If a boy "Sirs" me, he does it of his own free will. I believe that you cannot teach manners; taught manners are always forced, always overdone. My model of a true gentleman is a man with an innate good taste and artistry. My idea of a lady—well, one of the truest ladies I have yet known kept a dairy in the Canongate of Edinburgh.

I try to get my bairns to do to others as they would like

others to do to them. Shaw says "No: their tastes may not be the same as yours." Good old G. B. S.!

I once was in a school where manners were taught religiously. I whacked a boy one day. He said, "Thank you, sir."

I wonder how much influence on observation the so-called Nature Study has. . . . I got my scanty Nature Study from Grant Allen's little shilling book on plants. It was a delightful book full of an almost Yankee imagination. It theorised all the way—grass developed a long narrow blade so that it might edge its way to the sun; wild tobacco has a broad blade because it doesn't need to care tuppence for the competition of other plants, it can grow on wet clay of railway bankings. I think now that Grant Allen was a romancer not a scientist.

I do not see the point in asking bairns to count the stamens of a buttercup. (Dr. Johnson hated the poets who "count the streaks of the tulip.") But I do want . . . them to make a theory. Nature Study has but little result unless bairns get a lead. No boy will guess that the lines on a petal are intended to lead bees to the honey; at least, I know I would never have guessed it. I should never have guessed that flowers are beautiful or perfumed in order to attract insects. But . . . I could not tell at this moment the colour of my bedroom wallpaper; I can't tell whether my father wears a moustache or sidewhiskers. Until I began to teach Woodwork I never observed a mortise, or if I did, I never wondered how it was made. I never noticed that the tops of houses sloped downward until I took up Perspective.

Anyway, observation is a poor attainment unless it is combined with genius as in Darwin's case. Sherlock Holmes is a nobody. Observation should follow fancy. The average youth has successive hobbies. He takes up photography, and is led (sometimes) to enquire into the action of silver salts; he takes up wood-carving, and begins to find untold discoveries in the easy-chair.

I would advocate the keeping of animals at school. I would have a rabbit run, a pigeon loft, one or two dogs, and a few cats for the girls. Let a boy keep homers and fly them, and he will observe much. Apart from the observation side of the question, I would advocate a live stock school-farm on humanitarian grounds; every child would acquire a sense of duty to animals. . . . Incidentally, the study of pigeons and rabbits would conduce to a frank realisation of sex.

I have just bought the new shilling edition of H. G. Wells's *New Worlds for Old,* and I have come upon this passage: "Socialists turn to the most creative profession of all, to that great calling which, with each generation, renews the world's 'circle of ideas,' the Teachers!" . . . On the same page he says: "The constructive Socialist logically declares the teacher master of the situation."

If the Teachers are masters of the situation I wish every teacher in Scotland would get *The New Age* each week. Orage's *Notes of the Week* are easily the best commentary on the war I have seen. *The New Age* is so very amusing, too; its band of "warm young men" are the kind who "can't stand Nietzsche because of his damnable philanthropy" as a journalist friend of mine once phrased it. They despise Shaw and Wells and Webb—the old back-numbers. The magazine is pulsating with life and youth. Every contributor is so cock-sure of himself. It is the only fearless journal I know; it has no advertisements . . . [with which] a journal is muzzled.

One or two bairns are going to try the bursary competition of the neighbouring Secondary School, and I have just got hold of the last year's papers.

"Name an important event in British History for each of any eight of the following years:—1314, 1688, 1759, &c."—

and Wells says that teaching is the most creative profession of all!

"Write an essay of twenty lines or so on any one of these subjects: School, Holidays, Examinations, Bursaries, Books." The examiners might have added a few other bright interesting topics such as Truth, Morals, Faith, Courage.

"Name the poem to which each of the following lines belongs, and add, if you can, the next line in each case, &c." There are ten lines, and I can only spot six of them. And I am, theoretically, an English scholar; I took an Honours English Degree under Saintsbury. But my degree is only a second class one; that no doubt accounts for my lack of knowledge.

That the compilers of the paper are not fools is shown by the fact that they ask a question like this: "A man loses a dog, you find it; write and tell him that you have found it." . . .

X.

I tried an experiment to-day. I gave an exam in History, and each pupil was allowed to use a text-book. . . . I deprecate the usual exam system of allotting a prescribed time to each paper. Blyth Webster, the racy young lecturer in English in Edinburgh University, used to allow us an indefinite time for our Old English papers. I generally required a half hour to give him all I knew about Old English, but I believe that some students sat for five hours. Students write and think at different rates, and the time limit is always unjust.

I wish the Department would allow me to set the Higher Grade Leavings English papers for once. My paper would certainly include the following:

"If Shakespeare came back to earth what do you think would be his opinion of Women's Suffrage (refer to *The Taming of the Shrew*), Home Rule, Sweated Labour, the Kaiser?

"Have you read any Utopia? If not, it doesn't matter; write one of your own. (Note—a Utopia is an ideal country—this side the grave.)

"Discuss Spenser's idea of chivalry, and state what you think would be his opinion on table manners, Soho, or any slum you know, or 'the Present State of Ireland.'

"What would Burns have thought of the prevalence of the kilt among the Semitic inhabitants of Scotland? Is Burns greater than Harry Lauder? Tell me why you think he isn't or is.

"Discuss the following humorists and alleged humorists: Dickens, Jacobs, Lauder, Jerome, Leacock, Storer Clouston, Wells (in *Kipps,* and *Mr. Polly*), Locke (in *Septimus*), Bennett (in *The Card*), Mark Twain, your class teacher, the average magistrate.

"If you have not read any humour at all, write a humorous dialogue between a brick and the mongrel dog it came in contact with."

I hold that my exam paper would discover any genius knocking about in ignorance of his or her powers. I intend to offer it to the Department—when I am out of the profession.

It is extremely difficult for any teacher to keep from getting into a rut. The continual effort to make things simple and elementary for children is apt to deaden the intellect.

To-night I felt dull; I simply couldn't think. So I took up a volume of Nietzsche, and I now know the remedy for dullness. Nietzsche is a genius; he dazzles one . . . and he almost persuades. To-night I am doubting. Is my belief in a great democracy all wrong? Is it true that there is a slave class that can never be anything else? Is our Christian morality a slave morality which is evolving the wrong type of human?

I think of the pity and kindness which is making us keep alive the lunatic and the incurable; I am persuaded to believe that our hospitals are in the long run conducing to an unfit race. Unfit physically; but unfit mentally? Is Sandow the Superman? Will Nietzsche's type of Master man with his physical energy and warlikeness prove to be the best?

I think that the journalists who are anathematising Nietzsche are wrong; I don't believe the Kaiser ever read a line of his. But I think that every German is subconsciously a believer in energy and "Master Morality"; Nietzsche was merely one who realised his nature. The German religion is undoubtedly the religion of the Old Testament; to them "good" is all that pertains to power; their God is the tyrant of the Old Testament. Nietzsche holds that the New Testament code of morals was invented by a conquered race; the poor were meek and servile, and they looked forward to a time when they would be in glory while the rich man frizzled down below.

No man can scorn Nietzsche; you are forced to listen to him. Only fools can dismiss him with the epithet "Madman!"

But I cannot follow him; I believe that if pity and kindness are wrong, then wrong is right. Yet I see that Nietzsche is wise in saying that there must always be one stone at the top of the pyramid. The question is this: Will a democracy always be sure to choose the right man? I wonder.

I found one arresting statement in the book: "If we have a degenerate mean environment, the fittest will be the man who is best adapted to degeneracy and meanness; he will survive." That is what is happening now. I believe that the people will one day be capable of altering this basis of society; Nietzsche believed that the people are mostly of the slave variety, and that a better state of affairs could only come about through the breeding of Supermen—masters. "The best shall rule," says he. Who are the best? I ask, and I really cannot answer myself.

As I go forward with these notes, I find that I become more and more impelled to write down thoughts that can only have a remote connection with the education of children. I think the explanation lies in the fact that every day I realise more and more the futility of my school-work. Indeed, I find myself losing interest sometimes; I go through a lesson on Geography mechanically; in short, I drudge occasionally. But I always awake at Composition time.

I find it useless to do home correction; a bairn won't read the blue pencil marks. I must sit down beside him while I correct; and this takes too much time—from a timetable point of view.

But the mistakes in spelling and grammar are minor matters; what I look for are ideas. I never set a dull subject of the How-I-spent-my-holidays type; every essay must appeal to the imagination. "Suppose you go to sleep for a thousand years," I said, "and tell the story of your awaking." . . .

"Go to Mrs. Rabbit's Garden Party, and describe it." One boy went as a wolf, and returned with the party inside. A girl went as a weasel and left early because she could not eat the lettuce and cabbage on the table. One boy went as an elephant and could not get in. . . .

"Imagine that you are the last man left alive on earth." This essay produced some good work; most of the girls were concerned about the fact that there was no one to bury them when they died.

The best results of all came from this subject: "Die at the age of ninety, and write the paragraph about yourself to the local paper." Most of them made the present minister make a few pious remarks from the pulpit; one girl was clever enough to name a strange minister.

A newspaper correspondence interests a class. "Make a Mr. James Smith write a letter to *The Scotsman* saying that he saw a cow smoking a cigar one night; then write the replies." One boy made a William Thomson suggest that a man must have been standing beside the cow in the darkness. Smith replied that this was impossible, for any man standing beside a cow would be a farmer or a cattleman, and "neither of them can afford to smoke cigars."

I notice that many School Boards insist on having Trained
·Teachers. Is it possible to "train" a teacher? Are teachers not
born like poets? I think they are. I have seen untrained teachers at work, and I have seen trained teachers; I never observed
a scrap of difference. All I would say to a young teacher is:
"Ask questions. Ask why there is a fence round the field, ask
why there is a fence round that tree in the field, then ask
whether any plant or tree has a natural fence of its own."

And I think I should say this: "A good teacher will begin
a lesson on Cromwell [and] touch, in passing, Jack Johnson,
Charlie Chaplin, Votes for Women, guinea pigs, ghosts, and
finish up with an enquiry into Protective Coloration of Animals."

The Code seems to be founded on the assumption that the
teachers of Scotland don't know their business. Why specify
that Nature Study will be taught? Any good teacher will refer
to Nature every five minutes of the day. To me teaching is a
ramble through every subject the teacher knows. . . .

To-day I talked about crime and punishment. I told my
bairns that a criminal cannot help himself; heredity and environment make a man good or bad. I spoke of the environment that makes millions of children diseased morally and
physically, and of the law that punishes a man for the sins of
the community. I told them that there should be no prisons;
if a man is a murderer he is not responsible for his actions, and
he must be confined—but not in prison.

Our present system is not justice; it is vengeance. I once
saw a poor waif sent to prison for stealing a pair of boots, sent
to the care of warders, sent to acquire a hatred of his fellow-
men. Justice would have asked: "Why did he steal? Why had
he no boots? What sort of life has he been forced to lead?"

and I know that the waif would have been acquitted.

I told my bairns that to cure any evil you must get at the root of it. . . . I told them that their fathers have not tried to get at the root of evil, that their prisons and cats and oakum are cowardly expedients. . . . I told them that if I had been born in the Cowgate of Edinburgh I should have been a thief and a drunkard—and society would have added to my curse of heredity and environment the pains and brutishness of a prison. And yet men accuse me of attaching too much importance to material reforms.

I have not used the strap for many weeks now. I hope that I shall never use it again. I found a boy smoking a cigarette to-day. Four years ago I should have run him into the school and welted him. To-day I spoke to him. "Joseph," I said, "I smoke myself, and at your age I smoked an occasional Woodbine. But it isn't really good for a boy, and I hope you won't get into the habit of buying cigs with your pocket money." He smiled and told me that he didn't really like it; he just smoked for fun. And he tossed the cigarette over a wall.

A very clever friend of mine talks about the "Hamlet cramp." I've got it. Other men have a definite standard of right and wrong; I have none. The only original sin that I believe in is the cruelty that has come to man from the remote tree-dweller.

XI.

A villager stopped me on my way to school this morning. "Look at that," he cried, pointing to a broken branch on a tree in his garden, "that's what comes o' yer nae discipline ideas. That's ane o' yer laddies that put his kite into ma gairden. Dawm it, A'll no stand that! Ye'll jest go doon to the school and gie that boy the biggest leathering that he's ever had in his life."

I explained patiently that I was not the village constable, and I told him that the broken branch had nothing to do with me. He became angry, but he became speechless when I said, "I sympathise with you. Had it been my garden I should have sworn possibly harder than you have done. On the other hand, had it been twenty years ago and my kite, well, I should have done exactly what the boy did. Good morning."

Although it was no concern of mine I called the boy out, and advised him to try to think of other people. Then I addressed the bairns. "You might convey to your parents," I said, "that I am not the policeman in this village; I'm a schoolmaster."

I think that many parents are annoyed at my giving up punishment. They feel that I am not doing their work for them; they think that the dominie should do the training of children—other people's children, not their own. I find that I am trying to do a very difficult thing. The home influence is bad in many cases; the children hear their parents slight the teacher, and they do not know what to think. The average parent looks upon the teacher as an enemy. If I hit a boy the parents side with him, if I don't hit the boy who hit their boy, they indignantly ask what education is coming to. Many a night I feel disheartened. I find that I am on the side of the bairns. I am against law and discipline; I am all for freedom of action.

At last I have attained my ambition. As a boy my great ambition was to possess a cavalry trumpet and bugle. I have just bought both. I call the bairns to school with "Stables" or the "Fall In," and I gleefully look forward to playtime so that I may have another tootle. The bairns love to hear the calls, but I think I enjoy them most.

I try hard to share the bairns' joys. At present I am out with them every day flying kites, and I never tire of this. The boys bring me their comic papers, but I find that I cannot laugh at them as I used to do. Yet, I like to see *Chips;* Weary Willie and Tired Tim are still figuring on the front page, but their pristine glory is gone. When I first knew them they were the creation of Tom Browne, and no artist can follow Tom in his own line.

I miss the old "bloods"; I used to glory in the exploits of Frank Reade and Deadwood Dick. I have sat on a Sunday with *Deadwood Dick* in the covers of a family Bible, and my old grandmother patted my head and told me I was a promising lad.

Then there was Buffalo Bill—tuppence coloured; I never see his name now. I wonder why so many parents and teachers cuff boys' heads when they find them reading comic papers and "bloods." I see no harm in either. I wish that people would get out of the absurd habit of taking it for granted that whatever a boy does is wrong. I hold that a boy is nearly always right.

I see in to-day's *Scotsman* that a Sheriff substitute in Edinburgh has sentenced two brothers of nine and ten to twelve stripes with the birch rod for stealing tuppence ha'penny. The account remarked that the brothers had previously had a few stripes for a similar theft. That punishment is no prevention is proved in this case.

The Sheriff Substitute must have a very definite idea of righteousness; I envy him his conscience free from all remembrance of shortcomings in the past. For my part had I been sitting in judgment on the poor laddies I should have recollected the various times I have travelled first with a third ticket, sneaked into circuses by lifting the tent cover, laid farthings on the railway so that they might become ha'pennies, or, with a special piece of luck—a goods [freight] train—pennies. Then I should have invited the boys to tea, and sent them home with *Comic Cuts,* two oranges, and a considerable bit of chewing gum. Anyhow, my method would have brought out any good in the boys. The method of the judge will bring out no good; it may make the boys feel that they are enemies of society. And I should like to ask the gentleman what he would do if his young son stole the jam. I'm sure he would not send for the birch rod. The damnable thing about the whole affair is that he is probably a very nice kindly man who would not whip a dog with his own hand. His misfortune is his being part of a system.

I have just added a few volumes to my school library. I tried to recollect the books that I liked as a youth; then I wrote for catalogues of "sevenpennies." The new books include these: *The Prisoner of Zenda* and its sequel, *Rupert of Hentzau, King Solomon's Mines, Montezuma's Daughter, The Four Feathers, A Gentleman of France, White Fang, The Call of the Wild, The Invisible Man, The War of the Worlds,* . . . I find that the average bairn of thirteen cannot appreciate these stories. Margaret Steel was the only one who read *The Scarlet Pimpernel* and asked for the sequel. Most of them stuck half way with *Zenda*. Guy Boothby's novels, the worst of the lot possibly, appealed to them strongly. The love element bores the boys, but the girls rather like it. One boy sat and yawned over *King Solomon's Mines;* then he took out a coloured comic and turned to the serial. I took the book away and told him to read the serial. Violet Brown prefers a book about giants from the infant room to all the romantic stories extant. After all, they are but children.

I am delighted with my sketching results. We go out every Wednesday and Friday afternoon, and many bairns are giving me good work. We usually end up with races or wading in the sea. There was much wonder when first they saw my bare feet, but now they take my feet for granted.

Modesty is strong here. The other day the big girls came to me and asked if they could come to school slipshod.

"You can come in your nighties for all I care," I said, and they gasped.

We sit outside all day now. My classes take books and wander away down the road and lie on the banks. When I want them I call with the bugle. Each class has a "regimental call," and they come promptly. They most of them sit down separately, but the chatterers like to sit together.

I force no bairn to learn in my school. The few who dislike books and lessons sit up when I talk to the class. The slackers are not always the most ignorant.

I am beginning to compliment myself on having a good temper. For the past six weeks I have left the manual room open at playtime and the boys have made many toys. But they have made a woeful mess of the cutting tools. It is trying to find that your favourite plane has been cracked by a boy who has extreme theories on the fixing of plane irons. But it is very comforting to know that the School Board will have to pay for the damage. Yes, my temper is excellent.

On Saturday I went to a Bazaar, and various members of the aristocracy talked to me. They talked very much in the manner they talk to their gardeners, and I was led to muse upon the social status of a dominie. What struck me most was the fact that they imitate royalty in the broaching of topics of conversation; I knew that I presumed when I entered new ground of conversation. The ladies were very polite and very regal, and very well pleased with themselves. One of them said: "I hope that you do your best to make these children realise that there are classes in society; so many of their parents refuse to see the good in other classes!"

"For my part," I answered, "I acknowledge one aristocracy—the aristocracy of intellect. I teach my children to have respect for thinking." She stared at me, and went away.

I am not prejudiced against the county people, but any superiority of manner annoys me. I simply have no use for ladies who live drifting lives. The lady-bountifuls . . . of Britain would be much better as typists; in these days of alleged scarcity of labour they might come down and mix with the lower orders. Their grace and breeding would do much to improve us, and we might be able to help them in some ways. I am not being cynical, I have a genuine admiration for the breeding and beauty of some society women.

The doctor and the minister are seldom patronised. I cannot for the life of me see why it is more lowly to cure a child of ignorance than measles.

I have heard it said that the real reason of the teacher's low social status is the fact that very often he is the son of a humble labourer. There is some truth in this. At the Training College and the University the student meets men of his own class only; he never learns the little tricks of deportment that make up society's criterion of a gentleman. But for my part I blame the circumstances under which a dominie works. In Scotland he is the servant of a School Board, and a School Board is generally composed of men who have but the haziest notion of the meaning of education. That is bad enough, but very often there is a feud between one or two members and the teacher. Perhaps the teacher does not get his coals from Mr. Brown the Chairman, perhaps Mr. Brown voted for another man when the appointment was made. It is difficult for a man who is ruled by a few low-idealed semi-illiterate farmers and pig-dealers to emphasise his social position.

Larger areas have been spoken of by politicians. Personally, I don't want larger areas; I want to see the profession run by the members, just as Law and Medicine are. It is significant that the medical profession has dropped considerably in the social scale since allowing itself to work under the Insurance Act.

My ideal is an Education Guild which will replace the Scotch Education Department. It will draw up its own scheme of instruction, fix the salaries of its members, appoint its own inspectors, build its own schools. It will be directly responsible to the State which will remain the supreme authority.

I blame the teachers for their low social status. To-day they have no idea of corporate action. They pay their subscriptions to their Institute, and for the most part talk of stopping them on the ground that it is money wasted. The authorities of the Institute try to work for a better union, but they try clumsily and stodgily. They never write or talk forcibly; they resemble the Labour Members of Parliament in their having an eager desire to be respectable at any price. I don't know why it is, but when a professional man tries to put his thoughts on paper he almost always succeeds in saying nothing in many fine phrases.

What is really wrong with the Educational Institute of Scotland is hoary-headedness. It is run by old men and old wives. . . . If a man can teach under the present system for thirty years and retain any originality or imagination at the end of that time, he must be a genius.

I object to age and experience; I am all for youth and empiricism. After all, what is the use of experience in teaching? I could bet my boots that ninety-nine out of a hundred teachers use the methods they learned as pupil-teachers. Experience! I have heard dominies expatiate on innovations like Kindergarten and Blackboard Drawing. I still have to meet a dominie of experience who has any name but "fad" for anything in education later than 1880. . . .

A fad is a half-formed idea that a sub-inspector has borrowed from a bad translation of a distinguished foreigner's treatise on Education, and handed on to a deferential dominie.

An inspector called to-day; a middle-aged kindly gentleman with a sharp eye. His chief interest in life was tables.

"How many pence in fifty-seven farthings?" he fired at my highest class. When he found that they had to divide mentally by four, he became annoyed.

"They ought to know their tables," he said to me.

"What tables?" I asked.

"O, they should learn up that; why I can tell you at once what sixty-nine farthings are."

I explained humbly that I couldn't, and should never acquire the skill.

I did not like his manner of talking *at* the teacher through the class. When an inspector says, "You ought to know this," the scholars glance at the teacher, for they are shrewd enough to see that the teacher is being condemned.

He fired his parting shot as he went out.

"You must learn not to talk in school," he said.

I am a peaceful man, and I hate a scene. I said nothing, but I shall do nothing. If he returns he will find no difference in the school.

The bairns did talk to each other when the inspector talked to me, but when he asked for attention he got it.

I am surprised to find that his visit does not worry me; I have at last lost my fear of the terror of teaching—H.M.I.S.

XII.

I went "drumming" last night. I like the American word "drummer," it is so much more expressive than our "commercial traveller."

I made a series of postcards, and I went round the shops trying to place them. One man refused to take them up because the profits would not be large enough. As the profits work out at 41½ per cent, I begin to wonder what he usually makes.

To-day I talked to the bairns about commerce, and I pointed out that much in commerce was thieving.

"This is commerce," I said. "Suppose I am a pig-dealer. I hear one day from a friend that pigs will rise in price in a few days. I at once set out on a tour of neighbouring farms, and by nightfall I have bought twenty pigs at the market price. Next morning pigs have doubled in price, and these farmers naturally want to shoot me. Why don't they shoot me?"

"They would be hanged," said Violet Brown.

"Because they would buy pigs in the same way if they had the chance," said Margaret Steel.

I went on to say that buying pigs like that is stealing, and I said that the successful business man is usually the man who is most unscrupulous.

I told them of the murderous system that allows a big firm to place a shop next door to a small merchant and under-sell him till his business dies. It is all done under the name of competition, but of course there is no more competition about the affair than there is about the relationship between a wolf and a lamb.

I try very very hard to keep my bairns from low ideals. Some one—Oscar Wilde or Shaw, I think—says that love of money is the root of all good. That is the sort of paradox that isn't true, and not even funny. I see farmers growing rich on child labour: fifteen pence a day for spreading manure. I meet the poor little boys of thirteen and fourteen on the road, and the smile has gone from their faces; their bodies are bent and racked.

When I was thirteen I went to the potato-gathering at a farm. Even now, when I pass a field where potatoes are being lifted, the peculiar smell of potato earth brings back to me those ten days of misery. I seldom had time to straighten my back. I had but one thought all day: When will that sun get down to the west? My neighbour, Jock Tamson, always seemed fresh and cheerful, but, unfortunately, I did not discover the cause of his optimism until the last day.

"Foo are you feenished so quick, Jock?" I asked.

Jock winked and nodded his head in the direction of the farmer.

"Look!" he said, and he skilfully tramped a big potato into the earth with his right foot; then he surreptitiously happed it over with his left.

I have never forgiven Jock for being so tardy in spreading his gospel.

To-day I received from the Clerk the Report on my school.

"Discipline," it says, "which is kindly, might be firmer, especially in the Senior Division, so as to prevent a tendency to talk on the part of the pupils whenever opportunity occurs."

An earlier part runs thus: "The pupils in the Senior Division are intelligent and bright under oral examination, and make an exceedingly good appearance in the class subjects."

I scratch my head thoughtfully. If the inspector finds the bairns intelligent and bright, why does he want them to be silent in school? I cannot tell; I suspect that talking children annoy him. I fancy that stern disciplinarians are men who hate to be irritated.

"More attention, however, should be paid to neatness of method and penmanship in copybooks and jotters."

I wonder. I freely admit to myself that the jotters are not neat, but I want to know why they should be. I can beat most men at marring a page with hasty figures; on the other hand I can make a page look like copperplate if I want to. I find that my bairns do neat work on an examination paper.

The truth is that I am incapable of teaching neatness. My desk is a jumble; my sittingroom is generally littered with books and papers. Some men are born tidy: some have tidiness thrust upon them. I am of the latter crowd. Between the school charwoman and my landlady, I live strenuously.

I object to my report. I hate to be the victim of a man I can't reply to, even when he says nice things. But the main objection I have to the report is this: the School Board gets not a single word of criticism. If I were not almost proud of my lack of neatness, I might argue that no man could be neat in an ugly school. It is always filthy because the ashed playground is undrained. Broken windows stand for months; the plaster of the ceiling came down months ago, and the lathes are still showing. . . .

It would be a good plan to make teachers forward reports of inspectors' visits to the Scotch Education Department. I should love to write one.

"Mr. Silas K. Beans, H.M.I.S., paid a visit to this school to-day, and he made quite a passable appearance before the pupils.

"It was perhaps unfortunate that Mr. Beans laboured under the delusion that Mrs. Hemans wrote *Come into the Garden, Maud,* but on the whole the subject was adequately treated.

"The geography lesson showed Mr. Beans at his best, but it might be advisable for him to consider whether the precise whereabouts of Seville possesses the importance in the scheme of things that he attributes to it. . . .

"The school staff would have liked Mr. Beans to have stayed long enough to discover that a few of the scholars possessed imagination, and it hoped that he will be able to make his visit longer than four hours next time.

"Mr. Beans's knowledge of dates is wonderful, and his parsing has all the glory of Early Victorian furniture."

XIII.

To-night MacMurray invited me down to meet his former

head, Simpson, a big man in the Educational Institute, and a likely President next year. Mac introduced me as "a chap with theories on education; doesn't care a rap for inspectors and abominates discipline."

Simpson looked me over; then he grunted.

"You'll grow out of that, young man," he said sagely.

I laughed.

"That's what I'm afraid of," I said, "I fear that the continual holding of my nose to the grindstone will destroy my perspective."

"You'll find that experience doesn't destroy perspective."

"Experience," I cried, "is, or at least, should be one of Oscar Wilde's Seven Deadly Virtues. The experienced man is the chap who funks doing a thing because he's had his fingers burnt. 'Tis experience that makes cowards of us all."

"Of course," said Simpson, "you're joking. It stands to reason that I, for instance, with a thirty-four years' experience of teaching know more about education than you do, if you don't mind my saying so."

"Man, I was teaching laddies before your father and mother met," he added.

"If you saw a lad and a lass making love, would you arrange that he should sit near her?"

"Good gracious, no!" he cried. "What has that got to do with the subject."

"But why not give them chances to spoon?" I asked.

"Why not? If a teacher encouraged that sort of thing, why, it might lead to anything!"

"Exactly," I said, "experience tells you that you have to do all you can to preserve the morals of the bairns?"

"I could give you instances—"

"I don't want them particularly," I interrupted. "My main point is that experience has made you a funk. Pass the baccy, Mac."

"Mean to tell me that's how you teach?" cried Simpson. "How in all the world do you do for discipline?"

"I do without it."

"My goodness! That's the limit! May I ask why you do without it?"

"It is a purely personal matter," I answered. "I don't want anyone to lay down definite rules for me, and I refuse to lay down definite rules of conduct for my bairns."

"But how in all the earth do you get any work done?"

"Work," I said, "is an over-rated thing, just as knowledge is overrated."

"Nonsense," said Simpson.

"All right," I remarked mildly, "if knowledge is so important, why is a university professor usually a talker of platitudes? Why is the average medallist at a university a man of tenth-rate ideas?"

"Then our Scotch education is all in vain?"

"Speaking generally, it is."

I think it was at this stage that Simpson began to doubt my sanity.

"Young man," he said severely, "some day you will realise that work and knowledge and discipline are of supreme importance. Look at the Germans!"

He waved his hand in the direction of the sideboard, and I looked round hastily.

"Look what Germany has done with work and knowledge and discipline!"

"Then why all this bother to crush a State that has all the virtues?" I asked diffidently.

"It isn't the discipline we are trying to crush; it is the militarism."

"Good!" I cried. "I'm glad to hear it. That's what I want to do in Scotland; I want to crush the militarism in our schools, and, as most teachers call their militarism discipline, I curse discipline."

"That's all rubbish, you know," he said shortly.

"No it isn't. If I leather a boy for making a mistake in a sum, I am no better than the Prussian officer who shoots a Belgian civilian for crossing the street. I am equally stupid and a bully."

"Then you allow carelessness to go unpunished?" he sneered.

"I do. You see I am a very careless devil myself. I'll swear that I left your garden gate open when I came in, Mac, and your hens will be all over the road."

Mac looked out at the window.

"They are!" he chuckled, and I laughed.

"You seem to think that slovenliness is a virtue," said Simpson with a faint smile.

"I don't really, but I hold that it is a natural human quality."

"Are your pupils slovenly?" he asked.

"Lots of 'em are. You're born tidy or you aren't."

"When these boys go out to the workshop, what then? Will a joiner keep an apprentice who makes a slovenly job?"

"Ah!" I said, "you're talking about trade now. You evidently want our schools to turn out practical workmen. I don't. Mind you I'm quite willing to admit that a shoemaker who theorises about leather is a public nuisance. Neatness and skill are necessary in practical manufacture, but I refuse to reduce education to the level of cobbling or coffin-making. I don't care how slovenly a boy is if he thinks."

"If he is slovenly he won't think," said Simpson.

I smiled.

"I think you are wrong. Personally, I am a very lazy man; I have my library all over the floor as a rule. Yet, though I am lazy physically I am not lazy mentally. I hold that the really lazy teacher is your 'ring the bell at nine sharp' man; he hustles so much that he hasn't time to think. If you work hard all day you never have time to think."

Simpson laughed.

"Man, I'd like to see your school!"

"Why not? Come up tomorrow morning," I said.

"First rate!" he cried, "I'll be there at nine."

"Better not," I said with a smile, "or you'll have to wait for ten minutes."

He arrived as I blew the "Fall in" on my bugle.

"You don't line them up and march them in?" he said.

"I used to, but I've given it up," I confessed. "To tell the truth I'm not enamoured of straight lines."

We entered my classroom. Simpson stood looking sternly at my chattering family while I marked the registers.

"I couldn't tolerate this row," he said.

"It isn't so noisy as your golf club on a Saturday night, is it?" He smiled slightly.

Jim Burnett came out to my desk and lifted *The Glasgow Herald,* then he went out to the playground humming *On the Mississippi.*

"What's the idea?" asked Simpson.

"He's the only boy who is keen on the war news," I explained.

Then Margaret Steel came out.

"Please, sir, I took *The Four Feathers* home and my mother began to read them; she thinks she'll finish them by Sunday. Is anybody reading *The Invisible Man?*"

I gave her the book and she went out.

Then Tom Macintosh came out and asked for the Manual Room key; he wanted to finish a boat he was making.

"Do you let them do as they like?" asked Simpson.

"In the upper classes," I replied.

Soon all the Supplementary and Qualifying pupils had

found a novel and had gone out to the roadside. I turned to give the other classes arithmetic.

Mary Wilson in the front seat held out a bag of sweets to me. I took one.

"Please, sir, would the gentleman like one, too?"

Simpson took one with the air of a man on holiday who doesn't care what sins he commits.

"I say," he whispered, "do you let them eat in school? There's a boy in the back seat eating nuts."

I fixed Ralph Ritchie with my eye.

"Ralph! If you throw any nutshells on that floor Mrs. Findlay will eat you."

"I'm putting them in my pooch," he said.

"Good! Write down this sum."

"What are the others doing?" asked Simpson after a time.

"Margaret Steel and Violet Brown are reading," I said promptly. "Annie Dixon is playing fivies on the sand, Jack White and Bob Tosh are most likely arguing about horses, but the other boys are reading, we'll go and see." And together we walked down the road.

Annie was playing fivies all right, but Jack and Bob weren't discussing horses; they were reading *Chips*.

"And the scamps haven't the decency to hide it when you appear!" cried Simpson.

"Haven't the fear," I corrected.

On the way back to the school he said: "It's all very pleasant and picnicky, but eating nuts and sweets in class!"

"Makes your right arm itch?" I suggested pleasantly.

"It does," he said with a short laugh, "Man, do you never get irritated?"

"Sometimes."

"Ah!" He looked relieved. "So the system isn't perfect?"

"Good heavens!" I cried, "What do you think I am? A saint from heaven? You surely don't imagine that a man with nerves and a temperament is always able to enter into the moods of bairns! I get ratty occasionally, but I generally blame myself." I sent a girl for my bugle and sounded the "Dismiss."

"What do you do now?"

I pulled out my pipe and baccy.

"Have a fill," I said, "it's John Cotton."

To-night I have been thinking about Simpson. He is really a kindly man; in the golfhouse he is voted a good fellow. Yet MacMurray tells me that he is a very strict disciplinarian; he saw him give a boy six scuds with the tawse one day for drawing a man's face on the inside cover of his drawing book. I suppose that Simpson considers that he is an eminently just man.

I think that the foundation of true justice is self-analysis. It is mental laziness that is at the root of the militarism in our schools. . . .

It is strange that our boasted democracy uses its power to set up bullies. The law bullies the poor and gives them the cat if they trespass; the police bully everyone who hasn't a clean collar; the dominie bullies the young; and the School Board bullies the dominie. Yet, in theory, the judge, the constable, the dominie, and the School Board are the servants of democracy. Heaven protect us from the bureaucratic Socialism of people like the Webbs! It is significant that Germany, the country of the super-official is the country of the super-bully.

Paradoxically, I, as a Socialist, believe that the one thing that will save the people is individualism. No democracy can control a stupid teacher or a stupid judge. . . . Our cruel teachers and magistrates are good fellows in their clubs and homes; they are bad fellows in their schools and courts because they have never come to think, to examine themselves. In my Utopia self-examination will be the only examination that will matter.

. . .

I saw a good fight to-night. At four o'clock I noticed a general move towards Murray's Corner, and I knew that blood was about to be shed. Moreover I knew that Jim Steel was to tackle the new boy Welsh, for I had seen Jim put his fist to his nose significantly in the afternoon.

I followed the crowd.

"I want to see fair play," I said.

Welsh kept shouting that he could "fecht the hale schule wi' wan hand tied ahent 'is back."

In this district school fights have an etiquette of their own. One boy touches the other on the arm saying: "There's the dunt!" The other returns the touch with the same remark. If he fails to return it he receives a harder dunt on the arm with the words, "And there's the coordly!" If he fails to return that also he is accounted the loser, and the small boys throw divots at him.

Steel began in the usual way with his: "There's the dunt!" Welsh promptly hit him in the teeth and knocked him down. The boys appealed to me.

"No," I said, "Welsh didn't know the rules. After this you should shake hands as you do in boxing."

Welsh never had a chance. He had no science; he came on with his arms swinging in windmill fashion. Jim stepped aside and drove a straight left to the jaw, and before Welsh knew what was happening Jim landed him on the nose with his right. Welsh began to weep, and I stopped the fight. I told him that Steel had the advantage because I had taught my boys the value of a straight left, but that I would give him a few lessons with the gloves later on. Then I asked how the quarrel had arisen. As I had conjectured Steel and Welsh had no real quarrel. Welsh had cuffed little Geordie Burnett's ears, and Geordie had cried, "Ye wudna hit Jim Steel!" Welsh had no alternative but to reply: "Wud Aw no!" Straightway Geordie had run off to Steel saying: "Hi! Jim! Peter Welsh says he'll fecht ye!"

So far as I can remember all my own battles at school were arranged by disobliging little boys in this manner. If Jock Tamson said to me: "Bob Young cud aisy fecht ye and ca' yer nose up among yer hair!" I, as a man of honour, had to reply: "Aw'll try Bob Young ony day he likes!" And even if Bob were my bosom friend, I would have to face him at the brig at four o'clock.

I noticed that the girls were all on Steel's side before the fight began, and obviously on Welsh's side when he was beaten, the bissoms!

XIV.

I gave a lecture in the village hall on Friday night, and many parents came out to hear what I had to say on the subject of *Children and their Parents*. After the lecture I invited questions.

"What wud ye hae a man do if his laddie wudna do what he was bidden?" asked Brown the joiner.

"I would have the man think very seriously whether he had any right to give the order that was disobeyed. For instance, if you ordered your Jim to stop singing while you were reading, you would be taking an unfair advantage of your years and size. From what I know of Jim he would certainly stop singing if you asked him to do so as a favour."

"Aw dinna believe in askin' favours o' ma laddies," he said.

I smiled.

"Yet you ask them of other laddies. You don't collar Fred Thomson and shout: 'Post that letter at once!' You say very nicely: 'You might post that letter like a good laddie,' and Fred enjoys posting your letter more than posting a ton of letters for his own father."

The audience laughed, and Fred's father cried: "Goad! Ye're quite richt, dominie!"

"As a boy," I continued, "I hated being set to weed the garden, though I spent hours helping to weed the garden next door. A boy likes to grant favours."

"Aye," said Brown, "when there's a penny at the tail end o' them!"

"Yes," I said after the laughter had died, "but your Jim would rather have Mr. Thomson's penny than your sixpence. The real reason is that you boss your son, and nobody likes to be bossed."

"Believe me, ladies and gentlemen, I think that the father is the curse of the home. (Laughter.) The father never talks to his son as man to man. As a result a boy suppresses much of his nature, and if he is left alone with his father for five minutes he feels awkward, though not quite so awkward as the father does. You find among the lower animals that the father is of no importance; indeed, he is looked on as a danger. Have you ever seen a bitch flare up when the father comes too near her puppies? Female spiders, I am told, solve the problem of the father by eating him." (Great laughter.)

"What aboot the mothers?" said a voice, and the men cackled.

"Mothers are worse," I said. "Fathers usually imagine that they have a sense of justice, but mothers have absolutely no sense of justice. It is the mother who cries, 'Liz, ye lazy slut, run and clean your brother's boots, the poor laddie! Lod, I dinna ken what would happen to you, my poor laddie, if your mother wasna here to look after you.' You mothers make your girls work at nights and on Saturdays, and you allow your boys to play outside. That is most unjust. Your boys should clean their own boots and mend their own clothes. They should help in the washing of dishes and the sweeping of floors."

"Wud ye say that the mother is the curse o' the hame,

too?" asked Brown.

"No," I said, "she is a necessity, and in spite of her lack of justice, she is nearer to the children than the father is. She is less aloof and less stern. You'll find that a boy will tell his mother much more than he will tell his father. Speaking generally, a stupid mother is more dangerous than a stupid father, but a mother of average intelligence is better for a child than a father of average intelligence.

"This is a problem that cannot be solved. The mother must remain with her children, and I cannot see how we are to chuck the father out of the house. As a matter of fact he is usually so henpecked that he is prevented from being too much of an evil to the bairns.

"The truth is that the parents of to-day are not fit to be parents, and the parents of the next generation will be no better. The mothers of the next generation are now in my school. They will leave at the age of fourteen—some of them will be exempted and leave at thirteen—and they will slave in the fields or the factory for five or six years. . . . A mother who has never learned to think has absolute control of a growing young mind, and an almost absolute control of a growing young body. She can beat her child; she can starve it. She can poison its mind with malice, just as she can poison its body with gin and bitters." . . .

I cannot flatter myself that I made a single parent think on Friday night. Most of the villagers treated the affair as a huge joke.

I have just decided to hold an Evening School next winter. I see that the Code offers *The Life and Duties of a Citizen* as a subject. I shall have the lads and lasses of sixteen to nineteen in my classroom twice a week, and I guess I'll tell them things about citizenship they won't forget.

It occurs to me that married people are not easily persuaded to think. The village girl considers marriage the end of all things. She dons the bridal white, and at once she rises meteorically in the social scale. Yesterday she was Mag Broon, an outworker at Millside; to-day she is Mrs. Smith with a house of her own.

Her mental horizon is widened. She can talk about anything now; the topic of childbirth can now be discussed openly with other married wives. Aggressiveness and mental arrogance follow naturally, and with these come a respect for church-going and an abhorrence of Atheism.

I refuse to believe those who prate about marriage as an emancipation for a woman. Marriage is a prison. It shuts a woman up within her four walls, and she hugs all her prejudices and hypocrisies to her bosom. The men who shout "Women's place is the home!" at Suffragette meetings are fools. The home isn't good enough for women.

A girl once said to me: "I always think that marriage makes a girl a 'has been.'"

What she meant was that marriage ended flirtation, poor innocent that she was! Yet her remark is true in a wider sense. The average married woman is a "has been" in thought, while not a few are "never wasers." Hence I have more hope of my evening school lasses than of their mothers. They have not become smug, nor have they concluded that they are past enlightenment. They are not too omniscient to resent the offering of new ideas.

A man's marriage makes no great change in his life. His wife replaces his mother in such matters as cooking and washing and "feeding the brute." He finds that he is allowed to spend less, and he has to keep elders' hours. But in essentials his life is unchanged. He still has his pint on a Saturday night, and his evening crack at the Brig. He has gained no additional authority, and he is extremely blessed of the gods if he has not lost part of the authority he had.

The revolution in his mental outfit comes later when he becomes a father. He thinks that his education is complete when the midwife whispers: "Hi, Jock, it's a lassie!" He immediately realises that he is a man of importance, a guide and preacher rolled into one; and he talks dictatorially to the dominie about education. Then he discovers that precept must be accompanied by example, and he aspires to be a deacon or an elder.

Now I want to get at Jock before the midwife gets at him. I don't care tuppence whether he is married or not—but he mustn't be a father.

To-day I began to read Mary Johnston's *By Order of the Company* to my bairns. I love the story, and I love the style. It reminds me of Malory's style; she has his trick of running on in a breathless string of "ands." When I think of style I am forced to recollect the stylists I had to read at the university. There was Sir Thomas Browne and his *Urn Burial*. What the devil is the use of people like Browne I don't know. He gives us word music and imagery I admit, but I don't want word music and imagery from prose, I want ideas or a story. I can't think of one idea I got from Browne or Fisher or Ruskin, or any of the stylists, yet I have found many ideas in translations of Nietzsche and Ibsen. Style is the curse of English literature.

When I read Mary Johnston I forget all about words. I vaguely realise that she is using the right words all the time, but the story is the thing. When I read Browne I fail to scrape together the faintest interest in burials; the organ music of his *Dead March* drowns everything else.

When a man writes too musically and ornately I always suspect him of having a paucity of ideas. If you have anything important to say you use plain language. The man who writes to the local paper complaining of "those itinerant denizens of the underworld yclept hawkers, who make the day hideous with raucous cries," is a pompous ass. Yet he is no worse than the average stylist in writing. I think it was G. K. Chesterton who said that a certain popular authoress said nothing because she believed in words. He might have applied the phrase to 90 per cent of English writers.

Poetry cannot be changed. Substitute a word for "felicity" in the line: "Absent thee from felicity awhile" and you destroy the poetry. But I hold that prose should be able to stand translation. . . .

There must be something in style after all. I had this note from a mother this morning.

"DEAR SIR,

Please change Jane's seat for she brings home more than belongs to her."

I refuse to comment on this work of art.

I must get a cornet. Eurythmics with an artillery bugle is too much for my wind and my dignity. Just when the graceful bend is coming forward, my wind gives out, and I make a vain attempt to whistle the rest. Perhaps a concertina would be better than a cornet. I tried Willie Hunter with his mouth-organ, but the attempt was stale and unprofitable, and incidentally flat. Then Tom Macintosh brought a comb to the school and offered to perform on it. After that I gave Eurythmics a rest.

When the war is over I hope that the Government will retain Lloyd George as Minister of Munitions—for Schools. I haven't got a tenth of the munitions I should have; I want a player-piano, a gramophone, a cinematograph with comic films, a library with magazines and pictures. I want swings and see-saws in the playground, I want rabbits and white mice; I want instruments for a school brass and wood band.

I like building castles in Spain. The truth is that if the

School Board would yield to my importunities and lay a few loads of gravel on the muddy patch commonly known as the playground I should almost die of surprise and joy. . . .

XV.

. . . I wonder when the people will begin to realise what wagery means. When they do begin to realise, they will commence the revolution by driving women out of industry. To-day the women are used by the profiteer as instruments to exploit the men. Surely a factory worker has the right to earn enough to support a family on. The profiteer says "No! You must marry one of my hands, and then your combined wages will set up a home for you."

I spoke of this to the manager of Bruce's factory once.

"But," he said, "if we did away with female labour we'd have to close down. We couldn't compete with other firms."

"Not if they abolished female labour too?"

"I was thinking of the Calcutta mills where labour is dirt cheap," he said.

"I see," I said, "so the Scotch lassie is to compete with the native?"

"It comes to that," he admitted.

I think I see a very pretty problem awaiting Labour in the near future. As the Trade Unions become more powerful and show their determination to take the mines and factories into their own hands, capitalists will turn to Asia and Africa. The exploitation of the native is just beginning. At a time when Britain is a Socialistic State all the evils of capitalism will be reproduced with ten-fold intensity in India and China and Africa. I see an Asia ruled by lash and revolver; the profiteer has a short way with the striker in Eastern climes. The recent history of South Africa is sinister. A few years ago our brothers died presumably that white men should have the rights of citizenship in the Transvaal. What they seemed to have died for was the right of profiteers to shoot white strikers from the windows of the Rand Club. If white men are treated thus I tremble for the fate of the black man who strikes. . . .

"If," I said, "I have a factory, I have to pay out wages and money for machinery and raw material. When I sell my cloth I get more money than I paid out. This money is called profit, and with this money I can set up a new factory.

"Now what I want you to understand is this: Unless work is done by someone there is no wealth. If I make a fortune out of linen I make it by using the labour of your fathers, and the machinery that was invented by clever men. Of course, I have to work hard myself, but I am repaid for my work fully. Margaret Steel at this moment standing at a loom, is working hard too, but she is getting a wage that is miserable.

"Note that the owner of the factory is getting an income of, say, ten thousand pounds a year. Now, what does he do with the money?"

"Spends it on motor cars," said a boy.

"Buys cigarettes," said a girl.

"Please, sir, Mr. Bruce gives money to the infirmary," said another girl.

"He keeps it in a box beneath the bed," said another, and I found that the majority in the room favoured this theory. This suggestion reminded me of the limitations of childhood, and I tried to talk more simply. I told them of banks and stocks, I talked of luxuries, and pointed out that a man who lived by selling expensive dresses to women was doing unnecessary labour.

Tom Macintosh showed signs of thinking deeply.

"Please, sir, what would all the dressmakers and footmen do if there was no money to pay them?"

"They would do useful work, Tom," I said. "Your father

works from six to six every day, but if all the footmen and chauffeurs and grooms and gamekeepers were doing useful work, your father would only need to work maybe seven hours a day. See? In Britain there are forty millions of people, and the annual income of the country is twenty-four hundred million pounds. One million of people take half this sum, and the other thirty-nine millions have to take the other half."

"Please, sir," said Tom, "what half are you in?"

"Tom," I said, "I am with the majority. For once the majority has right on its side."

Bruce the manufacturer had an advertisement in to-day's local paper. "No encumbrances," says the ad. Bruce has a family of at least a dozen, and he possibly thinks that he has earned the right to talk of "encumbrances." I sympathise with the old chap.

But I want to know why gardeners and chauffeurs must have no encumbrances. If the manorial system spreads, a day will come when the only children at this school will be the offspring of the parish minister. Then, I suppose, dominies and ministers will be compelled to be polygamists by Act of Parliament.

I like the Lord of the Manor's damned impudence. He breeds cattle for showing, he breeds pheasants for slaughtering, he breeds children to heir his estates. Then he sits down and pens an advertisement for a slave without "encumbrances." Why he doesn't import a few harem attendants from Turkey I don't know; possibly he is waiting till the Dardanelles are opened up.

I have just been reading a few schoolboy howlers. I fancy that most of these howlers are manufactured. I cannot be persuaded that any boy ever defined a lie as "An abomination unto the Lord but a very present help in time of trouble." Howlers bore me; so do most school yarns. The only one worth remembering is the one about the inspector who was ratty.

"Here, boy," he fired at a sleepy youth, "who wrote *Hamlet?*"

The boy started violently.

"P—please, sir, it wasna me," he stammered.

That evening the inspector was dining with the local squire.

"Very funny thing happened to-day," he said, as they lit their cigars.

"I was a little bit irritated, and I shouted at a boy, 'Who wrote *Hamlet?*' The little chap was flustered. 'P—please, sir, it wasna me!' he stuttered."

The squire guffawed loudly.

"And I suppose the little devil had done it after all!" he roared.

Lawson came down to see me to-night, and as usual we talked shop.

"It's all very well," he said, "for you to talk about education being all wrong. Any idiot can burn down a house that took many men to build. Have you got a definite scheme to put in its place?"

The question was familiar to me. I had had it fired at me scores of times in the days when I talked Socialism from a soap-box in Hyde Park.

"I think I have a scheme," I said modestly.

Lawson lay back in his chair.

"Good! Cough it up, my son!"

I smoked hard for a minute.

"Well, Lawson, it's like this, my scheme could only be a success if the economic basis of society were altered. So long as one million people take half the national yearly income you can't have any decent scheme of education."

"Right O!" said Lawson cheerfully, "for the sake of argument, or rather peace, we'll give you a Utopia where there are no idle rich. Fire away!"

"Good! I'll talk about the present day education first.

"Twenty years ago education had one aim——to abolish illiteracy. In consequence the Three R.'s were of supreme importance. Nowadays they are held to be quite as important, but a dozen other things have been placed beside them on the pedestal. Gradually education has come to aim at turning out a man or a woman capable of earning a living. Cookery, Woodwork, Typing, Bookkeeping, Shorthand . . . all these were introduced so that we should have better wives and joiners and clerks.

"Lawson, I would chuck the whole blamed lot out of the elementary school. I don't want children to be trained to make pea-soup and picture frames, I want them to be trained to think. I would cut out History and Geography as subjects."

"Eh?" said Lawson.

"They'd come in incidentally. For instance, I could teach for a week on the text of a newspaper report of a fire in New York."

"The fire would light up the whole world, so to speak," said Lawson with a smile. . . .

"I would keep Composition and Reading and Arithmetic in the curriculum. Drill and Music would come into the play hours, and Sketching would be an outside hobby for warm days."

"Where would you bring in the technical subjects?"

"Each school would have a workshop where boys could repair their bikes or make kites and arrows, but there would not be any formal instruction in woodwork or engineering. Technical education would begin at the age of sixteen."

"Six what?"

"Sixteen. You see my pupils are to stay at school till they

are twenty. You are providing the cash you know. Well, at sixteen the child would be allowed to select any subject he liked.
Suppose he is keen on mechanics. He spends a good part of
the day in the engineering shop and the drawing room—
mechanical drawing I mean. But the thinking side of his education is still going on. He is studying political economy,
eugenics, evolution, philosophy. By the time he is eighteen he
has read Nietzsche, Ibsen, Bjornson, Shaw, Galsworthy, Wells,
Strindberg, Tolstoi, that is if ideas appeal to him."

"Ah!"

"Of course, I don't say that one man in a hundred will
read Ibsen. You will always have the majority who are averse
to thinking if they can get out of it. These will be good
mechanics and typists and joiners in many cases. My point is
that every boy or girl has the chance to absorb ideas during
their teens."

"Would you make it compulsory? For instance, that boy
Willie Smith in your school; do you think that he would learn
much more if he had to stay at school till he was twenty?"

"No," I said, "I wouldn't force anyone to stay at school,
but to-day·boys quite as stupid naturally as Smith stay at the
university and love it. A few years' rubbing shoulders with
other men is bound to make a man more alert. Take away, as
you have done for argument's sake, the necessity of a boy's
leaving school at fourteen to earn a living and you simply make
every school a university."

"And it isn't three weeks since I heard you curse universities!" said Lawson with a grin.

"I'm thinking of the social side of a university, I explained.
"That is good. The educational side of our universities is bad
because it is mostly cram. I crammed Botany and Zoo for my
degree and I know nothing about either; I was too busy trying
to remember words like Caryophylacia, or whatever it is, to ask
why flowers droop their heads at night. So in English I had to

cram up what Hazlitt and Coleridge said about Shakespeare when I should have been reading *Othello*. The university fails because it refuses to connect education with contemporary life. You go there and you learn a lot of rot about syllogisms and pentameters, and nothing is done to explain to you the meaning of the life in the streets outside. No wonder that Oxford and Cambridge dons write to the papers saying that life has no opening for a university man."

"But I thought that you didn't want education to produce a practical man. You wanted a theoretical chimney-sweep, didn't you?" said Lawson smiling.

"The present university turns out men who are neither practical nor theoretical. I want a university that will turn out thinkers. The men who have done most to stimulate thought these past few years are men like Wells and Shaw and Chesterton; and I don't think that one of them is a 'varsity man.' "

"You can't run a world on thought," said he.

"I don't know," I said, "we seem to run this old State of ours *without* thought. The truth is that there will always be more workers than thinkers. . . . Along with science and art I want the thinking part of education to go on."

"It goes on now."

"No," I said, "it doesn't. Your so-called educated man is often a stupid fellow. Doctors have a good specialist education, yet I know a score of doctors who think that Socialism means 'The Great Divide.' When Osteopathy came over from America a few years ago thousands of medical men pronounced it 'damned quackery' at once; only a few were wide enough to study the thing to see what it was worth. So with inoculation; the doctors follow the antitoxin authority like sheep. At the university I once saw a raid on an Anti-Vivisection shop, and I'm sure that not one medical student in the crowd had ever thought about vivisection. Mention Women's Freedom to the average lawyer, and he will think you a madman. . . .

"This is the age of the specialist. That's what's wrong with it. Somebody, Matthew Arnold, I think, wanted a man who knew everything of something and something of everything. It's a jolly good definition of education."

"That is the idea of the Scotch Code," said Lawson.

"Yes, perhaps it is. They want our bairns to learn tons of somethings about everything that doesn't matter a damn in life."

My talk with Lawson last night makes me realise again how hopeless it is to plan a system of education when the economic system is all out of joint. I believe that this nation has the wealth to educate its children properly. I wonder what the Conscriptionists would say if I hinted to them that if a State can afford to take its youth away from industry to do unprofitable labour in the army and navy it can afford to educate its youth till the age of twenty is reached.

The stuff we teach in school leads nowhere; the Code subjects simply lull a child to sleep. How the devil is a lad to build a Utopia on Geography and Nature Study and Woodwork? Education should prove that the world is out of joint, and it should point a Kitchener finger at each child and say, "Your Country Needs *You* . . . to set it Right."

XVI.

This has been a delightful day. About eleven o'clock a rap came at the door, and a young lady entered my classroom.

"Jerusalem!" I grasped. "Dorothy! Where did you drop from?"

"I'm motoring to Edinburgh," she explained, "on tour, you know, old thing!"

Dorothy is an actress in a musical comedy touring company, and she is a very old friend of mine. She is a delightful child, full of fun and mischief, yet she can be a most serious lady on occasion.

She looked at my bairns, then she clasped her hands.

"O, Sandy! Fancy you teaching all these kiddies! Won't you teach me, too?" And she sat down beside Violet Brown. I thanked my stars that I had never been dignified in that room.

"Dorothy," I said severely, "you're talking to Violet Brown and I must give you the strap."

The bairns simply howled, and when Dorothy took out her wee handkerchief and pretended to cry, laughter was dissolved in tears.

It was minutes time, and she insisted on blowing the "Dismiss" on the bugle. Her efforts brought the house down. The girls refused to dismiss, they crowded round Dorothy and touched her furs. She was in high spirits.

"You know, girls, I'm an actress and this big bad teacher of yours is a very old pal of mine. He isn't such a bad sort really, you know," and she put her arm round my shoulders.

"See her little game, girls?" I said. "Do you notice that this woman from a disreputable profession is making advances to me? She really wants me to kiss her, you know. She—" But Dorothy shoved a piece of chalk into my mouth.

What a day we had! Dorothy stayed all day, and by four o'clock she knew all the big girls by their Christian names. She insisted on their calling her Dorothy. She even tried to talk their dialect, and they screamed at her attempt to say "Guid nicht the noo."

In the afternoon I got her to sing and play; then she danced a ragtime, and in a few minutes she had the whole crowd ragging up and down the floor.

She stayed to tea, and we reminisced about London. Dear old Dorothy! What a joy it was to see her again, but how dull will school be tomorrow! Ah, well, it is a workaday world, and the butterflies do not come out every day. If Dorothy could read that sentence she would purse up her pretty lips and say, "Butterfly, indeed, you old bluebottle!" The dear child!

The school to-day was like a ballroom the "morning after." The bairns sat and talked about Dorothy, and they talked in hushed tones as about one who is dead.

"Please, sir," asked Violet, "will she come back again?"

"I'm afraid not," I answered.

"Please, sir, you should marry her, and then she'll always be here."

"She loves another man, Vi," I said ruefully, and when Vi whispered to Katie Farmer, "What a shame!" I felt very sad. For the moment I loved Dorothy, but it was mere sentimentalism. Dorothy and I could never love, we are too much of the pal to each other for emotion to enter.

"She is very pretty," said Peggy Smith.

"Very," I assented.

"P—please, sir, you—you could marry her if you really tried?" said Violet. She had been thinking hard for a bit.

"And break the other man's heart!" I laughed.

Violet wrinkled her brows.

"Please, sir, it wouldn't matter for him, we don't know him."

"Why!" I cried, "he is a very old friend of mine!"

"Oh!" Violet gasped.

"Please, sir," she said after a while, "do you know any more actresses?"

I seized her by the shoulders and shook her.

"You wee bissom! You don't care a rap about me; all you want is that I should marry an actress. You want my wife to come and teach you ragtimes and tangoes!" And she blushed guiltily.

Lawson came down to see me again tonight; he wanted to

tell me of an inspector's visit to-day.

"Why don't you apply for an inspectorship?" he asked.

I lit my pipe.

"Various reasons, old fellow," I said. "For one thing I don't happen to know a fellow who knows a chap who lives next door to a woman whose husband works in the Scotch Education Department.

"Again, I'm not qualified; I never took the Education Class at Oxford."

"Finally, I don't want the job."

"I suppose," said Lawson, "that lots of 'em get in by wire-pulling."

"Very probably, but some of them probably get in straight. Naturally, you cannot get geniuses by wire-pulling; the. chap who uses influence to get a job is a third-rater always."

Lawson reddened.

"I pulled wires to get into my job," he said.

"That's all right," I said cheerfully, "I've pulled wires all my days."

"But," I added, "I wouldn't do it again."

"Caught religion?"

"Not quite. The truth is that I have at last realised that you never get anything worth having if you've got to beg for it."

"It's about the softest job I know, whether you have to beg for it or not. The only job that beats it for softness is the kirk," he said.

"I wouldn't exactly call it a soft job, Lawson; a rotten job, yes, but a soft job, no. Inspecting schools is half spying and half policing. It isn't supposed to be you know, but it is. You know as well as I do that every teacher starts guiltily whenever the inspector shoves his nose into the room. Nosing, that's what it is."

"You would make a fairly decent inspector," said Lawson.

"Thanks," I said, "the insinuation being that I could nose

well, eh?"

"I didn't mean that. Suppose you had to examine my school how would you do it?"

"I would come in and sit down on a bench and say: 'Just imagine I am a new boy, and give me an idea of the ways of the school. I warn you that my attention may wander. Fire away! But, I say, I hope you don't mind my finishing this pie; I had a rotten breakfast this morning.' "

"Go on," said Lawson laughing.

"I wouldn't examine the kids at all. When you let them out for minutes I would have a crack with you. I would say something like this: 'I've got a dirty job, but I must earn my screw in some way. I want to have a wee lecture all to myself. In the first place I don't like your discipline. It's inhuman to make kids attend the way you do. The natural desire of each boy in this room was to watch me put myself outside that pie, and not one looked at me.

" 'Then you are far too strenuous. You went from Arithmetic to Reading without a break. You should give them a five minutes chat between each lesson. And I think you have too much dignity. You would never think of dancing a ragtime on this floor, would you? I thought not. Try it, old chap. Apart from its merits as an antidote to dignity it is a first-rate live stimulator.' Hello! Where are you going? Time to take 'em in again?

" 'O, I say, I'm your guest, uninvited guest, I admit, but that's no reason why you should take advantage of me. Man, my pipe isn't half smoked, and I have a cigarette to smoke yet. Come out and watch me play footer with the boys.' "

"You think you would do all that," said Lawson slowly, "but you wouldn't you know. I remember a young inspector who came into my school with a blush on his face. 'I'm a new inspector,' he said very gingerly, 'and I don't know what I am supposed to do.' A year later that chap came in like whirlwind,

and called me 'young man.' Man, you can't escape becoming
smug and dignified if you are an inspector."

"I'd have a darned good try, anyway," I said. "Getting
any eggs just now?"

. . . I don't advise a man to seize every opportunity for a
scrap. There is little use in arguing with an inspector who has
methods of arithmetic different to your methods; it is easier to
think over his advice and reject it if you are a better arithme-
tician than he. But if a man feels strongly enough on a subject
to write to the papers about it, he ought to write as a man, not
as a slave. Incidentally, the habit of using a pseudonym damns
the inspectorate at the same time. For this habit is universal,
and teachers must have heard tales of the victimising of bold
writers. Most educational papers suggest by their contributed
articles that the teachers of Britain are like a crowd of Public
School boys who fear to send their erotic verses to the school
magazine lest the Head flays them. No wonder the social status
of teachers is low. . . .

. . . The School Board here is theoretically a Socialistic
body. Its members are chosen by the people to spend the public money on education. No member can make a profit out of
a Board deal. Yet this board perpetrates all the evils of the private profiteer.

Mrs. Findlay gets ten pounds a year for cleaning the
school. To the best of my knowledge she works four or five
hours a day, and she spends the whole of each Saturday morning cleaning out the lavatories. This sum works out at about
sixpence a day or three ha'pence an hour. Most of her work
consists of carrying out the very considerable part of the playground that the bairns carry in on their boots. Yet all my re-
quests for a few loads of gravel are ignored.

The members do not think that they are using sweated
labour; they say that if Mrs. Findlay doesn't do it for the

money half a dozen widows in the village will apply for the job. They believe in competition and the market value of labour.

A few Saturdays ago I rehearsed a cantata in the school, and I offered Mrs. Findlay half a crown for her extra trouble in sweeping the room twice. She refused it with dignity, she didn't mind obliging me, she said. And this kindly soul is merely a "hand" to be bought at the lowest price necessary for subsistence.

Sometimes I curse the Board as a crowd of exploiters, but in my more rational moments I see that they could not do much better if they tried. If Mrs. Findlay had a pound a week the employees of the farmers on the Board would naturally object to a woman's getting a pound a week out of the public funds for working four hours a day while they slaved from sunrise to sunset for less than a pound. A public conscience can never be better than the conscience of the public's representatives. Hence I have no faith in Socialism by Act of Parliament; I have no faith in municipalisation of trams and gas and water. Private profit disappears when the town council takes over the trams, but the greater evil—exploitation of labour remains.

Ah! I suddenly recollect that Mrs. Findlay has her old age pension each Friday. She thus has eight and six a week. I wonder did Lloyd George realise that his pension scheme would one day prevent fat farmers from having conscience qualms when they gave a widow sixpence a day?

As I came along the road this morning I saw half a dozen carts disgorging bricks on one of Lappiedub's fields. Lappie-dub himself was standing by, and I asked him what was happening.

"Man," he cried lustily, "they've fund coal here and they're to sink pits a' ower the countryside."

When I reached the school the bairns were waiting to tell me the news.

"Please, sir," said Willie Ramsay, "they're going to build a town here bigger than London."

"Bigger than Glasgow even," said Peter Smith.

A few navvies went past the school.

"They're going to build huts for thousands of navvies," said a lassie.

"Please, sir, they'll maybe knock down the school and have a mine here," suggested Violet Brown.

"They won't," I said firmly, "this ugly school will stand until the countryside becomes as ugly as itself. Poor bairns! You don't know what you're coming to. In three years this bonny village will be a smoky blot on God's earth like Newcastle. Dirty women will gossip at dirty doors. You, Willie, will become a miner, and you will walk up that road with a black face. You, Lizzie, will be a trollop of a wife living in a brick hovel. You can hardly escape."

"Mr. Macnab of Lappiedub will lose all his land," said a boy.

"He didn't seem sad when I saw him this morning," I remarked.

"Maybe he's tired of farming," suggested a girl.

"Perhaps," I said, "if he is he doesn't need to worry about farming. He will be a millionaire in a few years. He will get a royalty on every ton of coals that comes up from the pit, and he will sit at home and wait for his money. Simply because he is lucky he will be kept by the people who buy the coals. If he gets sixpence a ton your fathers will pay sixpence more on every ton. I want you to realise that this is sheer waste. The men who own the mines will take big profits and keep up big houses with servants and idle daughters. Then Mr. Macnab will have his share. Then a man called a middleman will buy the coals and sell them to coal merchants in the towns, and he will have his share. And these men will sell them to the householders. When your father buys his ton of coals he is paying for these things:—the coalowner's income, Mr. Macnab's royalty, the middleman's profit, the town coal merchant's profit, and the miners' wages. If the miners want more wages and strike, they will get them, but these men won't lose their profits; they will increase the price of coals and the householders will pay for the increase.

"Don't run away with the idea that I am calling Mr. Macnab a scoundrel. He is a decent, honest, good-natured man who wouldn't steal a penny from anyone. It isn't his fault or merit that he is to be rich, it is the system that is bad."

Thomas Hardy somewhere talks about "the ache of modernism." I adapt the phrase and talk about the ache of industrialism. I look out at my wee window and I see the town that will be. There will be gin palaces and picture houses and music-halls—none of them bad things in themselves, but in a filthy atmosphere they will be hideous tawdry things with horrid glaring lights. I see rows of brick houses and acres of clay land littered with bricks and stones thrown down any way. Stores will sell cheap boots and frozen meat and patent pills, packmen will lug round their parcels of shoddy and sheen. And education! They will erect a new school with a Higher Grade department, and the Board will talk of turning out the type of scholar the needs of the community require. They will have for Rector a B.Sc., and technical instruction will be of first importance. When that happens I shall trek inland and shall seek some rural spot where I can be of some service to the community. I might be able to stand the smoke and filth, but before long there would be a labour candidate for the burgh, and I couldn't stand hearing him spout.

XVII.

. . . A magazine for my hundred and fifty bairns would

be useless; what I want is a magazine for parents and children. It would be issued weekly, and would mingle school gossip with advice. If Willie Wilson knew that Friday's edition might contain a paragraph to the effect that he had been discovered murdering two young robins, I fancy that he would think twice before he cut their heads off.

I imagine entries like the following:

"Peter Thomson said on Thursday that it was Lloyd George who said 'Father, I cannot tell a lie,' and he was caned by the master who, by the way, has just been appointed President of the Conservative Association."

"Mary Brown was late every morning this week."

"John Mackenzie is at present gathering potatoes at Mr. Skinnem's farm, and is being paid a shilling a day for ten hours. Mr. Skinnem has been made an elder of the Parish Kirk."

Someone has said that the most arresting piece of literature is your own name in print. . . . Publicity is the most pleasing thing in life, and that's why patent medicines retain their popularity. At present the village cobbler is figuring in the local paper as a "Cured by Bunkum's Bilious Backache Bunion Beans" example, and beneath his photograph (taken at the age of nineteen; he is fifty-four now) is a glowing testimonial which begins with these words: "For over a decade I have suffered from an excess of Uric Acid, from Neurotic Dyspepsia, and from Optical Derangements. Until I discovered that marvellous panacea—"

I marvel at his improved literary style; it is only a month since he wrote me as follows: "Sir, i will be oblidged if you will let peter away at three oclock tonight hoping that you are well as this leaves me i am your obidt servent peter Macannish."

The magazine would also contain interesting editorials for the parents. Art would have a prominent place; if a bairn made a good sketch or a bonny design it would be reproduced.

Of course, the idea cannot be carried out for lack of funds.

Yet I fancy that the money now spent on hounds and pet dogs would easily run a magazine for every school in Scotland.

The technical difficulties could easily be overcome. The bigger bairns could read the proofs and paste up the magazine, and the teachers would revise it before sending it to the printers.

I must get estimates from the printers, and if they are moderate I shall try to raise funds by giving a school concert.

I see that the Educational Institute is advertising for a man who will combine the post of Editor of *The Educational News* with the office of Secretary to the Institute. The salary is £450 per annum.

This combining of the offices seems to me a great mistake. For an editor should be a literary man with ideas on education, while a good secretary should be an organizer. Because a man can write columns on education, that is no proof that he is the best man to write to the office washerwoman telling her not to come on Monday because it is a holiday.

I could edit the paper (I would take on the job for a hundred a year and the sport of telling the other fellow that his notions of education were all wrong), but I couldn't organise a party of boys scouts. Kitchener is a great organiser, but I shouldn't care for the editorials of *The New Statesman* if he were editor.

I think that the Institute does not want a man with ideas. It wants a man who will mirror the opinions of the Institute. To do this is a work of genius, for the Institute has no opinions. No man can represent a body of men. Suppose the Institute decides by a majority that it will support the introduction of "Love" as a subject of the curriculum. The editor may be a misogynist, or he may have been married eight times, yet the poor devil has to sit down and write an editorial beginning: "Love has too long been absent from our schools. Who does not remember with holy tenderness his first kiss? . . ."

A paper can be a force only when it is edited by a man of force and personality. A man who writes at the dictation of another is a tenth-rater. That, of course, is why our press says nothing.

Little Mary Brown was stung by a wasp the other day as she sat in the class.

"Henceforward," I said, "the wasp that enters this room is to be slain. Tom Macintosh I appoint you commander-in-chief."

I begin to think that I prefer the wasp to the campaign against it. To-day I was in the midst of a dissertation on Trusts when Tom started up.

"Come on lads, there's a wasp!"

They broke a window and two pens; then they slew the wasp.

The less studious boys keep one eye on the window all day, and I found Dave Thomson chasing an imaginary wasp all round the room at Arithmetic time. Dave detests Arithmetic. But when I found that Tom Macintosh was smearing the inside window-sill with black currant jam, I disbanded the anti-wasp army.

The Inspectors refuse to allow teachers to use slates nowadays on the ground that they are unsanitary.

To-day I reintroduced slates to all classes. My one reason was that my bairns were missing one of the most delightful pastimes of youth—the joy of making a spittle run down the slate and back again. I always look back with tenderness to my old slate. It was such a serviceable article. By running my slate-pencil up it I got all the beats of a drum; its wooden sides were the acknowledged tests for a new knife, as a hammer it had few rivals. Then you could play at X-es and O-ies with impunity; you simply licked your palm and rubbed the whole game out when the teacher approached.

In the afternoon half a dozen bairns brought sponges, and I sighed for the good old days when sanitary authorities were plumbers on promotion.

I have given my bairns two songs—*Screw-Guns* and *Follow Me Home,* both by Kipling. I prefer them to the usual "patriotic" song that is published for school use. I don't see the force of teaching children to be patriotic; the man who imagines that a dominie can teach a bairn to love his neighbour or his country is fatuous. Flag-waving is the last futility of noble minds. The queer thing is that all these titled men who spout about Imperialism and Patriotism, and "Make the Foreigner Pay" are enemies of the worker. They don't particularly want to see a State where slums and slavery will be no more; they are so busy thinking out a scheme to extend the Empire abroad that they haven't time to think about the Empire at home. What is the use of an India or a South Africa if East Ham is to remain?

No, I refuse to teach my bairns to sing, "Britons never, never, never shall be slaves." My sense of humour won't allow me to introduce that song.

Although I like Kipling's verses I abominate Kipling's philosophy and politics. He is always to be found on the same platform with the Curzons and Milners and Roosevelts. He believes in "the big stick"; to him Britain is great because of her financiers, her viceroys, her engineers. He glories in enterprise and big ships. He believes with the late Lord Roberts that the Englishman is the salt of the earth. I should define Kipling as a Grown-up Public School Boy.

I always think that the "Patriot's" main contention is that a man ought to be ready to die for his country. I freely grant that it is a great thing to die for your country, but I contend that it is still greater to live for your country; and the man who tries to live for his country usually earns the epithet

"Traitor."

"What do they know of England who only England know?" Kipling says this, or words to this effect. That's the worst of these travelled Johnnies; they go out to India or Africa, and two months after their arrival they pity the narrow vision of the people at home. After having talked much to travelled men I have come to the conclusion that travel is the most narrowing thing on earth.

"If I went out to India," I remarked one day to an Anglo-Indian friend at College, "and if I started to talk about Socialism in a drawing-room, what would happen?"

"Oh," he said with a smile, "they would listen to you very politely, but, of course, you wouldn't be asked again."

When I went down to Tilbury to see this friend off to India I looked at the crowd on the first-class deck.

"Dick," I said, "these people are awful. Look at their smugness, their eagerness to be correct at any expense. They are saying good-bye to wives and mothers and sweethearts, and the whole blessed crowd of 'em haven't an obvious emotion among 'em. I'll bet my hat that they won't even wave their hands when the tender goes off."

As I left the boat the first-class passengers stood like statues, but one fat woman, with a delightfully plebeian face cried: "So long, old sport!" to a man beside me.

"Good!" cried Dick to me with a laugh.

"Lovely!" I called, and waved my hat frantically to the fat woman. Poor soul, I fear that society out East will be making her suffer for her lapse into bad form.

Travel is like a school-history reader; it forces you to study mere incident. The travelled man is an encyclopaedia of information; but I don't want to know what a man has seen; I want to know what he has thought. I am certain that if I went to live in Calcutta I should cease to think. I should marvel at the colour and life of the streets; I should find great pleasure in learning the lore of the native. But in a year I should very probably be talking of "damned niggers," and cursing the India Office as a crowd of asses who know nothing about India and its problems.

I once lent *Ann Veronica* [novel by H. G. Wells] to a clever young lady. Her father, an engineer who had been all over the world, picked up the book. Two days later he returned it with a final note dismissing me as a dangerous character for his daughter to know. The lady was clever, and had mentality enough to read anything with impunity.

No, travel doesn't broaden a man's outlook.

My writing is like my teaching, it is an irresponsible ramble. I meant to write about songs all the time to-night.

I curse my luck in not being a pianist. I want to give my bairns that loveliest of tenor solos—the *Preislied* from *The Meistersingers*. I want to give them Laurence Hope's *Slave's Song* from her *Indian Love Lyrics*—"*Less than the Dust beneath thy Chariot Wheel.*" And there are one or two catchy bits in *Gipsy Love* and *The Quaker Girl* that I should like them to know. I am sure that they would enjoy *Mr. Jeremiah, Esquire,* and *The Gipsy's Song.*

XVIII.

The essay I set to-day was this: "Imagine that you are an old lady who ordered a duck from Gamage's, and imagine that they sent you an aeroplane in a crate by mistake. Then describe in the first person the feelings of the aviator who found the duck awaiting him at breakfast time."

One girl wrote: "Dear Mr. Gamage, I have not opened the basket, but it seems to be an ostrich that you have sent. What will I feed it on?"

A boy, as the aviator, wrote: "If you think I am going to

risk my life on the machine you sent you are wrong. It hasn't
got a petrol tank."

The theme was too difficult for the bairns; they could not
see the ludicrous side. I don't think one of them visualised the
poor old woman gazing in dismay on the workmen unloading
the crate. H. M. Bateman would have made an excellent drawing of the incident.

I tried another theme.

"A few days ago I gave you a ha'penny each," I said.
"Write a description of how you spent it, and I'll give sixpence to the one who tells the biggest lie."

I got some tall yarns. One chap bought an aeroplane and
torpedoed a Zeppelin with it; one girl bought a thousand
motor-cars. But Jack Hood, the dunce of the class, wrote these
words: "I took it to the church on sunday and put it in the
clecshun bag."

I gave him the tanner, although I knew that he had won
it by accident. I don't think that Jack will ever get so great a
surprise again in this life.

We rambled out to sketch this afternoon. It was very hot,
and we lay down under a tree and slept for half-an-hour. Suddenly Violet Brown started up.

"Here's Antonio!" she cried, and the Italian drew his van
to the side of the road.

"A slider for each of us," I said, and he began to hustle.
My turn came last.

"You like a glass, zir, instead of a zlider?" said Antonio.

"Yes," I replied, "a jolly good suggestion; I haven't had
the joy of licking an ice-cream glass dry for many a long day."

It was glorious.

On the way back a girl bought sweets at the village shop.
She gave me one.

"Please, sir, it's one of them changing kind," she said.

"Eh?" I hastily took it out and looked at it.

"By George, so it is, Katie!" I cried, "I thought they were dead long since." It was white at first but it changed to blue, then red, then green, then purple. Unfortunately, I bit it unthinkingly, and I never discovered its complete spectrum.

I call this a lucky day; ice cream and changing balls in one afternoon are the quintessence of luck. But man is insatiable; to-night I have a great craving for a stick of twisted sugarelly— the polite call it liquorice.

A couple of Revivalists came to the village a week ago, and they have made a few converts. One of them stopped me on the road to-night and asked if I were saved.

"I am, or, at least, was, a journalist." I said, and walked on chuckling. Of course he gaped, for he did not know why I chuckled. I was thinking of the reporter sitting in the back seat at a Salvationist Meeting. A Salvation lass bent over him. "Are you saved, my friend?" she whispered. He looked up in alarm.

"I'm a journalist," he said hastily.

"O! I beg your pardon," she said, and moved on. . . .

I have no sympathy with all this "saving" business. It's a cowardly selfish religion that makes people so anxious about their tuppence-ha'penny souls. When I think of all the illiterate lay preachers I have listened to I feel like little Willie at the Sunday School.

"Hands up all those who would like to go to Heaven!" said the teacher. Willie alone did not put his hand up.

"What! Mean to tell me, Willie, that you don't want to go to Heaven?"

Willie jerked a contemptuous thumb towards the others.

"No bloomin' fear," he muttered, "not if that crowd's goin'."

Shelley says that "most wretched men are cradled into

poetry through wrong." I think that most wretched preachers
are cradled into preaching through conceit. It is thrilling to
have an audience hang upon your words; we all like the lime-
light. Usually we have to master a stiff part before we can
face the audience. Preaching needs no preparation, no thinking,
no merit; all you do is to stand up and say: "Deara friendsa,
when I was in the jimmynasium at Peebles, a fellow lodger of
mine blasphemeda. From that daya, deara friendsa, that son
of the devila nevera prospereda. O, friendsa! If you could only
looka into your evila heartsa. . . ."

I note that when Revivalists come to a village the so-
called village lunatic is always among the first to give his testimony. Willie Baffers has been whistling *Life, Life, Eternal Life*
all the week, but I was glad to note that he was back to *Stop
yer Ticklin', Jock,* to-night.

I have introduced two new text-books—*Secret Remedies,*
and *More Secret Remedies.* These books are published by the
British Medical Association at a shilling each, and they give
the ingredients and cost of popular patent medicines.

These books should be in every school. Everyone should
know the truth about these medicines, and unless our schools
tell the truth, the public will never know it. No daily newspaper would think of giving the truth, for the average daily
is kept alive by patent medicine advertisements.

I marvel at the mentality of the man who can sell a farthing's worth of drugs for three and sixpence. I don't blame
the man; I merely marvel at him. What is his standard of
truth? What does he imagine the purpose of life to be?

Poor fellow! I fancy he is a man born with a silver knife
in his mouth, as Chesterton says in another context; either that,
or he is born poor in worldly goods and in spirit. He is
dumped down in an out-of-joint world where money and power
are honoured, where honesty is never the best policy; the poor,

miserable little grub realises that he has not the ability to earn money or power honestly; but he knows that people are fools, and that a knave always gets the better of a fool.

Our laws are really funny. I can swindle thousands by selling a nostrum, but if I sign Andrew Carnegie's name on a cheque I am sent to Peterhead Prison. Britain is individualistic to the backbone. The individual must be protected, but the crowd can look after itself. If I steal a pair of boots and run for it, I am a base thief; if I turn bookie and become a welsher I have entered the higher realms of sport, and I get a certain amount of admiration—from those who didn't plunge at my corner. I have seen a cheap-jack swindle a crowd of Forfarshire ploughmen out of a month's earnings, but not one of them thought of dusting the street with him.

Honesty must be a relative thing. Personally I will "swick" a railway company by travelling without a ticket on any possible occasion; yet, when a cycle agent puts a new nut on my motor-bike and charges a shilling I call him a vulgar thief. Of course he is; there is no romance in making a broken-down motor-cyclist pay through the nose, but a ten mile journey without a ticket is the only romantic experience left in a drab world.

I once saw an article on *Railway Criminals* in, I think, *Tit-Bits*. It pointed out that the men who are convicted of swindling the railway companies have well marked facial characteristics. I recollect going to the mirror at the time and saying "Tu quoque!"

In these days I had a firm belief in physiognomy; I believed that you had only to gaze into a person's eyes to see whether he was telling the truth or not. I am wiser now that I know Peter Young. Pete is ten, and he has a clear, honest countenance. To-night I found him tinkering with the valve of my back tyre.

"Who loosened that valve?" I demanded.

"Please, sir, it was Jim Steel," he said unblushingly, and he looked me straight in the eyes.

"All right, George Washington," I remarked. "There's a seat in the Cabinet, waiting for you, my lad." And I meant it too. I believe in the survival of the fittest, and I know that Peter is the best adapted to survive in a modern civilisation. It is said of his father that he bought an old woman's ill-grown pig, a white one, and promised her a fine piebald pig in a week's time. He brought her the piebald. Then rain came—

I often condemn the press for not seeking truth, yet no man has a greater admiration for a good liar than I have. When I hear a fellow break in on a conversation with the words: "Talking of Lloyd George, when I was in the Argentine last winter. . . ." I grapple him to my soul with hoops of steel. I can't stand the common or garden liar with his trite expressions. . . . "So the missis is keeping better, old man? Glad to hear it." "Your singing has improved wonderfully, my dear." "I was kept late at the office," and all that sort of lie. All the same I recognise that we are all liars, and few of us can evade the trite manner of lying.

I met a man on the road to-night, and he stopped to talk. I hate the fellow; he is one of those mean men who would plant potatoes on his mother's grave if the cemetery authorities would allow it. Yet I shook his greasy hand when he held it out. If I had had the tense honesty of Ibsen's *Brand* I should have refused to see his hand. But we all lie in this way; indeed, life would be intolerable if we were all *Brands* and cried "All or Nothing!" We all compromise, and compromise is the worst lie of all. Compromise I can pardon, but not gush. I know men who could say to old greasy-fist: "Man, I'm glad to see you looking so well!" Men who would cut his throat if they had the pluck. Nevertheless gush is not one of the Scot's chief characteristics.

There is a shepherd's hut up north, and George Broon

lives there alone. Once another shepherd came up that way, and he thought he would settle down with George for a time. The newcomer, Tam Kennedy, came in after his day's work, and the two smoked in silence for two hours. Then Tam remarked: "Aw saw a bull doon the road the nicht."

Next morning George Broon said: "It wasna a bull; it was a coo."

Tam at once set about packing his bag.

"Are ye gaein' awa?" asked George in surprise.

"Yus," said Tam savagely, "there's far ower much argybargying here."

Summer holidays at last! Many a day I have longed for them, but now that they are here I feel very very sad. For to-day some of these bairns of mine sat on these benches for the last time. When I blow my bugle again I shall miss familiar faces. I shall miss Violet with her bonny smile; I shall miss Tom Macintosh with his cheery face. Vi is going to the Secondary School, and Tom is going to the railway station. They are sweethearts just now, and I know that both are sad at leaving.

"Never mind, Tam," I heard her say, "Aw'll aye see ye at the station, ilka mornin' and nicht."

"We'll get married when Aw'm station mester, Vi," said Tom hopefully, and she smiled and blushed.

Poor Tom! I'm sorry for you my lad. In three years you will be carrying her luggage, and she won't take any notice of you, for she is a lawyer's daughter.

Confound realism!

Once I felt as Tom feels. I loved a farmer's daughter, and I suffered untold agony when she told me that her father's lease expired in seventeen years.

"Then we're flittin' to Glesga," she said, and I was wretched for a week. She was ten then; now she is the mother of four.

Annie and her seventeen years reminds me of the professor who was lecturing on Astronomy to a village audience.

"In seven hundred million years, my friends," he said solemnly, "the sun will be a cold body like the moon. There will be no warmth on earth, no light, no life . . . nothing."

A chair was pushed back noisily at the back of the hall, and a big farmer got up in great agitation.

"Excuse me, mister, but hoo lang did ye say it wud be till that happened?"

"Seven hundred million years, my friend."

The farmer sank into his chair with a great sigh of relief.

"Thank Goad!" he gasped, "Aw thocht ye said seven million."

They say that when a man dies after a long life he looks back and mourns the things that he's left undone. I suppose that some teachers look back over a year's work and regret their sins of omission. I do not.

I know that I have had many lazy days this session; I know that there were exercises that I failed to correct, subjects that I failed to teach. I regret none of these things, for they do not count.

Rachel Smith is leaving the district, and to-day Mary Wilson shook her hand. "Weel, by bye, Rachel, ye'll have to gang to anither schule, and ye'll maybe have to work there," she said.

"Eh?" I cried, "do you mean to say, Mary Wilson, that Rachel hadn't to work in this school?"

"No very much," said Mary, "ma father says that we just play ourselves at this school."

Mary's father is right; I have converted a hard-working school into a playground. And I rejoice. These bairns have had a year of happiness and liberty. They had done what they liked; they have sung their songs while they were working at graphs, they have eaten their sweets while they read their books.

They have hung on to my arms as we rambled along in search of artistic corners. It was only yesterday that Jim Jackson marched up the road to meet me at dinner-time with his gun team and gun, a log of wood mounted on a pair of perambulator wheels. As I approached I heard his command: "Men, lay the gun!" and when I was twenty yards off he shouted "Fire!"

"Please, sir," he cried, "you're killed now, but we'll take you prisoner instead." And the team lined up in two columns and escorted me back to the school to the strains of *Alexander's Ragtime Band* played on the mouth-organ.

"Is it usual, Colonel," I asked, "for the commander of the gun team to act as the band?"

Jim scratched his head.

"The band was all killed at Mons," he said, "and the privates aren't musical." Then he struck up *Sister Susie's Sewing Shirts for Soldiers*.

I know that I have brought out all the innate goodness of these bairns. When Jim Jackson came to the school he had a bad look; if a girl happened to push him he turned on her with a murderous scowl. Now that I think of it I realise that Jim is always a bright cheery boy now. When I knew him first I could see that he looked upon me as a natural enemy, and if I had thrashed him I might have made him fear me, but the bad look would never have left his face.

If I told anyone that I had made these bairns better I should be met with the contemptuous glance that usually greets the man who blows his own horn. Stupid people can never understand the man who indulges in introspection; they cannot realise that a man can be honest with himself. If I make a pretty sketch I never hesitate to praise it. On the other hand I am readier than anyone else to declare one of my inferior sketches bad. Humility is nine-tenths hypocrisy.

I do have a certain amount of honesty, and I close my log with a solemn declaration of my belief that I have done my work well.

As for the work that the Scotch Education Department expected me to do—well, I think the last entry in my official Log Book is a fair sample of that.

"The school was closed to-day for the summer holidays. I have received Form 9b from the Clerk."

VI

LETTERS TO
THE TIMES

Unless otherwise specified, the following letters of A. S. Neill have appeared in THE (LONDON) TIMES EDUCATIONAL SUP- PLEMENT. *Each is preceded by its date of publication.*

FREEDOM AND LICENCE:
PLIGHT OF THE PIONEER SCHOOL

July 26, 1957

Pioneer schools have been allowed inside the framework of the State. We have the famous experiment of E. F. O'Neill as one of the best examples. But the scope was usually limited; the teacher could experiment with methods of teaching, not with methods of living. A year or two ago the head of a secondary modern school in East Anglia told his classes that they could make their own timetables. I believe that his committee told him that he must not do such a thing again.

Pioneering has so far been most free outside the State system. My own school, Summerhill, has been, as I said to an H.M.I. the other day, not a school but a way of community living. In its 36 years' existence it has proved that when children are free to be themselves they play for a long period and then make up in academic work in about two years; pupils who have played for the best part of their time until the age of 14 have often passed School Certificate at 16 with distinction and ease. But some H.M.I.'s, even today, seem to hold the narrow view that academic success is the criterion of education. The criterion we hold is one of happiness, balance, sincerity, originality; and these qualities cannot easily be inspected. Many people hold that Summerhill has been a success. I think it has been myself, naturally.

But now comes this year of 1957 when all schools have to register and submit to the Ministry's criterion of their value. Any inspection will be mainly concerned with lessons, and I agree that, in a system which allows any child to play all day long until it wants lessons, good lessons should be there to be had. Apart from what the Ministry may say, parents will demand a school in which their children can pass G.C.E. if they want to. Hence the future of my school at least depends on having a good staff. And to a great extent, a good staff depends on salaries. That is the rub. I have 45 pupils and should have at least a staff of seven to give them the best chance of passing exams. My parents are not in the main rich, so that my fees have never allowed me to pay Burnham Scale.

In the past this did not seem to matter. Before the war, I had an excellent staff working then for only £8 a month with board, laundry, etc. I had plenty of choice, for many wanted to work in Summerhill. Today . . . well, I had an advertisement in this journal a week or two ago: I had two replies, both unsuitable. I tried another weekly and again had two replies; when I told the salary, one said she would not come for the money. I await with trepidation the reply from the second applicant.

Why is it that today no one wants to sacrifice money for an interesting experience? I think that the reasons are several. When Summerhill began in Germany in 1921, the new psychology was sweeping the West; Freud's discovery of the unconscious was to revolutionize the world; Homer Lane's wonderful work in The Little Commonwealth inspired scores of teachers, myself included. It was all so new. Then gradually the idea of freedom in education grew, and although apparently the public schools retained their barbarous system of allowing prefects to beat small boys (who could not hit back), many a State day school burned its cane and treated children humanely. Freedom spread and is still spreading. True, freedom had to be limited; you cannot say to a school of a thousand children in East London: "Play all day if you like." But the *Stimmung* of freedom penetrated schools, so that perhaps teaching in a place like Summerhill is no longer so exciting as it was 20-odd years ago.

Then, again, there is the training of teachers. The State expects teachers to teach in State schools for at least two years after finishing training. Fair enough, but it makes my problem difficult. I expect that most young teachers after their two years in State schools settle down in the system and do not wish to change. They would lose their superannuation for the period they were in a private school.

The biggest factor militating against my getting staff must be the financial one. Since the war, wages have become of great importance. It may be that the general sense of insecurity . . . is partly allayed by financial security. I am sure that all private schools are having the same difficulties . . . only some of the bigger co-educational schools get fees that make my Scottish mouth water.

I cannot see much future for the pioneer school. Without staff, it must die, and in a world that more and more becomes totalitarian, the death of pioneer schools would be a tragedy, for the world needs citizens who know freedom and are able to distinguish it from licence. Freedom is such a delicate plant. Look at the school freedom in the U.S.S.R. in the twenties and thirties, and compare it with the mass character-moulding there to-day. We need not go so far away. What Ministry of Education in this country would support any free enterprise in education? It could not dare; after all, it represents many millions of parents, while my school has only about 35 of them. I think that one of the proofs of advancing totalitarianism is the increasing struggle to live of minority movements in education, art, science—think of Reich in prison in the United States—humanism, health, food reform.

Freedom in school grows, but how far can it go against the big battalions—McCarthyism (hate), apartheid (fear), U.S.S.R. in Hungary (power), race hatred, political wangling—all the anti-life elements in society? And it may take a long time before it is realized that a B.A. or an M.A. is not necessarily an educated man. . . .

The first requisite for good character is freedom from within, and no external discipline can give it. But, alas, the sad truth is that affording an atmosphere in which this inner free-dom can grow depends on hard cash, and again, alas, the richer one gets, the less one seems to believe in freedom. But as a man who has never been able to afford anything better than a third-hand car, I may be prejudiced.

Since writing the above, I have just seen the reference to my school in Comment in Brief last week. Yes, the H.M.I. Report of 1949 was fair and generous, but because of shortage of staff, I doubt if Summerhill would get as good a report to-day. A lot depends on the individual inspector; obviously an inspector whose horizon was bounded by lessons would not be the best person to evaluate a pioneer school. Quite frankly, I am not worried about the H.M.I.'s. My worry will possibly be the medical officers, with their standard requirements of so many lavatories, so many inches between beds, etc. But that bridge can wait till it is crossed. After all, I may get a Scottish M.O.H.!

WHY HAVE EXAMS? CULTURE AND FUTILITY

May 8, 1959

An H.M.I. said to me: "What would you teach if there were no G.C.E. exams?" I could not think of an answer, pos-sibly because when one has been conditioned from infancy to accept school subjects as education, he is not free enough to reply.

That the products of schools are much more interested in things outside the school system—football pools, cheap press, television, sex, crime—than they are in all the subjects we teach, suggests that our schools are never adapted to the life outside. This is primarily due to the fact that emotion is of infinitely more moment than intellect. . . . We see the extreme result of this imbalance in books like *Blackboard Jungle* and *The Young Devils*. Raising the leaving age has too often meant adolescents having to continue studying what has no appeal to their heads or senses. It is just nonsense to say that our schools give children culture—the sales of our most sensational newspapers prove this point; education precedes a national interest in the inferior and nonessential.

Cultures! Thousands of our pupils learn French. Few will ever go to France, fewer will ever read French books; in two years most of what they learnt has gone. So with other subjects. Maths! What passer of the 0 level maths could do a quadratic equation five years later? English! What proportion of G.C.E. passers read whodunnits instead of the cultured reading their grammar schools gave them—Lamb's Essays, Shakespeare, Milton, Coleridge? Geography! How do we apply what we learn after we leave school? When I motor to Scotland I cannot get rid of the notion that I am going uphill: the wall map had Scotland at the top. The only geography we use is of the place-on-the-map variety and that vaguely, to be sure. How many of us know exactly where these places are— Thursday Island, Vermont, Salzburg? Post-school life does not concern itself with the exports of Brazil or the climate of Timbuctu.

I feel like replying to the H.M.I. by saying: "I'd scrap the lot," but then would have the painful task of saying what my school would teach; painful, because it is so difficult to assess change of values. In my youth, a university education was the criterion of an educated man; the scholar with his Latin and Greek and philosophy was the man to respect and emulate. Today that is not so. The standard has altered, mainly because of the great and rapid advance in mechanical theory and practice. In terms of utility today, the expert who can make or even repair a television set is of more importance than an M.A. who has specialized in—say—English, for the M.A. can only teach in a small circle while the other man can do in a large one. We see the same in music. Whatever a school may do to give pupils a love of classical music, the fact [probably] remains that records of the rock 'n' roll singers far exceed in volume and sale those of all the classics lumped together.

Given freedom from examinations, I should aim at catching the children's interests and following them. Rock 'n' roll? Good, the music of the school would start with Elvis Presley and Tommy Steele. Reading would be all the whodunnits the school could procure. I should reverse the process by which the school begins with Addison and goes on to the post-graduate *News of the World,* feeling uneasily that my pupils' daily perusal of the *News of the World* might not automatically lead later to the reading of Addison.

But perhaps I should teach nothing at all on the ground that you cannot teach anything of importance. I know of no school that has been free enough to follow in its teaching the dictates of child nature. Adults must work and therefore children must be taught to work. Since the importance of play in a child's life has been recognized, no fundamental alteration of the timetable has been made. I can fantasy a nonexam school which would be a large playground—not playing fields, which are not really play at all; play with books and tools and music and dance and—in Utopia—play with love. I doubt if the adage that the hard way forms character has any validity in psychology. I see rock 'n' roll as a flight from the hard way of schooling with its insane demand for homework; yet, to be honest, I do not think that is the whole truth. My pupils who are as free as they can be in a school today, love rock 'n' roll records. But to be honest again, they do not seem to carry on the interest into the later teens. Nor are my own pupils free from the G.C.E. obstacle to real education.

The only importance in education lies in character formation, and here many a teacher will agree. But not many will agree that character formation must come from inside. No study will form a good character. Indeed, character is seldom mentioned by teachers; the cry today is not for better character but for better science, better science in an era in which knowing has run far ahead of emotion, and science has almost become synonymous with keeping up with the Joneseskis.

This insistence on the importance of playhood may sound mad to many a teacher. Maybe it is mad, but it is at least a tentative suggestion for coping with a most dangerous situation, that of a sick world whose values have little or nothing to do with schooling. And I do not mean Britain alone; the news of anti-social rebellious youth in Sweden, America, Russia, shows that schooling is failing in many lands. Personally I think that conscious or, more probably, unconscious fear is at the bottom of youth's revolt. Let us eat, drink, and be merry, for tomorrow we die. Sex repression is not enough to account for it; we had sex repression long before the H-bomb appeared, and it did not seem to go so far as flick knives and cycle chains.

Is youth rebelling because of its education or in spite of it? I suggest the former. I question if a lessonless school would produce any anti-social, any criminal products; I feel sure that most hateful coshings and stabbings are the result of unlived-out play, but again that cannot be the whole truth, for children of the upper and middle classes are not usually teddy boys. I am not wise enough to pose as an authority, but in the days when I had to deal with many antisocial adolescents, I saw most of them go out cured, not by lessons, not by my analyses, but cured because they had freedom to live out their playhood, cured because allowed to be themselves. And of moment, cured because relieved of guilt about sex. An odd thought to end up with: When any madman or fool of a statesman can press the button that could kill us all, why does such a small thing as sex retain its Victorian significance? Until the guilt complex of youth is relieved, all or nearly all of our school subject teaching will remain useless and a matter of indifference to the young.

REALITIES OF LIFE:
PRACTICAL APPROACHES IN THE SCHOOL

May 6, 1960

If a letter appears in these columns about the teaching of mathematics, there will most likely be some replies, but if a letter concerns "The Emotions of the Adolescent" there might be no reply. . . . Teachers are trained primarily in school subjects, and they feel that psychology is outside their knowledge and experience.

Thus the sad situation has arisen that teachers of specific subjects have to ignore most of the things that are of greater importance. They can tell if Bob is good at English and bad at French, but they know nothing of Bob's real inner life; he is almost certainly suffering from guilt about masturbation; his home life may be a hell of parental hate or at least everyday quarrelling; he may be odd man out in his family. His emotional life has no contact with his school life, and one result, patent to all, is that when he leaves school he drops all his subjects in favour of cheap reading, e.g., the average Sunday newspaper. The pornography, the crime stories, the scandals of the gutter press appeal to the student's infantile emotions, emotions that had no chance of finding a healthy outlet. What good is our secondary and grammar school education when the Press Council condemns papers for pornography, papers that must have well over 10 million readers?

Is it right that teachers should stick to their special jobs teaching subjects and by-pass so much in a child's life that is

vital? I can hear one honest answer: "We aren't qualified."
I can hear another: "We haven't the time; heavens above,
haven't we enough to do correcting papers, preparing lessons?"
Both answers are true, yet the unhappy thought comes—have
these home exercises any validity? Apart from examinations,
do they really matter?

Even if the teacher has considerable knowledge of child
psychology, how can he use it? Even if he has been psycho-
analysed himself, he cannot analyse his pupils. Therapy implies
complete objectivity; the therapist must be completely detached,
accepting all confessions without criticism or blame. The teacher
can never be outside; the mere fact that he has to keep discipline in class makes the child identify him with the father (or
in the case of a woman teacher, the mother). And as every
child is tied up emotionally with his parents, resistance will
keep him from allowing the substitute parent to analyse him.
Anyway, analysis is not the answer; you cannot analyse the
world, or a single class.

Luckily, children can be helped to psychic health by other
means. Freedom is the best remedy, and even in schools that
have little or no freedom, the teacher who is "on the side of"
the child can accomplish much. If a teacher inspires any fear,
he can help no child, and should not be in a noble profession.
To help an unhappy child, the teacher must be gentle, un-
dignified, human, sincere; he must be capable of inspiring
trust; he must be able to distinguish between freedom and
licence; and he should have a sense of humour.

Without having read Freud, Jung, Adler, or Reich, a
teacher can approach children through psychology. In fact, . . .
the more he studies psychology, the greater [may be] his difficulties. Suppose a young teacher, influenced by Reich, sees our
social system as a patriarchal one, anti-sex, anti-life, inhibiting
the children with evil Verbots and repressive religion; suppose he sees the compulsive family as the enemy of young life,

castrating it with moral taboos. What can he do about it? If a boy confides in him about his masturbation guilt, dare he tell him that his parents have lied when they told him he would become mad, stop growing, or something of the sort? Dare he tell him the truth, that the only bad thing about masturbation is the guilt feeling?

Or suppose an adolescent tearfully tells her sympathetic woman teacher that she is cuffed at home by her parents, that her life there is a misery. Dare the teacher explain that her parents hate each other and themselves? I hasten to add that in both cases telling will do no good. The early Freudian belief that knowing the cause of a complex cured it, [has] proved to be erroneous. The male teacher mentioned could help the boy by telling him masturbation is universal in "civilized" countries, and is harmless; but the girl would not be helped by being told the truth about her ugly home because, for one thing, she has an ambivalent attitude toward her parents, love and hate.

Here I am, quite arbitrarily, ruling out the practical use of psychology by the class teacher. His use of his knowledge should be an indirect one, approving instead of condemning. You have much more chance of curing a young thief by giving him sixpence every time he steals than by punishing him. You will help the young liar by showing him that you are a much better liar than he is. I recognize the limits; it might be difficult to get any reaction by giving out love to the near morons pictured in *Blackboard Jungle*. Only a genius like Homer Lane would try. Teachers of tough lads tell me that they had to give up treating with love because the toughs thought them sissies. . . .

I now realize why teachers evade the psychological issue. Even with the best intentions, what can a teacher do about the cosh merchants and rapists of the adolescent world— a world that embraces East and West? Why do adolescents rebel today? Unconscious fear of the H-bomb—let us eat, drink and be merry for tomorrow we die? Is it the family constellation breaking up; parental moral authority gone with nothing to replace it?

I think that all this rock 'n' roll, this knee-wagging singer craze with its hysterical reception, this coshing and knifing, are primarily outlets for sex that is hated because of adult moral teaching. Repressed sex so often appears as sadism. I think that youth rebels partly because it has at last realized that it has been lied to by its elders. And, in parenthesis, I suggest that raising the school age has been evil because it has made adolescents who want to be out and doing sit at the old desks and learn the old dull subjects. I feel that after 14, compulsory education should be mainly for doing—music, dance, handwork, hiking, swimming, play of all kinds. If the *Blackboard Jungle* had been a huge workshop, even the morons would have been less anti-social.

But what should the class teacher do? Rather he should know what not to do: "Your brother wouldn't get his sums wrong like you do." "Stop crying; be a man." He must be honest. "Please, teacher, did you ever wet the bed when you were a kid?" I have known one bedwetter who improved a lot when his honest father told him that he had been enuritic until he was 19.

Psychology, teachers? Don't practice it: live it.

USING THE EXTRA YEAR,
OR DAYDREAMING OF FREEDOM?

February 14, 1964

What is the nation to do about the curriculum for the

fifteeners? . . . Much of school learning has little to do with the outside world. The thousands who study Shakespeare, Hardy, Tennyson help later to swell the millions who read the most sensational Sunday papers. Naturally, for in a school system that makes emotion inferior to intellect, the sensational tales of crime and sex touch the starved emotions. The hysteria about the Beatles is another manifestation of primitive emotions. . . .

Youth will hate any system that does not provide some outlet for emotion . . . The schools for the fifteeners should be largely workshops and art schools. Not entirely, of course. I can imagine a group of that age taking part in discussions on subjects they have some interest in. A topic like local government might lead to head-nodding, while a debate on the relative merits of Elvis Presley and the Beatles would surely be an exciting one. In short: the new schooling for the new agers should be linked up with life outside the school.

Doing and creation do not necessarily help the emotional life. . . . I am advocating creation, not for curative purposes, but because it does compel interest and effort . . . By the way, I would like to see what results would appear in a typically "dead" school if the essay subject were: "The Influence of the Camel on European Art."

I can visualize new schools for the older pupils, wonderful places with cookery, pottery, painting, music, dance, engineering, and science, with mathematics for the engineers. I can see many of both sexes liking to be in these schools. The great danger would be the teacher who wanted to show how things are done, one who ruined initiative by attaching too much importance to method and not enough to creation. . . .

There is the other way. I had a pupil in Dresden who left to go into a big furniture factory. The foreman gave him the plan of a roll-top desk, showed him how to do a dovetail joint, and said: "You'll get as long as you like to make this desk. Carry on." When finished, it was pretty good.

I would like to see the suggesting teacher abolished, the kind who says: "Now, children, you'll paint Walter Raleigh laying his cloak in the mud for Queen Elizabeth." If any child in my school asked: "What shall I paint?" I would get a shock. A teacher . . . must never give a child a sense of inferiority by showing his own dexterity . . . that is why I, with a degree in English, Second Class by the way, teach maths.

I am old enough to remember the terrible sense of inadequacy children had in the days when the copy books had wonderful copperplate specimens to copy. Yet . . . no one wants to see [them] these days.

No, the problem for the fifteeners is not one of classrooms and subjects so much as one of teachers who will not stand by and observe. . . . More than once [have] I said that my pet aversion is the teacher who sees a kid making mud pies and immediately improves the shining hour by giving a lesson on coast erosion. . . .

The new schools should do something about civics, not teach them but allow the pupils to live them, and that means a considerable amount of self-government. True, in a day school, self-government is not easy . . . what is there to govern anyway? You can have true self-government only when living in a community all the time. In the thousand self-government meetings I have attended I cannot recall one in which lessons were mentioned. But in a day school the adolescents should have the right to choose what they will do.

Why should not a boy of 15 spend his whole day painting or playing the fiddle or simply reading? Ah, but he must have a broad education. Who has? I think it nonsense to argue that school subjects teach a child to reason. This argument is often used in connexion with maths, yet I have never seen a staffroom in which the maths master was considered a fount of rational opinion.

And what is the new school going to do about morals? Is it to compel adolescents to have religious instruction in a nation that is not Christian at all? Is it to have a department in which troubled boys and girls can tell their sex problems to a non-moral sympathetic teacher? Sex is the only vital subject ignored by education. Hence, pornography, hence music-hall jokes, hence far too much pregnancy, hence an anti-life society.

I am really asking this question: Will the raising of the school age mean a continuation of an education that evades most of the things most vital to the young? Is its aim going to be teaching a child how to make a living instead of letting him discover how to live? I know of nobody good enough to tell a child how to live. Is education to mean better scientists, engineers, doctors, instead of more balanced, happier, more tolerant human beings? A good education would mean both.

Somebody will tell me I am out of touch with schools in general. Possibly, but if anyone wants to tell me that I am writing about schools as they were 60 years ago, I quote a letter I had the other day from a teacher in a state school: "Six were caned today for bad work." Exceptional, no doubt, but the fact that a county council allows any such school to exist shows that such things are tolerated in an era in which many teachers are humane and balanced and kindly.

LEARNING OR LIVING?

June 17, 1966

I am casting no aspersions on my good friend the editor when I say that much of *Times Educational Supplement* is to me unreadable. His job is to run a journal that will interest teachers, and he has to depend on his contributors. I am taking the prerogative of an old man to shoot out my neck when I say that apparently teachers are interested in the wrong things.

The fundamental factor in education is the child, and I do not often see the word *child* in these columns. Salaries, organization, comprehensive schools, sometimes methods of teaching, but where is the child? Let us face the fact that education primarily means learning. Tories and Labour both want to build a fine educational system, but they think in terms of learning, of better scientists, of exams and exams. Education today begins at the neck and goes upwards.

But the world is not populated by scientists and university graduates. What a child learns in school is for the most part forgotten almost immediately. How many of you readers, who are not teachers of mathematics, could solve a quadratic equation or even do a square root? I can because I teach maths, although not a trained mathematician, but I have long forgotten the exports of Peru and the tributaries of the Rhine.

So have you, dear fellow teachers. It trained us to think, some will say. Nonsense; it trained us to be bored. Learning by itself is of little consequence in a sick world. The Mods and Rockers, once free of the hated system, get on scooters and motorbikes with birds behind and find expression for their starved emotions in bashing each other at seaside resorts.

I hold that education should concern itself with the emotions and leave the intellect to look after itself. But what chance have the emotions in a system that makes school subjects of [greater] importance? Think of *Lord of the Flies,* a most damaging criticism (unconscious on the part of Golding) of our education. His boys were drilled in subjects; they were disciplined; their emotions were never allowed to be expressed, so little wonder that once free on an island they killed each other. The "Hitler" was the head choir boy, the religious lad.

No one who has seen free children could visualize their becoming little barbarians when wrecked on an island. By free children, I mean children whose emotions have not been killed by outside discipline, subject compulsion, punishment, moralizing, fear. True, our big schools are not turning out a majority of killers and savages, but they must be turning out docile members of society who never challenge . . . One aim of education should be to make children challenge.

I get mail from the United States that is almost Beatle-size, and the most saddening letters are from school kids—"I hate my school. The teachers make the lessons dull, and if you try to do anything original, they jump on you. We are being fitted into a mould." I don't get letters from home children, possibly because they have so many home lessons that they can't find the time to write.

In my school, where lessons are voluntary, a new boy or girl of 13 will skip all formal lessons but will attend lessons in art, drama, handwork. This to me is proof that lessons are forced on a few million children all over the world. Yet to read *Times Educational Supplement,* one would think that lessons are the be-all and end-all of schooling. How many teachers know what a child feels? How many guess the enormous guilt about sex, especially masturbation? How many know what fears a child has? How can they anyway, in big classes?

But a child after leaving school does not drop his fears and his guilt as he drops his book learning; they go on with him through life. Education should deal with life and not with acquiring knowledge. . . . I fail to answer at least half the questions in the TV Top of the Form competition.

I ask what our system is doing for the children who become delinquents. What is it doing for the poor adolescents who accept sex as something dirty and sinful? The pages of this journal seldom mention things like that. Why plan comprehensive schools for children if the meal offered is a dull, heady one? Michael Duane tried to put emotions first in his school, and we know what happened to him. We know what

R. F. Mackenzie had to face when, in Scotland, he thought
that his pupils would benefit more from roaming the glens
than from sitting at a desk. Duane and Mackenzie believed that
living is more important than knowing. . . .

Teachers flee from emotional things; they find it easy to
rationalize—"My job is to teach French, not to worry about
whether Tommy is bullying his sister or not." The damned subject kills a teacher. It becomes a be-all; think of the bitter rows
in staffrooms when the mathematics man finds he has three
periods less than the English teacher. The teacher cannot see
the educational wood for subject trees.

It is all reflected weekly in these pages. And it is all so
disappointing. The G.C.E. papers seem to me to be the same old
papers I knew over 60 years ago, the same old rubbish about
parsing and analysis. It is a sick world, my masters, and our
schooling system is not doing a thing to make people more
balanced, more charitable, more conscious.

DRAMA IN SUMMERHILL

December 30, 1966

We have had a theatre for 40 years, a building that might
have tempted .us to convert it into a dormitory had we not
believed so strongly in play-making and acting. The children
write their own plays, dress them, stage them without any help
from teachers. We have an unwritten law that any play performed must have been written in the school. I myself think

that Shakespeare is too difficult for children, at least pre-
adolescent ones. Years ago we staged *The Dream,* and our most
gifted actress of 12 made a mess of Puck. "I didn't understand
the language," she said.

Our seniors read plays together—we get them from the
Drama League—but the centre of our drama is our spontaneous
acting on Sunday nights. I begin with easy situations . . . be
a blind man crossing the street, load and wheel a barrow of
sand, and then on to speaking parts. I give only the skeleton.
"You are a father, you a mother, and you have been expelled
from school. Carry on." We have a rule that two heads cannot
get together first to decide about the situation and the dialogue.

One can imagine many situations. Ask a London bobby
the way. A London girl of 10 asked the way to the station and
we had to explain to over three dozen American pupils that
London had umteen stations. Strike up a conversation with a
fellow traveller in a train. Phone the doctor and get the
butcher by mistake . . . one boy carried on a confused conversation about liver and heart. Burgle a safe, and the owner
comes in.

"What the devil do you think you are doing?"

A bright boy of twelve: "Are you the owner of the house?
Good, glad you came."

"But you are robbing my safe."

"Ah, you have got it all wrong. I am from the safe company
and we go round testing our safes."

"And come in by the window instead of ringing the
front-door bell. It won't do. I'll call the police."

"Got me wrong again. We have to test to see if your
windows are burglar proof."

Such acting possibly does more for the imagination than
for the acting, yet of course they are combined. I find that
children shy away from serious situations. I can think of only
one in which they are always deadly serious. Alf has done

seven years for robbery. He was framed by the gang leader. Released, he gets a gun and sets out to kill the leader. Slowly he realizes that the man he is to kill is blind. The last attempt went thus.

"Hullo, Spike."

"That's Alf's voice. Hallo, Alf, so you're out at last."

"Nice place you've got here, Spike. That grand piano must have cost a packet. In the money, ain't you? Get up. Put your hands up, you dirty swine. Move over there."

Spike stumbles over a chair and Alf moves forward to look at him.

"My God, you are blind!"

I have tried this one out many times but no one ever shot the gangster.

The best one we ever had I put into one of my books. I said to a girl: "You are a young lady with toothache, and you set out to find a dentist, but in the blackout you mistake the door and get into the office of the undertaker. Carry on."

She comes in looking wretched.

"This is awful," she says.

"Sit down, madam, and tell me about it."

She sits down. "I think it's decaying."

"Good heavens, how long have you had it?"

"About a month."

"But haven't you done anything about it?"

"I tried stuffing it with cottonwood."

"But, madam, this is impossible. You must have it removed."

"I'll have it removed if you promise to give me a gold plate."

"Madam, we only make brass plates."

"But it will go all verdigris."

"That won't matter, madam, no one will see it."

Our second best effort was when I was St. Peter at the

Celestial Gate interviewing intended tenants of heaven. A boy of 14 went past me whistling.

"Hi," I cried, "you can't go in there."

He stopped and looked at me.

"Oh, you are a new man on the job," he said. "Do you know who I am?"

"And who exactly are you?" I asked.

"God," and he walked into heaven.

I hasten to say that one seldom gets bright efforts such as these, but the game is always fun, and it does offer much scope for originality. One difficulty is the young exhibitionist, the boy or girl of nine who wants to try every part. Only older children can act a honeymoon Channel crossing on a rough sea.

Any school could use the system, but two State school teachers have said that it is almost impossible with disciplined children to have them act naturally and freely. Certainly if children have any fear of their teacher, they will not be able to act with originality. How much should acting be taught? In spontaneous acting never, but when a play is being produced, the producer, adult or child, must have the right to give directions as to position, movement, etc., but not as to interpretation of character.

Criticism is a different matter. Our children will give their opinion. . . . Willie smiled when he was told his father was dead (children don't allow for such things as Oedipus complexes). "Start a quarrel with the woman over your garden wall." "Mary screamed too much over a trifling episode . . . the non-return of a borrowed saucepan." "The dentist pulled the tooth as if he were opening a wine bottle." So it is not only an acting school, it is a school for embryonic dramatic critics.

Some children who act well in plays cannot act spontaneously. I recall a theatre group which, many years ago, had a summer school at Summerhill. One night I suggested to the leader that he should try spontaneous acting. He did and there was a cry of dismay, but since then we have had Stanislavsky, and I fancy that today every dramatic school uses the spontaneous method. I do not think that children should act grown-up plays.

Once a visitor suggested a Shaw play. Miles Malleston, whose son was with us then, said: "No, no, if I want to see Shaw, I go to a play produced by professionals. In Summerhill I want to see plays written and produced in the school." I love Ibsen but it would break my heart to see children attempting to act *The Doll's House.*

I have had many a good actor, many a good actress in the school, but I can think of only three who took up acting as a profession. Why? I cannot say. Maybe an actor is a man who is discontented with his own personality and has to play the part of another. Certainly a child who stutters seldom stutters on the stage; he is another person, and perhaps when children are free in themselves, they do not need to flee from themselves into a fictional character. But school acting does not aim at producing stage casts. Its fun and games, its originality and imagination, are all that it needs to justify itself.

Euripides' *Trojan Women* is timeless. For his contemporaries, Troy could have been the ransacked Melos; for us, a village in Vietnam. Hecuba's is a tragedy of all women who outlive their meaningful lives and, with their children dead, come to bury a grandson. A brave choice, then, for a school play by the girls of Ensham School and boys of Spencer Park.

True, it would have been happier if the chorus in particular had not had to struggle with Gilbert Murray's mechanical Georgian verse, especially now that Philip Vellacott's much more direct and forcible translation is so easily available. And a dramatic opportunity was missed by dressing the women so prettily. Their torn, dishevelled despair should contrast with the spruce men of the Greek army and the still well-kempt Helen. Yet these seemed minor faults compared with Hecuba's

beautifully sustained performance and [the producer's] skill-
ful use of emotional contrast.

WHAT SHORTAGE?

January 6, 1967

How many teachers are we short of—40,000 or so? Not
enough young folks wanting to teach; not enough training
colleges to house the ones who do. I make the humble suggestion that we put the clock back and return to the days of pupil
teachers. . . . My father had four classes in one room. I learned
my trade by seeing how he taught. . . . I learned the system
with all its faults and its merits, and I have often wondered
if training would have made me a better teacher. In my school
during the past 45 years I have had trained and untrained
teachers. I had good ones and bad ones in both categories, and
I have often wondered whether a teacher is born, and if not,
whether he can be trained.

One merit the pupil-teacher system had . . . it weeded
out the unfit; it resembled Judge Lindsay's trial marriages. I
question if the training-college systems of sending out students
to schools for practice teaching is anything so good as the
apprenticeship way, where the young teacher was doing every
day what he would do all his life.

I may offend when I say that teaching is the least important
part of a teacher's life and job. A gramophone could hand out
most of the useless encyclopedic knowledge that passes for
schooling. How much contact with children do training-college
students have? How many go out with little knowledge of
child psychology? I asked a visiting student recently what they
taught him about children. "In our psychology class we only

learn about rats and their behaviour," he said.

We do not learn psychology from books; we learn it by living with children. A man can read all of Freud and Jung and Adler and have not the least idea what to do with a kid who is stealing or lazy or cheeky. I wonder sometimes if the stupid gulf that separates so many teachers from their pupils stems from the comparative isolation of the training colleges—the gulf that makes a teacher stand on his dignity, that makes him an authority to be feared. . . .

I have many a time lectured to training colleges, and every time I have felt depressed at the lack of challenge among young students. So many appeared to be already in the Establishment. But perhaps it is just as well, seeing that education in general is a preparation for entering the rat race of degrees and jobs and uniformity . . . of school uniforms and the ban on jeans and Beatle hair.

I am not contending that a pupil-teacher system would produce a crop of young challengers, but it might produce a race of teachers more interested in practice than in theory, a race that never lost contact with the young.

But what is teaching anyway? When I was younger, I was more than once called a brilliant teacher. I was nothing of the kind. I was doing all the work instead of letting the class do it. I was Billy Grahaming and the poor unsaved boobs were hearkening to my gospel when they should have been telling me all about it. . . .

One great danger is that a teacher may [be] afraid that his pupils will find he is not omniscient. After lecturing at a university I was mobbed by a crowd of cheering students. I asked why. "Because someone asked you a question and you said you didn't know. No professor in this university would ever admit that he didn't know the answer."

I have more than once suggested to friendly training-college heads that they should send some of their students to

Summerhill for a six months' course in actual living with children, but they all said that the powers above would not countenance the experiment. More teachers? I have a strong belief that what we need is fewer teachers, for no one can teach anything of deep importance—how to lessen the hate in humanity, for instance. One can by living with children, but not by teaching children.

THE INDEPENDENT SCHOOL

August 11, 1967

The private school must be a class affair. When a gardener's wife writes me saying that she wants her boy of 10 to come to Summerhill, I have to reply sadly that I can take only pupils who can pay full fees. If it were the law that all independent schools should be abolished, then logically the law would have to tell well-off parents that they cannot give their children expensive clothes and motor bikes. Under capitalism, if you have the money you can buy what you like, whether it be diamond necklaces or education; rumour says that you can buy a title. That the system is grossly unfair we all know, but it is the wish of the Establishment that the system remain and we cannot do much about it.

The recent B.B.C. television programme *Your Witness* was rather feeble. It dwelt on the snobbery angle of private schools, a very old angle indeed. . . . A public school accent is likely to open more gates to jobs than an East End secondary modern one. During the war I spoke with a man whose job was to select candidates for commissions in the Army. He said: "My orders are to say no to any provincial accent—Lancashire, Cockney, Somerset, etc., but to say yes to a Scottish or North

Ireland accent." . . .

Fom the teaching point of view, I fancy it is difficult to justify the existence of many a private school. It is likely that the . . . secondary modern and grammar schools have better teaching apparatus than the average private school. In my own school I lack so much in the way of apparatus, books, etc. I cannot afford to employ teachers who should be necessary: teachers of dance, music, domestic economy; my physics lab could not possibly take a pupil through A level. Postulating for the moment that education means school subjects, I can see no justification for independent schools. However, the defenders dwell on the advantages of character formation . . . [and] some of us might argue that one of the main purposes of education is to preserve the individuality of the pupil. . . . The boarding school has more opportunity to mould character than the day school has. . . . My feelings prompt me to side with the teachers who seek to abolish all private education. But here comes the rub; if there are no independent schools, there can be no trying of new ways. Oh, yes, one can experiment in teaching subjects but not in living. . .

Kenneth Barnes wrote in the *Guardian:* "[If there had not been private schools] there would never have been a Summerhill or a Bedales." Later on he wrote: "Is it certain that in large-scale organization, the odd-man-out on the school staff, the chap with the queer ideas, will some day be given a headship to show whether he is a creator or only mad?" I am pretty sure that Kenneth himself would never have gone far up the ladder in a State school.

The fact is that experiment within a national system is impossible, or nearly so, apart from Michael Duane and R. F. MacKenzie. To be fair, the blame is not wholly attributable to the school authorities. Few parents would agree to new ways of living, and some even object to free methods in primary schools. Fifty years ago in a Scots village the parents came to me—"I send my laddie to the schule to lairn, not to play." I overheard a woman say almost the same words recently—translated into English, of course.

The N.U.T could say: Okay, we'll abolish private schools, but make an exception in the case of pioneer schools. Fine, but who is to decide what a pioneer school is? Naturally I think that Summerhill is a pioneer school, but the headmaster of some prep school might well call it a disgrace to education. No, the only way seems to be to retain the independent schools in the hope that a few of them may suggest new paths. But again, what sort should be retained? Only those that are "recognized"? Recently a widow wrote me saying that her local council would pay half the fees for her boy at Summerhill. Then came a second letter. The council had refused on the ground that my school is not "recognized as efficient," only registered.

Summerhill is recognized in much of the Western world. My latest books are required reading, I am told, in many U.S. and Israeli training colleges and universities. I am not trying to sell Summerhill; I am simply wondering why the standard of recognition by the Ministry is different from that of Henry Miller, Sir Herbert Read, Erich Fromm, and a few score professors of psychology and education. Personally I don't care if my school is recognized or not, but I do care that a poor widow cannot select the school she wants for her child.

I don't know what the Ministry's word *efficient* means, and can only guess that it means in the main efficient teaching, and possibly is connected with premises—my teaching rooms are outside huts mostly. It may also refer to enough water closets and fire escapes. I simply do not know; visits from inspectors suggest to me that their chief interest is in learning, not in living, but one cannot generalise. John Blackie and Lady Helen Asquith, when they inspected Summerhill, showed in their reports that they saw things that were more important than teaching methods and 0 levels. The sad truth is that one can inspect teaching methods but cannot easily inspect happiness, sincerity, balance—in short, freedom. The intangible cannot be taken out and examined. One of my daydreams is that the Minister invites me to meet his inspectors in a lecture hall and tell them, not what education is, but what it isn't, and this daydream only goes to show that even at nearly 84 a man can have *Grossenwahn.*

ALL OF US ARE PART OF THIS SICK CENSORSHIP

March 29, 1968

I have just read the banned book *Last Exit to Brooklyn* [by Hubert Selby]. It has many four-letter words, many instances of perverted sex, many instances of sheer brutality, but pornographic it is not, if by pornography we mean a way of exciting people sexually. It is a grim, honest picture of a side of society that we know nothing about, and for this very reason it ought to be read by millions.

It is the society of *Blackboard Jungle* when the inhabitants have left school; a society ruled by ignorance, hate, brutality, illiteracy; a society of young people who sat for years on school benches. To ban such a book is to rob the people of a necessary knowledge of the dregs of a world society: the Brooklyn perverts exist in all big cities.

I cannot see that there has ever been a case for censorship. No modern young person is shocked by a four-letter word, and if elders are shocked, it must be because "there is nothing either good or bad but thinking makes it so." Old wives of both sexes should not know bad words anyway. Ah, but books can corrupt. Henry Miller's *Tropic of Cancer, Lady Chatterley's*

Lover, Ulysses, not to mention the *Canterbury Tales* and the Elizabethan drama.

I make the guess that not one of these books induced a young person of either sex to go out seeking sexual intercourse; I also make the guess that 1,001 sex films have led young people to masturbation or promiscuous sex adventures. . . . D. H. Lawrence pointed this out long ago.

Incidentally, I wonder how much the four-letter word has to do with snobbery. Navvies don't have *intercourse;* farm boys do not say *excrement.* But why class distinctions should make the Anglo–Saxon words obscene, I cannot guess.

Censorship is wrong because it postulates repression, because it accepts repression as a normal factor. In a sane world, no one would be shocked; by cruelty and violence, yes, but not by words dealing with sex and bodily functions. My own pupils are unshockable. We have *Lady C* in the school library, and those adolescents who tried to read it stuck half way. . . . "Too boring" the general verdict.

The cure for censorship is a healthy non-guilty orientation about sex. When a young person has that, he or she automatically senses what is mere filth in a book, for sick sex books are written by sick sex authors, and a healthy child easily feels that sick sex is too dull a subject. Obviously, then, censorship is necessary only when the people above—the elders, the politicians, the judges—in short, the Establishment—think that sex is so obscene that the innocent young must be protected from its temptation.

However, when one comes to what are called horror comics, it is not easy to be objective. I have seen American "comics"— they should be called "tragics"—that showed men gouging out eyes, men lashing young half-naked women with whips. My 45 American pupils never get such magazines sent from home, but if they did I should wonder what to do. Older children could take them in their stride, but I do not know what effect they would have on—say—children of 10 or 11. Possibly very little, since they come from enlightened homes, but I can imagine small children in a Brooklyn slum accepting the pictures as the normal features of real life.

But here again, censorship is not the answer. The answer is . . . but is there an answer? It would mean abolishing slums and poverty and squalor; it would mean educating parents to some form of pro-life culture; it would mean abolishing the dreary subjects in school that have as a main result boredom. Deeper, it would mean a new attitude to life.

Six million tortured and slain Jews shocked us years ago, but today we read of babies incinerated by napalm in Vietnam, gas in the Yemen, police torture of blacks in the United States, conflicts all over the world involving hate and savagery; we read of them and almost take them for granted; we read of them without any emotion and then switch on the television.

Our emotions are blunted. We are all aware that at any time there may be a war that will destroy us all, but we sit and wait for the big ones, the politicians and the generals, to decide our fate. The few who care march in protest, knowing well that the Pentagon or Moscow will never hear of their protest.

It is this mass indifference that is alarming. The Roman Catholic Church stops the Pill because it kills life, but how many religious bodies ever protest against the death of thousands of young men in modern war? The hippies rise in protest but against what? Our educational system, our religious morals, our politics? Nay, the hippies protest against length of hair; against conventional clothes; in short, against everything that does not matter.

Four pop-singer lads in flowery clothes saw a short film of Summerhill. They indignantly condemned it. . . . "Neill is exploiting kids to make money. Breeding a lot of bloody anarchists." But are we any more advanced? Front-page news is seldom news of a world of sickness and death; millions are more interested in the Saturday football matches than in wars and race hatred—or crime.

Any cheap daily is a list of all that is banal and futile in society. Our television programmes are geared to an average age of 11. The sales returns of papers show that society is divided into the great majority that is interested in banalities and the tiny minority that reads the book reviews, the theatre criticisms, the political arguments in the *Observer* or *The Sunday Times*.

I am not trying to say that such higher-brow readers should be accepted as a criterion of culture, but I am saying that the masses have a component that has affinities with the Brooklyn toughs and roughs . . . witness the savagery so prevalent at football matches. Brooklyn hoodlums kick in the face; the football gangs throw bottles. The readers of the highbrow Sunday papers are not likely to be bottle throwers, and if and when they are crooks, they act in respectable circles like the Stock Exchange or Parliament.

Censorship is of a sick civilization, and most people are content to live in this sick society. Few can ever challenge, because early indoctrination seems to work 95 per cent successfully. If the teaching profession were to challenge, they would make every school a place of activity, a place of happy faces and voices, a place without fear, as they do in many a primary school.

O dear me, what a hope! When more than 80 per cent of teachers want to retain the cane . . . the symbol of violence and fear and hate. . . . Still, there may be a case for censorship. Censor the criminal code that deprives a man of freedom and of love; censor the teachers who cane and strap; censor the ministers who bless battleships, censor the primitives who hunt the hare and the fox, who shoot and wound deer. I took a few children to see *Bambi*. A small boy said: "How can anyone shoot a deer after seeing a film like that?" I couldn't answer him.

We are all in it. I eat meat that someone else kills, and so do most of you. Even G.B.S. had to wear leather shoes. We are all sick, and the more our sickness is portrayed in books like *Last Exit to Brooklyn,* the more chance we have of coming to see ourselves in the raw.

MY UNRECTORIAL ADDRESS

November 22, 1968

(The Editor has asked me what I would have said had I been made Lord Rector of Edinburgh University. I apologize to Kenneth Allsop for anticipating what I am sure will be an excellent address when he comes to give it.)

Students of Edinburgh. Why do you need a Lord Rector, and since you apparently do need one, why invite people with publicity names to be candidates? Had Alf Garnett been available, he might have been elected. Why do you need a representative to state your case? I'll tell you why. Because your lives have been moulded since cradle days. They castrated you when you were an infant: they told you how to live. They spanked you, they made you feel sinful, guilty: in short, they killed your life for you. By their sex taboos they made you anti-sex for life: they made sex a matter of pornography and dirt. School simply was an extension of home moulding. Obey authority, respect adults who do not merit respect, fear your teachers, accept their verdict that O and A levels mean education. In other words, be underlings and remain underlings. And that is your position now, you young ones. Few of you can challenge anything: your indoctrination has been too successful.

Ah, you say, what about the world revolt among students? I am all for it: I am optimistic to see the challenge, yet I fear too often the challenge is against all that does not matter— length of hair, colour of jacket. To be fair, this refers more to pop hippies than to students. But what are you seeking? It is 60 years since I matriculated, and I am long out of touch with you. I ask myself what I would challenge if I were a student today. Firstly the gulf between staff and students, really the same gulf that exists in any state school. . . .

Students, you cannot be free as long as you have to show "respect" to your teachers. It makes a barrier that kills social contact and free association. This is not theory. For 48 years in my school I have been plain Neill to pupils, staff, parents, visitors, but then my Summerhill is a pure democracy where there is no partriarchal authority, where the laws are made by popular vote. Perhaps it isn't fair to make a comparison of a small school with a large university. We meet to make laws once a week, but you students cannot all meet in the Usher Hall and vote for laws. . . .

Students should have a big say in the curriculum they have to follow. I can see limitations here: I cannot see students tell a professor of surgery how to teach his subject. Here there is expert knowledge that has to be tested by examinations . . . I don't want my appendix to be removed by the man who wheels me into the operating theatre. But the teaching of some subjects should be challenged. . . .

Take the degrees in psychology today. I ask a B.A. Psychology what they taught him to do with a thief. "Good God, they don't tell us things like that: they only tell us what happens to rats when you condition them." I have met graduates in psychology who knew almost nothing about Freud or Jung or Reich.

How much value any protest would have I do not know.

In my own school, if a teacher's lessons are dull, he or she has to leave, for in a school where lessons are not compulsory, a poor teacher has no class. I'd like to see the system obtain in the university.

How to get democracy in such a heterogeneous mob? It is beyond me. Yet more important than any democratic structure is the freedom of youth, the inner freedom, the urge to be rational. The urge to keep asking why . . . but not like Malcolm Muggeridge and his Sunday night "Why"? For he always knows his own answers. . . . I wonder how many of you are grown up. Two of my old pupils came to Edinburgh to study medicine. I asked them separately how they got on with their fellow students. Their answers were similar. "I can't get on with chaps my own age: they are too infantile—they do things I lived out at 10—cat-calling, chucking paper darts, stamping when a student comes in late."

It is true. You never had a real childhood. Childhood is playhood, and you never had time to play. Football and cricket maybe, but they are not play: real play has a fantasy behind it. That is why you youngsters behave like sooty five-year-olds on election night in the old quad.

Students, your job is to grow up, and all the courses in the faculties will not help you to do so. The fact that you elect a rector proves that you need a rector, a symbol of old Oedipus, the all-knowing and all-powerful father. Shame on ye. You cannot stand on your own feet because you have had to have crutches all your days—teachers, policemen, politicians, sex repressors. "Fear of freedom," wrote Erich Fromm, and also Wilhelm Reich. You all seek freedom and you fear to have it because it means responsibility, aloneness, guts.

Freedom? You can ask what the word means. To be primitive, if you like; to be natural and out-going, to love and not to hate. The world is full of hate because each and every one of us is fashioned by ignorant elders. When black children came to Summerhill, not even the youngest child seemed to notice their colour, but our television showed the hateful faces of deep south white children stoning black children, with hate given to them as babies. Racialism, crime wars appear to have no promise in the eyes of a new-born babe. My own opinion is that the salvation of the world depends on freedom from moulding. Free children are not aggressive, not hateful; they are tolerant and understanding.

You live in a very sick world and a most uncertain one. That is half the tale of delinquency today. Let us eat, drink, and be merry, for tomorrow the bomb may end everything. Young friends, in your struggle for freedom, do try to think out your priorities. Oppose everyone who seeks to make you feel that sex is guilty or that obedience is a virtue, or that bishops should bless Polaris subs. Challenge all things and when they restrict your natural growth, reject them. Remember that rebellion in itself is feeble unless it has a practical outcome. Violence is simply negative and never gets anywhere because it is hate and never cured a thing. Violence, if necessary, should go into things and not people. Hitler put many of my old Jewish pupils into his *gaswagen,* but hating Hitler gets nowhere: one should hate all that he stood for.

Freedom? It isn't enough to demand freedom in a university, one must demand it in a wide world. Really I am beginning to feel that a lord rectorship is a very minor matter. For that matter so is a university education, so narrow: I have my M.A. Honours degree (2nd class), but even if it were a first class one my ignorance of art and music and philosophy would be as profound as it is now. Students, your trouble is that of all of us, a head education that leaves the emotions untouched: and if you think that is bosh ask why millions of people think and talk of nothing but football all week long, why thousands who read Shakespeare and Hardy for O level now read nothing but thrillers and the pictorial press. The press and television are now our universities: they serve up the food for emotion that the classrooms in school and university ignore. *The Man from Uncle* will beat the Long Parliament any day.

I fear I have gone over my time limit. I have only enough time to announce that I hereby resign my rectorship and invite you students to figure out how you are going to find your own style of freedom without having to rely on any stage or author personality to tell you what to do. Muggeridge, or Allsop, or Sims, or I cannot tell you what to do. Forget names. Get together and thrash it all out. Above all, make up your minds what sort of freedom you want. But do not be content to have "ordered freedom." It doesn't exist. All or nothing.

LIFE WITHOUT FATHER

April 11, 1969

The revolt of the students, and now the school children, is primarily one against paternalism. It is also a protest against an education that is mostly a head affair. This was shown the other night on a B.B.C. television programme about why so few are taking up science. More than one student spoke of the absence of any human contact, any emotional one. They might well have given a similar criticism of school learning. That it does not grip anything fundamental in a child is proved by the reaction of new pupils to Summerhill.

When they learn that classes are not compulsory, everyone of every age immediately drops all lessons for weeks, for months—in a few cases, for years. When they begin to attend, it is usually to go to creative lessons—workshop, pottery, art, music, if we had it—but the difficulty is that a private school depending on fees cannot afford the teachers who deal with creation and the arts. I'd like to sack my English and history teachers and employ teachers of music, dance, drama, but the old bugbear of O level forces me to have teachers of subjects that will be examined.

Granted that a good teacher can make a subject interesting, the sad truth is that school subjects do not really interest children. Why teach history that we all forget? In 1908 I got a high mark in history as a degree subject, but I have no idea who won the Wars of the Roses or what the Long Parliament did. And I do not miss the knowledge. I would consign history and English to the library, at least for pupils over 12 or so.

Unconsciously, often consciously, the pupils realize that they are getting nothing of value from their subjects. I have often wondered why these subjects, why not gardening or chicken farming or photography or film-making? When Bob MacKenzie took his Braehead pupils out to live on the moors, he found a wave of interest that never appeared in the desk school. By the way, Bob is now head of a comprehensive school in Aberdeen—named Summerhill. Good for Aberdeen!

How much connexion is there between schooling and life? When I go to our local, I never hear the workmen discuss history or geography, and the only mathematical conversation I hear is about the number of pigs or cows they work with. I am convinced that the majority of teachers would not agree with this argument, but I am sure that the majority of schoolchildren would. And the school is theoretically for children, and only secondarily for teachers.

In the past nine years I must have had a thousand letters from American children complaining about the incubus of dull lessons. Children and university students are demanding the right of self-determination, the right to have a big say in what they will learn and how it should be taught. They belong to a society that is much more conscious than it was 60 years ago. Today many students studying psychology are against the courses that study rats and not humans. They can do nothing under a paternal system.

I am not a Freudian and cannot claim that the basis is a sexual one but there is a sex element in this new wave of enthusiasm. Muggeridge resigned his Lord Rectorship of Edinburgh University because he would not subscribe to the demand for the issue of the Pill to women students. The educational upsurge is accompanied by the female demand to have their desire for a sex life recognized. In my young days, a woman was not supposed to have any sex desire until she married the wonderful man who would awaken her. (Here I write of universities, not schools.)

Youth feels frustrated. I can imagine a youth's looking around and saying: "Our elders made this—Vietnam, racialism, super-rich and super-poor, a society founded on grab and wealth and social injustice. Who the hell are they to tell us how to live?"

Ah, but what about practice? How can pupils use freedom? In Summerhill it is easy; 80 of us sit round every Saturday night and make laws by show of hands. But a comprehensive school cannot meet in its hundreds and make laws. Our democracy is as true as it can be, but the large school would have to elect members of parliament, and then the rank and file would lose interest. That is a practical problem that could be solved.

I doubt if there would be much unrest among schoolchildren if they felt that their teachers were on their side, that they were human. In our international school in Germany, 1921-24, our German teachers used to hide their cigarettes if they met a pupil on the street. To many children, teachers are not human; they are robots . . . What dehumanizes teachers? The training colleges? No, I think it is fear, fear of losing their little authority, their dignity. And vaguely the pupils feel it, but they have to act their parts . . . say Sir or Miss, answer

in an insincere voice, show manners that mean nothing to a
child, in short be underlings.

Some teachers accuse me of being unfair to the profession.
Some tell me that I am ignorant of many advances in schools.
I have been delighted with a few new-method primary schools,
longing to see the free and easy ways introduced into O level
schools. I know that many teachers are doing excellent work.
Alas, I seldom hear of them; my mail tells about the other
kind, the fear-makers, the stiff ones, the caners, the tawsers.
They are not evil men and women, just unaware people who
have no real contact with, no sympathy for children.

May 2, 1969

I have had many an article in these columns, usually about
psychology or children or living, and seldom was there much
of a reaction, but now that I attack the sacred-cow school subjects, there is considerable reaction. . . . I am not against learning . . . but I want to put learning in its place; I want it to
be asked for. I asked a pupil of eight what he did with his
pocket-money. He said he didn't spend it [but] saved it to buy
history books. He is now a professor of history. Two other
boys in the same class were interested in maths and science.
One is now a professor of maths and the other a lecturer in
physics. These boys sought learning without any suggestion
from parents or staff. . . .

But I am thinking [of] the millions who will simply drop
most of what they learnt in school. How many Tennysons and
Shakespeares will one find in the homes of the thousands who
watch the Cup Final? Will the Top of the Form teams remem-

ber all the useless encyclopedic knowledge when they are 40? What do school subjects do for the children depicted in that disturbing book by Sir Alec Clegg, *Children in Distress?* All the O and A levels in the world do nothing to better this very sick society. Walker's paternalism can easily be a basis for Fascism. When I had my school in Dresden, I saw a nation whose education was lessons, discipline, obedience, suppression of the instincts. It was Wilhelm Reich who said that the ruling classes, by supressing the sexuality of children, make a proletariat that is symbolically castrated and without the guts to challenge or rebel. And it is not only sex repression. A whole nation raised its Heil Hitler arms when all their interests were being killed. It could happen in any country. Didn't [George] Wallace get ten million votes? Didn't [Joseph] McCarthy have much success?

I cannot think of education in terms of schooling. Like everyone else I have a bee in my bonnet . . . the belief that what is wrong with the world is the killing of the life force of the young by the old. I sincerely believe that this is the source of the hate in the world. And I don't think it is all theory. I have been in my small Suffolk town since 1927. For years I had crooks of all kinds thrown out of other schools. I have never had a child brought before a juvenile court for delinquency, but at the moment the town is having a wave of public-lavatory vandalism by young lads. They are under external discipline, [whereas] my pupils make their own discipline. The law—or maybe better to say, the discipline—makes the crime.

I cannot look at a class of sixth formers and see bright scholars. I see a bunch of boys who most probably have a guilt about masturbation, a guilt about the gulf between them and their parents. I see lads who have no idea of what freedom is, lads who fear freedom. I had to give up taking boys of 15 and 16 because, after years of suppression, they went haywire when they came into a free society. Boys from "nice" schools often reacted to freedom by destroying, for the subject school does nothing to reach the emotional part of the child psyche. That is why so few people can ever challenge anything; their conditioning was too powerful all the way from cradle days. . . .

True, the teacher has had a raw deal. How can a teacher with a class of 40 know anything about the character structure of each pupil? How can he or she know about a child's home life? A sane system would make 10 the limit of pupils for each teacher, but with an insane system of Polaris Subs and moon rockets, what hope is there for teachers? And would small classes solve the problem so long as teachers think that lessons are of great importance? I doubt it because I have a nasty suspicion that many teachers have no interest in depth psychology. How many have read Homer Lane or Wilhelm Reich? How many have studied Freud and Jung and Adler? One teacher put it thus: "My job is to teach history, not worry my arse about whether Willie is beaten up at home by a drunken father." And with large classes he is right.

The school carries on the life murder of the young; it instils obedience, perhaps the worst of the seven deadly virtues; it ignores all that is vital in a child's character—the play instinct, the natural noisiness of children; it inhibits the child's natural sincerity by forcing it to "respect" its teachers, to act a part, really to be a hypocrite. . . .

PSYCHOLOGY

May 16, 1969

David Holbrook apparently assumes that psychologically I am' in "the dark backward and abysm of time." Let me explain how I got there.

In 1919 Homer Lane said that every teacher ought to be analysed and offered to take me on free of charge. . . . I cannot recall having any emotional reaction in his consulting room. So I went to Dr. Maurice Nicoll, then a leading Jungian. Same result—no reaction. In 1921, I went to Dresden to help found an international school, read a book by Stekel, and decided to go to Vienna to be his patient. He was a brilliant interpreter of symbols, but again I got it with my head but not my guts.

In spite of my failures I still thought that analysis was the answer, and in the early days of Summerhill, when I could get only problem pupils, I analysed them. A lad of 15, expelled from a public school for stealing, went out in two years an honest boy; and I thought that analysis was wonderful, until it slowly dawned on me that other crooks, boys and girls, who would not come for analysis, also went out cured. I concluded that it was not therapy that was the active agent; it was freedom. Doubts arose, augmented by reading men like Suttie and Malinowski.

In 1937, I met Wilhelm Reich in Oslo. He was the first psychologist I had heard of who linked up the somatic and the psychological and I asked him to take me as a pupil, which meant going through what he then called Vegetotherapy. Reich held that Freudian analysis dealt with words and memories, whereas the damage is done before a child can talk or remember. He did not analyse dreams. His theory was that neurosis betrays itself in tension of the muscles, facial expression, posture, and he attacked these with energy. I got more emotional reaction in six weeks with Reich than I had ever had in talky analysis.

So if David thinks that I am dyed-in-the-wool Freudian, I wonder how he would explain the fact that in 48 years no British analyst, Freudian, Adlerian, Jungian, Kleinian, has ever recommended a parent to send a child to Summerhill. Among my 40 American pupils, a few have been sent by Reich therapists.

One of my doubts about Freudianism was this: Freud rightly said that there was a conflict between the instinct, life force, libido—whatever we call life's energy—and the cultural environment. Freud did nothing about it, and his disciples kept analysis for the private patient; only a few, like Anna Freud and Susan Isaacs, tried to do something to change the inhibiting external forces.

David jibes at my use of the term "depth psychology." I have read a lot about Fascism, how it arose from economic misery, nationalism, etc., but in his book *The Mass Psychology of Fascism* Reich goes deeper; he traces it to the symbolic castration of babies in their cradles, producing Pavlovised masses that have not the guts to challenge authority. That to me is depth psychology. When I said that teachers did not read the pioneers of the psychology of the unconscious, I did not mean that they should follow them, only know what they said and did, and make up their own minds about them. In my ignorance, when I analysed problem children, I sought for the famous trauma that caused the damage. In over 20 years I found it only once, in a girl of 12 who had a sex phobia due to her having seen an exhibitionist when she was four. The search for the trauma is almost a futile one, for a child is not made neurotic by one trauma but by a plethora of traumas all the way through childhood and later in school.

I never heard of the men mentioned by David and have a suspicion that they belong to the new computerized psychology that is mechanistic and scientific. But I am prejudiced, for I fear the growth of Skinnerism and its rats and pigeons. Who could make a scientific study of, say—the Little Commonwealth, or for that matter, Summerhill? Oh, yes, one can tabulate the number of academic scholars and artists and engineers, but how to tabulate the cultural and emotional I have no idea. Have the men mentioned by David any new way of dealing with a

young thief or a kid deprived of love?

David writes: "Homer Lane and even Reich are no longer central and significant figures." Tut, tut, David, don't you know that 50 years ago Lane showed that disturbed children can best be treated by love and freedom, while today the Establishment treats young delinquents with the methods that made many of them delinquent—strict discipline, punishment, often fear—and poor old Lane is a back number.

THE WAY OF VIOLENCE

June 13, 1969

One argument for the retention of the cane or tawse is clear and logical. Take the situation of the teacher in, say, a slum of any big city. He has a large class, and in that class there are almost certainly bound to be a few tough guys who upset the class and the teaching. What can the teacher do?

Michael Duane solved the matter when he refused to use the cane, but he was no ordinary teacher. The average teacher sees no way out but the way of violence, and caning is violence and must breed violence. And, indeed, the poor man is in a hole.

There is a solution. In Sweden, apparently, the young tough is taken out of the school and sent to one run on psychological lines which attempts to help the child to overcome his anti-social ways. It could be done here; it should be done here. Over 50 years ago Homer Lane showed the way in his Little Commonwealth where very "bad" boys and girls were given self-government, making their own laws.

I saw it only once and it staggered me to see slum children living socially in a society that was as free as it could be.

Later, I came to know some of the ex-pupils and a pleasant lot of social youth they were.

Not having seen them, I cannot fairly judge Borstals and approved schools. A few may be very good, but from what I read, I take it that the methods used are those that made the inmates crooks—discipline from above, strenuous work, obedience without question, shortage of free time. Punishment cannot cure what is individual and social sickness, so that if special schools were set up for the misfits, they would have to be on Little Commonwealth lines.

It could be done in the state system. A man like Howard Case in Herts deals with his junior maladjusted children with understanding and affection. Others . . . undoubtedly are doing so also. True, the job is much more difficult with teenagers of both sexes, and, by the way, such schools should be for both sexes.

The chief difficulty, as we all know, is the environment that makes young delinquents, the bad homes, the ignorant parents, so that such schools would have to be boarding ones well away from slumland. But one snag would be the question of staff. There are not many Homer Lanes and Aichhorns around.

I would suggest that such schools should be run by psychologists if I did not have the disturbing fear that many trained psychologists are taught more about rats and pigeons than about child psychology, meaning that if a man is a B.A. (Psychology), it does not follow that he can understand children.

Such a system would lead naturally to a change in our present inhuman prison system for adults, when men and women are shut away from love and sex and companionship, cut off from hope. I know it is all a daydream; I know that society will go on seeking its pound of flesh, its scapegoats, for I fancy very few of us see crime as a sickness and not as

a sin.

One day, if this sick society does not blow itself up, delinquency and crime will be treated as tenderly and humanely as bodily sickness is treated in our hospitals. I hate being so old if only because I won't live to see love ruling instead of hate and fear.

PRIVATE SCHOOLS

I hope that the new Education Secretary will take a new look at the term "recognized as efficient." Recognition is given if the Ministry decides that a school meets its standard of education. This, I take it, means good premises, good teaching, modern methods. I have not applied for recognition because my view of education is not that of the Ministry, and because I could not see myself getting it.

Recognition means nothing to me personally, but if I had it, poor parents could send their children to Summerhill. A poor widow wanted to send her boy, saying that her county council had offered to pay half the fees. Then the council discovered that we were not recognized and therefore could not pay the fees. So I continue being ashamed that I have to take middle-class pupils only.

I am not trying to sell my school when I say that it is "recognized" in a dozen countries. An American professor of education tells me that there are hundreds of new schools in the United States claiming to run on Summerhill principles. What pains me is this: if I had a private school with ideal premises and teaching, plus fear and the cane, I could be recognized. It would be great if Mrs. Thatcher [Education Secretary] were to begin her reign by abolishing the barbarity and cowardliness of corporal punishment in all schools, but if she tried to, she would have many teachers against her.

I appeal to her to drop the Ministry yardstick that makes all schools fit into its criterion of education, or should I say learning? The new freedom in many primary schools should encourage her to put school-subject education in its uncreative place.

VII

INDEX